CW01512760

Anglo-Saxon Studies 32

'CHARMS', LITURGIES, AND SECRET RITES IN EARLY MEDIEVAL ENGLAND

Anglo-Saxon Studies

ISSN 1475-2468

GENERAL EDITORS
John Hines
Catherine Cubitt

'Anglo-Saxon Studies' aims to provide a forum for the best scholarship on the Anglo-Saxon peoples in the period from the end of Roman Britain to the Norman Conquest, including comparative studies involving adjacent populations and periods; both new research and major re-assessments of central topics are welcomed.

Books in the series may be based in any one of the principal disciplines of archaeology, art history, history, language and literature, and inter- or multi-disciplinary studies are encouraged.

Proposals or enquiries may be sent directly to the editors or the publisher at the addresses given below; all submissions will receive prompt and informed consideration.

Professor John Hines, School of History, Archaeology and Religion, Cardiff University, John Percival Building, Colum Drive, Cardiff, Wales, CF10 3EU, UK

Professor Catherine Cubitt, School of History, Faculty of Arts and Humanities, University of East Anglia, Norwich, England, NR4 7TJ, UK

Boydell & Brewer, PO Box 9, Woodbridge, Suffolk, England, IP12 3DF, UK

Previously published volumes in the series are listed at the back of this book

'CHARMS', LITURGIES, AND SECRET RITES
IN EARLY MEDIEVAL ENGLAND

Ciaran Arthur

THE BOYDELL PRESS

© Ciaran Arthur 2018

All Rights Reserved. Except as permitted under current legislation
no part of this work may be photocopied, stored in a retrieval system,
published, performed in public, adapted, broadcast,
transmitted, recorded or reproduced in any form or by any means,
without the prior permission of the copyright owner

The right of Ciaran Arthur to be identified as
the author of this work has been asserted in accordance with
sections 77 and 78 of the Copyright, Designs and Patents Act 1988

First published 2018
The Boydell Press, Woodbridge

ISBN 978-1-78327-313-3

The Boydell Press is an imprint of Boydell & Brewer Ltd
PO Box 9, Woodbridge, Suffolk IP12 3DF, UK
and of Boydell & Brewer Inc.
668 Mt Hope Avenue, Rochester, NY 14620–2731, USA
website: www.boydellandbrewer.com

A CIP catalogue record for this book is available
from the British Library

The publisher has no responsibility for the continued existence or accuracy
of URLs for external or third-party internet websites referred to in this book,
and does not guarantee that any content on such websites is, or will remain,
accurate or appropriate

This publication is printed on acid-free paper

Printed and bound in Great Britain by
TJ International Ltd, Padstow, Cornwall

Contents

Illustrations

Acknowledgements

I am indebted to several people for their unfailing encouragement over the course of years in the writing of this book. My sister Dr Catherine Arthur, to whom this book is dedicated, deserves special attention for all of the support and sympathy we have shared with each other through both fruitful and difficult stages of our studies together. I owe most of my success to my parents for their many sacrifices over the years. Within the academic community, I would like to thank Dr Helen Gittos for her careful scrutiny of my work, and her persistent interest in my research. Dr Sarah James has been very helpful in pushing me to explore exciting possibilities, and I thank her for her endless enthusiasm. I am also extremely grateful to Dr Stephen Kelly for his ever critical interest and good humoured discussions that invigorate my work ethic; he has gone beyond reasonable expectations to keep supporting me long after I had ceased to be a student of his. I also owe special thanks to Dr Ivan Herbison for his intellectual stimulation and often mind-blowing insights; I am not likely to ever meet another intellectual like him. I am also indebted to Ivan for proof-reading my Latin translations, all remaining infelicities are my own. For their inspiring discussions during the preparation of this book, I thank Professors Karen Jolly, Katy Cubitt, Roy Liuzza, John Hines, Hugh Magennis, James Carley, Sarah Hamilton, and Mary Clayton; and Doctors Alaric Hall, Leonie Hicks, Rebecca Stephenson, Pádraic Moran, Tom Birkett, Sinead O'Sullivan, Ryan Perry, Marilina Cesario, Frances McCormack, Nicky Tsougarakis, Vicky Symons, Patricia McCann, and Craig Wallace. Dr Mike Bintley should get special mention for his warm friendship and generous encouragement over the years. I am also greatly indebted to Aoife and the boys for their endless entertainment during periods of isolated research. Finally, I would like to thank the institutions that have provided invaluable assistance in the preparation of this book, particularly the AHRC, the British Library, Queen's University Belfast, and the Centre of Medieval and Early Modern Studies at the University of Kent.

Abbreviations

ANQ	*American Notes and Queries*
ASE	*Anglo-Saxon England*
ASPR	Anglo-Saxon Poetic Records
BL	British Library
CSEL	*Corpus Scriptorum Ecclesiasticorum Latinorum*
EEMF	Early English Manuscripts in Facsimile
EETS	Early English Text Society
EHR	*English Historical Review*
ES	*English Studies*
HBS	Henry Bradshaw Society
JEGP	*Journal of English and Germanic Philology*
N&Q	*Notes and Queries*
OE	Old English
OEN	Old English Newsletter
OHG	Old High German
ON	Old Norse
PL	Patrologia Latina
PMLA	*Publications of the Modern Language Association*
PQ	*Philological Quarterly*
RES	*Review of English Studies*
SP	*Studies in Philology*

Introduction

'Anglo-Saxon charms prove that Christianity could not hold back the pagans' faith in their magical powers and attest to the enduring quality of a deep-seated belief in magic.'[1]

The early medieval period continues to fascinate modern audiences on a global scale, and it is consistently presented as a strange and mysterious world teeming with sorcerers, witches, druids, monks, monsters, malignant supernatural creatures, and even the walking dead. According to popular understandings, the medieval world, both visible and invisible, was held together through constant battles between cosmologically opposing forces of good and evil, white and black magic, Christianity and paganism. So superstitious were medieval people that everybody – whether Christian or pagan, cleric or lay, learned or illiterate, nobleman or peasant – turned to magical spells, objects, talismans, folk remedies, and old wives' tales in their attempts to survive the many hardships of a filthy, plague-ridden life. The charm is presented as perhaps the most important tool in the medieval survival kit; every conceivable situation could be influenced by a specific charm. They were used to guarantee good harvests, prevent natural disasters, influence important authorities, forcibly win somebody's love, curse enemies and bring about their ruin, find thieves, heal the sick, drive away death, and so forth. Ideas of medieval paganism, occultism, magic, and charms have profoundly influenced the entertainment industry through creative reconstructions in historical novels, fantasy literature, gaming, television, and cinematic productions. Popular representations of medieval magic have great market potential and they continue to shape modern understandings of the past.

Traditional scholarship has also sought to uncover evidence of medieval magic and pre-Christian religion in mysterious texts and artefacts. These surviving materials are seen to be magical precisely because of their enigmatic nature, and as such they have come to encapsulate an elusive medieval world that remains shrouded in a veil of superstition. Sources range extensively from Late Antiquity to much

---

[1] Paola Tornaghi, 'Anglo-Saxon Charms and the Language of Magic', *Aevum*, 84 (2010), 439–64, p. 464.

later Old Norse saga literature, but traditional scholarship has consistently returned to one vital repository of evidence in discussions of medieval magic and paganism. The so-called corpus of Anglo-Saxon charms has been venerated as a vault that houses rare evidence of surviving pre-Christian magical practices.

The Anglo-Saxon 'charms' have been traditionally understood as witnesses to a continued paganism that became Christianised in the tenth and eleventh centuries. The genre of 'charms' is constantly used as a point of entry for discussions of paganism and heterodox Christianity, but these texts provide very important information about the diverse nature of late Anglo-Saxon liturgical practices and ecclesiastical culture. A new critique of this topic is worthwhile because when traditional perceptions of Anglo-Saxon paganism are challenged, the vibrant nature of early medieval Christianity can be exposed. This book offers a re-evaluation of the concept of 'charms' in Anglo-Saxon culture and proposes an alternative reading of these rituals as mainstream Christian texts.

The book engages with three principal issues that lie at the heart of the 'charms' genre: the translation of the Old English noun 'galdor' as 'charm'; the manuscript contexts of the rituals that are included in this corpus; and the phenomenon of 'gibberish' writing that is used as a defining characteristic of 'charms'. These core issues also parallel three important aspects of late Anglo-Saxon Christianity, when the majority of these texts were written. Firstly, there was considerable concern about the spiritual nature of the *galdor* as it is presented as both a powerful Christian utterance and a dangerous ritual practice. Secondly, the manuscripts in which 'charms' were written elucidate experimentations with Christian literary traditions and liturgical practices, rendering a study of these rituals in their manuscript contexts extremely important. Finally, the study of language gained great momentum in the tenth and eleventh centuries, and understandings of the cosmological power of letters were significantly developed by English theologians. Taking account of these approaches to language opens alternative readings of obscure writing and 'gibberish' in Anglo-Saxon texts.

In this book I argue that 'charms' were written down as experimental Christian rituals in late Anglo-Saxon England. Even the most obscure features of these texts – particularly their use of 'gibberish' writing – can be understood as belonging to Christian philosophical traditions that were being taught in late Anglo-Saxon minsters. Once 'charms' are re-read in their manuscript contexts, they reveal information about the particular ecclesiastical milieus in which they were written, they raise critical questions about Anglo-Saxon paganism, and they offer important insights into early English Christianity. In order to reconsider 'charms', it is first necessary to outline how these texts have been understood and classified to date. This introductory chapter pro-

2

vides an overview of the historiography of this genre before plotting important historical events that seem to have influenced perceptions of ritual practices when these texts were written down.

Editions of 'Charms'

Collections of Anglo-Saxon 'charms' have been gathered for almost 150 years, and this genre of ritual texts has now been firmly established. In 1866, the antiquarian Thomas Oswald Cockayne completed his seminal three-volume work *Leechdoms, Wortcunning, and Starcraft of Early England*.[2] Cockayne identified a total of thirty-two rituals from ten Anglo-Saxon manuscripts as belonging to the 'charm' tradition, which he described as follows:

> We may perchance wonder at the slavery in which people were held by the Church, during the earlier ages of our modern period; at the saying of medicine masses, at the blessing the worts out of the field, at the placing them upon the altar; but the Church had delivered men from a worse servitude than this, from the tyranny and terror of the poisoner and the wizard... Let the scornful reader, in good health, not toss his head on high at the so called superstition of the simple Saxon, but consider rather how audacious an infidel that man, in those ages, would have seemed, who had refused to pray in the received manner for the restoration of his health... The Catholic Church of the day, unequal to root out these superstitions and rarely beneficial ideas, tried to fling a garb of religion round them to invoke holy names to drive out devils by exorcisms.[3]

Cockayne's opening discussion of these texts reflects attitudes to early medieval religion in the mid-nineteenth century. He did not explicitly define the 'charm' but he saw it as a form of ritual that incorporated Christian elements into an otherwise superstitious, folk custom.

Cockayne's work gave careful consideration to the content and ordering of the manuscripts in which the rituals survive, and he edited the entirety of two other manuscripts (London, British Library, MSS Harley 585, Royal 12 D. xvii), which later became key sources in charm studies. Cockayne's edition reflects the diverse range of texts that co-exist with 'charms' in manuscripts, including medical works, Patristic writings, computus, prognostications, riddles, poetry, and liturgical texts. Later editions of Anglo-Saxon 'charms' extracted these

---

[2] Thomas Oswald Cockayne, ed. and trans, *Leechdoms, Wortcunning, and Starcraft of Early England: Being a Collection of Documents, for the Most Part Never Before Printed, Illustrating the History of Science in this Country Before the Norman Conquest*, 3 Vols. (London, 1864–66).
[3] Cockayne, *Leechdoms*, Vol. I, pp. xxviii, xxxiii. The 'charms' are printed in Vol. I, pp. 384–405; Vol. III, pp. 286–95.

rituals from their manuscript contexts and separated them from their surrounding materials.[4]

In 1909, Felix Grendon published the first exclusive corpus of 146 Anglo-Saxon 'charms' from nineteen manuscripts, although only sixty-two rituals were printed in the edition.[5] Grendon did not define what he understood by the word 'charm', but the extent to which this genre was imposed on these texts is clear from titles which he made up for some rituals. He used the Old English term *galdor* to form the titles 'Siðgaldor' ('A Journey Spell'), 'Nigon wyrta galdor' ('Nine Herbs Charm'), and 'Be galdorstafum' ('Concerning Magic Writings').[6] Grendon's terminology was left largely undefined, but he associated incantations, remedies, 'gibberish', and superstition with the 'charm' tradition.[7] The edition is divided into five categories of magic, and it is claimed that the texts' magical elements reveal a native Germanic religion that was subsumed into English Christianity:

> Pagan charms had to be met by Christian charms; and wherever heathen names of deities were used, authorized canonical names had to be substituted. From this want of single-hearted aim in its war on magic usages, the Church met with but slight success; so that Christian and Pagan ceremonies came to be strangely mingled… A sequel to the conciliatory policy of the Church was the active participation of the clergy in the old superstitious customs. This was not as unnatural as it may seem. The very air of the time was heavy with irrational beliefs; and priests, like other people, breathed in what they were far from recognizing as Pagan superstitions.[8]

These rituals were presented as evidence of a heterodox Christianity that embraced animism and the irrational superstitions of pre-Christian religion. Anglo-Saxon clergymen are also depicted as susceptible to superstitions that saturated early English culture.

Grendon attempted to trace diachronic connections between these native English customs and contemporary folklore.[9] He claimed that modern children's rhymes have their origins in heathen formulas that were deliberately corrupted in 'gibberish' words and phrases:

---

[4] On the value of Cockayne's edition for other genres in Anglo-Saxon studies, see Lázló Sándor Chardonnens, *Anglo-Saxon Prognostics, 900–1100: Study and Texts* (Leiden, 2007), pp. 17–20.

[5] Felix Grendon, 'The Anglo-Saxon Charms', *Journal of American Folk-Lore*, 22 (1909), 105–237, pp. 160–4. Most of the eighty-seven unprinted 'charms' are taken from Cockayne and Günther Leonhardi, ed., *Kleinere angelsächsische Denkmäler I*, Bibliothek der Angelsächsischen Prosa, Vol. 6 (Hamburg, 1905).

[6] Grendon, 'Anglo-Saxon Charms', pp. 176–7, 190–1, 202–3.

[7] Grendon, 'Anglo-Saxon Charms', pp. 110–22.

[8] Grendon, 'Anglo-Saxon Charms', pp. 144–5, see also pp. 124–39.

[9] Grendon, 'Anglo-Saxon Charms', pp. 123–7.

This fact points to the possibility of a common Germanic origin for the rhymes, – an origin which must be set at a remote pre-Christian period... The permitted survival both of the jingle spells and of the children's rhymes is explicable enough: for whether the original theurgic phraseology was replaced by outright gibberish, as in the spells, or by harmless lingo, as in the rhymes, the obtrusive Heathenism of the Anglo-Saxon compositions would alike have disappeared, so that the Church could afford to wink at the persisting forms.[10]

Grendon viewed 'gibberish' as a remnant of the heathen past in both the rituals and his contemporary society. Little is known about his personal life and beliefs, and further research on his other publications may reveal interesting information about his interest in pre-Christian religion.[11] For example, Grendon was an apologist for Samuel Butler's animistic philosophy (*God the Known and God the Unknown*, 1917), and there are indications of non-conformist, socialist sympathies in his commentary on Harry Laidler's *Socialism in Thought and Action* (1920).[12] Grendon's personal interests seem to have influenced much of his scholarly edition of 'charms', and more research on his academic, religious, social, and political environments would reveal more about his historiographical agendas.[13]

In 1919, Charles Singer – a British historian of science and medicine – expanded Grendon's discussion of 'charms' to a wider corpus of magical texts from early medieval England.[14] Singer identified a number of different sources that he believed had influenced the 'charms', and he claimed that these were transmitted to Anglo-Saxon England from Continental monasteries.[15] Singer emphasised that native Teutonic

---

[10] Grendon, 'Anglo-Saxon Charms', pp. 125–6.

[11] A summary of his main work can be found in *The Campus* journal of the City University of New York (between 1909 and 1923), and his obituary in *The Shaw Review*, 8 (1965), 110.

[12] Felix Grendon, 'Samuel Butler's God', *North American Review*, 208 (1918), 227–86; 'Socialism in Thought and Action by Harry W. Laidler', *Political Science Quarterly*, 35 (1920), 484–6.

[13] A good starting point for this research could begin by considering the following relevant works: chapters in Allen J. Frantzen and John D. Niles, eds, *Anglo-Saxonism and the Construction of Social Identity* (Gainesville, FL, 1997); chapters in Marie-Françoise Alamichel and Derek Brewer, eds, *The Middle Ages After the Middle Ages in the English Speaking World* (Cambridge, 1997); J. R. Hall, 'Anglo-Saxon Studies in the Nineteenth Century: England, Denmark, America', in *A Companion to Anglo-Saxon Literature*, Phillip Pulsiano and Elaine Treharne, eds (Oxford, 2001), pp. 434–54; chapters in Timothy Baycroft and David Hopkin, eds, *Folklore and Nationalism in the Long Nineteenth Century* (Leiden, 2012); and chapters in Graham A. Loud and Martial Staub, eds, *The Making of Medieval History* (York, 2017).

[14] Charles Singer, 'Early English Magic and Medicine', *Proceedings of the British Academy*, 9 (1919), 341–74.

[15] Singer, 'Magic and Medicine', pp. 346–7, 352–3.

magic had the greatest influence on Anglo-Saxon 'charms', and he argued that this could be identified by four 'obviously pagan' doctrines of specific venoms, the number nine, the disease-causing worm, and elf-shot.[16] Singer also believed that 'charms' were influenced by Celtic magic, European plant-lore, Byzantine magic (including 'gibberish'), and pagan Roman spells.[17] Like Grendon before him, he maintained that once all classical and ecclesiastical elements are removed from the rituals, the remains of original, pagan Anglo-Saxon compositions are exposed.[18]

In 1942, Elliot Van Kirk Dobbie included twelve 'charms' in his collection of Anglo-Saxon poetry and grouped them according to their use of metre, which he associated with the Old English term *galdor*.[19] He provided descriptions for the five manuscripts from which the rituals were selected, and he criticised Grendon's system of classification as 'far from satisfactory'.[20] However, Dobbie did not reject Grendon's corpus of charms, and he also followed previous editors in identifying their non-Christian features, arguing that their metre reflects original heathen elements.[21] His collection of metrical 'charms' associated the Old English noun *galdor* with poetic features of seemingly pagan rituals.

The second principal corpus of Anglo-Saxon 'charms' was published in 1948 by Godfrid Storms. This work drew upon a wider range of sources than Grendon's edition, as it used twenty-three manuscripts for its eighty-six rituals.[22] Storms followed Singer in attempting to uncover features of native Germanic religion in 'charms', which he defined according to James Frazer's anthropological theory of magic.[23] Storms believed that the Old English noun *galdor* defines a tradition of magic in Anglo-Saxon England, and that cognates of this word also uncover Germanic magical practices in Old Norse, Old Saxon, and Old High German contexts.[24] Although only twelve surviving rituals from Anglo-Saxon England actually identify a *galdor* as a ritual performance, Storms used this term to define an entire corpus of 'charms'. He also associated the following pagan characteristics with this genre: vernacular instructions; a 'magical atmosphere'; alliterating verse;

---

[16] Singer, 'Magic and Medicine', pp. 351–9.
[17] Singer, 'Magic and Medicine', pp. 360–73.
[18] See in particular Singer, 'Magic and Medicine', pp. 358–60.
[19] Elliot Van Kirk Dobbie, ed., *The Anglo-Saxon Minor Poems*, ASPR, Vol. 6 (New York, 1942), pp. cxxxii–cxxxiii, 116–28.
[20] Dobbie, *Minor Poems*, pp. cxxx–cxxxii.
[21] Dobbie, *Minor Poems*, p. cxxxvi.
[22] Godfrid Storms, ed. and trans, *Anglo-Saxon Magic* (The Hague, 1948), pp. vi–viii, 25–6.
[23] Storms, *Anglo-Saxon Magic*, pp. 36–40, 117–18; see also James G. Frazer, *The Golden Bough: A Study in Magic and Religion*, abridged edn (London, 1974), p. 14.
[24] Storms, *Anglo-Saxon Magic*, p. 113.

surviving references to Germanic deities; 'gibberish' and 'incomprehensible doggerel'; and superstitious beliefs in herbal power.[25] While Storms outlined some of the predominant Christian elements that are found throughout these texts – such as invocations of saints, liturgical objects, and the use of Latin and Greek – he also maintained that co-existing elements of a Christian and seemingly pagan nature should be separated 'because both have marked characteristics that have little in common with each other'.[26] Storms firmly believed that all of these pagan elements can be easily identified in Anglo-Saxon rituals, and that they collectively define a genre of 'charms' and magic.

Storms' pursuit of a pure, Germanic religion was inspired by the earlier scholarly endeavours of German philologists. There are also indications that his contemporary environment heavily influenced his approach to these early English texts because he traced the historical unity of Germanic nations through the idea of the pre-Christian 'charm':

> If we want to know how magic was performed among the Germanic peoples we must go to the O.E. charms... The original unity existing between the Anglo-Saxons and other Germanic tribes makes it pretty certain that they all used the same charms... Leaving out of account a few minor differences the same charm is found in England, Scotland, Germany, Denmark, Norway, Sweden, the Netherlands, Esthonia, Finland and Hungary... There are positive proofs that an Indo-European linguistic unity existed, comprising both the Germanic and the Aryan peoples, which, even if we reject the unity of race, admits the possibility of a common origin of the charm.[27]

Storms viewed Anglo-Saxon 'charms' as the oldest surviving evidence of Germanic magic that can be traced back to an Indo-European past when the Teutonic nations were united. With the exceptions of England and Scotland, all of the countries that he included in this history were either occupied by the Nazis or allied to Germany during the Second World War. Storms worked on this edition during the war before its publication in 1948 and, given that he was living in Holland throughout the country's occupation, these sentiments about Anglo-Saxon 'charms' may have been influenced by his contemporary political environment.[28] Like Grendon's first edition of 'charms', Storms'

---

[25] See Storms, *Anglo-Saxon Magic*, pp. 116–25.
[26] Storms, *Anglo-Saxon Magic*, p. 117.
[27] Storms, *Anglo-Saxon Magic*, pp. 108–11.
[28] Storms was to later resume this approach to Germanic history in an article on *Beowulf*, where he patriotically situated his hometown Nijmegen in the drama of the Anglo-Saxon poem, Godfrid Storms, 'How Did the *Dene* and the *Geatas* Get Into *Beowulf*?', *ES*, 80 (1999), 46–9, p. 47. On the nationalist agendas of the early German philologists, see Eric G. Stanley, *Imagining the Anglo-Saxon Past:*

edition may reveal more about his academic, social, and political pressures than it does about Anglo-Saxon ritual practices. More research could be conducted on Storms' historiographical agendas, but for the sake of this study it is important to note how he used the idea of the Anglo-Saxon *galdor* to reconstruct a history of a Germanic cultural legacy that survived the conquests of Rome and the Roman Catholic Church.

Scholarly Understandings of Galdor and 'Charms'

The definition of *galdor* as a magical performance prompted a rich tradition of charm scholarship in Anglo-Saxon studies. In their 1952 edition of magic and medicine, George Grattan and Charles Singer defined *galdor* as 'a common word always associated with singing for a magical purpose'.[29] Other studies developed this view of Anglo-Saxon magic and argued that evidence of continued pagan worship can be found in the 'charms', as seen, for example, in William Chaney's influential 1960 article:

> the terms in which the newly converted Anglo-Saxons interpreted the Christian religion were shaped by the tribal culture, impregnated, as it was, by the heathenism of the old religion… However much the merging of the two strands [of Christianity and paganism] complicates the problem of survival, the latter is well attested – perhaps especially in the Anglo-Saxon charms – and the resulting syncretism at times makes for a virtual neo-polytheism… One need not go so far, however, to see more heathenism lurking behind the manuscripts and artefacts than is visible to the twentieth-century eye.[30]

Case studies of individual 'charms' also reflect Chaney's views of paganism, as seen in Bruce Rosenberg's 1966 analysis of the eleventh-century *Æcerbot* field ritual: 'old West Saxon magic is mixed with the new because the worshipper, be he shaman or plowman, has not yet accepted Christianity exclusively nor rejected paganism completely'.[31] Indeed,

---

The Search for Anglo-Saxon Paganism and Anglo-Saxon Trial by Jury (Cambridge, 1975); Robert Leventhal, 'The Emergence of Philological Discourse in the German States 1770–1810', *Isis*, 77 (1986), 243–60; Jeffrey M. Peck, '"In the Beginning Was the Word": Germany and the Origins of German Studies', in *Medievalism and the Modernist Temper*, R. Howard Bloch and Stephen G. Nichols, eds (Baltimore, 1996), pp. 127–47.

[29] George H. G. Grattan and Charles J. Singer, eds and trans, *Anglo-Saxon Magic and Medicine* (London, 1952), p. 38.

[30] William Chaney, 'Paganism to Christianity in Anglo-Saxon England', *Harvard Theological Review*, 53 (1960), 197–217, pp. 197, 199, 217.

[31] Bruce A. Rosenberg, 'The Meaning of *Æcerbot*', *Journal of American Folklore*, 79 (1966), 428–36, p. 431. For other case studies, see Wilfrid Bonser, 'The Seven

in 1967 Paul Taylor went so far as to claim that the Anglo-Saxons recognised a form of ritual that is equivalent to the modern understanding of a 'charm'.[32] The scholarship that immediately followed the two main editions of 'charms' consistently depicted these rituals as evidence of a reluctance or refusal to abandon pagan beliefs.

In 1963, Jane Crawford upheld the view that *galdor* denotes a magical practice but she also remarked that the word is 'irrevocably linked' to the word *sige* (victory) in other Christian texts.[33] She emphasised the importance of the historical contexts of 'charms' and their manuscripts, and highlighted that it is easy to discern the Christian elements in these ritual texts but almost impossible to find convincing evidence of paganism.[34] In 1966 Audrey Meaney also took this approach to the apparent evidence of pagan cults in medieval England, arguing that it is unhelpful to reconstruct anything more than attenuated half-memories of paganism in later Anglo-Saxon texts.[35] Like Crawford, Meaney emphasised the need for caution when discussing supposed pagan practices in England and the importance of a source's historical, political, and ecclesiastical contexts.[36] Thomas Hill has also offered alternative sources of inspiration for these rituals from liturgical texts.[37] These counter-arguments are still crucial for understanding

Sleepers of Ephesus in Anglo-Saxon and Later Recipes', *Folklore*, 56 (1945), 254–6; *The Medical Background of Anglo-Saxon England: A Study in History, Psychology, and Folklore* (London, 1963); Howell Chickering, 'The Literary Magic of *Wið Færstice*', *Viator*, 2 (1972), 83–104; Marie Nelson, 'An Old English Charm against Nightmare', *Germanic Notes*, 13 (1982), 17–18; and, more recently, Lázló Sándor Chardonnens, 'An Arithmetical Crux in the Woden Passage in the Old English *Nine Herbs Charm*', *Neophilologus*, 93 (2009), 691–702.

[32] Paul Beekman Taylor, 'Some Vestiges of Ritual Charms in *Beowulf*', *Journal of Popular Culture*, 1 (1967), 276–85, p. 277.

[33] Jane Crawford, 'Evidences for Witchcraft in Anglo-Saxon England', *Medium Ævum*, 32 (1963), 99–116, p. 103.

[34] Crawford, 'Evidences for Witchcraft', pp. 105, 108. For a study of the Christian construction of paganism, see Carl S. Watkins, *History and the Supernatural in Medieval England* (Cambridge, 2007), pp. 68–107.

[35] Audrey L. Meaney, 'Woden in England: A Reconsideration of the Evidence', *Folklore*, 77 (1966), 105–15, p. 109.

[36] See also Audrey L. Meaney, 'Women, Witchcraft, and Magic in Anglo-Saxon England', in *Superstition and Popular Medicine in Anglo-Saxon England*, Donald G. Scragg, ed. (Manchester, 1989), pp. 9–40; '"And we forbeodað eornostlice ælcne hæðenscipe": Wulfstan and Late Anglo-Saxon and Norse "Heathenism"', in *Wulfstan, Archbishop of York: The Proceedings of the Second Alcuin Conference*, Matthew Townend, ed. (Turnhout, 2004), pp. 461–500.

[37] See Thomas D. Hill, 'An Irish-Latin Analogue for the Blessing of the Sods in the Old English *Æcer-bot* Charm', *N&Q*, 213 (1968), 362–3; 'The *Æcerbot* Charm and its Christian User', *ASE*, 6 (1977), 213–21; 'The Theme of the Cosmological Cross in Two Old English Cattle Theft Charms', *N&Q*, 25 (1978), 488–90; 'Invocation of the Trinity and the Tradition of the Lorica in Old English Poetry', *Speculum*, 56 (1981), 259–67. See also Heather Barkley, 'Liturgical Influences on the Anglo-Saxon Charms against Cattle Theft', *N&Q*, 44 (1997), 450–2.

when, why, how, and by whom these rituals were written. Their most important contribution to the field is that they highlight the ecclesiastical environments in which many of these rituals were written down that were previously discarded by their editors.

Since the mid-1980s, Karen Jolly has become a leading authority on the religious nature of Anglo-Saxon 'charms'. She noted that in other didactic sources *galdor* is condemned because it is used illegitimately, and that these sources replace the saying of a *galdor* with Christian liturgical prayers.[38] In 1996, Jolly argued that *galdor* denoted a vocal production and, given its surrounding liturgical context in 'charm' rituals, it may have been chanted in a similar way to the Gregorian chant used in public liturgies.[39] According to Jolly, *galdor* was not always condemned as a harmful supernatural practice and it could have strong liturgical connections. In her more recent work, she abandons the term 'charm' and refers to these rituals as medicinal and protective 'formulas'.[40]

Despite Jolly's extensive work on the Christian nature of some 'charms', traditional views of pre-Christian magic have persisted. Numerous scholars returned to Dobbie's edition to define metrical 'charms' as magical poetry that depends primarily upon heathen incantation.[41] In 1993, Louis Rodrigues produced another edition of twelve metrical 'charms', arguing that they survived because their Christian substitutions 'hardly differed in spirit from the magical atmosphere of their pagan originals'.[42] The view that these ritual texts provide examples of surviving paganism has also been upheld in very recent years.[43]

Other approaches to 'charms' have traced diachronic and geograph-

---

[38] Karen Jolly, 'Anglo Saxon Charms in the Context of a Christian Worldview', *Journal of Medieval History*, 11 (1985), 279–93, pp. 285–6. See also Karen Jolly, 'Magic, Miracle, and Popular Practice in the Early Medieval West: Anglo-Saxon England', in *Religion, Science, and Magic: In Concert and Conflict*, Jacob Neuser and Ernest S. Frerichs, eds (Oxford, 1989), pp. 166–84.

[39] Karen Jolly, *Popular Religion in Late Saxon England: Elf Charms in Context* (Chapel Hill, NC, 1996), p. 99.

[40] See Karen Jolly, 'On the Margins of Orthodoxy: Devotional Formulas and Protective Prayers in Cambridge, Corpus Christi College MS 41', in *Signs on the Edge: Space, Text and Margin in Medieval Manuscripts*, Sarah L. Keefer and Rolf Bremmer, eds (Paris, 2007), pp. 135–83, esp. pp. 143–6.

[41] See L. M. C. Weston, 'The Language of Magic in Two Old English Metrical Charms', *Neuphilologische Mitteilungen*, 86 (1985), 176–86; Judith A. Vaughan-Sterling, 'The Anglo-Saxon Metrical Charms: Poetry as Ritual', *JEGP*, 82 (1983), 186–200; Stephen Glosecki, *Shamanism and Old English Poetry* (New York, 1989).

[42] Louis J. Rodrigues, ed. and trans, *Anglo-Saxon Verse Charms, Maxims, and Heroic Legends* (Pinner, Middlesex, 1993), pp. 29–30.

[43] See Tornaghi, 'Language of Magic'; James Paz, 'Magic that Works: Performing *Scientia* in the Old English Metrical Charms and Poetic Dialogues of *Solomon and Saturn*', *Journal of Medieval and Early Modern Studies*, 45 (2015), 219–43.

ical connections between the Old English *galdor* and its cognates in other languages. Lea Olsan connected its Indo-European root *ghel-* to Modern English 'yell' and 'yelp', and defined *galdor* according to the Latin *carmen*, which later became *charme* in Middle English.[44] Olsan highlighted geographical and chronological connections between English and Latin ritual traditions, and usefully acknowledged the porosity of any distinction between 'charms' and prayers. However, she also maintained that *galdor* and *carmen* distinguish 'charms' from other genres in both early and late medieval rituals.[45] Jonathan Roper has traced historical changes in the meaning of *galdor* from its origins as an ancient Germanic magical practice to its connotations of trickery in Middle English and its final association with singing in the Modern English 'nightingale'.[46] He also drew semantic connections between these nouns and terms in other European languages denoting 'speech' (Slavic *govor*, German *besprechen* and *spruch*, Czech *zařikat*, and Estonian *sõnad*).[47] Roper's approach brings together different European ritual traditions in an effort to establish a cross-cultural and trans-historical corpus of 'charms'.[48]

For the focus of this study, the most important insight of these scholars is that certain types of English rituals were labelled as 'charms' after the Anglo-Saxon period. Olsan and Roper follow conventional scholarship in claiming that *galdor* denoted a magical performance, and they believe that this Old English term is a direct precedent of later 'charm' traditions. The original Germanic root of *galdor* seems to have denoted a supernatural ritual utterance but the meaning of this word and its cognates seem to have undergone significant change over time. Furthermore, later recensions of English rituals were classified as 'charms' *after* the Anglo-Saxon period, but this does not necessarily mean that *galdor* had the same significance as later understandings of charms. Indeed, the latest prescriptions of a *galdor* are found in mid-eleventh-century manuscripts, and none survive after the Norman Conquest. The precise (but lost) meaning of this word is perhaps the

---

[44] Lea Olsan, 'Latin Charms of Medieval England: Verbal Healing in a Christian Oral Tradition', *Oral Tradition*, 7 (1992), 116–42, pp. 116–17.

[45] See also Lea Olsan, 'The Inscriptions of Charms in Anglo-Saxon Manuscripts', *Oral Tradition*, 14 (1999), 401–19, pp. 401–2; 'Charms and Prayers in Medieval Medical Theory and Practice', *Social History of Medicine*, 16 (2003), 343–66; Lori-Ann Garner, 'Anglo-Saxon Charms in Performance', *Oral Tradition*, 19 (2004), 20–42; Rebecca M. C. Fisher, 'Genre, Prayers, and the Anglo-Saxon Charms', in *Genre – Text – Interpretation: Multidisciplinary Perspectives on Folklore and Beyond*, Frog and Kaarina Koski, eds (Helsinki, 2013), pp. 1–25.

[46] Jonathan Roper, 'Towards a Poetics, Rhetorics, and Proxemics of Verbal Charms', *Folklore*, 24 (2003), 7–49, pp. 38–9.

[47] Roper, 'Towards a Poetics', p. 8.

[48] See also Jonathan Roper, 'Typologising English Charms', in *Charms and Charming in Europe*, Jonathan Roper, ed. (Basingstoke, 2004), pp. 128–44.

most elusive piece of information that would have significant ramifications for historians and enthusiasts of early English magic, paganism, Christianity, and liturgy. Despite the pivotal significance of the meaning of *galdor*, traditional definitions of this Old English word have not taken into account its full range of semantic meanings that do not satisfactorily reflect modern understandings of a 'charm'.

Since the first collection of Anglo-Saxon 'charms' by Thomas Cockayne in 1866, scholars have consistently added more rituals to this corpus, extracted them from their manuscript contexts and isolated them from other texts, and regrouped them according to traditional understandings of magic and paganism. The genre has been defined according to definitions of the Old English noun *galdor* and other features such as their use of verse, 'heathen' elements, and obscure 'gibberish' language. However, an approach that has thus far not been fully explored in contemporary research is to consider how the scribes themselves organised each of these rituals in their manuscripts. While several scholars have discussed some of these texts in their manuscript contexts, unhelpful distinctions between 'charms' and other rituals have been upheld, and this approach has not been applied to the genre as a whole. This book offers a starting point for such an endeavour. An investigation into how Anglo-Saxon ecclesiastics understood and recorded these rituals requires a brief overview of the historical contexts in which they were written.

Historical Contexts of 'Charms'

From the middle of the tenth century, the movement known as the Benedictine Reform was underway in key monastic centres in England, and most of the manuscripts containing 'charms' were written at this time. Some of the main objectives of the Benedictine Reform were to regularise liturgical observances, improve monastic training and study, and increase pastoral care in the wider community. The principal leaders of this movement were Dunstan, Æthelwold, and Oswald; and King Edgar (r. 959–75) was one of the Reform's leading patrons.[49]

After Dunstan's appointment as archbishop of Canterbury (959–88), Christ Church cathedral gradually became a monastic community, and Dunstan established strong connections with Continental monasteries.[50] Several manuscripts containing 'charms' were written

---

[49] See Simon Keynes, 'Edgar, rex admirabilis', in *Edgar, King of the English 959–975: New Interpretations*, Donald G. Scragg, ed. (Woodbridge, 2008), pp. 3–59.

[50] John Blair, *The Church in Anglo-Saxon Society* (Oxford, 2005), p. 352. See also Nicholas Brooks, 'The Career of St Dunstan', Tim Tatton-Brown, 'The City and Diocese of Canterbury in St Dunstan's Time', and Alan Thacker, 'Cults

at Christ Church after Dunstan's reforms, indicating their approval in this high-status ecclesiastical minster. Æthelwold was bishop of Winchester from 963 to 984 and he began his career by dramatically expelling clerics from the Old Minster, replacing them with monks from Abingdon in 964.[51] One of Æthelwold's most important initiatives was the production of the *Regularis Concordia* that outlines how the *Rule of Benedict* should be observed in English monasteries.[52] Æthelwold seems to have advocated the use of the vernacular in the liturgy, and he translated the *Rule of Benedict* into English for the education of monks.[53] A programme of standardising Old English vocabulary also took place at Æthelwold's school in Winchester and, as will be seen in Chapter 1, *galdor* may have been one of the terms that became restricted in usage to signify a dangerous spiritual practice. Many manuscripts containing 'charms' were written in Winchester at important reforming ecclesiastical centres, particularly the Old and New Minsters, indicating that these rituals were incorporated into Æthelwold's programmes for education and liturgical observances. The third of these English reformers was Oswald, who was a politically active figure during his archiepiscopacy in York (972–92). As Oswald was born of a Danish family, his kinship made him a well-connected political and religious leader in the aftermath of the Danish settlements, and his elevation to the archbishopric of York testifies to his abilities as a politician.[54] Many

At Canterbury: Relics and Reform under Dunstan and His Successors', in *St Dunstan: His Life, Times and Cult*, Nigel Ramsay, Margaret Sparks, and Tim Tatton-Brown, eds (Woodbridge, 1992), pp. 1–24, 75–88, and 221–46.

[51] 'Cleric' is used throughout to signify the ecclesiastics who did not observe the monastic *Rule of Benedict*. They are also referred to as Canons and secular clergy in scholarship.

[52] Thomas Symons, ed. and trans, *The Monastic Agreement of the Monks and Nuns of the English Nation: Regularis Concordia* (New York, 1953). On a version of the *Concordia* which was probably written for nuns at Nunnaminster, see Sarah Foot, *Veiled Women I: The Disappearance of Nuns from Anglo-Saxon England* (Aldershot, 2000), pp. 85–110, 145–98, 199–208; Joyce Hill, 'Rending the Garment and Reading by the Rood: *Regularis concordia* Rituals for Men and Women', in *The Liturgy of the Late Anglo-Saxon Church*, M. Bradford Bedingfield and Helen Gittos, eds, HBS Subsidia Series, Vol. 5 (Woodbridge, 2005), pp. 53–64; Julia Barrow, 'The Chronology of the Benedictine "Reform"', in *Edgar, King of the English 959–975*, Scragg, ed., pp. 211–23; Stephen Vanderputten, 'Debating Reform in Tenth- and Early Eleventh-Century Female Monasticism', *Zeitschrift für Kirchengeschichte*, 125 (2014), 289–306.

[53] Henri Logeman, ed., *The Rule of S. Benet: Latin and Anglo-Saxon Intelinear Version*, EETS Original Series, Vol. 90 (London, 1888), p. xxxiv. See also Patrick Wormald, 'Æthelwold and his Continental Counterparts: Contact, Comparison, Contrast', Barbara Yorke, 'Æthelwold and the Politics of the Tenth Century', and Michael Lapidge, 'Æthelwold As Scholar and Teacher', in *Bishop Æthelwold: His Career and Influence*, Barbara Yorke, ed. (Woodbridge, 1988), pp. 13–42, 65–88, and 89–117.

[54] See Nicholas Brooks and Catherine Cubitt, eds, *St Oswald of Worcester: Life and Influence* (London, 1996); Catherine Cubitt, 'The Tenth-Century Benedictine

of the most vehement condemnations of *galdor* as a heathen custom were written in monasteries under Oswald's rule, and these indicate his strict stance on religious practices in their surrounding areas.

Ælfric of Eynsham, Wulfstan the Homilist, and Byrhtferth of Ramsey continued the efforts of these leading reformers into the eleventh century. Ælfric (d. circa 1010) became Abbot of Eynsham in 1005 under the patronage of a nobleman called Æthelmaer the Stout.[55] He wrote an extensive number of works, most notably his series of *Catholic Homilies* and *Lives of Saints* which contain many condemnations of *galdru*.[56] Ælfric significantly developed Æthelwold's 'Winchester vocabulary', he wrote homilies for Wulfstan of York, and he was also a strong opponent of religious customs that were not sanctioned by ecclesiastical authority.[57] Wulfstan ruled as bishop of Worcester and archbishop of York from 1002 to 1016, during which time he wrote the *Canons of Edgar* for the instruction of clerics, which contains proscriptions against practising *galdru*.[58] In 1016, Wulfstan relinquished the see of Worcester, ruling only in York until his death in 1023. As archbishop, he drew up law codes for King Æthelred (r. 978–1013 and 1014–16) and Cnut (r. 1016–35), and he wrote many homilies with further condemnations of *galdru*.[59] Like his contemporary Ælfric, Wulfstan wrote extensively in English to reinforce Christian principles that were put forward by his reformist predecessors. Byrhtferth of Ramsey (c. 970–1020) was also a strong proponent of the Reform's agendas. He was a pupil of Abbo of Fleury and a friend of Dunstan's, and he also promoted the use of the vernacular in monastic education

---

Reform in England', *Early Medieval Europe*, 6 (1997), 77–94, p. 84; 'Sites and Sanctity: Revisiting the Cult of Murdered and Martyred Anglo-Saxon Royal Saints,' *Early Medieval Europe*, 9 (2000), 53–83.

[55] See Joyce Hill, 'Ælfric: His Life and Works', in *A Companion to Ælfric*, Hugh Magennis and Mary Swann, eds (Leiden, 2009), pp. 109–37.

[56] Ælfric, *Ælfric's Lives of Saints*, Walter W. Skeat, ed. and trans, 2 Vols., EETS Original Series, Vols. 76, 82, 94, 114 (London, 1881–91); *Ælfric's Catholic Homilies: The Second Series*, Malcolm Godden, ed., EETS Supplementary Series, Vol. 5 (London, 1979); *Ælfric's Catholic Homilies: The First Series, Text*, Peter Clemoes, ed., EETS Supplementary Series, Vol. 17 (Oxford, 1997).

[57] See Malcolm Godden, 'Ælfric's Changing Vocabulary', *ES*, 61 (1980), 206–23; Mechthild Gretsch, 'Ælfric, Language, and Winchester', in *A Companion to Ælfric*, Magennis and Swann, eds, pp. 35–66.

[58] Wulfstan, *Wulfstan's Canons of Edgar*, Roger Fowler, ed., EETS Original Series, Vol. 266 (London, 1972).

[59] Wulfstan, *The Homilies of Wulfstan*, Dorothy Bethurum, ed. (Oxford, 1971); *Wulfstan's Canon Law Collection*, James E. Cross and Andrew Hamer, eds (Cambridge, 1999). For further, see Dorothy Whitelock, 'Wulfstan and the So-Called Laws of Edward and Guthrum', *EHR*, 56 (1941), 1–21; 'Wulfstan and the Laws of Cnut', *EHR*, 63 (1948), 433–52; M. K. Lawson, 'Archbishop Wulfstan and the Homiletic Element in the Laws of Æthelred II and Cnut', *EHR*, 107 (1992), 565–86.

and study.[60] Byrhtferth's most famous work, the *Enchiridion*, demonstrates his extensive interest in computus, cosmology, and grammar.[61] Many 'charms' appear in manuscripts that also contain computus, astronomical materials, and multilingual texts, demonstrating that some of these rituals were produced in scholarly environments like Byrhtferth's in the late tenth and eleventh centuries.

Despite the efforts of some reformers who condemned uncensored ritual practices – in particular *galdru* – several manuscripts containing 'charms' were written in reforming minsters in Winchester, Canterbury, Worcester, Exeter, and Ramsey. I explore this perhaps surprising outcome of the Reform in the first three chapters before taking a case study of a Winchester manuscript that is believed to contain 'charms' in Chapter 4. In Chapter 5, I consider possible sources of inspiration for obscure 'gibberish' writing in Patristic and medieval theologies of language that assigned great cosmological significance to alphabets and letters.

The historical context of the Benedictine Reform is of paramount importance for situating some 'charms' and their manuscripts in their respective ecclesiastical milieus. However, there has been a tendency in scholarship to represent the Reform as a highly successful movement that had a widespread impact throughout Anglo-Saxon England.[62] A number of important factors should be borne in mind when considering manuscript evidence from this period: monastic centres underwent reform at different times;[63] reformed minsters had distinctive individual leaders and ritual customs;[64] not all minsters were exclusively run by reformed monks and some appear to have had a mix of clerics, monks, and lay people;[65] and reformed monastic communities were

---

[60] See Rebecca Stephenson, 'Scapegoating the Secular Clergy: The Hermeneutic Style as a Form of Monastic Self-Definition', *ASE*, 38 (2009), 101–35; *The Politics of Language: Byrhtferth, Ælfric, and the Multilingual Identity of the Benedictine Reform* (Toronto, 2015).

[61] Byrhtferth of Ramsey, *Byrhtferth's Enchiridion*, Peter S. Baker and Michael Lapidge, eds and trans, EETS Supplementary Series, Vol. 15 (Oxford, 1995).

[62] For a very good recent criticism of this view, see Jesse D. Billett, *The Divine Office in Anglo-Saxon England, 597–c. 1000*, HBS Subsidia Series, Vol. 7 (Woodbridge, 2014), pp. 6–10.

[63] See Christopher Hohler, 'Some Service-Books of the Later Saxon Church', in *Tenth-Century Studies: Essays in Commemoration of the Millenium of the Council of Winchester and 'Regularis Concordia'*, David Parsons, ed. (London, 1975), pp. 60–83; Christopher A. Jones, 'The Book of the Liturgy in Anglo-Saxon England', *Speculum*, 73 (1998), 659–702.

[64] See Blair, *Church in Anglo-Saxon Society*, pp. 291–340; Helen Gittos, 'Sources for the Liturgy of Canterbury Cathedral in the Central Middle Ages', *British Archaeological Association*, 35 (2013), 41–58.

[65] See Blair, *Church in Anglo-Saxon Society*, p. 352; Christopher A. Jones, 'Ælfric and the Limits of "Benedictine Reform"', in *Companion to Ælfric*, Magennis and Swann, eds, pp. 67–108; Julia Barrow, *The Clergy in the Medieval World: Secular Clerics, Their Families and Careers in North-Western Europe, c. 800–c. 1200* (Cambridge, 2015), pp. 269–309.

even replaced by clerics, as seen in mid-eleventh-century Exeter under Bishop Leofric.[66] Considering these factors, great care must be taken to avoid generalising how certain ritual practices were understood, as each manuscript provides unique information about a particular compiler, community, or scribe at a particular time.

Karen Jolly has argued that 'charms' were Christianised during the Reform to increase pastoral care in the wider community, and that these rituals reflect the efforts of reformers to control and censor religious practice.[67] While Jolly usefully highlighted the Christian nature of 'charms', she presented these texts as evidence of a somewhat heterodox Christianity that reflects religious practice on a grassroots level in rural areas.[68] Some of these rituals may have been re-written to control both public and private practices beyond reforming minsters, but I argue that the manuscript evidence of 'charms' in fact provides information about how the Church hierarchy understood and experimented with rituals for a wide range of different occasions.

There are texts from the corpus of 'charms' that lie beyond the scope of this work. Some 'charms' were written down after the Norman Conquest, appearing as twelfth-century additions, and others are found in seventeenth-century transcriptions.[69] Scholars must be cautious when using these sources, as the appearance of 'charms' in later books reveals more about the interests of later scribes and collectors than it does about the activities of Anglo-Saxon scribes. Furthermore, pre-Conquest exemplars that do not survive may have been altered by later scribes; at the very least, the later titles that were given to these copied texts suggest that they were perceived in a different way to their original composers (who did not specify the type of ritual performance in the title).[70] While the afterlives of these 'charms' would be fascinating studies in their own right, this book cannot pursue a recep-

---

[66] Richard W. Pfaff, *The Liturgy in Medieval England: A History* (Cambridge, 2009), p. 130. See also Elaine M. Treharne, 'Producing a Library in Late Anglo-Saxon England: Exeter 1050–1072', *RES*, 54 (2003), 155–72; 'Bishops and Their Texts in the Later Eleventh Century: Worcester and Exeter', in *Essays in Manuscript Geography: Vernacular Manuscripts of the English West Midlands from the Conquest to the Sixteenth Century*, Wendy Scase, ed. (Turnhout, 2007), pp. 13–28; 'The Bishops' Book: Leofric's Homiliary and Eleventh-Century Exeter', in *Early Medieval Studies in Memory of Patrick Wormald*, Stephen Baxter, Catherine E. Karkov, Janet L. Nelson, and David Pelteret, eds (Farnham, 2009), pp. 521–37.

[67] Jolly, *Popular Religion*, pp. 40–66.

[68] Jolly, *Popular Religion*, p. 58.

[69] Seventeenth-century transcripts are found in London, British Library, MS Cotton Julius C. ii and London, British Library, MSS Harley 438, 464. See *A Catalogue of the Harleian Manuscripts in the British Museum*, 4 Vols. (London, 1808–12), Vol. I, pp. 311–13, 323; Storms, *Anglo-Saxon Magic*, pp. 204, 276.

[70] See, for example, two twelfth-century 'charm' rituals with the added titles 'Exorcismus ad Febres expellendas' and 'Medicine contra Febres', Storms, *Anglo-Saxon Magic*, pp. 295–6, 306.

tion history of 'charms' after the Anglo-Saxon period. I include manuscripts that were still being read and used in the twelfth century, as the Anglo-Saxon period did not simply end with the Norman invasion of 1066, as Elaine Treharne and others have demonstrated.[71] However, it is important to note that nine of the twenty-three manuscripts that Godfrid Storms used for his edition contain rituals that were written down *after* the Conquest, and at a time when ritual practices may have been understood in different ways. Furthermore, these texts are scripts for performance and they may not have been followed closely, thus the rituals that survive indicate only an intended performance and do not reflect possible innovations in actual practice.

This study begins by addressing the first core issue of the 'charms' genre and reconsiders the meaning of the Old English noun *galdor*. The first part opens a number of alternative interpretations of this word that impact directly on how these 'charms' could have been seen as liturgical texts. The second part compares the so-called 'charms' to other contemporary Anglo-Saxon liturgical rites and reconsiders them in their manuscript contexts. This approach is fundamental to understanding how scribes recorded 'charms', it reunites the texts with their manuscript sources, and it uncovers the intertextual relationships that exist between these rituals and their surrounding materials. The third part of the book then reconsiders the important characteristic of 'gibberish' that has been used to identify pre-Christian 'charms', and it offers a different way of interpreting this obscure writing as belonging to Patristic philosophies of language. These three approaches to 'charms' address fundamental issues with this constructed genre.

Traditional understandings of 'charms' have imposed connotations of magic, paganism, occultism, and superstition onto definitions of the Old English noun *galdor*. However, when we return to the primary texts themselves and read this word in its wider literary and manuscript contexts, it becomes clear that Anglo-Saxon ecclesiastics valued *galdor* as a very powerful ritual performance that could be used in explicitly Christian and liturgical ways. This word lies at the very heart of the 'charms' genre and a reconsideration of its meaning will dispel modern assumptions of texts that have been seen to embody a heathen medieval past.

---

[71] Elaine M. Treharne, *Living Through Conquest: The Politics of Early English, 1020–1220* (Oxford, 2012); Elaine M. Treharne, Orietta Da Rold, and Mary Swan, eds, *Producing and Using English Manuscripts in the Post-Conquest Period* (Turnhout, 2013).

Part I

1

Kill or Cure:
Anglo-Saxon Understandings of *Galdor*

> 'connotations of *gealdor* in sophisticated, and Christian, literature seem to be entirely evil'.[1]

The first part of this book engages with one core issue of the 'charms' genre: the translation of the Old English noun *galdor* (pl. *galdru*) as 'charm'. It explores the different non-ritual texts that use this word and the surrounding contexts that inform its meaning, before re-evaluating the meaning of *galdor* in Anglo-Saxon rituals. The corpus of Old English highlights the range of texts in which *galdor* appears, and in a small number of cases the word is endorsed as a Christian concept denoting spiritual wisdom, discernment, and divine revelation. However, the noun mainly occurs in proscriptive contexts in glosses and didactic prose texts such as law codes, homilies, and religious guides, where it is condemned as a dangerous form of spiritual knowledge that leads Christians astray. Given that *galdor* is a crucial word for modern historiographies of 'charms', this chapter reconsiders its meanings in non-ritual texts to investigate how various Anglo-Saxon scribes understood this term.

The Etymology of 'Galdor'

The *Toronto Dictionary of Old English* (hereafter *DOE*) offers several different definitions of *galdor*, according the many variants of this noun that are found in homilies, saints' lives, law codes, wisdom poems, riddles, and heroic poetry. These definitions include: 'poem', 'song', 'incantation', 'charm', 'spell', 'illusion', 'deception', 'snake-charmer', 'enchanter', 'wizard', 'divination', 'soothsaying', 'prophe-sying', 'necromancy', 'communication with the dead', 'sorcery', and 'sound / call of a horn'.[2] According to the *DOE*, forms of this word

---

[1] Wulfstan, *Homilies of Wulfstan*, p. 319.
[2] *Dictionary of Old English Corpus* (Toronto, 2009): <http://0-tapor.library. utoronto.ca/doecorpus/> accessed 26 September 2017. Forms of the noun that are recorded in the *DOE* include *galdor, galdra, galdras, galdre, galdres, galdru, galdrum, galdur, gealdor, gealder, gealdra, galder, galdere, galendes, galyndra, galendra, galdrigean, galdriggan, galere, galeres, galunge, gælstre*. See also Joseph

could signify general sounds and utterances as well as supernatural knowledge and practices.

The noun *galdor* and its verbal counterpart *galan* have cognates in other Germanic languages that indicate many different original meanings for these words before they were used to denote specific religious concepts in the late Anglo-Saxon period. In his collection of Proto-Germanic lexemes, Vladimir Orel reconstructs the form 'galðran' from the Old English (OE) *gealdor*, Old Norse (ON) *galdr*, and Old High German (OHG) *galtar* and defines it as 'incantation', 'charm', 'song', 'witchcraft'.[3] He also reconstructs the verb 'galanan' from OE and OHG *galan* and ON *gala*, defining it as 'to crow', 'to sing', and 'to incantate' in an imitative way.[4] Orel also draws comparisons between 'galanan' and the Slavic verb *galiti* ('to triumph, to laugh'), thus presenting the Proto-Germanic roots of *galdor* and *galan* as signifying vocalised sounds, ritual performances, and utterances of exultation.[5]

Other related cognates of *galdor* provide more information about wider meanings of this noun. ON *galdr* (pl. *galdar*), for example, is defined by Mindy MacLeod and Bernard Mees as 'incantation' and 'magical charm', and other compound forms of this word may reflect positive supernatural qualities, such as *galdraumr* ('great sorcerer'), as well as curses and harmful rituals.[6] Indeed, the later endorsement of *galdr* in Iceland as an approved and useful component of ritual practice is witnessed by the fifteenth-century *Galdrabók*, which contains a large collection of ritual texts.[7] Other cognates of OE *galdor* can be found in the OHG nouns *galtar* ('chant'), *gougalari* ('fortune-teller'), *gougal* ('deception, magic'), *galstar(āra)* ('magic, magician'), *agalstra*

Bosworth, *A Compendious Anglo-Saxon and English Dictionary* (London, 1848), p. 102; John R. Clark-Hall, *A Concise Anglo-Saxon Dictionary*, 2nd rev edn (New York, 1916), p. 115.

[3] Vladimir Orel, *A Handbook of Germanic Etymology* (Leiden, 2003), p. 124. For more detailed etymological studies of 'galder-forms' across Scandinavian languages, see Ivar Lindquist, *Galdrar: De gamla germanska trollsångernas stil undersökt I samband med en svensk runinskrift från folkvandringstiden* (Göteborg, 1923); F. Ohrt, 'Om Galdersange', *Danske Studier*, 23 (1923), 186–9; 'Om Merseburgformlerne som Galder', *Danske Studier*, 35 (1938), 125–37.

[4] Orel, *Handbook*, pp. 123–4.

[5] Orel, *Handbook*, p. 124.

[6] Mindy MacLeod and Bernard Mees, *Runic Amulets and Magic Objects* (Woodbridge, 2006), p. 10; Geir T. Zoëga, *A Concise Dictionary of Old Icelandic* (Oxford, 1910), p. 158. For other nouns that are linked with *galdr*, such as *formáli* ('formula, charm'), *seiðr* ('spell, enchantment') and *taufr* ('charms, talismans'), see E. V. Gordon, ed., *An Introduction to Old Norse*, 2nd rev edn (Oxford, 1957), pp. 345, 379, 389; Nils Århammar, ed., *Aspects of Language: Studies in Honour of Mario Alinei, Vol. 1: Geolinguistics* (Amsterdam, 1986), pp. 372–3; Alaric Hall, *Elves in Anglo-Saxon England: Matters of Belief, Health, Gender and Identity* (Woodbridge, 2007), pp. 130–7.

[7] For an edition see M. V. Sæmundsson, ed., *Galdrar á Íslandi: Íslensk Galdrabók*, 2nd edn (Reykjavik, 1992).

('magpie'), *tougali* ('secrecy'), and *swegala* ('sound of a flute').[8] These cognates are inclusive of supernatural practices, secrecy, prophecy, and more general vocalised sounds.

The OE verb *galan* likewise has many different definitions such as 'to sing, cry, yelp, chant', 'speak formally', 'cast a spell', and it is used in contexts 'of birdsong' and of 'the sound of a horn'.[9] The ON verb *gala* is defined as 'to scream, sing, chant, chant magic songs over one' and is related to the verb *kalla* ('to call, shout, cry').[10] OHG cognates are found in *gougalōn* ('bewitch, conjure, foretell'), *bigalstarōn* ('bewitch, enchant'), *fogalōn* ('tell fortunes from the flight of birds'), *tougalen* ('conceal'), and *galan* ('conjure, enchant'), showing common linguistic roots for spiritual practices, prophecy, and secrecy.[11] The Germanic forms of *galan* are indicative of religious rituals and verbal performances but they are also sometimes applied to signify other, more general vocal expressions of humans, birds, and inanimate objects. While *galan* is clearly a verbal form of *galdor*, the verb appears much more frequently in Old English than the noun, suggesting that it had wider, more general meanings for vocal utterances. This chapter can therefore consider only forms of the noun, but it should be noted that *galan* is often closely related to *galdor*.

Other Germanic languages reveal that cognates of OE *galdor* and *galan* could signify supernatural vices like bewitchment and curses, and supernatural virtues like prophecy and wisdom. They are also linked to secrecy, singing, and sounds of objects. It is unwise to limit the meaning of these words to 'charm' and 'chant' exclusively when other, more varied meanings are possible through their Germanic cognates. These original linguistic roots developed different meanings over time, and *galdor* in particular seems to have denoted several specific concepts in early medieval England. In late Anglo-Saxon texts and contexts, *galdor* is mainly used to describe a type of spiritual knowledge or practice that threatened Christian authority, but it is also

---

[8] All OHG definitions are taken from Gerhard Köbler, *Neuenglisch-althochdeutsches Wörterbuch* (2006): <http://www.koeblergerhard.de/germanistischewoerter-buecher/althochdeutscheswoerterbuch/neuenglisch-ahd.pdf> accessed 26 September 2017, 'galtar', p. 74; 'gougalari', p. 175; 'gougal', pp. 111, 273; 'galstar(āra)', p. 273; 'agalstra', p. 273; 'galāri', p. 273; 'tougali', p. 389; 'swegala', p. 169.

[9] *DOE*, s.vb. 6, galan.

[10] Zoëga, *Dictionary of Old Icelandic*, pp. 158, 235. Interestingly, the metrical verses that are chanted in the sagas are commonly signified by the verb *kveða* ('to say, utter, compose, say aloud, sound'), rather than *gala* or *kalla*.

[11] Köbler, *Wörterbuch*, 'gougalōn', pp. 46, 91, 174; 'bigalstarōn', pp. 46, 141; 'fogalōn', p. 47; 'tougalen', p. 89; 'galan', pp. 91, 141. The second Old High German *Merseburg Charm* employs triple repetition of the verb *bigalan* in a ritual to bind a sprain, see Susan Fuller, 'Pagan Charms in Tenth-Century Saxony? The Function of the Merseburg Charms', *Monatschefte*, 72 (1980), 162–70.

used in other ways to promote Christian ideologies, indicating a wider semantic range of possible meanings that have not been considered in previous translations of this word.

Appearances of 'Galdor' in Old English

In order to understand the meaning of *galdor* in Anglo-Saxon ritual texts, it is essential to trace the occurrences of all forms of this word in the corpus of Old English. Most surviving appearances of *galdor* show that the term was condemned because of a clear concern over its spiritual usage, and these proscriptions are constructed in formulaic ways. There are, however, a number of texts that present *galdor* in Christian terms where it signifies wisdom, spiritual discernment, and a medium through which divine secrets are revealed. Although only a few such appearances of *galdor* survive, it is beneficial to begin with a discussion of these Christian depictions because they indicate a greater range of meanings for this word than has been traditionally perceived.

Non-Condemnatory Uses of 'Galdor'

Some scholars have argued that *galdor* is always condemned by Christian writers in non-ritual texts.[12] However, this is not always the case, as some sophisticated Christian works use *galdor* in a non-condemnatory way. Indeed, the contexts that surround this word reflect its rich connotations with spiritual power, wisdom, liturgy, and sacramental mystery. These non-proscriptive occurrences of *galdor* are found in *Beowulf*, saints' lives, wisdom poems, and two riddles.

Beowulf

In the Old English epic poem *Beowulf*, *galdor* is used to describe the sound of a horn in battle and a supernatural barrier that protects the dragon's hoard. These instances indicate broader and more general meanings of this word than its later usage in didactic prose texts. The first appearance occurs after Beowulf's death, when a messenger recounts past glories of the Geats. This messenger describes how the horn of King Hygelac once declared the Geats' victory over the Swedes:

---

[12] See, for example, Bethurum, ed., *Homilies of Wulfstan*, p. 319; Rebecca M. C. Fisher, 'Writing Charms: The Transmission and Performance of Charms in Anglo-Saxon England', Unpublished Doctoral Thesis (University of Sheffield, England, 2011), p. 9.

Frofor eft gelamp
sarig-modum somod ær-dæge,
syððan hie Hygelaces horn ond byman,
gealdor ongeaton, þa se goda com
leoda dugoðe on last faran (2941–5).[13]

With break of day
what comfort came to those care-oppressed men
when they heard Hygelac's horn and trumpet
giving voice [*gealdor ongeaton*], as that valiant man came up
with the flower of his host, following on their tracks![14]

Ongentheow, king of the Swedes, killed Hygelac's brother Hathkin and drove the surviving Geats into a forest. Hygelac then arrived to rescue them and avenged the death of his brother by killing Ongentheow. The victory was signalled by the *galdor* of Hygelac's horn, and the term is evidently used to denote a heroic victory. The meaning of *galdor* in this passage reflects its broader semantic range, and it is evidently connected with ideas of victory, sound, and knowledge (in this case knowledge of victory; 'ongietan', to know, recognise, behold, perceive).

Following the messenger's description of the Geats' previous victories and his prophecy of their impending doom, Beowulf's retainers seek out their lord's body, which is found lying beside the corpse of the dragon. Surrounding the dragon are objects from the treasure-hoard that it guarded with the aid of a supernatural *galdor*:

Þonne wæs þæt yrfe eacen-cræftig,
iu-monna gold, galdre bewunden,
þæt ðam hring-sele hrinan ne moste
gumena ænig, nefne God sylfa,
sigora Soð-cyning, sealde þam ðe he wolde
– he is manna gehyld – hord openian (3051–7).[15]

And this gold of former men was full of power,
the huge inheritance, hedged about with a spell [*galdre*]:
no one among men was permitted to touch
that golden store of rings unless God Himself,
the true King of Victories, the Protector of mankind,
enabled one He chose to open the hoard.[16]

The hoarded wealth of an ancient tribe is guarded by both a dragon and a *galdor* ('galdre bewunden', 3052), and this passage has been used

---

[13] Charles L. Wrenn, ed., *Beowulf*, 2nd edn (London, 1958), p. 172.
[14] Michael Alexander, trans, *Beowulf* (Harmondsworth, 1973), p. 144.
[15] Wrenn, *Beowulf*, p. 175.
[16] Alexander, *Beowulf*, p. 147.

to explicate the word's 'magical' connotations.[17] In this context, the *galdor* is a protective force that has been activated by some entity with supernatural power. John Tanke argued that the thief who stole a cup from the hoard – thus awaking the dragon – simultaneously unleashed a curse that ultimately led to Beowulf's death.[18] This type of curse may be the kind of practice that is elsewhere wholeheartedly condemned as heathen by Anglo-Saxon ecclesiastics, but the surrounding context of this passage indicates that this *galdor* is subject to the Christian God. God alone ('God sylfa', 3055) may decide who accesses the hoard and nobody but His chosen one is permitted to touch it. It may be that the *galdor* surrounding the hoard is multivalent, as it protects the wealth of a pre-Christian people but simultaneously works according to the will of the Christian God. If this is a later embellishment of the poem, the function of this *galdor* remained compatible with a Christian framework. Rather than providing evidence of an explicitly 'magical', pagan, or even non-Christian concept, the *galdor* that protects the hoard may be more neutral in meaning than has previously been considered.

The Exeter Book

The remaining non-condemnatory uses of *galdor* are found in poems from the Exeter Book and the Vercelli Book. These two manuscripts contain similar texts that are thematically related, and they use *galdor* in similar ways. It is important to note that both of these manuscripts also contain texts that describe *galdor* in a condemnatory way, indicating that this word was employed for different purposes. The Exeter Book (Exeter, Cathedral Library, MS 3501) is a collection of spiritual texts and wisdom poetry, containing elegies, riddles, biblical poems, saints' lives, homilies, and maxims. These genres are not as distinct as printed editions have indicated and all demonstrate a focus on wisdom, Christian discernment, and spiritual edification. A number of these texts use *galdor* to signify explicitly Christian concepts, although one other poem in this manuscript uses it in a condemnatory way, suggesting that the *galdor* was a powerful spiritual practice that was harnessed by both God's saints and enemies. It is therefore important to try to situate when and where the manuscript was written so that we may understand how a particular community or group of individuals perceived this term.

The Exeter Book was written by a single scribe in the second half of the tenth century but there has been great disagreement over its place

---

[17] See Taylor, 'Ritual Charms in *Beowulf*', p. 277. For a criticism of this interpretation, see Crawford, 'Evidences for Witchcraft', p. 109.
[18] John Tanke, 'Beowulf, Gold-Luck, and God's Will', *SP*, 99 (2002), 356–79, p. 363.

of origin. The manuscript dates to the early years of the Benedictine Reform, and this is important because it was written at a time when *galdor* seems to have been restricted in meaning in didactic prose texts to signify a dangerous spiritual practice that led Christians astray. Some scholars believe that it was written in a small minster in the south-west of England which was not influenced by the Reform movement, whilst others have argued that it was copied from an earlier exemplar in a major ecclesiastical centre associated with the Reform. The scribe who copied these texts evidently did not see any problem with using *galdor* to signify explicitly Christian concepts, whether he was working in a non-Reform scriptorium or in a minster under the authority of leading reformers.

There is a reference to this manuscript in a famous inventory of gifts donated to Exeter cathedral library by Leofric (bishop of Exeter 1050–72), and this has led scholars to believe that the manuscript was written in Exeter.[19] The same handwriting of the Exeter Book scribe has also been identified in two other early eleventh-century manuscripts: London, Lambeth Palace, MS 149; and Oxford, Bodleian Library, MS Bodley 319.[20] Neil Ker believed that these manuscripts were written in Exeter, which was a monastic house from 968 until Leofric's episcopacy in 1050.[21] However, Richard Gameson has more recently demonstrated that Lambeth 149 and Bodley 319 have strong palaeographical connections with books from Christ Church, Canterbury.[22] After his appointment as archbishop of Canterbury in 959, Dunstan maintained close contact with his previous monastery at Glastonbury, and Gameson concludes that the Exeter Book was likely

---

[19] See R. W. Chambers, Max Förster, and Robin Fowler, eds, *The Exeter Book of Old English Poetry* (London, 1933), p. 28; George Philip Krapp and Elliot Van Kirk Dobbie, eds, *The Exeter Book*, ASPR, Vol. 3 (New York, 1936), p. x; Benjamin J. Muir, ed., *The Exeter Anthology of Old English Poetry: An Edition of Exeter Dean and Chapter MS 3501*, 2 Vols. (Exeter, 1994), Vol. I, p. 3. See also P. W. Conner, *Anglo-Saxon Exeter: A Tenth-Century Cultural History* (Woodbridge, 1993), pp. 1–20, 48–147. On the contents of Leofric's inventory, see Richard Gameson, 'The Origin of the Exeter Book of Old English Poetry', *ASE*, 25 (1996), 135–85, pp. 140–3, 162–3; Michael Lapidge, *The Anglo-Saxon Library* (Oxford, 2005), pp. 56–7, 139–40.

[20] Neil R. Ker, *Catalogue of Manuscripts Containing Anglo-Saxon* (Oxford, 1957), pp. 153, 340, 360–1. See also Jane A. Roberts, ed., *The Guthlac Poems of the Exeter Book* (Oxford, 1979), pp. 12–13.

[21] See Ker, *Catalogue*, p. 153; David Knowles, C. N. L. Brooke, and Vera C. M. London, *The Heads of Religious Houses England and Wales I: 940–1216*, 2nd edn (Cambridge, 2004), p. 48.

[22] Gameson, 'Origin of the Exeter Book', p. 177, see also pp. 163–8, 173–5; Helmut Gneuss, *Handlist of Anglo-Saxon Manuscripts: A List of Manuscripts and Manuscript Fragments Written or Owned in England up to 1100* (Tempe, AZ, 2001), p. 54; Helmut Gneuss and Michael Lapidge, *Anglo-Saxon Manuscripts: A Bibliographical Handlist of Manuscripts and Manuscript Fragments Written or Owned in England up to 1100* (Toronto, 2014), pp. 201–2.

to have been produced at this major ecclesiastical centre associated with the Reform.[23] Robert Butler also argues that the literary milieu of Glastonbury under Dunstan and the contents of the Exeter Book indicate that the manuscript was written at Glastonbury during or shortly after Dunstan's abbacy there.[24] If this was the case, there are important implications about how *galdor* was perceived as a term that was entirely compatible with Christianity at a high-status minster and at a time when the term was being used in condemnatory ways by other reformers.

Elaine Treharne has proposed Exeter, Crediton, and Glastonbury as possible places of production for the Exeter Book, all of which were monastic houses at the time of writing.[25] Treharne concludes that the manuscript was written by one highly skilled scribe who had access to a good range of resources, and that the manuscript's thematic content reflects clerical as well as monastic interests, thus indicating that it was written for a variety of audiences in the early years of the Reform in one of these south-western monasteries.[26]

Different spellings in the Exeter Book and Bodley 319 indicate that the scribe was able to write in more than one standardised version of English, with West-Saxon being his native language.[27] This is an important point to note because Æthelwold's school in Winchester promoted the standardisation of West-Saxon spelling during the Reform which, as Helmut Gneuss has convincingly argued, gave rise to a conscious revision of language in the second half of the tenth century.[28] This project had a significant impact on the redefinition of certain words and their use in written sources, and it may have been the case that *galdor* was one such word that came to be reconceived as a forbidden spiritual practice. The non-condemnatory uses of *galdor* in the Exeter Book, therefore, perhaps reflect earlier views of this word before its

---

[23] Gameson, 'Origin of the Exeter Book', p. 179. See also Matthew T. Hussey, 'Dunstan, Æthelwold, and Isidorean Exegesis in Old English Glosses: Oxford, Bodleian Library Bodley 319', *RES*, 60 (2009), 681–704.

[24] Robert M. Butler, 'Glastonbury and the Early History of the Exeter Book', in *Old English Literature in its Manuscript Context*, Joyce Tally Lionarons, ed. (Morgantown, 2004), pp. 173–215, p. 215.

[25] Elaine M. Treharne, 'Manuscript Sources of Old English Poetry', in *Working with Anglo-Saxon Manuscripts*, Owen-Crocker, ed., pp. 88–111, pp. 90, 99.

[26] Treharne, 'Manuscript Sources', pp. 99–101.

[27] See N. F. Blake, 'The Scribe of the Exeter Book', *Neophilologus*, 46 (1962), 316–19.

[28] Helmut Gneuss, 'The Origin of Standard Old English and Æthelwold's School at Winchester', *ASE*, 1 (1972), 63–83, p. 69. See also W. Hofsetter, 'Winchester and the Standardization of Old English Vocabulary', *ASE*, 17 (1988), 139–61; Helmut Gneuss, 'The Study of Language in Anglo-Saxon England', *Bulletin of the John Rylands Library*, 72 (1990), 3–32, pp. 25–6; Ursula Lenker, 'The Monasteries of the Benedictine Reform and the "Winchester School": Model Cases of Social Networks in Anglo-Saxon England', *European Journal of English Studies*, 4 (2000), 225–38, p. 231.

revised usage spread from Winchester; the manuscript was copied from one or more exemplars, the term is found in poetry that almost certainly predates the time when the first exemplar was written, and the scribe may not have wished to make alterations to the texts' poetic vocabulary.[29]

From the evidence that is available, we are dealing with a manuscript that was probably copied from an earlier, pre-Reform codex in a reforming minster after it was commissioned by patrons or leading ecclesiastics of the Reform movement. The Exeter Book provides important information about how those involved in the manuscript's production understood and viewed the Christian nature of *galdor* before it became predominantly associated with dangerous religious knowledge and practices in the 'Winchester' vocabulary. This word is used to describe wisdom, Christian discernment, and spiritual revelation in poems about St Guthlac, Christian morality, the transient nature of the earthly life, and two riddles for liturgical objects. As will be seen later, this manuscript also contains one instance where *galdor* is used in a particular way to describe the actions of God's enemies, suggesting that it signified a powerful spiritual performance that could help or hinder Christian authorities.

GUTHLAC B

Galdor is used to describe spiritual wisdom and foresight in the Exeter Book's *Guthlac B*. This poem is usually considered to be separate from *Guthlac A* (lines 1–818) according to differences in style and sources.[30] *Guthlac B* is based on Chapter 50 of Felix's Latin *Life of Saint Guthlac* and it gives an account of the saint's relationship with his disciple Beccel. Catherine Clarke argues that the poem presents a model of the ideal relationship between a spiritual patron and a disciple, and that it was written for a monastic audience to underscore these values for seniors and novitiates.[31] Guthlac's superior authority is the central focus of the poem and his wisdom is demonstrated through his edifying lessons to his disciple. Daniel Calder has argued that this focus on authority serves to distinguish the saint from the ordinary man to the

---

[29] See Kenneth Sisam, *Studies in the History of Old English Literature* (Oxford, 1953), pp. 102–3.

[30] For an overview of these differences, see Krapp and Dobbie, *Exeter Book*, pp. xxx–xxxi. On *Guthlac A*, see Alaric Hall, 'Constructing Anglo-Saxon Sanctity: Tradition, Innovation and Saint Guthlac', in *Images of Sanctity: Essays in Honour of Gary Dickson*, Debra Higgs Strickland, ed. (Leiden, 2007), pp. 207–35. Catherine A. M. Clarke provides a very good discussion of the relationships between the two poems in *Writing Power in Anglo-Saxon England: Texts, Hierarchies, Economies* (Cambridge, 2012), pp. 11–43. See also Roberts, *Guthlac Poems*, pp. 19–48.

[31] Clarke, *Writing Power*, p. 16.

point where 'Beccel does not, nor will he ever, grasp the meaning of the mystical transfiguration that will occur in his presence.'[32] However, although Guthlac is a mystical figure who edifies and reveals divine mysteries to his servant, Beccel does in fact come to spiritual enlightenment when he affirms that he has grasped the meaning of Guthlac's mystical *galdrum*.

The poem uses *galdor* to describe the saint's words of spiritual wisdom. When Guthlac is on the point of death, Beccel begs him for comfort before he dies:

> Ongon þa ofostlice
> to his winedryhtne wordum mæðlan:
> 'Ic þec halsige, hæleþa leofost
> gumena cynnes, þurh gæsta weard,
> þæt þu hygesorge heortan minre
> geeþe, eorla wyn. Nis þe ende feor,
> þæs þe ic on galdrum ongieten hæbbe.
> Oft mec geomor sefa gehþa gemanode,
> hat æt heortan, hyge gnornende
> nihtes nearwe, ond ic næfre þe,
> fæder, frofor min, frignan dorste' (1201–11).[33]

> Hurriedly then he addressed these words to his friend and master: 'I beg you, most beloved man among humankind, by the Guardian of souls, that you, men's joy, might ease the anxious curiosity in my heart. The end is not far from you, according to what I have understood from your divinations [*galdrum*]. Often my troubled understanding, ardent at heart, my nagging thought would remind me of these anxieties in the confine of the night, but I have never dared to question you, my father and comforter.'[34]

Beccel laments the fact that he had not asked Guthlac about some conversations which he had overheard. We are then told that the saint spoke with God's angel during his time in retreat (1227–69). A little earlier in the poem, Guthlac describes this exchange of divine speech, and it is referred to as a revelation of the lord's mystery: 'ne swa deoplice dryhtnes geryne / þurh menniscne muð areccan on sidum sefan' (1121–2).[35] Clarke claims that this passage describing Guthlac's spiritual revelation is climactic in the poem, and that it emphasises Guthlac's role as a pupil of divine teaching, mirroring Beccel's

---

[32] Daniel G. Calder, 'Theme and Strategy in *Guthlac B'*, *Papers on Language and Literature*, 8 (1972), 227–42, p. 237.

[33] Krapp and Dobbie, *Exeter Book*, p. 83.

[34] S. A. J. Bradley, trans., *Anglo-Saxon Poetry* (London, 1982), p. 279.

[35] Krapp and Dobbie, *Exeter Book*, p. 81; 'nor the mystery of the Lord so deeply expounded in breadth of understanding out of human mouth', Bradley, *Anglo-Saxon Poetry*, p. 277.

discipleship of Guthlac.[36] Guthlac is shown to be a mediator between God's messengers and his fellow men, and Beccel is given spiritual insight into the saint's death because Guthlac spoke to him in *galdrum* (1206–7).

This description in *Guthlac B* departs slightly from the account found in Felix's *Life of Guthlac*:

> Audiens autem haec praefactus frater exorsus inquit: 'Obsecro mi pater, quia infirmitatem tuam intelligo, et moriturum te audio, ut dicas mihi unum, de quo olim te interrogare non ausus diu sollicitabar. Nam ab eo tempore, quo tecum, domine, habitare coeperam, te loquentem vespere et mane audiebam, nescio cum quo. Propterea adiuro te, ne me sollici- tum de hac re post obitum tuum dimittas.'

> When the same brother heard this he began to say: 'I beseech you, father, since I understand that you are ill, and I hear that you are like to die, that you will tell me one thing which I have long been troubled about but have not dared to ask you. From the time I first began to live with you, my lord, I have heard you talking, evening and morning, with someone, I know not whom. Therefore I adjure you not to leave me troubled about this matter after your death.'[37]

In Felix's version, Beccel says that he understands the saint's mortal condition ('quia infirmitatem tuam intelligo') according to what he hears ('moriturum te audio'). He grasps the situation through his intel- lect and hearing, but *Guthlac B* diverges from Felix's *Vita* to stress that it is the saint's *galdrum* that are grasped and understood. These *galdrum* describe the prophecy of a saint who has conversed with angels and is about to leave the human world, perhaps suggesting an acceptable form of divination because it came from an exemplary Christian saint. Guthlac's *galdrum* bring spiritual knowledge and wisdom to men on earth, reflecting one of the primary functions of this poem in its late tenth- and eleventh-century monastic context.[38]

VAINGLORY

The Exeter Book's *Vainglory* also links *galdor* to concepts of wisdom. This poem concerns the discernment of good and evil, and it instructs its reader or listener in Christian moral values. At the beginning of *Vainglory* the poet explains how a wise person, who is learned in the teaching of prophets, taught him how to discern the good man:

---

[36] Clarke, *Writing Power*, pp. 25–6.
[37] Felix, *Felix's Life of Saint Guthlac*, Bertram Colgrave, ed. and trans (Cambridge, 1956), pp. 156–7.
[38] See Clarke, *Writing Power*, p. 42.

Hwæt, me frod wita on fyrndagum
sægde, snottor ar, sundorwundra fela!
Wordhord onwreah witgam larum
beorn boca gleaw, bodan ærcwide,
þæt ic soðlice siþþan meahte
ongitan bi þam gealdre godes agen bearn (1–6).[39]

Listen, an old advisor in former days,
a wise messenger, told me of many special wonders.
The man learned in books opened his word-hoard,
with prophetic teachings, an ancient saying of the prophet,
so that I may now truly know
by these *gealdre* God's own son.[40]

Vainglory is a homiletic poem about the dangers of pride and its remedy of humility.[41] The proud and the humble man are contrasted throughout the poem, and it has been referred to as one of the 'poems of advice' that has strong resonances with the teachings of the Church Fathers.[42] The word *gealdre* is inextricably linked to surrounding phrases denoting wise men and their learning: 'frod wita' (1), 'snottor ar' (2), 'witgam larum' (3), 'boca gleaw' (4), 'bodan ærcwide' (5). The special wonders of divine knowledge ('sundorwundra fela', 2) are also revealed through these *gealdre*, in a similar way to the saint's *galdrum* in *Guthlac B. Vainglory* explicitly uses *galdor* to signify the ancient sayings of the prophets, and true knowledge of God's sons.

RIMING POEM

The *Riming Poem* of the Exeter Book also uses *galdor* to signify wisdom and poetic skill. This poem is a very enigmatic text and bears strong resemblances to the riddles. It opens with an expansive range of blessings that were enjoyed by a leader during his or her reign, and half way through the poem the ruler describes how he or she lost everything and fell into misery. Critics have claimed that the poem is merely about this ruler's series of misfortunes and loss of earthly wealth and lordship.[43] Others have claimed that it is an allegory of death and time in

---

[39] Krapp and Dobbie, *Exeter Book*, p. 147.

[40] Unless otherwise indicated, all translations are my own.

[41] See Roy M. Liuzza, *Old English Poetry: An Anthology* (Ontario, 2014), p. 59.

[42] Tom A. Shippey, *Old English Verse* (London, 1972), p. 67; Catharine A. Regan, 'Patristic Psychology in the Old English "Vainglory"', *Traditio*, 26 (1970), 324–35.

[43] W. C. Robinson, *Introduction to Our Early English Literature* (London, 1885), p. 181; Doris Grübl, *Studien zu den angelsächsischen Elegien* (Marburg: Elwert-Gräfe, 1948), pp. 61–3.

purgatory, and that its overall message is about God's will and human existence.[44]

Among the many blessings that the leader enjoyed, we are told that he or she sang *galdorwordum* in the height of his or her glory:

Swa mec hyhtgiefu heold, hygedryht befeold,
staþolæhtum steold, stepegongum weold
swylce eorþe ol, ahte ic ealdorstol,
galdorwordum gol. Gomen sibbe ne ofoll,
ac wæs gefest gear, gellende sner,
wuniendo wær wilbec bescær.
Scealcas wæron scearpe, scyl wæs hearpe,
hlude hlynede, hleoþor dynede,
sweglrad swinsade, swiþe ne minsade (21–9).[45]

So joy dwelt within me, a family troop encompassed me, I possessed estates, where I stepped I had command over whatever the earth brought forth, I had a princely throne, I sang with charmed words [*galdorwordum*], old friendship did not grow less. Moreover, there was a year rich in gifts, a resounding harp-string, lasting peace cut short the river of sorrow. The servants were active, the harp was resonant, loudly rang; sound pealed, music made melody, did not greatly abate.[46]

This passage focuses on the leader's joys in family life, friendship, leadership, and music. The hall occupies the centre of this narrative where the leader sat upon a throne and sang *galdorwordum* (23–4), where harps were played (27), and where music resounded (28–9). The passage evidently connects the *galdorwordum* to both the music in the hall and the ruler's authority. A little later the speaker also describes the quality of wisdom ('freaum frodade', 32), echoing other associations of *galdor* with wise words.

Karl Wentersdorf interprets this *galdor* and the poem's musical imagery as references to liturgical performances, and he claims that when the speaker recalls singing or chanting *galdorwordum*, 'he is probably thinking either of participation in Christian liturgies or of his spontaneous offering of prayers of thanksgiving'.[47] If this is a reference to a liturgical performance, it could be a description of the singing

---

[44] G. K. Anderson, *Literature of the Anglo-Saxons* (Princeton, NJ, 1949), p. 175; Kemp Malone, 'The Old English Period (to 1100)', in *A Literary History of England*, A. C. Baugh, ed., 2nd edn (London, 1967), pp. 1–106, p. 84; R. P. M. Lehmann, 'The Old English Riming Poem: Interpretation, Text, and Translation', *JEGP*, 64 (1970), 437–49, pp. 440–1.

[45] Krapp and Dobbie, *Exeter Book*, p. 167.

[46] Translation from W. S. Mackie, 'The Old English "Rhymed Poem"', *JEGP*, 21 (1922), 507–19, p. 513.

[47] Karl P. Wentersdorf, 'The Old English "Rhyming Poem": A Ruler's Lament', *SP*, 82 (1985), 265–94, p. 281.

of psalms in a church setting. The hall is used as a metaphor for the church building elsewhere in the Exeter Book (*Riddles* 55, 56, 59), and these *galdorwordum* may perhaps be the prayers that were sung each day within the church.[48] The compounding of *galdor* and *wordum* in this context is interesting as 'wordum' may imply literate sounds and 'galdor' may signify a type of oral performance of spiritual significance, suggesting the chanting of the psalms or the Word of God.

The Christian nature of these *galdorwordum* is also established in the opening lines of the poem, where the speaker associates his or her previous prosperity and glory with God's grace: 'Me lifes onlah se þis leoht onwrah, / ond þæt torhte geteoh, tillice onwrah' (1–2).[49] It is clear that the leader's singing of *galdorwordum* is included among nostalgic memories of the past and other aspects of a well-ruled kingdom. The songs, hymns, or prayers of this fallen kingdom and bygone, glorious era reinforce the association of this word with right-ruling and Christian wisdom.

RIDDLES

Two riddles from the Exeter Book use *galdor* in perhaps the most intriguing ways to describe explicitly Christian concepts. They share features with other riddles that concern 'writing as a material form of speech' but their uses of *galdor* distinguish them in a particular way.[50] In *Riddle* 48 a 'hring' is said to cry out in *galdorcwide*:

> Ic gefrægn for hæleþum hring endean,
> torhtne butan tungan, tila þeah he hlude
> stefne ne cirmde, strongum wordum.
> Sinc for secgum swigende cwæð:
> 'Gehæle mec, helpend gæsta.'
> Ryne ongietan readan goldes
> guman galdorcwide, gleawe beþencan
> hyra hælo to gode, swa se hring gecwæð (1–8).[51]

> I heard of a ring singing for heroes,
> bright without a tongue, rightly though he cried out
> without a voice, with strong words.
> The treasure for men spoke silently:

---

[48] For a discussion of these riddles, see Dieter Bitterli, *Say What I Am Called: The Old English Riddles of the Exeter Book and the Anglo-Latin Riddle Tradition* (Toronto, 2009), pp. 124–31.

[49] Krapp and Dobbie, *Exeter Book*, p. 166; 'He granted me life who revealed the sun, and formed that brightness, well displayed.'

[50] Peter Ramey, 'Writing Speaks: Oral Poetics and Writing Technology in the Exeter Book Riddles', *PQ*, 92 (2013), 335–56, p. 336.

[51] Krapp and Dobbie, *Exeter Book*, pp. 205–6.

'Save me, Helper of souls!'
May men perceive the mystery [*ryne*] of the red gold,
the enchanting song [*galdorcwide*], may the wise entrust
their salvation to God, as the ring said.[52]

The 'hring' that speaks in this riddle could refer to a ring bearing the inscription 'Gehæle mec, helpend gæsta', which may have been worn as an amulet. The generally accepted solution to this riddle is 'chalice', and the words that it speaks are interpreted as a liturgical formula inscribed on this object.[53]

One of the fascinating features of this riddle is that the object speaks without a tongue ('butan tungan', 2), without a voice ('stefne ne cirmde', 3), and silently ('swigende cwæð', 4). *Riddle* 59 also describes a chalice that is dumb but is able to bring the name of the Saviour to the listener's mind: 'dumba brohte / ond in eagna gesihð'.[54] The use of paradox is characteristic of riddling texts and it often misguides the reader or listener through prosopopoeia.[55] Elizabeth Okasha has highlighted the possible connection between the silent 'hring' and the verb 'hringan' (to sound).[56] Interestingly, the 'hring' cries silently in *galdorcwide* so that the wise may be directed towards God through its words (7–8). Peter Ramey offers an important insight into the affectivity of the paradoxical silent voice:

> the mysterious riddle-object is not presented as a message decoded by a reader but as an utterance *enacted* upon a hearer or group of listeners... speech is conferred upon an article of a profoundly sacred character (probably an engraved communion chalice), which imbues its religious function with a deepened sense of mystery and power... silent declaration, perceptible only to those capable of understanding it, obviously refers to writing.[57]

---

[52] Translation from Ramey, 'Writing Speaks', p. 344. Ramey emends 'hring endean' of line 1 to 'hring gyddian', rendering the ring as a singing object. See also Krapp and Dobbie, *Exeter Book*, p. 347.

[53] See Marie Nelson, 'The Paradox of Silent Speech in the Exeter Book Riddles', *Neophilologus*, 62 (1978), 609–15; Wentersdorf, 'Ruler's Lament', p. 281; Bitterli, *Say What I Am Called*, p. 26; Patrick J. Murphy, *Unriddling the Exeter Book Riddles* (Pennsylvania, 2011), p. 100. John Niles and Megan Cavell interpret the word 'hring' as 'husel-disc' to pose the solution of a paten, John Niles, *Old English Enigmatic Poems and the Play of the Texts* (Turnhout, 2006), p. 112; Megan Cavell, 'Powerful Patens in the Anglo-Saxon Medical Tradition and Exeter Book *Riddle 48*', *Neophilologus*, 101 (2017), 129–38.

[54] Krapp and Dobbie, *Exeter Book*, p. 209. 'Dumb, it brought the Lord's name clearly into the mind', translation from Ramey, 'Writing Speaks', p. 345.

[55] See especially Miriam Edlich-Muth, 'Prosopopoeia: Sharpening the Anglo-Saxon Toolkit', *ES*, 95 (2014), 95–108.

[56] Elizabeth Okasha, 'Old English hring in Riddles 48 and 59', *Medium Ævum*, 62 (1993), 61–9, pp. 64–5.

[57] Ramey, 'Writing Speaks', pp. 344–5.

Ramey's insight is extremely useful for interpreting this riddle. However, the object's silent declaration and its *galdorcwide* are not necessarily limited to a written message. The chalice was used during an inaudible performance in the Mass as the Canon was said quietly by a priest, and evidence for this dates as early as the sixth century in Frankish liturgies.[58] This is also implied in an Anglo-Saxon Chrism Mass *ordo* from the late tenth-century *Sacramentary of Ratoldus*: 'et canatvr secreto secvndvm ordinem. Vsque sed ueniam quaesumus largitor admitte' (Paris, Bibliothèque Nationale, Lat. 12052, fol. 117r).[59] This may suggest that the silent *galdorcwide* of *Riddle* 48 does not indicate an 'enchanting song', as Ramey translates but, rather, an inaudible utterance.[60] The chalice's speech may also refer to these silent utterances of the liturgy.

The Christian, liturgical nature of this *galdor* is further emphasised in its direct relation to spiritual mystery: 'Ryne ongietan readan goldes / guman galdorcwide' (6–7).[61] The word for divine secret or mystery ('geryne') is elsewhere used in glosses to translate 'sacramento' (sacrament), *'misterio'* (mystery), and 'typicum, .i. mysticum' (symbolic and mystical).[62] The term is also used in *Guthlac B* to describe the angelic revelation of the Lord's mystery ('dryhtnes geryne', 1121).[63] *Ryne* could have liturgical and doctrinal meaning and its correlation with *galdorcwide* demonstrates that *galdor* is used in this context to denote another type of spiritual mystery. If 'chalice' is the correct solution to this riddle – which is highly plausible, given its close connections with the other chalice riddle (*Riddle* 59) – then the mystery that is

---

[58] See Geoffrey G. Willis, *Further Essays in Early Roman Liturgy* (London, 1968), p. 125; Joseph A. Jungmann, *The Mass of the Roman Rite: Its Origins and Development*, Francis A. Brunner, trans, 2 Vols. (New York, 1951), Vol. II, pp. 90–7.

[59] Nicholas Orchard, ed., *The Sacramentary of Ratoldus: (Paris, Bibliothèque nationale de France, lat. 12052)*, HBS, Vol. 116 (London, 2005), pp. 194–5; 'And the Secret shall be sung (cf. Ratoldus "and [the Mass shall be sung inaudibly"?] in the usual way, down to "sed ueniae quaesumus largitor admitte"', translation from Christopher A. Jones, 'The Chrism Mass in Later Anglo-Saxon England', in *The Liturgy of the Late Anglo-Saxon Church*, M. Bradford Bedingfield and Helen Gittos, eds, HBS Subsidia Series, Vol. 5 (Woodbridge, 2005), pp. 105–42, p. 124.

[60] 'Cwide' can be translated as 'speech', 'word', 'utterance', and 'homily'; Clark-Hall, *Dictionary*, p. 63. Nelson translates *galdorcwide* literally as 'sound-saying' to further the riddle's paradox with silence, 'Silent Speech', p. 612.

[61] It is worth noting that 'ongietan' is the same verb used to describe Beccel's understanding of Guthlac's *galdrum* ('galdrum ongieton hæbbe').

[62] For examples, see Arthur S. Napier, ed., *Old English Glosses* (Oxford, 1900), pp. 30, 56, 78. See also Christine Fell, 'Runes and Semantics', in *Old English Runes and their Continental Background*, Alfred Bammesberger, ed. (Heidelberg, 1991), pp. 195–229, p. 206.

[63] Krapp and Dobbie, *Exeter Book*, p. 81. For the use of 'ryne' in the Exeter Book riddles, see Bitterli, *Say What I Am Called*, pp. 121–4.

communicated through this *galdor* has sacramental and Eucharistic significance. It has been assumed that the voice of this object comes from an inscription on a communion chalice but it may also be the case that this *galdor* represents the sacramental presence of Christ, which is brought about through the words of the priest ('cwide'; speech, saying, word).

The final occurrence of *galdor* in the Exeter Book is found in *Riddle 67*:

> Ic on þinge gefrægn þeodcyninges,
> wrætlice wiht, wordgaldra [...
> ...] snytt[...] hio symle deð
> fira gehw[...
> ...] wisdom. Wundor me þæt [...
> ...] nænne muð hafað,
> fet ne [...
> ...] welan oft sacað,
> cwiþeð cy[...] wearð
> leoda lareow. Forþon nu longe m[ ]g
> [...] ealdre ece lifgan
> missenlice, þenden menn bugað
> eorþan sceatas. Ic þæt oft geseah
> golde gegierwed, þær guman druncon,
> since ond seolfre. Secge se þe cunne,
> wisfæstra hwylc, hwæt seo wiht sy (1–16).[64]

> I have heard of a splendid thing,
> Of the Lord of peoples, a word of incantation [*wordgaldra*]...
> (Several defective lines and then the conclusion):
> I have become
> a teacher of peoples, live an eternal life
> in many lands, while men inhabit
> the bosom of the earth. I have often seen it
> adorned with gold where men were drinking,
> with treasures and silver. Say if you can,
> if you are wise enough, what this thing is.[65]

This is an extremely difficult text to translate, as it is missing many words in its opening lines. However, the surviving text has strong connections with *Riddle 48*, as it speaks without a mouth ('nænne muð hafað', 6), and it probably describes a liturgical object (most likely a decorated Bible).[66] The term 'wordgaldra' appears in the second line

---

[64] Krapp and Dobbie, *Exeter Book*, p. 231.
[65] Paull F. Baum, trans, *Anglo-Saxon Riddles of the Exeter Book* (Durham, NC, 1963), p. 62.
[66] See Frederick Tupper, *The Riddles of the Exeter Book* (Boston, MA, 1910), pp. 207–8; Craig Williamson, *The Old English Riddles of the Exeter Book* (Chapel Hill, NC,

and it is surrounded by other words denoting wisdom in 'snytt' ('wise', 3), 'wisdome' (5), and 'wundor' (5). If the solution to this riddle is the Bible it evidently refers to a written object, but the riddle also draws upon the paradox of silence and speech in much the same way as the chalice. The speaker says that they have heard through *wordgaldra* that this object has no mouth (6) but is able to speak ('cwiþeð', 9) so that it teaches people of many different lands (10). Like the chalice riddle, the holy book of *Riddle 67* uses *galdor* to signify spiritual wisdom, discernment, and the revelation of mysteries. These two riddles in the Exeter Book inextricably associate the word *galdor* with liturgical objects and performances.

These appearances of *galdor* in the Exeter Book indicate that the word could be used in poetry to denote divine revelations, Christian wisdom and morality, and possibly even powerful liturgical words and utterances. The Exeter Book indicates that Anglo-Saxon perceptions of *galdor* were not limited to proscribed spiritual practices at all, and that the term was sometimes actively incorporated into explicitly Christian contexts.

The Vercelli Book

The Vercelli Book (Vercelli, Biblioteca Capitolare, MS cxvii) contains saints' lives, homilies, and wisdom poems, and it was also written by a single scribe in the second half of the tenth century, and in the early years of the Benedictine Reform.[67] The manuscript's place of origin is greatly disputed, as some scholars believe that it contains pro-reformist materials whilst others believe that it contains texts that were written as a reaction against the Reform movement. Like the Exeter Book, this manuscript contains some texts that endorse *galdor* as a Christian concept and others that use it in a condemnatory way.

While there are strong similarities between the Exeter and Vercelli Books – both contain a *Soul and Body* poem, signed poems by Cynewulf, a text on St Guthlac, among other textual similarities – Pamela Gradon argued that there is 'no cogent reason for associating the Vercelli Book with the west' on these grounds.[68] She instead proposed Canterbury as

---

1977), p. 334; Bitterli, *Say What I Am Called*, pp. 126–7; Ramey, 'Writing Speaks', p. 340.

[67] See George Philip Krapp, ed., *The Vercelli Book*, ASPR, Vol. 2 (London, 1932), pp. xvi–xvii; Ker, *Catalogue*, pp. 460–4; Michelle P. Brown, *Manuscripts from the Anglo-Saxon Age* (London, 2007), p. 137. For a digitization of this manuscript, see *Vercelli Book Digitale*: <http://vbd.humnet.unipi.it/?p=2047> accessed 26 September 2017.

[68] Pamela O. E. Gradon, ed., *Cynewulf's Elene* (London, 1958), pp. 3–5. George Krapp claimed that the manuscript was commissioned by the same patron as the Exeter Book, suggesting that a supporter of the Reform from the south-

a probable place of origin on the basis of the scribe's Kentish spellings and the abbreviation 'xb' that is common to the Vercelli Book and other Canterbury manuscripts.[69] Donald Scragg and Elaine Treharne propose St Augustine's, Canterbury as the most likely place of production according to evidence from other manuscripts that have connections with some of the Vercelli Book's homilies, and possible ninth- and tenth-century sources that would have been available in Canterbury minsters.[70] Treharne further argues that some homilies contain 'Benedictine prejudices' which indicate that it was a product of the Reform movement, and that the manuscript may have been written for public use by an abbot or bishop, possibly even for Dunstan.[71] This possibility places the manuscript firmly within the context of a reforming minster during Dunstan's archiepiscopacy in Canterbury (959–88), and at a time when *galdor* was predominantly used to denote a dangerous spiritual practice. Most recently, Richard North and Michael Bintley have proposed that the manuscript was written in Canterbury under Dunstan's instruction, and that one of the exemplars used (containing *Andreas* and the *Fates of the Apostles*) was written by Edith, daughter of King Edgar, in Wilton Abbey, according to evidence of the erased 'eadgiþ' colophon at the bottom of folio 41r, among other thematic reasons.[72]

Other scholars have, however, contested that the Vercelli Book was written in a reforming minster. Charles Wright situated the manuscript within the context of the early years of the Reform, arguing that *Homilies XI–XIII* reveal a pointed clerical reaction against the principles of the movement, in particular the prohibition of private property.[73] Éamonn

---

west of England was also responsible for this collection, Krapp, *Vercelli Book*, p. xvi.

[69] Gradon, *Elene*, pp. 3, 5. See also Sisam, *History of Old English*, p. 153. Karen Jolly also notes that this abbreviation is used in the *Durham Collectar*, 'Prayers from the Field: Practical Protection and Demonic Defence in Anglo-Saxon England', *Traditio*, 61 (2006), 95–147, p. 104.

[70] Donald G. Scragg, 'The Compilation of the Vercelli Book', *ASE*, 2 (1973), 189–207; *The Vercelli Homilies and Related Texts*, EETS Original Series, Vol. 300 (Oxford, 1992), pp. xxxviii–xxxix, xli–lxxiii, lxxv–lxxvi; Elaine Treharne, 'The Form and Function of the Vercelli Book', in *Text, Image, Interpretation: Studies in Anglo-Saxon Literature and its Insular Context in Honour of Éamonn Ó Carragáin*, Alastair J. Minnis and Jane Roberts, eds (Turnhout, 2007), pp. 253–66. For a more thorough study of these connections, see Donald G. Scragg, 'Studies in the Language of Copyists of the Vercelli Homilies', in *New Readings in the Vercelli Book*, Samantha Zacher and Andy Orchard, eds (Toronto, 2009), pp. 41–61.

[71] Treharne, 'Manuscript Sources', p. 102; 'Function of the Vercelli Book', pp. 265–6.

[72] Richard North and Michael D. J. Bintley, eds, *Andreas: An Edition*, Exeter Medieval Texts and Studies (Liverpool, 2016), pp. 8–26. See also Patrick McBrine, 'The Journey Motif in the Poems of the Vercelli Book', in *New Readings in the Vercelli Book*, Zacher and Orchard, eds, pp. 298–317.

[73] Charles D. Wright, 'Vercelli Homilies XI–XIII and the Anglo-Saxon Benedictine Reform: Tailored Sources and Implied Audiences', in *Preacher, Sermon, and*

Ó Carragáin likewise made a compelling argument about the Vercelli Book's origin in an unreformed minster according to the manuscript's thematic organisation. He argued that the manuscript was not suitable for public use, that its varied materials reflect the preoccupations of a single compiler, and that the compilation as a whole indicates that it was produced in an ecclesiastical centre against which the reforms were directed.[74] Ó Carragáin concluded by speculating on the possibility that the manuscript was taken away to Vercelli shortly after the Reform because its texts were seen to be out of date by reformers.[75] These suggestions have implications for the meaning of *galdor* in this manuscript; if the compilation of the Vercelli Book reflects the views of an individual in a non-Reform setting, the non-condemnatory uses of *galdor* may reflect its endorsement as a Christian concept before it came to be associated with forbidden practices by reformers, particularly via the 'Winchester' vocabulary.

The Vercelli Book was copied from at least five different exemplars, and some items – particularly its poems – seem to have been copied from earlier sources.[76] There are also disruptions of continuous copying that are evident throughout the manuscript, suggesting that the collection was written over a long period of time.[77] The scribe copied his texts mechanically, paying little attention to errors in the exemplars and faithfully copying the source materials that appear to

---

Audience in the Middle Ages, Carolyn Meussig, ed. (Leiden, 2002), pp. 203–27, p. 224. For similar interpretations, see Celia Sisam, ed., *The Vercelli Book: A Late Tenth-Century Manuscript Containing Prose and Verse, Vercelli Biblioteca Capitolare CXVII*, EEMF, Vol. 19 (Copenhagen, 1976), p. 220; David Dumville, 'English Square Miniscule Script: The Mid-Century Phases', *ASE*, 23 (1994), 133–64, p. 140; Samantha Zacher, *Preaching the Converted: The Style and Rhetoric of the Vercelli Book Homilies* (Toronto, 2009), pp. 17–21; Samantha Zacher and Andy Orchard, 'Introduction', in *New Readings in the Vercelli Book*, Zacher and Orchard, eds, pp. 3–11, p. 3.

[74] Éamonn Ó Carragáin, 'Rome, Ruthwell, Vercelli: "The Dream of the Rood" and the Italian Connection', in *Vercelli tra Oriente ed. Occidente tra Tarda Antichità e Medioevo*, Vittora D. Corazza, ed. (Alessandria, 1999), pp. 59–99, pp. 94–9.

[75] Ó Carragáin, 'Rome, Ruthwell, Vercelli', p. 96. A scribbled note indicates that it was in Italy by at least the twelfth century, see Ker, *Catalogue*, p. 464; Sisam, *History of Old English*, pp. 113–16; Scragg, *Vercelli Homilies*, p. xxiv; Zacher and Orchard, 'Introduction', p. 3. Scragg, however, notes two Canterbury hands in a pen-trial from the first half of the eleventh century and interlinear insertions from the second half of the eleventh century, suggesting that the manuscript remained in England until this time, Donald G. Scragg, *A Conspectus of Scribal Hands Writing English, 960–1100* (Cambridge, 2012), p. 85. North and Bintley state that it was in Italy by no later than c. 1150, North and Bintley, *Andreas*, pp. 10–11.

[76] See Treharne, 'Manuscript Sources', p. 102; Scragg, 'Compilation of Vercelli Book', p. 205; *Vercelli Homilies*, pp. xxiv, xxxviii–xxxix.

[77] See Krapp, *Vercelli Book*, pp. xi–xii; Scragg, *Vercelli Homilies*, pp. xxiv, lxxiii.

have been in late West-Saxon.[78] There therefore seems to be very little (if any) scribal interference with the materials that were used during the manuscript's production, whether they were much earlier in date or roughly contemporary with the time of writing.

The Vercelli Book provides important information about how *galdor* was endorsed as a Christian concept before the Reform, and how certain individuals who were involved in the manuscript's production understood this word at the time of writing during the Reform movement (most likely at St Augustine's, Canterbury according to palaeographical, linguistic, textual, and contextual evidence). The manuscript's different uses of this word perhaps reflect a transitional stage in its redefinition, as two poems depict it as a powerful spiritual performance that is harnessed by Christian authorities, whilst other texts portray it as a harmful practice that is used by God's enemies.

THE FATES OF THE APOSTLES

Galdor is used in the *Fates of the Apostles* to signify Christian exegesis. The poem is a martyrology of the twelve apostles in verse and it provides a brief account of each of their martyrdoms. At the end of the poem and immediately following Cynewulf's runic signature, the poet concludes by asking the reader to pray for him:

> Nu ðu cunnon miht,
> hwa on þam wordum wæs werum oncyðig.
> Sie þæs gemyndig, mann se ðe lufige
> þisse galdres begang, þæt he geoce me
> ond frofre fricle (105–9).[79]

> Now you may know,
> in these words, those who were known to men.
> May that man be mindful, he who loves
> this *galdres* veneration, so that he seeks for me
> help and comfort.

The speaker refers to their account of the apostles' deaths after Christ's Ascension as 'þisse galdres begang' (108). He or she claims to have edified the audience and asks them to be mindful of the martyrology (107) before asking for prayers in return (108–9). The noun 'begang' generally denotes 'course', 'practice', or 'exercise' but it can also mean 'reverence' or 'veneration'.[80] The *galdor* of this poem is explicitly associated with reverencing the apostles and venerating their deaths.

---

[78] Scragg, 'Compilation of Vercelli Book', p. 196; *Vercelli Homilies*, pp. xliii, lxxi–lxxii; Treharne, 'Manuscript Sources', pp. 101–2.
[79] Krapp, *Vercelli Book*, p. 54.
[80] Clark-Hall, *Dictionary*, p. 32.

Like *Vainglory* in the Exeter Book, the poet's Christian knowledge is transmitted through this *galdor* so that the audience may come to greater spiritual understanding through exegesis. The word signifies a poetic skill that expounds Christian hagiography and reveals divine knowledge to its audience.

ELENE

The only other text that uses *galdor* to signify Christian wisdom in the Vercelli Book is *Elene*, which is another poem marked with Cynewulf's runic signature. *Elene* recounts the finding of the true cross in the Holy Land by St Helen and it concludes with the conversion story of a Jew called Judas. The legend is traceable to Patristic writings from the fourth and fifth centuries, and the source of the Old English poem is believed to be the *Acta Cyriaci*.[81] *Elene* opens with a description of the Emperor Constantine's victory over the Hunnish peoples ('Hunna leode', 128).[82] The Huns are defeated when the cross is raised as a battle standard, and Constantine's army sings a song of victory ('sigeleoð galen', 124).[83] In the Exeter Book's *Guthlac B*, the angels also sing a 'sigeleoð' as the saint's soul enters heaven (1314–15).[84] After the battle, Constantine summons a council of men skilled in wisdom ('snyttro cræft', 154) to explain why the sign of the cross brought such a crushing victory:

> Þa þæs fricggan ongan folces aldor,
> sigerof cyning ofer sid weorod,
> wære þær ænig yldra oððe gingra
> þe him to soðe secggan meahte
> galdrum cyðan hwæt se god wære (157–61).[85]

> Then the people's lord began to ask,
> the king strong in victory over the expansive host,
> if there were any old or young
> who could say to him in truth,
> to reveal through *galdrum*, what god it was.

Constantine's advisors are depicted in terms of their ability to offer counsel through *galdrum*. Gradon defines *galdrum* as 'speech', and Bradley translates it as 'divination', but 'wise words' or 'spiritual discernment' may be a better translation in this context.[86] However, as

---

[81] See Gradon, *Elene*, p. 15.
[82] Gradon, *Elene*, p. 31.
[83] Gradon, *Elene*, p. 31.
[84] Krapp and Dobbie, *Exeter Book*, p. 86.
[85] Gradon, *Elene*, p. 33.
[86] Gradon, *Elene*, p. 91; Bradley, *Anglo-Saxon Poetry*, p. 169.

seen in other wisdom poems, the term also evokes the ability to interpret divine revelations. This is made explicit when the wisest among
them affirms that this spiritual power could only have come from the
King of Heaven (169–71). The counsellors are then inspired to recall
Christ's Passion and Resurrection and they are described as being
wise in spiritual mysteries: 'Ðus gleawlice gastgerynum / sægdon'
(189–90).[87] As seen in the Exeter Book, these *galdrum* are directly connected to spiritual mysteries as Constantine's advisors respond with
'gast-gerynum'. These advisors are described only as wise men but
their ability to discern mysteries leads them to the truth ('soðe', 160)
about the omnipotence of the Christian God.

This connection between *galdor* and *ryne* is further extended when
Elene later lands on the shores of the Holy Land and also calls a
council:

> Heht ða gebeodan burgsittendum,
> þam snoterestum side and wide,
> geond Iudeas gumena gehwylcum,
> meðelhegende on gemot cuman
> þa ðe deoplicost dryhtnes geryno
> þurh rihte æ reccan cuðon (276–81).[88]

> Then she ordered the hall-sitters muster,
> the wisest far and wide
> of every man throughout Judea
> to come to council, those deliberating ones,
> most deeply skilled in the lord's secrets [*geryno*],
> who were able to expound the law through truth.

Elene summons advisors to expound Christian doctrine in the same
way that Constantine summons his council. Emphasis is placed on
the counsellors' wisdom and their ability to interpret spiritual signs
(280). In a similar way to the angelic revelation in *Guthlac B* and the
Eucharistic mystery in *Riddle* 48, *Elene* connects *galdrum* with *ryne* to
denote ways of discerning Christian mysteries and divine secrets.

Observations

These surviving occurrences of *galdor* in *Beowulf*, wisdom poems, and
enigmatic riddles cast much light on how the word was understood

---

[87] Gradon, *Elene*, p. 34; 'Thus they wisely said in spiritual mysteries'. On the significance of this passage for a contemporary Anglo-Saxon audience, see Heide
Estes, 'Colonization and Conversion in Cynewulf's *Elene*', in *Conversion and
Colonization in Anglo-Saxon England*, Catherine E. Karkov and Nicholas Howe,
eds (Tempe, AZ, 2006), pp. 133–51, p. 144.
[88] Gradon, *Elene*, pp. 37–8.

as a non-condemnatory concept by some Anglo-Saxon poets and by the scribes who copied these texts. It is noteworthy that all of these examples occur in Old English poetry, and it may be the case that such uses of *galdor* were part of a poet's repertoire.[89] When *galdor* appears in verse, it usually denotes the acquisition and explication of concealed, mystical knowledge. These mysteries are nearly always made explicitly Christian through the surrounding context of the poem, and *galdor* functions as a medium through which these divine secrets are expounded through exegesis. There is even evidence to suggest that it could describe the transformative words used in the Mass through which Christ becomes present in the Eucharist. The non-condemnatory appearances of *galdor* indicate a broader range of meanings for this word before it became predominantly associated with harmful religious practices, especially with the development of the so-called 'Winchester' vocabulary.

Although these surviving texts may reflect older poetic uses of *galdor*, such endorsements of this word in Christian contexts should not be seen as a result of mere archaism among particular poetic milieus. As will be seen in Chapter 2, instructions to perform a *galdor* are also found in Christian ritual texts that are overtly Christian and that were written by scribes in reforming minsters at a time when some ecclesiastics were evidently concerned about this particular concept, most notably in Winchester. What can be gleaned from the surviving evidence is that the scribes and compilers of these manuscripts did not see any problem with copying texts that use *galdor* to denote Christian wisdom, discernment, and even sacramental mystery. Indeed, the manuscripts were also likely to have been written in monasteries that were undergoing reform or that were closely associated with leading reformers. Aside from ritual texts, which will be considered in the next chapter, all other appearances of *galdor* in the Old English corpus occur in proscriptive contexts. In these cases, the word has been interpreted as referring to evidence of pagan practices that inform our understanding of 'charms' in early medieval England.

---

[89] On the shared formulaic epithets used and reused by Anglo-Saxon poets, see especially Andy Orchard, *The Poetic Art of Aldhelm* (Cambridge, 1994), esp. pp. 126–238; 'Old Sources, New Resources: Finding the Right Formula for Boniface', *ASE*, 30 (2001), 15–38; 'The Word Made Flesh: Christianity and Oral Culture in Anglo-Saxon Verse', *Oral Tradition*, 24 (2009), 293–318. For later poetic milieus at Cnut's court in the eleventh century, see Matthew Townend, 'Contextualizing the *Knútsdrapur*: Skaldic Praise-Poetry at the Court of Cnut', *ASE*, 30 (2001), 145–79; 'Cnut's Poets: An Old Norse Literary Community in Eleventh-Century England', in *Conceptualizing Multilingualism in Medieval England, c. 800 – c. 1250*, Elizabeth M. Tyler, ed. (Turnhout, 2011), pp. 197–215.

Condemnations of 'Galdor'

The *DOE* records over one hundred occurrences of *galdor* in a proscriptive context, and these are found in hagiography, homilies, laws,
guides, glosses, and translations.[90] In these texts, *galdor* is used alongside other terms denoting dangerous religious practices to explicitly
condemn specific types of spiritual knowledge. The proscriptions are
constructed in similar ways and many forms of the word are compounded, indicating particular types of *galdor* that are condemnable.
When the word does not appear as a compound, it is described as a
harmful spiritual practice in formulaic ways. *Galdor* is also employed
in word-for-word translations and glosses to describe evil customs
according to the surrounding contexts of Latin sources. To avoid laborious repetition, I will consider examples that are representative of the
key literary techniques which are employed in all of these texts.

Hagiography

Despite the non-condemnatory meanings of *galdor* in the poems of
the Exeter and Vercelli Books, these manuscripts also contain poems
that use the term to depict the evil utterances of God's enemies. The
hagiographical poem known as the *Old English Martyrology* is the only
other verse composition that uses *galdor* in this way.

Juliana

The Old English poem *Juliana* is found in the Exeter Book and, like
the *Fates of the Apostles* and *Elene*, it is also marked with Cynewulf's
signature. This poem is based on a lost Latin source but it introduces
some minor differences to Latin versions of the story.[91] The poem tells
the story of the virgin daughter of Africanus of Nicomedia who is
promised in marriage to a pagan senator, Eleusias. As Juliana had
converted to Christianity, she refuses to marry and is subjected to a
long list of tortures. Her sanctity is proved through her ability to overcome physical and spiritual trials until she is martyred. When Juliana

---

[90] The numbers from the *DOE* record do not take into account multiple copies
of a text in different manuscripts. For example, Wulfstan's homily *On Baptism*
appears in five different manuscripts but I have included it as only one text,
according to the *DOE* record. For variant spellings of the noun, see note 2.

[91] See Krapp and Dobbie, *Exeter Book*, pp. xxxvi–xxxvii. *Juliana* may be based on
the *Acta Sanctorum*, see Shippey, *Old English Verse*, p. 167. There are also two
twelfth-century English versions of this life, neither of which use *galdor*, see
Joseph Hall, ed., *Selections from Early Middle English 1130–1250*, 2 Vols. (Oxford,
1920), Vol. I, pp. 138–49.

is put into prison, she is visited by a demon and heroically overcomes its temptations (236–88). The demon reappears just before Juliana is decapitated, and it exhorts her executioners to take revenge on the saint for her defiance:

> Ða cwom semninga
> hean helle gæst, hearmleoð agol,
> earm ond unlæd, þone heo ær gebond
> awyrgedne ond mid witum swong,
> cleopade þa for corþre, ceargealdra full (614–18).[92]

> Then suddenly an abject spirit from hell arrived and wailed a song of woe, wretched and miserable – the cursed creature whom she had previously snared and scourged with torments; full of anxious incantations [*ceargealdra*], he cried out in front of the crowd.[93]

This passage describes the demon as a vile spirit from hell who chants harmful songs and *ceargealdra* to rouse the people against Juliana (615, 618). The advice of this cursed demon contrasts with other descriptions of *galdor* in the Exeter Book but it is also formed in a different way. In *Juliana*, the noun appears in compound form with the adjective 'cear' ('anxious', 'sorrowful'), it is surrounded by terms denoting evil counsel ('inwitrune', 610) and an abject spirit from hell ('hean helle gæst', 615), and it is directly associated with the harmful songs it chants through the preterite form of *galan* ('hearmleoð agol', 615). This type of *galdor* is compounded and placed in direct relation to other terms denoting evil so that it signifies wicked advice and exhortation, thus distinguishing it from other Christian *galdru* found in the Exeter Book.

ANDREAS

The Old English *Andreas* is found in the Vercelli Book and it likewise uses *galdor* in the opposite way to the *Fates of the Apostles* and *Elene*. *Andreas* is based on a Latin version of a Greek source, and it recounts the apocryphal life of St Andrew the Apostle and his conversion of the Mermedonians.[94] Andrew undergoes many trials at sea, he rescues

---

[92] Krapp and Dobbie, *Exeter Book*, p. 130.
[93] Bradley, *Anglo-Saxon Poetry*, p. 317.
[94] On the Greek source, see Krapp, *Vercelli Book*, p. xxxvi. There are two other Old English prose versions of this text, but only this poem uses *galdor*. The prose versions are contained in the manuscript of the *Blickling Homilies* (Princeton, Princeton University Library, Scheide Library 71, s. x/xi, Mercia) and Cambridge, Corpus Christi College, MS 198 (s. xi[1], Worcester?), see Richard J. Kelly, ed. and trans, *The Blickling Homilies: Edition and Translation* (London, 2003), pp. xlvi–xlvii.

St Matthew and other Christians who are being killed and eaten, he is tortured for three days before exacting God's punishment on the Mermedonians, and finally he converts the repentant enemy.

Before Andrew travels across the sea to save his fellow apostle Matthew from prison, the Mermedonians have been voraciously eating their prisoners; meanwhile, Matthew's time is almost up. The imprisoned apostle is comforted by Christ, who takes pity on him and remembers his own imprisonment by the Jews:

> Þa wæs gemyndig, se ðe middangeard
> gestaðelode strangum mihtum,
> hu he in ellþeodigum yrmðum wunode,
> belocen leoðubendum, þe oft his lufan adreg
> for Ebreum ond Israhelum,
> swylce he Iudea galdorcræftum
> wiðstod stranglice (161–7).

> Then was He mindful, Who had founded
> the middle world with strong powers,
> how in foreign miseries the man remained,
> locked in limb-bonds who often had shown
> love for Him before Hebrews and Israelites,
> just as He the Jews' arts of enchantment [*galdorcræftum*]
> had strenuously withstood.[95]

The contrast between the Christians and their enemies is clearly established; as the Jews imprisoned and killed Christ in a foreign land, so too does Matthew undergo imprisonment in Mermedonia and he faces the threat of being eaten by his captors. Interestingly, Christ is said to have strongly withstood the Jews' *galdorcræftum* (166). Unlike the Christian *galdru* in other poems of the Vercelli Book, the word is compounded and related to Christ's miseries ('yrmðum', 163) to signify harmful spiritual knowledge or an evil craft that is used by the Jews to attack Christ.[96]

The poem also uses the verb *galan* to describe the cry of a boy who is offered in sacrifice by his father to save his own life: 'ða se geonga ongann geomran stefne, / gehæfted for herige, hearmleoð galan, / freonda feasceaft, friðes wilnian' (1126–8).[97] As seen in other poetic formulas, like the demon's cry in *Juliana*, the boy's lament over

---

[95] North and Bintley, *Andreas*, p. 126.
[96] On the differing uses of 'cræft' compounds in Old English poetry, see Peter Clemoes, *Interactions of Thought and Language in Old English Poetry* (Cambridge, 1995), pp. 78–9.
[97] Krapp, *Vercelli Book*, p. 34; 'Then the youth, enchained in front of the crowd, with plaintive voice began to wail a lament and, being badly off for friends, to plead for a reprieve', Bradley, *Anglo-Saxon Poetry*, p. 139.

his father's offering is an outcome of the demonic practices of the Mermedonians. The same formula appears later when a demon tries to rouse the Mermedonians to attack Andrew: 'Ongan eft swa ær ealdgeniðla, / helle hæftling, hearmleoð galan' (1341–2).[98] Like *Juliana*, *Andreas* compounds *galdor* and also uses *galan* in a formulaic way to describe God's evil enemies and their harmful spiritual knowledge and practices, and this condemnatory use of *galdor* is further borne out from the surrounding context of the poem.

OLD ENGLISH MARTYROLOGY

The *Old English Martyrology* provides short narratives of saints' martyrdoms throughout the liturgical year. This text has also been viewed as a Cynewulfian composition, suggesting that *galdor* was employed for various purposes by an individual composer.[99] There are six surviving fragments of the *Old English Martyrology* that date from the late ninth to late eleventh centuries.[100] The *galdor* reference is found in a late tenth- or early eleventh-century manuscript London, British Library, MS Cotton Julius A. x, which is possibly from Glastonbury.[101] This is the most extensive of the fragments and it contains an entry for the feast of Saints Anatolia and Audax on 10 July, which summarises how Anatolia was imprisoned on account of her faith:

> Þeahhwæþre sum hæþen dema het hi belucan on stænenum cleofan, ond he het sumne wyrmgaldere micle næddran hire into gelædan þæt seo hi abitan sceolde ond hire ban begnagan… Ða gelyfde se wyrmgaldere to Gode þurh þæt wundor, ond he sealde his feorh for Criste mid þære fæmnan, ond his noma wæs Sanctus Audax.

> Nevertheless a pagan judge ordered her to be locked into a stone cell, and he ordered a snake-charmer [*wyrmgaldere*] to put in a big snake along with her so that it would bite her and knaw at her bones… Then the snake-charmer [*wyrmgaldere*] believed in God on account of that miracle, and together with that virgin he gave up his life for Christ, and his name was St Audax.[102]

---

[98] Krapp, *Vercelli Book*, p. 40; 'Again as before, the old enemy, hell's captive, began to wail a lament', Bradley, *Anglo-Saxon Poetry*, p. 144.

[99] Christine Rauer, ed. and trans, *The Old English Martyrology: Edition, Translation and Commentary* (Cambridge, 2013), p. 14.

[100] Rauer, *Martyrology*, pp. 18–23.

[101] Christine Rauer, 'Usage of the *Old English Martyrology*', in *The Foundations of Learning: The Transfer of Encyclopaedic Knowledge in the Early Middle Ages*, Rolf H. Bremmer Jr and Kees Dekker, eds (Leuven, 2007), pp. 125–46, pp. 130–1; *Martyrology*, p. 20. See also Ker, *Catalogue*, pp. 205–6; Gneuss, *Handlist*, p. 64; Gneuss and Lapidge, *Bibliographical Handlist*, pp. 259–60; Scragg, *Conspectus*, pp. 40–1.

[102] Rauer, *Martyrology*, pp. 134–7.

In a striking parallel with Juliana, Anatolia is put into prison because she refused to marry a pagan. She is also attacked by an evil agent during her imprisonment, and she overcomes a harmful type of *galdor*. Unlike Juliana, Anatolia is able to convert her adversary and this *wyrmgaldere* forsakes his heathen beliefs to die with her. Interestingly, the attacker is named as Audax once he becomes a Christian; prior to his conversion he is only identified by his sinful profession. Once again, *galdor* is compounded to signify its harmful spiritual nature, and this is made explicit by the surrounding terms for snakes ('wyrm', 'næddran') and snake-attacks ('abitan', 'begnagan'). This emphasis on the serpent recalls the Fall and explicitly associates this type of *galdor* with Satan.

In the same way as *Juliana* and *Andreas*, the meaning of *galdor* in the *Old English Martyrology* is dependent upon its surrounding vocabulary. This fragment may have been written in Glastonbury – which may also be the place of the Exeter Book's production – suggesting that different types of *galdor* could be used to signify both Christian wisdom and knowledge of evil practices. *Galdor* itself does not signify a condemnable practice in Old English poetry but a medium through which spiritual knowledge is revealed and practices are performed in opposing ways.

Homilies, Rules, and Guides

Didactic prose texts that condemn *galdor* include the laws of *Ine* and *Alfred*, the *Penitentials* of *Pseudo-Theodore* and *Egbert*, the *Vercelli* and *Blickling* homilies, homilies by Ælfric and Wulfstan, Wulfstan's *Canons of Edgar*, a confessor's *Handbook*, and the *Ancrene Wisse*. Some of these sources reflect early condemnations of *galdor*, as the laws of *Ine* were drawn up in the late seventh century, and those of *Alfred* date to the late ninth century.[103] The Penitentials of *Pseudo-Theodore* and *Egbert* are also probably translations of ninth-century Frankish sources, indicating that *galdor* was used in English translations of Continental materials.[104] Many condemnations of *galdor* are found in texts from the tenth and eleventh centuries, which may simply be due to a larger number of surviving written sources from this time. However, it may also suggest that ecclesiastics from key Benedictine monasteries were drawing

---

[103] F. L. Attenborough, ed. and trans, *The Laws of the Earliest English Kings* (Cambridge, 1922), p. 34; Eric G. Stanley, 'On the Laws of King Alfred: The End of the Preface and the Beginning of the Laws', in *Alfred the Wise*, Jane Roberts, Janet L. Nelson, and Malcolm Godden, eds (Cambridge, 1997), pp. 211–21.

[104] Thomas Pollock Oakley, *English Penitential Discipline and Anglo-Saxon Law in their Joint Influence* (Clark, NJ, 2003), p. 201.

upon earlier English laws and Continental writings to regulate, censor, and improve Christian observances during the Reform.[105]

WULFSTAN AND THE DANES

Many of the texts listed above are found in manuscripts that also contain writings by Wulfstan, bishop of Worcester (1002–16) and archbishop of York (1002–23). Although the manuscripts originate in minsters outside of the old Danelaw – predominantly in Canterbury, Winchester, Worcester, and Exeter – they were written for audiences in many other parts of England.[106] As archbishop of York, Wulfstan's works show an acute sensitivity to the Danish presence in England and the threat of non-Christian religious beliefs. In addition to many homilies, Wulfstan wrote laws for King Æthelred and King Cnut which, according to Bethurum, were written to counter re-emerging pagan practices following Danish settlements.[107] Wulfstan included *galdor* among popular customs that he perceived were infiltrating Christian communities, and his writings show that he intended to leave his audiences in no doubt about what types of practices could be spiritually harmful to their Christian faith.

Wulfstan always condemned *galdor* in relation to other forbidden practices but he never renounced it in isolation. This suggests that he constructed a general but accumulative opposition to approved Christian beliefs and rituals in his writings – which he repeated for rhetorical effect – rather than explicitly condemning distinct catego-

---

[105] See Jolly, *Popular Religion*, pp. 49–58.

[106] These include Cambridge, Corpus Christi College, MSS 173, 190, 201, 265, 320, 419; London, British Library, MSS Burney 277, Cotton Nero A. i, Cotton Otho B. xi, Cotton Vespasian D. xv; Oxford, Bodleian Library, MSS Bodley 343, 718, Junius 121, Laud Misc. 482. Only Cotton Nero A. i may have been written in York. See Ker, *Catalogue*, pp. 57–9, 70–3, 82–90, 92–4, 105–6, 115–17, 171–2, 211–15, 230–4, 277–8, 368–75, 412–22; Gneuss, *Handlist*, pp. 32–6, 38, 61, 64, 67, 71–2, 96, 101, 103; Scragg, *Conspectus*, pp. 7–10, 12–16, 33, 42, 44, 77–8. Interestingly, Part A of Corpus 190 contains a 'charm' against theft of cattle (fol. 130), which, according to palaeographical evidence, was added to the manuscript when it was in Exeter by the mid-eleventh century along with a hymn, Decrees and Councils, excerpts from an Irish collection of Canon Law, and records of the Councils of Winchester and Windsor (1070). Part A also contains Wulfstan's Canon Law collection and *Homily VIII*, the *Penitentials of Pseudo-Theodore and Egbert*, Ælfric's pastoral letters, an *Ordo Romanus*, writings by Alcuin, Hrabanus Maurus, Amalarius, and Abbo of Saint-Germain, and excerpts from the *Regularis Concordia*, see Ker, *Catalogue*, p. 70; see also James M. Ure, ed., *The Benedictine Office: An Old English Text* (Edinburgh, 1957), pp. 3–46. Although a *galdor* is not prescribed in the ritual, this manuscript indicates that texts which have been classified as 'charms' were perceived by scribes as completely compatible with liturgical *ordines* and didactic writings that condemn this term.

[107] Bethurum, ed., *Homilies of Wulfstan*, p. 319.

ries of spiritual practices that threatened Christians. Consider, for example, how *galdor* is dependent upon many other terms denoting the Antichrist in Wulfstan's homily *De Temporibus Anticristi*:

> Antecrist hæfð mid him drymen and unlybwyrhtan and wigleras and þa, ðe cunnan galder agalan, þa ðe hine mid deofles fultume fedað and lærað on ælcre unrihtwisnesse and facne and manfullum cræfte.[108]

> The Antichrist has with him sorcerers and poison-workers and sooth-sayers and those who know how to chant *galder*, those who with the devil's aid feed and tempt him to every iniquity and wretchedness and evil craft.

Interestingly, Wulfstan does not use or compound a proper noun for those who chant *galder* and he condemns such practitioners through their association with the devil ('deofles'), sorcerers ('drymen'), poison-workers ('unlybwyrhtan'), and soothsayers ('wigleras'). In another homily on baptism (*Sermo de Baptismate*), Wulfstan included *galdru* among the many illusions of the devil in his warning to catechumens: 'And ne gyman ge galdra ne idelra hwata, ne wigelunga ne wiccecræfta; 7 ne weorðian ge wyllas ne ænige wudutreowu, forðam æghwylce idele syndon deofles gedwimeru'.[109] These may perhaps be practices that emerged during the acculturation of Danish communities in or near Wulfstan's episcopal jurisdictions.[110]

These types of condemnation follow a formulaic structure that appears to be reminiscent of Revelations 21. 8 and 22. 15:

> 'timidis autem et incredulis et execratis et homicidis et fornicatoribus et veneficis et idolatris et omnibus mendacibus pars illorum erit in stagno ardenti igne et sulphure quod est mors secunda... foris canes et venefici et inpudici et homicidae et idolis servientes et omnis qui amat et facit mendacium.'[111]

> 'However, the fearful and unbelieving and accursed and murderers and fornicators, and sorcerers and idolators and all the deceitful will have their share in the burning lake of fire and sulphur which is the second death... Outside are dogs and sorcerers and the lustful and murderers and slaves of idolatory and all those who love and create deceit.'

It seems likely that condemnations from the Bible, like these from Revelations, were reworked by ecclesiastics like Wulfstan in homilies

---

[108] Wulfstan, *Wulfstan: Sammlung Englischer Denkmäler*, Arthur S. Napier, ed. (Berlin, 1883), p. 194.

[109] Wulfstan, *Homilies of Wulfstan*, p. 184; 'And do not heed *galdra* nor the soothsayer, nor enchantments nor witchcrafts; and do not venerate wells nor any trees of the wood, because all the devil's illusions are empty.'

[110] See Crawford, 'Evidences of Witchcraft', pp. 110–11.

[111] *Biblia Sacra: iuxta Vulgatam versionem*, Bonifatio Fischer, Iohanne Gribomont, H. F. D. Sparks, W. Thiele, et al, eds, 2 Vols. (Stuttgart, 1969), Vol. II, pp. 1903, 1905.

to instruct catechumens and warn of the coming of the Antichrist during a time of social, cultural, and political unrest in England. Furthermore, Wulfstan's homily for Rogation Tuesday contains very similar descriptions to the laws of Alfred, suggesting that he drew upon earlier proscriptions of *galdor* from law codes and formulaically reused them for his homilies and other didactic texts.[112]

Wulfstan also wrote the *Canons of Edgar*, which is a collection of ecclesiastical law codes compiled around 1005–8.[113] This text associates *galdor* with other heathen practices like the veneration of objects and creatures: 'forbeode wilweorþunga, and licwiglunga, and hwata, and galdra, and manweorðunga, and þa gemearr ðe man drifð on mistlicum gewiglungum... and eac on oðrum mistlicum treowum and on stanum'.[114] Another version of this text in Oxford, Bodleian Library, MS Junius 121 (s. xi², Worcester) adds the detail of pulling children through the earth ('þær man þa cild þurh þa eorðan tihð'), indicating that these law codes forbade more localised practices in English territories.[115] It is evident that there is great textual overlap between the *Canons of Edgar* and Wulfstan's other homilies, demonstrating the formulaic rhetoric that he employed in his exhortations.

Other texts that circulated with writings by Wulfstan also condemn *galdor* in similar ways. In a mid-eleventh-century manuscript from Worcester (Oxford, Bodleian Library, MS Laud Misc. 482), a copy of the *Penitential of Pseudo-Egbert* is included with other writings by Wulfstan.[116] This *Penitential* is a translation of a Latin text by Halitgar, bishop of Cambrai 817–31, and it contains one law code that proscribes 'wyrta gaderunga mid nanum galdre butan mid pater noster and mid credo oððe mid sumon gebede þe to gode belimpe'.[117] From the

---

[112] See Felix Liebermann, ed., *Die Gesetze der Angelsachsen: Herausgegeben im Auftrage der Savigny-Stiftung*, 2 Vols. (Halle, 1916), Vol. I, p. 38; Wulfstan, *Sammlung Englischer Denkmäler*, p. 253.

[113] Two eleventh-century copies are found in Corpus 201, from Winchester, and Oxford, Bodleian Library, MS Junius 121, from Worcester. See Ker, *Catalogue*, pp. 82–90, 412–18; Ure, *Benedictine Office*, pp. 3–14; Gneuss, *Handlist*, pp. 34, 101; Scragg, *Conspectus*, pp. 12–13, 77–8.

[114] Wulfstan, *Canons of Edgar*, p. 4; 'We forbid well-worship, and necromancy, and witchcrafts, and *galdra*, and man-worship, and those errors that men practise in various sorceries... and also about many other trees and stones.'

[115] Wulfstan, *Canons of Edgar*, p. 5; 'where he draws those children through the earth'. Ælfric also expressed remarkably similar concerns, indicating a common source for these Old English didactic writings, see Jolly, 'Context of a Christian World View', pp. 285–7.

[116] On Wulfstan's indebtedness to Frankish writings, see Wulfstan, *Homilies of Wulfstan*, p. 70.

[117] J. Raith, ed., *Die alternglische Version des Halitgar'schen Bussbuches* (Hamburg, 1933), p. 29; 'herb gathering with no *galdre* except with the Paternoster and the Creed or with some prayer that belongs to God'. See also Francisco José Álvarez López, 'Monastic Learning in Twelfth-Century England: Marginalia,

evidence of this passage, it seems that in some proscriptive contexts *galdor* simply refers to a spiritual song, saying, or chant, as it is here implied that the Paternoster is an acceptable *galdor* to be used in the summoning of a herb's remedial power. As will be seen in the next chapter, there is another surviving example of an explicitly approved *galdor* that is prescribed for performance with a 'gebed' because it is directly attributed to St John the Evangelist and is associated with the Christian God. The specification that *galdru* are not to be practised without clear reference to Christian prayer indicates that Wulfstan's condemnations were also directed towards unauthorised *galdru*. It is probable that Wulfstan believed that *galdru* should be censored or at the very least supervised by Christian authorities.

ÆLFRIC

Although Ælfric (d. circa 1010) uses *galdor* in similar ways to Wulfstan, Christopher Jones has highlighted the differing approaches of these writers to religious reform according to the environments in which they worked.[118] Ælfric was educated under Æthelwold in Winchester during the standardisation of vernacular writing before he became a novice master at Cerne Abbey around 987 and eventually abbot of Eynsham in 1005.[119] Catherine Cubitt claims that Ælfric's didactic writings reflect much of the evangelising efforts of the monastic community at Cerne, and it is also evident that he targeted wider readerships beyond local audiences in the diocese of Sherborne.[120] For instance, Ælfric corresponded with Wulfstan and wrote homilies for his usage.[121] He also dedicated homilies to Sigeric (archbishop of Canterbury, 990–94), he had connections with Æthelmær the Stout (an ealdorman of Devonshire), and he addressed a certain Ealdorman Æthelweard in his preface to his translation of the book of Genesis.[122]

Provenance and Use in London, British Library, Cotton MS. Faustina A. X, Part B', *Electronic British Library Journal* (2012), no. 11, 1–8, p. 5.

[118] Jones, 'Limits of "Benedictine Reform"', pp. 67–108.

[119] See Gneuss, 'Origin of Standard Old English', pp. 70–83; Malcolm Godden, 'Ælfric's Changing Vocabulary', *ES*, 61 (1980), 206–23; Mechthild Gretsch, 'Ælfric, Language and Winchester', in *Companion to Ælfric*, Magennis and Swann, eds, pp. 35–66.

[120] Catherine Cubitt, 'Ælfric's Lay Patrons', in *Companion to Ælfric*, Magennis and Swan, eds, pp. 165–92, p. 178. See also Jonathan Wilcox, 'Ælfric in Dorset and the Landscape of Pastoral Care', in *Pastoral Care in Late Anglo-Saxon England*, Francesca Tinti, ed., Anglo-Saxon Studies, Vol. 6 (Woodbridge, 2005), pp. 52–62.

[121] See especially Ælfric, *Die Hirtenbriefe Ælfrics in Altenglischer und Lateinischer Fassung*, Bernhard Fehr, ed. and trans, 2 Vols. (Hamburg, 1914), Vol. II, pp. 68–9; Wulfstan, *Homilies of Wulfstan*, pp. 83, 87.

[122] See Mary Swan, 'Identity and Ideology in Ælfric's Prefaces', in *Companion to Ælfric*, Magennis and Swan, eds, pp. 247–70.

Ælfric had great influence beyond Cerne abbey and Eynsham, and his high-ranking connections indicate that he had ambitions of reaching nationwide audiences of monks, secular clergy, and laity, as well as the Latinate and those who knew no Latin.[123]

In Ælfric's sermon *On Auguries*, he outlines dangerous religious practices that threaten the Christian soul:

> Nu alyse ic me sylfne wið god and mid lufe eow for-beode
> þæt eower nan ne axie þurh ænigne wicce-cræft
> be ænigum ðinge oððe be ænigre untrumnysse
> ne galdras ne sece to gremigenne his scyppend
> forðan se ðe þys deð se forlysð his cristen-dom
> and bið þam hæðenum gelic þe hleotað be him sylfum
> mid ðæs deofles cræfte þe hi fordeð on ecnysse.

> Now I deliver myself as regards God, and with love forbid you, that any of you should enquire through any witchcraft concerning anything, or concerning any sickness, or seek *galdras* to anger his Creator; for he that does this lets go his Christianity, and is like the heathen who casts lots concerning themselves by means of the devil's art, which will destroy them for ever.[124]

This passage inextricably connects 'galdras' with witchcraft ('wicce-cræft'), heathens ('hæðenum'), casting lots ('þe hleotað'), and the devil's arts ('deofles cræfte'). In a similar way to Wulfstan, Ælfric warns Christians against dangerous spiritual practices that would imperil their souls. This passage is drawn from the *Penitential of Pseudo-Egbert* and Ælfric also used material by Caesarius, Hrabanus Maurus, and Martin of Braga throughout the homily, further suggesting that *galdor* was incorporated into conventional formulaic reworkings of homiletic materials from the Continent.[125]

Ælfric also uses the term in his hagiographical writings. His saint's life *Natale Sancti Mauri* describes an accusation made against St Maurus that he illegitimately healed a priest through heathen *galdrum*: 'cwædon þæt he mid galdrum na mid godes cræftum þyllice geworhte'.[126] Another type of usage can be seen in Ælfric's homily for the *Feast of St Lucy*. Like *Juliana* and the *Old English Martyrology*, this *vita* describes a spiritual attack on a saintly virgin who refuses to apostatise: 'het

---

[123] See especially Helen Gittos, 'The Audience for Old English Texts: Ælfric, Rhetoric and "the Edification of the Simple"', *ASE*, 43 (2014), 231–66, pp. 234–6, 240, 253–4.

[124] Ælfric, *Lives of Saints*, Vol. I, pp. 368–71. I have slightly altered Skeat's translation.

[125] See Audrey L. Meaney, 'Ælfric's Use of his Sources in his Homily on Auguries', *ES*, 66 (1985), 477–95, p. 486; Leslie K. Arnovick, *Written Reliquaries: The Resonance of Orality in Medieval English Texts* (Amsterdam, 2006), pp. 65–8.

[126] 'saying, that he, by enchantments [*galdrum*], not by God's power had wrought this', Ælfric, *Lives of Saints*, pp. 158–9.

him gelangian þa leasan drymen to þæt hi þæt godes mæden mid heora galdrum oferswyðdon'.[127] The *galdrum* that are used against St Lucy come from 'leasan drymen' who are in complete opposition to God. Ælfric included *galdor* in his repertoire for translating formulaic source materials but, unlike Wulfstan, he perhaps took a stronger stance against the use of all *galdru* as illegitimate forms of spiritual knowledge that led Christians astray and thwarted the Church.

OTHER HOMILIES, RULES, AND GUIDES

Galdor is also explicitly associated with evil practices in other didactic prose writings. One of the *Vercelli Homilies* condemns 'dryicgan and scinlacan and gealdorcræftigan and lyblacan', and another proscribes the veneration of *galdor*-songs: 'ne lufian we ne scyncræftas, ne herien we ne galdorsangas, ne unriht lyblac onginnen we'.[128] The meaning of *galdor* in these descriptions is once again dependent on compounding ('gealdor-cræftigan', *galdor*-craft, -skill, -science; 'galdor-sangas', *galdor*-songs, -chants) and the surrounding words denoting a range of evil concepts.

The homily for the fifth Sunday in Lent in the *Blickling Homilies* (probably written in late tenth- or early eleventh-century Glastonbury) also states that those who practise *galdor* are damned to hell:

> On helle beoþ þeofas, ond flyteras, ond gitseras þe on mannum heora æhta on woh nimaþ, ond þa ofermodan men, ond þa scinlæcan þa þe galdorcræftas ond gedwolan begangaþ, ond mid þæm unwære men beswicaþ ond adwellaþ, ond hi aweniaþ from Godes gemynde mid heora scinlacum ond gedwolcræftum.

> There are in hell thieves, gangsters and covetous men who deprive men wrongfully of their property, proud men, and magicians who practise enchantments [*galdorcræftas*] and deceptions and deceive and mislead unwary men thereby and wean them from the contemplation of God by means of slights and deceptions.[129]

This passage places *galdorcræftas* in the context of theft and deception ('þeofas', 'scinlacum', 'gedwolan', 'gedwolcræftum') to describe it as a form of misleading knowledge that threatens the Christian.[130]

---

[127] '[He] bade false magicians be brought unto him, that they with their enchantments [*galdrum*] might overpower the virgin of God', Ælfric, *Lives of Saints*, pp. 216–17.

[128] Scragg, *Vercelli Homilies*, pp. 92, 198; 'sorcery and *gealdor*-crafts and poisons'; 'Nor do we love sorcery, nor do we glorify *galdor*-songs, nor do we try wicked poisons.'

[129] Kelly, *Blickling Homilies*, pp. 42–3. For the dating of this manuscript, see pp. xlvi–xlvii and Gneuss, *Handlist*, p. 139.

[130] See also Jolly, *Popular Religion*, pp. 75–6.

Those who lead others astray, target the ignorant, and rob them of true knowledge of God ('Godes gemynde') will undoubtedly face the spiritual consequences of this disobedience to the Church and its authorities. Another attempt to overpower somebody through a *galdor* can be found in an interesting entry in the so-called *Handbook for a Confessor*: 'Gyf hwa wiccige ymbon oðres lufu and him sille on æte oððe on drence on galdorcræftum, gif hit beo læwede man fæste healf gear Wodnesdagum and Frigedagum on hlafe and on wætere'.[131] The *Handbook* is a spiritual guide for penance that has close connections with Wulfstan's writings and the *Penitentials* of *Pseudo-Theodore* and *Egbert*.[132] This text provides an insight into the atonement that should be made in this life if one gives in to the temptation of using a *galdor* for one's own gain.[133] Despite the paucity of evidence, one cannot help but wonder whether such spiritual punishments were meted out on a frequent basis by priests residing in areas that were targeted by reforming ecclesiastics.

The great overlaps between these prohibitions indicate that *galdor* was used in formulaic reworkings of biblical passages and earlier materials from law codes and Continental writings, suggesting that reforming ecclesiastics copied these texts as they came to hand and as the need arose. It seems likely that this word was incorporated into a larger repertoire of didactic prose that was promulgated by ecclesiastics during the Benedictine Reform. Although *galdor* predominantly appears in proscriptive contexts, where it is depicted as a religious practice that ought to be supervised, if not censored completely, the term is never denounced in isolation or employed as a category term.

---

[131] Roger Fowler, 'A Late Old English Handbook for the Use of a Confessor', *Anglia*, 83 (1965), 1–34, p. 25; 'If any were to use witchcraft for another's love and were to give him *galdorcræftum* in food or in drink, if it is a layman, fast for half a year on Wednesdays and Fridays with bread and water.'

[132] See Fowler, 'Old English Handbook'; Melanie Heyworth, 'The "Late Old English Handbook for the Use of a Confessor": Authorship and Connections', *N&Q*, 54 (2007), 218–22; Joyce Tally Lionarons, *The Homiletic Writings of Archbishop Wulfstan* (Woodbridge, 2010), pp. 9–22, 133. On penitential literature more generally in Anglo-Saxon England, see Sarah Hamilton, 'Remedies for "Great Transgressions": Penance and Excommunication in Late Anglo-Saxon England', in *Pastoral Care in Late Anglo-Saxon England*, Tinti, ed., pp. 83–105.

[133] In another manuscript (London, British Library, MS Cotton Vespasian D. xx), a Latin 'charm' against toothache (fol. 93r) was added in the mid- to late eleventh century at the end of a confessor's manual, see Storms, *Anglo-Saxon Magic*, pp. 289–90; Ker, *Catalogue*, p. 278; Gneuss, *Handlist*, p. 72. Although this text does not prescribe a *galdor*, this manuscript indicates that some scribes perceived these types of rituals as compatible with mainstream liturgical and devotional texts. Sarah Hamilton argues that confessionals were intended for public use by a bishop, and the large writing space of 152 x 95mm in 15 long lines with large Anglo-Saxon miniscule handwriting suggests that this ritual was written for a bishop's use, see Hamilton, 'Remedies for "Great Transgressions"', p. 92.

If the meaning of *galdor* were to be isolated in these didactic texts, we may safely conclude that this word refers simply to a powerful but unauthorised spiritual song or chant.

Glosses

According to the *DOE*, over eighty of the proscriptive uses of *galdor* are found in glosses and translations of Latin texts, but it also lists two instances where *galdor* appears in glosses in a non-condemnatory way. In a copy of Bede's *Historia Ecclesiastica* the Latin word 'optimatibus' (nobles, advisors) is glossed with the Old English 'galdermonnum', and in a copy of Boethius' *De Consolatione Philosophiae* the Latin word 'senatorii' (senators) is glossed with the Old English 'gealderdomlic-es'.[134] However, these two glosses appear to be prefixed forms of the nouns 'aldermonnum' (aldermen) and 'aldordomlices' (judgement of an alderman) respectively, and do not in fact reflect any meaning of *galdor*.[135]

Aside from these two exceptions, all other occurrences of *galdor* in glosses are found in condemnatory contexts. In her study of the *Durham Collectar* (Durham, Durham Cathedral Library, MS A.IV.19), Karen Jolly emphasises the importance of glosses in expounding a word or phrase for the purposes of reflective reading, particularly in Patristic and ecclesiastical traditions.[136] *Galdor*-glosses also function to encourage a reader to reflect on forbidden and dangerous practices in their own cultural environments. The majority of these glosses were added to copies of Aldhelm's *De Laude Virginitatis* and to Psalm 57 in glossed psalters, while others appear in three alphabetical glossaries, Ælfric's *Glossary* and translation of the *Heptateuch*, Wærferth's translation of Gregory the Great's *Dialogues*, the *Meters* of Boethius, Bede's *Historia Ecclesiastica*, and a gloss to a prognostic text.[137]

---

[134] Herbert Dean Meritt, ed., 'Old English Glosses: A Collection (Oxford, 1945), p. 10; W. C. Hale, ed., 'An Edition and Codicological Study of CCCC MS. 214', Unpublished Doctoral Thesis (University of Pennsylvania, USA, 1978), pp. 3, 4, l. 56.

[135] This is borne out by the Old English version of Bede's *Historia Ecclesiastica* and other Old English glosses to Boethius, see Thomas Miller, ed., *The Old English Version of Bede's Ecclesiastical History of the English People*, 2 Vols., EETS Original Series, Vols. 95–6, 110–11 (London, 1890–91, 1898), Vol. II, p. 250; Boethius, *The Old English Boethius: An Edition of the Old English Versions of Boethius'* De Consolatione Philosophiae, Malcolm Godden and Susan Irvine, eds and trans, 2 Vols. (Oxford, 2009), Vol. I, pp. 300, 447; Vol. II, pp. 353–4.

[136] Jolly, 'Prayers from the Field', p. 134. See also Gernot R. Wieland, 'The Glossed Manuscript: Classbook or Library Book?', *ASE*, 14 (1985), 153–73.

[137] J. H. Hessels, ed., *An Eighth-Century Latin-Anglo-Saxon Glossary: Preserved in the Library of Corpus Christi College, Cambridge (MS No. 144)* (Cambridge, 1890), p. 69; W. G. Stryker, ed., 'The Latin–Old English Glossary in MS. Cleopatra A. III', Unpublished Doctoral Thesis (Stanford University, USA, 1951), pp. 113, 246,

The glossators of these texts chose *galdor* to translate and expound particular Latin terminology. Aldhelm's prose *De Laude Virginitatis* is a collection of female saints' lives that survives in twelve Anglo-Saxon manuscripts.[138] Some of the manuscripts seem to have been produced for personal use (like London, British Library, MS Royal 7 D. xxiv, s. x[1], Glastonbury?), while others appear to be classroom study books (like Brussels, Royal Library MS 1650, s. xi[in], Abingdon).[139] Given that Aldhelm's Latin is 'explicitly religious and didactic, if highly polished and self-consciously ornate', thus making for difficult reading, the Old English glosses were probably added to guide its readers through the text.[140] Some of these glosses seem to have been coined to translate particular phrasing by Aldhelm, and these may reflect specific socio-cultural concerns of the glossator and target reader.[141] However, other than a few exceptions, *galdor* is used in these glosses to cover a multitude of Latin nouns.

Some examples of *galdor*-glosses in Aldhelm's prose *De Laude Virginitatis* include the following:

324, 1264, 3891; J. J. Quinn, ed., 'The Minor Latin-Old English Glossaries in MS. Cotton Cleopatra A. III', Unpublished Doctoral Thesis (Stanford University, USA, 1956), 1191, 1277, 2005; R. T. Oliphant, ed., *The Harley Latin–Old English Glossary* (The Hague, 1966), C 218; Richard Marsden, ed., *The Old English Heptateuch and Ælfric's Libellus de Veteri Testamento et Novo*, EETS Original Series, Vol. 330 (London, 2008), pp. 98, 134, 165; Ælfric, *Ælfrics Grammatik und Glossar*, Julius Zupitza, ed. (Berlin, 1880), p. 303; H. Heht, ed., *Bischof Waerferths von Worcester Üebersetzung der Dialoge Gregors des Grossen* (Leipzig, 1900), p. 73; George Philip Krapp, ed., *The Paris Psalter and the Meters of Boethius*, ASPR, Vol. 5 (New York, 1932), p. 194; Miller, *Old English Version of Bede's Ecclesiastical History*, Vol. II, p. 362; Max Förster, 'Vom Fortleben antiker Sammellunare im Englischen und in anderen Volkssprachen', *Anglia*, 67 (1944), 1–171, pp. 92–6.

[138] Five manuscripts are from Canterbury, two are from Abingdon, and the remainder have provenance in Waltham abbey (Essex), Glastonbury / Winchester, Worcester, Exeter, and the origin of one has not yet been identified; see Ker, *Catalogue*, pp. 6–7, 107–8, 321–3, 330, 356–7, 381–3, 449; Gneuss, *Handlist*, pp. 36, 80–2, 87, 91, 98, 109, 120, 132. See also Mechthild Gretsch, *The Intellectual Foundations of the English Benedictine Reform* (Cambridge, 1999), pp. 137–9, 142–9.

[139] See Scott Gwara, 'Further Old English Scratched Glosses and Merographs from Corpus Christi College, Cambridge MS 326 (Aldhelm's *Prosa De Virginitate*)', *ES*, 3 (1997), 201–36; J. A. Kiff-Hooper, 'Classbooks or Works of Art? Some Observations on the Tenth-Century Manuscripts of Aldhelm's *De Laude Virginitatis*', in *Church and Chronicle in the Middle Ages: Essays Presented to John Taylor*, Ian Wood and G. A. Laud, eds (London, 1991), pp. 15–26.

[140] Clare A. Lees and Gillian R. Overing, 'Women and the Origins of English Literature', in *The History of British Women's Writing, 700–1500*, Liz Herbert McAvoy and Diane Watt, eds (New York, 2012), pp. 31–40, p. 34. On the origin of the glossing tradition in Theodore's Canterbury school in the seventh century, see Gneuss, 'Study of Language', pp. 19–20.

[141] See Alaric Hall, 'Glosses, Gaps and Gender: The Rise of Female Elves in Anglo-Saxon Culture', in *Change in Meaning and the Meaning of Change: Studies in Semantics and Grammar from Old to Present-Day English*, Matti Rissanen, ed. (Helsinki, 2007), pp. 139–70, p. 153.

necromantia(e) ('necromancy'); *deofolices galdres, galdres, mid galdre, galdre*;
marsorum, marsi, marsum ('incantations'); *wyrmgalera, wyrmgalere, iugeleras*;
auruspicum / aruspicibus ('soothsayer'); *iugelera, galdrum*;
prestrigiarum, prestigie ('delusions'); *galdra, galdres*;
incantationum ('incantation'); *galdra, galunge*.[142]

Like other didactic writings in Old English, some of these forms of *galdor* are compounded (e.g. 'wyrmgalere' and 'iugalera') to signify certain types of spiritual knowledge. As seen in the *Old English Martyrology*, the association of 'wyrm' with *galdor* evokes the Fall and the evil serpent. The 'iugalera' glosses are very interesting because the prefix 'iu' (former, ancient) links the concept of *galdor* with the distant past. This may indicate that some ecclesiastics associated this concept with a pre-Christian era, perhaps reminiscent of the *galdor* that protects the dragon's hoard in *Beowulf* ('iu-monna gold, galdre bewunden', 3052).[143] Aside from these compounds, *galdor* appears to have been used as a generic term to gloss different Latin words denoting evil knowledge, practices, and professions in Aldhelm's *De Laude Virginitatis*.

Galdor-glosses also appear in a large number of psalters. These books reflect a consistent transmission of liturgical glossing that began with the mid-tenth-century *Royal Psalter* from Winchester (London, British Library, MS Royal 2 B. V).[144] Mechthild Gretsch notes that the glossator of this psalter was remarkably competent in Latin and often coined Old English 'interpretamenta' of Latin terms.[145] Despite differences in style, register, and method, Gretsch also noted strong correspondences between the psalter and Aldhelm glosses, suggesting that there were networks of glossators and translators in key ecclesiastical centres that introduced the standardised 'Winchester' vocabulary and Old English 'interpretamenta' of particular Latin terminology.[146] The glosses that differ from the *Royal Psalter* draw upon the earlier ninth-century glosses of the *Vespasian Psalter* (London, British Library, MS Cotton Vespasian

---

[142] Napier, *Old English Glosses*, pp. 52, 54, 78, 87, 106–7, 109–10, 116, 121, 126. Additional glosses are recorded in Louis Goosens, ed., *The Old English Glosses of MS. Brussels, Royal Library, 1650 (Aldhelm's* De Laudibus Virginitatis*)* (Brussels, 1974).

[143] Wrenn, *Beowulf*, p. 175.

[144] For the date and origin of the *Royal Psalter* in Winchester with later Canterbury additions, see Ker, *Catalogue*, pp. 318–20; Phillip Pulsiano, *Anglo-Saxon Manuscripts in Microfiche Facsimile, Vol. 2: Psalters I*, A. N. Doane, ed. (Binghamton, 1994), p. 57. See also Gretsch, *Intellectual Foundations*, pp. 17–131; Gneuss, *Handlist*, p. 79; Scragg, *Conspectus*, pp. 55–6.

[145] Mechthild Gretsch, 'The Roman Psalter, its Old English Glosses and the English Benedictine Reform', in *Liturgy of the Late Anglo-Saxon Church*, Gittos and Bedingfield, eds, pp. 13–28, p. 19.

[146] Gretsch, *Intellectual Foundations*, p. 185.

A. i, Mercia),[147] and the early tenth-century glosses of the *Lambeth Psalter* (London, Lambeth Palace Library, MS 427, late West-Saxon origin).[148] The appearances of *galdor* in these glosses are restricted to Psalm 57, verse 6, which describes the evil but futile spiritual practices of God's enemies: 'quae non exaudiet uocem incantantium et uenefici quae incantantur a sapiente'.[149] The slight variations in Old English glosses to this verse reflect different terms favoured by glossators and their gloss-exemplars.

The psalters that use *galdor*-glosses and draw upon the *Royal Psalter* are from the tenth to twelfth centuries, and are of late West-Saxon origin.[150] These manuscripts were written in Winchester, except for the *Salisbury Psalter* (Salisbury, Cathedral Library, MS 150), which was written in south-west England (probably Shaftesbury or Wilton), and the *Eadwine Psalter* (Cambridge, Trinity College, MS R. 17. 1), which was produced in Christ Church, Canterbury.[151] The *Royal Psalter* glosses this verse from Psalm 57 with 'þa na gehyrað stefne ongalendra 7 ætrene þa beoð begalene fram wisum'.[152] All of the psalters that draw on *Royal* have this wording, with the exception of the later *Eadwine Psalter* that has the minor difference of no prefix in 'galdendra'.[153] The translations of 'incantantium' as *ongalendra* and 'incantantur' as

---

[147] Ker, *Catalogue*, pp. 266–7; Pulsiano, *Psalters I*, pp. 43–9; Gretsch, *Intellectual Foundations*, p. 35; Gneuss, *Handlist*, p. 70; Scragg, *Conspectus*, p. 50. Scholars have also proposed a Canterbury origin but Pulsiano argued that there is little evidence for this, *Psalters I*, p. 43.

[148] Ker, *Catalogue*, pp. 342–3; Gretsch, *Intellectual Foundations*, pp. 19, 27; Gneuss, *Handlist*, p. 87; Scragg, *Conspectus*, p. 63. The *Paris Psalter*, written in Canterbury in the twelfth century, also uses a different gloss with *galdor* ('heahgealdor'), and this psalter is different to all others in that it provides a full prose translation of Psalms 1–50 (attributed to Alfred) and a full verse translation of Psalms 51–150, see Krapp, *Paris Psalter*, pp. xvii, 10; Peter J. Lucas and Jonathan Wilcox, *Anglo-Saxon Manuscripts in Microfiche Facsimile, Vol. 16: Manuscripts Relating to Dunstan, Ælfric, and Wulfstan; the 'Eadwine Psalter' Group*, A. N. Doane, ed. (Tempe, AZ, 2008), pp. 111–18.

[149] Fritz Roeder, ed., *Der Altenglische Regius-Psalter: Eine Interlinearversion in HS. Royal 2 B. 5 des Brit. Mus.* (Halle, 1904), p. 104; 'so that it does not hear the voice of *incantantium* nor the wise enchanter's *incantantur*'.

[150] These are the *Salisbury* (x²), *Vitellius* (xi^med), *Arundel* (xi²), *Tiberius* (xi^med / xi³⁄₄), and *Stowe* psalters (xi^med / xi³⁄₄), and the second set of glosses in the *Eadwine Psalter* (c. 1155–1160); see Ker, *Catalogue*, pp. 135–6, 167–71, 262, 298–301, 336–7, 449–51; Pulsiano, *Psalters I*, pp. 13, 38, 50, 65; Lucas and Wilcox, *Dunstan, Ælfric, and Wulfstan*, p. 43; Gretsch, *Intellectual Foundations*, pp. 26–7; Scragg, *Conspectus*, pp. 33, 49, 52, 60, 83.

[151] Daphne Stroud, 'The Provenance of the Salisbury Psalter', *The Library*, 6 (1979), 225–35; Gretsch, *Intellectual Foundations*, pp. 18–20; Scragg, *Conspectus*, p. 83.

[152] Roeder, *Regius-Psalter*, p. 104; 'then it does not hear strong *ongalendra* and when poison is *begalene* by the wise'.

[153] Fred Harsley, ed., *Eadwine's Canterbury Psalter*, EETS Original Series, Vol. 92 (London, 1889), p. 97.

begalene came from Winchester and probably became the standardised gloss for this psalm.

Another recension of glosses that use *galdor* comes from the *Vespasian Psalter* (s. ix, Mercia). The *Vespasian* gloss was copied in the *Junius Psalter* (Oxford, Bodleian Library, MS Junius 27, s. x[1], Winchester) and the *Cambridge Psalter* (Cambridge, University Library, MS Ff. 1. 23, c. 1000, Ramsey).[154] The *Vespasian Psalter* glosses the psalm with 'sie ne gehered stefne galendra 7 galdurcreftas ða bioð agalæne from ðæm snottran'.[155] The *Junius Psalter* follows this gloss in its word formation but it has different spellings in 'galdorcræftas' and 'agelene', and the *Cambridge Psalter* also differs with 'galyndra'.[156] Despite the differences in spellings, these three psalters show an alternative approach to glossing the psalm with forms of *galdor* and *galan*, indicating that glossators were experimenting with different formations of this noun and verb.

The *Lambeth Psalter* (s. x[in]) is also of late West-Saxon origin but it is different from all of these manuscripts as it demonstrates an 'encyclopaedic character' in its vocabulary.[157] Gretsch believes that this psalter's glosses provide important evidence of standardised vocabulary that was taught at Bishop Æthelwold's school at the Old Minster, Winchester.[158] Multiple glosses are given in places and some freely draw upon the *Royal* and *Vespasian* traditions. The *Lambeth Psalter* glosses the verse from Psalm 57 with 'seo ne geherð stemne galendra 7 atterwyrhtan galendes wislice'.[159] This variance from other glosses suggests that different *galdor*-glosses were being used in eleventh-century Winchester.

As seen from the Aldhelm and psalter glosses, various forms of *galdor* were used to translate specific Latin terminology that denoted dangerous spiritual knowledge that is in opposition to God. Like all other proscriptive uses of *galdor*, the glosses demonstrate a dependency upon surrounding vocabulary and contexts in both the Latin

---

[154] Ker, *Catalogue*, pp. 11–12, 408–9; Gretsch, *Intellectual Foundations*, p. 18; Gneuss, *Handlist*, pp. 26, 101; Scragg, *Conspectus*, pp. 19–20.

[155] Conrad Grimm, ed., *Glossar zum Vespasian-Psalter und den Hymnen* (Heidelberg, 1906), pp. 4, 77; 'may it not be heard strong *galendra* and *galdurcreftas* which are *agalæne* by the wise'.

[156] Eduard Brenner, ed., *Der Altenglische Junius-Psalter: Die Interlinear-Glosse der Handschrift Junius 27 der Bodleiana zu Oxford* (Heidelberg, 1909), p. 74; Richard Jente, ed., *Die Mythologischen Ausdrücke im Altenglischen Wortschatz* (Heidelberg, 1921), p. 316.

[157] Gretsch, *Intellectual Foundations*, p. 27.

[158] Gretsch, *Intellectual Foundations*, p. 27.

[159] U. Lindelöf, ed., *Der Lambeth-Psalter: Eine Altenglische Interlinearversion des Psalters in der HS. 427 der Erzbischöflichen Lambeth Palace Library*, 2 Vols. (Helsingfors, 1909–14), Vol. I, p. 91; 'may it not hear strong *galendra* and poison-workers (who) *galendes* wisely'.

original and the Old English translation for the condemnation of this word.

Observations

Condemnatory uses of *galdor* make it difficult to reach a definition for this word because it is never condemned in isolation and it is consistently surrounded by other forbidden practices like 'wiccecræft' and 'scinlac' (witchcraft), 'lyblacan' (poisons), 'hæðenum' (heathens), 'wigelunga' (enchantments), 'hwata' (soothsayer), and 'leasung' (deceit). When the word appears in glosses and translations of Latin, it is generally used as an umbrella term to describe diabolical concepts like 'necromantia' (necromancy), 'marsorum' (incantations), 'auruspicum' (soothsayer), 'prestrigiarum' (delusions), and 'incantatium' (incantations). Aside from some exceptions where specific concepts are used in compounds, *galdor* appears to have increasingly become a 'go-to' word in late Anglo-Saxon didactic writings that provide long lists of unauthorised, unsupervised, or simply evil practices that unwary Christians are to avoid.

Many of the condemnatory uses of *galdor* were written by networks of reforming ecclesiastics – including Ælfric and Wulfstan – who sought to censor religious observances. There are indications that sometimes a *galdor* was permitted in ritual practices if it consisted of liturgical prayers, like the Paternoster. In most other contexts, it is employed in formulaic ways alongside a myriad of other vocabulary. When one simplifies its probable meaning in these texts, *galdor* seems to refer to a spiritual song or chant that requires special skill and authority for its performance. The sheer volume of texts that condemn the use of an unauthorised *galdor* suggests that high-ranking ecclesiastics understood it to be a powerful ritual performance that should be performed by proper Christian authorities, if by anybody at all.

Conclusions

This chapter has sought to reconsider the meaning of an Old English word that has been used to define the entire corpus of Anglo-Saxon 'charms'. It has become clear from etymological evidence and entries in the Old English corpus that *galdor* cannot simply be equated with modern understandings of a 'charm' and its connotations of suspicious pagan or heterodox practices. The noun has etymological connections with secrecy, wisdom, prophecy, and more general vocalised sounds. In Old English texts it could denote a wide range of concepts from a supernatural force that works according to divine providence, to Christian wisdom, discernment, prophecy, and even Eucharistic mystery. These meanings are mainly found in manuscripts that were written on the cusp of the Benedictine Reform, indicating that *galdor* was endorsed as an explicitly Christian concept in older poetic vocabulary before it was predominantly associated with dangerous, forbidden practices. This revision of meaning was quite possibly a result of Æthelwold's programme of standardised vernacular writings at his school in the Old Minster, Winchester. While these examples form a minority of entries in the Old English corpus, they provide invaluable insight into the developments of this word and its meanings, and are therefore perhaps the most crucial pieces of information that have so far not been fully considered in modern historiographies of early English ritual practices.

Nearly all other appearances of *galdor* occur in proscriptive contexts, and this has been well documented in scholarship. Some law codes and translations of Latin sources were written before the Benedictine Reform, indicating that *galdor* was sometimes used to describe forbidden beliefs and customs prior to this movement. Later evidence indicates that reformers drew upon earlier English laws and Continental writings to rework and promulgate condemnations of knowledge and rituals that were harmful to Christians. However, these proscriptions never condemn *galdor* in isolation and they are very formulaic, revealing nothing in particular about what exactly this ritual practice involved other than the uttering or chanting of powerful words in illicit contexts. Using these many condemnatory examples as evidence of surviving pagan ritual practices is therefore unsatisfactory, particularly because these texts were written by ecclesiastics who mechanically reworked Continental writings and constructed notions of paganism and heresy to censor unauthorised religious observances. *Galdor* is clearly employed as a standardised didactic trope in these texts, and it cannot be used as a category term in itself on this basis.

Galdor signifies spiritual knowledge and words of power that could be enlightening or deceptive. When a saint or ecclesiastical authority used a *galdor*, it was seen to be a powerful Christian utterance or performance that could lead to profound spiritual insight. When it was used by a malignant religious leader or unauthorised layperson, it led the soul astray and condemned the Christian to a spiritual death, and some provisions seem to have been made for atonements for this sin. It follows from the evidence of this chapter that *galdor* should simply be defined as a spiritual utterance or chant, and when it is found in an overtly Christian context, it could take on a prophetic, liturgical, or even sacramental significance. Scholarship must therefore include these meanings of *galdor* in its pursuit of new interpretations of Anglo-Saxon paganism, magic, and heterodox religion with a trajectory towards mainstream Christian ritual practices.

Having seen how this word is used in texts from across the Old English corpus, it is important to return to the rituals that actually prescribe the performance of a *galdor*. Nearly all of these rituals were, perhaps surprisingly, written down in reforming minsters during the late tenth and eleventh centuries, when this word was probably being restricted in meaning by reformers. These ritual texts underscore the conclusions of this chapter that *galdor* was not universally condemned. Indeed, it could signify a powerful, legitimate Christian ritual that was often accompanied by other liturgical prayers and objects, even in the very monasteries that simultaneously produced texts forbidding its unlawful use.

2

By the Power Vested in Me:
Galdor in Authorised Rituals

'galdor took on a Christian and even liturgical meaning'.[1]

There are twelve surviving Anglo-Saxon rituals that instruct a reader to write or recite a *galdor*. These are found in four manuscripts, at least three of which were written at major ecclesiastical centres in the late tenth and eleventh centuries. The word *galdor* is used in these manuscripts to refer to an explicitly Christian ritual performance. As seen in Chapter 1, many texts use *galdor* to signify dangerous and forbidden spiritual customs, but these manuscripts show that the term was also used in rituals with liturgical formulas and objects. Indeed, these *galdru* actually counter the same hostile forces that are connected to the noun in other proscriptive texts, such as 'lyblace' (poison), 'egsa' (monster), 'lað' (enemy), 'drycræft' (witchcraft), 'malscrunge' (enchantments), and 'leodrunan' (sorceresses). The meaning of *galdor* in these rituals reflects the poetic uses of the term in the Exeter and Vercelli Books to denote Christian wisdom, discernment, divine revelation, and sacramental mystery. Nearly all of these prescriptions were written in high-status monasteries associated with the Benedictine Reform, and this suggests that this ritual practice was endorsed by some ecclesiastics in explicitly Christian, liturgical contexts. This chapter reconsiders how some Christian scribes understood *galdor* in the late Anglo-Saxon period when these rituals were written down.

Ten out of twelve rituals that prescribe a *galdor* are found in two of these four manuscripts, which are books of healing. Many of these texts contain medical recipes as well as ritual utterances, gestures, and liturgical prayers. As such, the *galdor* forms one part of the ritual process and it is closely associated with other liturgical prayers and objects. The difference with some *galdru* is that their speech is unintelligible, possibly even to those who were required to perform them. However, it may be the case that their obscure language was precisely what protected them from being easily accessed, so that only those who could read them correctly could unlock their power.

All references to *galdor* in these two collections appear in the main writing space, indicating that this ritual performance was conceived of

---

[1] Wentersdorf, 'Ruler's Lament', p. 281.

as an intricate component of the collection as a whole by a compiler. These two manuscripts contain the majority of these *galdor* rituals, and they can be confidently located in reforming minsters in Winchester, possibly in the same scriptoria that were producing condemnations of this term. The final two references to *galdor* occur in rituals that are marginal texts and later additions to the other two manuscripts, and these require more speculation. As is the case with all later additions to manuscripts, these rituals may have been added to simply fill blank spaces, they may have no obvious connections with other texts in the manuscript, and it is often difficult to date when such additions were made. These possibilities limit what we can say about how a scribe understood these references to *galdor*, but information can be gathered from the rituals' surrounding manuscript contexts.

London, British Library, MS Royal 12 D. xvii

London, British Library, MS Royal 12 D. xvii, commonly known as *Bald's Leechbook*, consists of remedial prescriptions for a comprehensive range of illnesses. The manuscript is made up of three books, and its single scribe has been identified as one of the scribes of the *Parker Chronicle* (Cambridge, Corpus Christi College, MS 173), who was working at the Old Minster, Winchester in the third quarter of the tenth century.[2] The manuscript was copied shortly after the expulsion of clerics from the Old Minster in 964, and at a time when written Old English was being standardised at Æthelwold's school. Given that Ælfric was educated at the Old Minster before 987,[3] and that he seems to have been deeply suspicious of *galdor* practices, the manuscript's endorsement of this ritual performance suggests that some ecclesiastics in the Old Minster perceived the *galdor* in a different way to authorities like Ælfric.

Different dates have been suggested for the original composition of the texts in this collection. One reference to King Alfred's trade with Elias, Patriarch of Jerusalem, on folios 105v–106r may indicate that the original compilation was made in the late ninth or early tenth century.[4] Stephanie Hollis suggests that it originated in Theodore's

---

[2] See Alger N. Doane, *Anglo-Saxon Manuscripts in Microfiche Facsimile, Vol. 1: Books of Prayers and Healing* (Binghamton, 1994), p. 60. See also Ker, *Catalogue*, pp. 332–3; Gneuss, *Handlist*, p. 83; Thomas A. Bredehoft, 'The Boundaries Between Verse and Prose in Old English Literature', in *Old English Literature in its Manuscript Context*, Lionarons, ed., pp. 139–72, p. 150; Brown, *Manuscripts*, p. 144.

[3] Hill, 'Ælfric: His Life and Works', p. 35.

[4] See Malcolm L. Cameron, 'Bald's *Leechbook*: Its Sources and their Use in its Compilation', *ASE*, 12 (1983), 153–82, p. 153; 'Bald's *Leechbook* and Cultural

school at Canterbury in the seventh century on the basis of its classical content, and she dates the manuscript's exemplar to c. 900 on linguistic grounds.[5] The end of Book II also contains a verse colophon concerning a certain 'Bald' who ordered 'Cild' to copy the manuscript (fol. 109r):

Bald habet hunc librum cild quem conscribere iussit;
Hic precor assidue cunctis in nomine Xristi.
Quo nullus tollat hunc librum perfidus a me.
Nec ui nec furto nec quodam famine falso.
Cur quia nulla mihi tam cara est optima gaza.
Quam cari libri quos Xristi gratia comit.[6]

Bald is the owner of this book, which he ordered Cild to write;
earnestly here I beg everyone in the name of Christ
that no deceitful person should take this book from me,
neither by force nor by stealth nor by any false statement.
Why? Because no richest treasure is so dear to me
As my dear books which the grace of Christ attends.[7]

This declaration indicates Bald's personal ownership of the first two books but no further information is known about these two people.[8] Robert Nokes thinks that Books I and II were originally conceived of as a single unit and compiled by a network of medical practitioners as a catalogue for future use, with Book III being added later by the scribe.[9] The original version of this book of healing was likely to have been compiled by highly literate individuals with important royal and ecclesiastical connections, and at a centre with a substantial library.[10] Charles Singer traced the wide range of sources that would have been available for the compilation of this collection, and there are elements of classical, Irish, Byzantine, Continental, and ecclesiastical influences throughout the manuscript.[11] The individuals who were involved in the original compilation plundered a significant amount of material that was available to them, and the later scribe who copied Books I and

Interactions in Anglo-Saxon England', *ASE*, 19 (1990), 5–12, p. 6; Robert Scott Nokes, 'The Several Compilers of *Bald's Leechbook*', *ASE*, 33 (2004), 51–76.

[5] Stephanie Hollis, 'Scientific and Medical Writings', in *Companion to Anglo-Saxon Literature*, Pulsiano and Treharne, eds, pp. 188–208, pp. 194–8.

[6] Cockayne, *Leechdoms*, Vol. II, p. 298.

[7] Charles E. Wright, ed. and trans, *Bald's Leechbook: British Museum Royal Manuscript 12.D.xvii* (Copenhagen, 1955), p. 13.

[8] Cameron proposes that Bald was a lay physician, Malcolm L. Cameron, *Anglo-Saxon Medicine* (Cambridge, 1993), pp. 20–1 and see pp. 20–4 for two other names that appear in the manuscript. See also Richard Gameson, *The Scribe Speaks? Colophons in Early English Manuscripts* (Cambridge, 2001), p. 51.

[9] See Nokes, 'Compilers of *Bald's Leechbook*', pp. 51–2, 74.

[10] For details about the later reception of this manuscript, see James P. Carley, *The Libraries of King Henry VIII* (London, 2000), p. 329.

[11] Singer, 'Magic and Medicine', pp. 341–74.

II, and seems to have added Book III, had access to similar sources. The inclusion of remedies with components called *galdor* suggests that this ritual practice was perceived to be an important part of a collection of ancient, learned wisdom.

The possible origins of this collection in Theodore's school or Alfred's court indicate that *galdor* was endorsed as an important Christian ritual practice in earlier centuries. As the manuscript was probably copied during Æthelwold's episcopacy in the Old Minster, the term also seems to have been understood in this way by members of a reforming monastic community. This has significant implications for perceptions of *galdor*, as the term was also being used to denote forbidden spiritual practices in Æthelwold's school, and Ælfric condemned *galdru* which were not performed by Christian authorities after he was educated at the Old Minster. Indeed, Wulfstan condemned *galdor* in similar ways to Ælfric, but he may also have known about *Bald's Leechbook* because he owned an eleventh-century manuscript (London, British Library, MS Harley 55) which seems to have been copied from Book II of *Bald's Leechbook*.[12] Although Book II contains no references to *galdor*, reforming ecclesiastics like Wulfstan valued such collections of medical knowledge, and it seems likely that other monks in reforming minsters valued *galdor* as a ritual practice that could harness ancient Christian wisdom.[13]

Royal 12 D. xvii contains the largest number of rituals that prescribe a *galdor*; this word appears twelve times in six rituals from Books I and III. Importantly, all of these prescriptions occur in the manuscript's list of contents and main writing space, showing that these *galdru* were seen to be completely compatible with both the original collection (Books I and II) and the final manuscript as a whole (with Book III added later). All three books in the manuscript have their own list of contents, and that of Book I provides an entry for a remedy against sorcery and elf-sickness (fols. 5rv):

> LXIIII. Læcedomas wiþ ælcre leodrunan and ælfsidenne þæt is fefer-cynnes gealdor and dust and drencas and sealf and gif sio adl netnum sie and gif sio adl wyrde mannan oððe mare ride and wyrde seofon ealles cræfta.[14]

[12] See Hollis, 'Medical Writings', p. 197.

[13] Christine Voth has undertaken a comprehensive analysis of this manuscript from its compilation before the Benedictine Reform to its later uses after the Anglo-Saxon period, 'An Analysis of the Tenth-Century Anglo-Saxon Manuscript London, British Library, Royal 12. D. xvii', Unpublished Doctoral Thesis (Cambridge University, England, 2014).

[14] Cockayne, *Leechdoms*, Vol. II, p. 14. All translations for this manuscript are my own.

Leechdoms against all sorcery and elf-sickness; that is a fever *gealdor*, and powder, and drinks, and a salve; and if the disease is on cattle and if it harms a man, or if a mare ride him and hurts [him], [there are] all seven crafts.

This contents description separates the *galdor* from the powder, liquid, and salve treatments. The text to which this entry refers (fols. 52v–53r) does not use the word *galdor*, and the first part of this ritual against elf-sickness prescribes the writing of Greek letters ('greciscum stafum').[15] This is followed by a series of instructions to make the powder, drink, and salve from a wide range of ingredients. The *galdor* of this ritual is therefore the series of Greek letters that include Christ's title as Alpha and Omega: '++ A ++ O + γ°HρBγM +++++ BερρNN | κNεTTAN |'.[16] It is unclear whether these letters were to be vocalised or written down and carried like an amulet. This obscure sequence may be a corruption of a Greek phrase that is now illegible, as Malcolm Cameron believes: 'there is no evidence that Anglo-Saxons other than those under the immediate teaching or influence of Theodore and Hadrian at Canterbury could handle Greek well enough to be able to use medical texts in Greek'.[17] Despite Cameron's reservations, there is an evident attempt to signify Christ in the alpha and omega as well as the cruciform markings. Furthermore, Oda and Æthelwold are known to have developed grecisms and neologisms at their respective schools in Canterbury and Winchester in the second half of the tenth century, an effort undoubtedly inspired by intellectual engagements with Greek in Carolingian monasteries.[18] Greek was used in rituals for its associated spiritual power as one of the three sacred languages of Scripture, and it is used in some *galdru* because of their association with ancient words of Christian wisdom.

It may also be the case that these letters were deliberately obscured to conceal the meaning of this *galdor*, especially if it was meant to be vocalised (as seen in the previous chapter). There are many examples of encrypted writings in Anglo-Saxon manuscripts – including some

---

[15] Cockayne, *Leechdoms*, Vol. II, p. 138.

[16] Jolly, *Popular Religion*, p. 149. See also Cockayne, *Leechdoms*, Vol. II, p. 138.

[17] Cameron, *Anglo-Saxon Medicine*, p. 65.

[18] Michael Lapidge, 'The Hermeneutic Style in Tenth-Century Anglo-Latin Literature', *ASE*, 4 (1975), 67–111. For Carolingian interests in Greek, see Jan M. Ziolkowski, 'Theories of Obscurity in the Latin Tradition', *Mediaevalia*, 19 (1996), 101–70, pp. 116–24; Alessandro Zironi, 'Marginal Alphabets in the Carolingian Age: Philological and Codicological Considerations', in *Rethinking and Recontextualizing Glosses: New Perspectives in the Study of Late Anglo-Saxon Glossography*, Patrizia Lendinara, Loredana Lazzari, and Claudia Di Sciacca, eds (Turnhout, 2011), pp. 353–71; Mariken Teeuwen, 'Carolingian Scholarship on Classical Authors: Practices of Reading and Writing', in *Manuscripts of the Latin Classics 800–1200*, Erik Kwakkel, ed. (Leiden, 2015), pp. 23–52, pp. 45–6. See also Chapter 5.

that have direct connections with *Bald's Leechbook* – and this ritual's use of a different alphabet may indicate that its meaning is concealed within the graphemes (as will be discussed further in Chapters 4 and 5). Whatever the meaning of these Greek letters, it is clear that they form the 'fefercynnes gealdor' which counters the hostile spiritual forces of 'leodrunan' and 'ælfsidenne'.[19] The Christian, liturgical nature of this *galdor* is also confirmed by ensuing instructions to sing nine Masses, administer the drink at monastic hours (Terce, Sext, None), and use holy water and incense in the remedies that follow.[20]

The next entry after this text is a ritual against spring fever ('lencten adle', fol. 53r), and it combines a *galdor* with a *gebed* (prayer). The text opens with instructions to make a drink and sing many Masses over it ('fela mæssan').[21] The *galdor* of this ritual is then given and it is intricately connected to prayer and the evangelists:

+++

Feower godspellara naman y gealdor y gebed +++ Matheus +++++

+++

+++

Marcus +++++ lucas +++ Iohannes ++ Intercedite

+++ ++++

pro me. Tiecon. leleloth. patron. adiuro uos. Eft godcund gebed. In nomine domini sit benedictum. beronice. beronicen. et habet In uestimento et In femore suo scriptum rex regum et dominus dominantium. Eft godcund gebed. In nomine sit benedictum. D E E R E þ . N y . þ T X D E R E þ N y . þ T X. Eft sceal mon swigende þis writan and don þas word swigende þis on þa winstran breost and ne ga he in on þæt gewrit ne in on ber and eac swigende þis on don. HAMMANẏEL . BPONice . NOẏepTAẏEPΓ.[22]

The names of the four evangelists and a *gealdor* and prayer + Matthew + Mark + Luke + John + Intercede for me. Tiecon, Leleloth, patron, I urge you. Again a divine prayer. In the lord's name be blessed. Veronica. Veronica. And he has written on his robe and on his thigh 'king of kings and lord of lords'. Again a divine prayer. D E E R E þ . N and . þ T X D E R E þ N and . þ T X. Again, a man shall write this silently, and silently put these words on the left breast, and he [should] not go in [with]

---

[19] On the spiritual nature of these illnesses, see Alaric Hall, 'Calling the Shots: The Old English Remedy Gif Hors Ofscoten Sie and Anglo-Saxon "Elf-Shot"', *Neuphilologische Mitteilungen*, 106 (2005), 195–209; *Elves in Anglo-Saxon England*, pp. 105, 119–22. Jolly defines 'leodrunan' as 'evil wise woman', Jolly, *Popular Religion*, p. 146.

[20] See Cockayne, *Leechdoms*, Vol. II, pp. 138–40.

[21] Cockayne, *Leechdoms*, Vol. II, p. 140.

[22] Transcription follows that in Cockayne, *Leechdoms*, Vol. II, p. 140. Storms interprets different runic markings, which can be transliterated as 'D E E R E þ. N S. P T X D E R F P N S. P T X', Storms, *Anglo-Saxon Magic*, p. 270.

that writing, nor into bed, and [he should] also silently put this on. ΠAMMANŷEL . BPONice . NOŷepTAŷEPΓ.

The *galdor* of this ritual begins after the invocation of the four evange-lists and it seems to be a solemn adjuration, reading 'Tiecon. leleloth. patron. adiuro uos'. There is no indication of how this *galdor* is to be performed but the surrounding Latin petitions and commands and the presence of cross markings indicate a vocal utterance with bodily gestures. The later instructions for silence also indicate that this first performance is vocal. Two divine prayers ('godcund gebed') that follow use obscure language and echo the use of Greek in the previ-ous ritual against elf-sickness. The ritual's repetition of 'eft godcung gebed' ('again a divine prayer') is interesting in that these prayers are prescribed as additions to the *galdor* and complement the first ritual performance. In some ways the *galdor* is treated in the same way as the *gebed*, but distinctions between the two ritual performances remain unclear. The *galdor* may have been vocalised in a different manner, and it is not clear whether it was also seen to be a 'godcund' (divine, sacred, heaven-sent) performance.

The first divine prayer consists of passages from Scripture (Ps. 112; Rev. 19: 16) and most likely an invocation of St Veronica. The second *gebed* is formed by a sequence of runic and Roman letters and, unlike the previous sections of the ritual, it is specified that these letters must be written down in silence ('Eft sceal mon swigende þis writan'). The final inscription that is to be carried on the body in silence also uses obscure Greek. However, no satisfactory rendering of the prayers and inscription has been proposed. Thomas Cockayne translated the runic prayer as 'thine hand vexeth, thine hand vexeth' ('DEEREÞ HAND ÞIN DEREÞ HAND ÞIN') but this interpretation requires a liberal reading of the runes.[23] Felix Grendon called these letters 'mystic' and thought that they 'may have been substituted for earlier runes'.[24] Malcolm Cameron believed that the runes are 'pagan symbols' that were combined with other Christian elements like the 'attempt to write *Emmanuel* and *Veronica* and a third undecipherable word or phrase all in Greek letters' in the final inscription.[25] Once again, it is poss-ible that these obscure phrases are corrupted and that their surviving forms stem from a misunderstanding of their meanings. However, in a similar way to the ritual against elf-sickness, the sequences in this ritual for spring fever may have been deliberately obscured to conceal

---

[23] Cockayne, *Leechdoms*, Vol. II, p. 141.
[24] Grendon, 'Anglo-Saxon Charms', p. 223. He also argued that the same sequences of letters are to be used in another remedy in this manuscript (fol. 111v, Book III) that works against a range of physical and spiritual illnesses including 'lenctenadle' and 'yfelum gealdorcræftum', pp. 200–1.
[25] Cameron, *Anglo-Saxon Medicine*, pp. 133–4.

their meaning. This is implied in the runic prayer by the inclusion of the abbreviated conjunction 'y' (and) among the runes 'N y þ' (N and þ), which may indicate that the sequence is anagrammatic or that the names of the runes should be pronounced aloud.[26] Karen Jolly believes that the ritual's prescriptions for silence and prayer 'evoke a monastic setting', and this may imply that the ritual's overall performance was secretive.[27] It seems likely that the different parts of this ritual deliberately use obscure words and multiple alphabets to conceal utterances that were to be correctly discerned by a performer who knew how to interpret the letters, and who could vocalise its *galdor* and secret divine prayers.

Whatever the meaning of these runic and Greek letters, the ritual clearly associates its key components with Christian prayer. The *galdor* follows the names of the four evangelists and precedes two prayers ('gebed'), and multiple signings of the cross accompany the performance. The *galdor* is an urging of 'Tiecon', 'Leleloth', and 'patron', which are perhaps the names of two angels and a protector, indicating that it harnesses divine power.[28] This first ritual performance is followed by prescriptions for two 'godcund gebed', implying that the *galdor* was understood in a similar – if not the same – way as divine prayers. The focus on silence in the last section of the ritual and the final instructions that restrict locations in which the powerful letters can be carried further indicate that the *galdor* also conceals its powerful meaning. All of these stages of the ritual demonstrate that the *galdor* was intimately connected with Scripture, the names of important biblical figures, the sign of the cross, divine prayers, and secrecy.

Book I of *Bald's Leechbook* also contains a series of rituals against poison (fols. 42r–43r), and each entry prescribes specific ingredients to make drinks and salves. The description of these rituals in the contents (fol. 4r) says that they include 'þæs halgan cristes þegnes Iohannes gebed and gealdor and eac oþer scyttisc gecost gealdor gehwæþer wiþ ælcum attre'.[29] The prayer lists a variety of venomous reptiles that the ritual effectively counters, and it is based upon the *Virtutes Iohannis* from the *Book of Cerne* (fol. 79r, Cambridge, Cambridge University

---

[26] This is a feature of other runic signatures in the Exeter Book riddles and the *Husband's Message*, see Tom Birkett, 'Runes and *Revelatio*: Cynewulf's Signatures Reconsidered', *RES*, 65 (2014), 771–89.

[27] Jolly, *Popular Religion*, p. 150.

[28] See Cockayne, *Leechdoms*, Vol. II, p. 141. See also Eleanour Sinclair Rohde, *The Old English Herbals* (London, 1922), p. 33. Grendon claimed that these are the names of Arabian gods, Grendon, 'Anglo-Saxon Charms', p. 114.

[29] Cockayne, *Leechdoms*, Vol. II, p. 10; 'a prayer and *gealdor* of John, the holy thane of Christ, and also another proven Irish *galdor* against each and every poison'. For other contexts in which this prayer of St John occurs, see Edward Pettit, ed. and trans, *Anglo-Saxon Remedies, Charms, and Prayers from British Library MS Harley 585: The 'Lacnunga'*, 2 Vols. (New York, 2001), Vol. II, pp. 77–9.

Library, MS Ll.l.10, 820 × 840, Worcester) that begins: 'Item alia oratio: Tunc beatus iohannis iacentibus mortuis qui uenenum biberunt intrepidus et constans accipit calicem et signaculum crucis facians in eo et dixit'.[30] This apocryphal text connects the Eucharist, the sign of the cross, and John the Evangelist in a liturgical prayer ('oratio') that uses exorcism formulas to counteract poison. The *Book of Cerne* has Irish materials, and the entry in *Bald's Leechbook* uses this prayer of St John in conjunction with an Irish *galdor* ('scyttisc gecost gealdor').[31]

The invocation of St John in an exorcism of poison may have been inspired by Mark 16: 17–18, where Christ gives his Apostles power over all evil creatures:

'signa autem eos qui crediderint haec sequentur in nomine meo daemonia eicient linguis loquentur novis serpentes tollent et si mortiferum quid biberint non eos nocebit super aegrotos manus inponent et bene habebunt.'[32]

'These signs shall follow those who believe: in my name demons will be cast out; they will speak in new tongues; they will lift up serpents, and if they drink anything deadly it will not harm them, over the sick they will lay their hands, and they will recover.'

In this gospel passage Christ empowers his disciples so that they become immune to snakes and poison, and the association of St John with these Anglo-Saxon rituals lends Scriptural authority to the texts. The contents entry in *Bald's Leechbook* claims that these rituals against poison contain 'Iohannes gebed and gealdor' (John's prayer and *galdor*), which was said to be spoken by the Apostle himself to counteract venom.

In addition to this Scriptural passage, objects that came from Ireland were seen to possess special power against snakes, and this probably developed from legends about St Patrick. In Book I of his *Historia Ecclesiastica*, Bede describes the practice of scraping parchment from Irish manuscripts into water to concoct an efficacious potion against venomous reptiles:

---

[30] A. B. Kuypers, ed., *The Prayerbook of Aedeluald the Bishop Commonly Called the Book of Cerne: Edited from the MS in the University Library, Cambridge with Introduction and Notes* (Cambridge, 1902), p. 157; 'then, as those who had drunk the poison lay dead, holy John, fearless and persevering, took the chalice and, making the sign of the cross over it, said', translation from Aideen M. O'Leary, 'Apostolic *Passiones* in Early Anglo-Saxon England', in *Apocryphal Texts and Traditions in Anglo-Saxon England*, Kathryn Powell and Donald G. Scragg, eds (Cambridge, 2003), pp. 103–20, p. 116. On the dating of this manuscript, see Kuypers, *Prayerbook*, pp. xi–xiv; Michelle P. Brown, *The Book of Cerne: Prayer, Patronage, and Power in Ninth-Century England* (London, 1996), pp. 18–44; Gneuss, *Handlist*, p. 29.

[31] On Irish influence in the *Book of Cerne*, see Brown, *Book of Cerne*, pp. 117–20, 137–8.

[32] *Biblia Sacra*, Vol. II, p. 1605.

Nullum ibi reptile uideri soleat, nullus uiuere serpens ualeat. Nam saepe illo de Brittania adlati serpentes, mox ut proximante terris nauigio odore aeris illius adtacti fuerint, intereunt; quin potius omnia pene quae de eadem insula sunt contra uenenum ualent. Denique uidimus, quibusdam a serpente percussis, rasa folia codicum qui de Hibernia fuerant, et ipsam rasuram aquae inmissam ac potui datam talibus protinus totam uim ueneni grassantis, totum inflate corporis absumsisse ac sedasse tumorem.

No reptile is found there nor could a serpent survive; for although serpents have often been brought from Britain, as soon as the ship approaches land they are affected by the scent of the air and quickly perish. In fact almost everything that the island produces is efficacious against poison. For instance we see how, in the case of people suffering from snake-bite, the leaves of manuscripts from Ireland were scraped, and the scrapings put in water and given the sufferer to drink. These scrapings at once absorbed the whole violence of the spreading poison and assuaged the swelling (I, 1).[33]

The legend reported by Bede offers an example of practices involving written amulets scraped into a drink that found their way into some Anglo-Saxon rituals.[34] Although this *galdor* in *Bald's Leechbook* is to be sung and not scraped off an object, its explicit association with Ireland in the contents entry evidently enhances its claim to successfully counteract poison.

The first *galdor* in this series of texts to which the contents entry refers is found in a ritual against 'nædran slege' (snake strike). This text begins with a prescription to put earwax on the wound before singing 'þriwa þæs halgan Sancte Iohannes gebed and gealdor'.[35] Unlike the ritual against spring fever, this ritual does not distinguish the *galdor* from the *gebed* and there is no break in the text to indicate any difference between the two, suggesting that the *galdor* is here equated with the prayer of John the Evangelist. The *galdor* is very close to the version found in the *Book of Cerne*; it opens with an address to the Trinity ('deus meus et pater et filius et spiritus sanctus'), it is composed entirely in Latin, and it lists poisonous creatures over which God has power. It concludes by claiming that St John used this *galdor* before signing himself with the cross and receiving the Eucharist, thus embellishing the version found in the *Book of Cerne*: 'Et cum hoc dixisset, totum semet ipsum signo crucis armavit, et bibit totum quod erat in

---

[33] Bede, *Ecclesiastical History of the English People*, Bertram Colgrave and R. A. B. Mynors, eds and trans, Oxford Medieval Texts (Oxford, 1969), pp. 18–21.
[34] See, for example, Storms, *Anglo-Saxon Magic*, pp. 232–5.
[35] Cockayne, *Leechdoms*, Vol. II, p. 112; 'thrice the holy Saint John's prayer and *gealdor*'.

calice'.[36] This *galdor* is intricately related to the gospel (through reference to the Evangelist), the sign of the cross, and the Eucharist, and it harnesses Christian power to overcome the evil poison of a snake. It is worth remembering that in the *Old English Martyrology* St Audax was a 'wyrmgaldere' before he converted to Christianity, and he used *galdru* to summon snakes to attack St Anatolia. This *galdor* of St John is used in the opposite way to counteract evil snakes, further indicating that that *galdru* were perceived to be dangerous and illegitimate if they were not used by Christian authorities. Interestingly, the close connection between this *galdor* and the chalice ('bibit totum quod erat in calice') may also be compared with the *galdorcwide* that is uttered by a chalice in *Riddle* 48.[37]

The second ritual that is called a 'proven Irish *gealdor*' ('scyttisc gecost gealdor') is against flying venom or infection ('fleogendrum atre', fol. 43r). It opens with an instruction to prepare a salve for the wound, and continues with prescriptions to sing nine litanies, nine Paternosters, and 'þis gealdor' nine times.[38] The passage that follows is yet another sequence of obscure words and phrases:

> Acræ ærcræ ærnem nadre ærcuna hel ærnem niþærn ær afan buiþine adcrice ærnem meodre ærnem æþern ærnem allū honor ucus idar adcert cunolari raticamo helæ icas xpita hæle tobært tera fueli cui robater plana uili.[39]

The obscure Irish words of this *galdor* echo the use of other exotic and ancient languages in the manuscript.[40] Felix Grendon stated that this passage is 'plainly a rhythmical one of the jingle type', indicating that he thought this *galdor* was to be uttered rather than written.[41] Jacqueline Borsje also claims that it is a vocal utterance and offers a literal word-for-word interpretation of it:

> The urging of a claim (*acra(e)*)
> against gore (*ar crú*),
> against the poison (*ar nem*) of a snake
> against wounding (*ar guin*) [is] his *éle*
> against the poison of a snake
> *aer . asan . bui þine . adcrice*
> against the poison of a snake
> against the poison of a snake (or: against venomous poison).

---

[36] Cockayne, *Leechdoms*, Vol. II, p. 112; 'And when he had said this, he armed his whole self with the sign of the cross, and drank all that was in the chalice.'
[37] See Chapter 1.
[38] Cockayne, *Leechdoms*, Vol. II, p. 112.
[39] Cockayne, *Leechdoms*, Vol. II, p. 112.
[40] See also Gameson, *The Scribe Speaks?*, p. 21.
[41] Grendon, 'Anglo-Saxon Charms', p. 230.

against poison
allū . honor . and (*ucus = ocus*) water (*idar*)
ad cert with the drink (*cu n-ol*) against them (? *ari = airi*)
May my *éle* heal you. [It is] Christ in whom is (*i ta*) healing.
Put (or: I will put; *tobær*) the *ttera* of urine (*fuel*) in (*i[n]*) a place (for *cui* read *ait*).
They have all become healthy.
[Or:] I placed / uttered [it] (*tobært*) upon (*ter* = OIr. *tar*) his (*a*) wounds (*fueli* for *fuili*) so that (*cui* = OIr. *co*?) they have all become healthy.[42]

Borsje thinks that the words to be uttered conclude at 'ærnem æþern ærnem' and that the words from 'allū honor ucus' signal instructions for a separate performance that have connections with other Irish rituals, including a holy salve in London, British Library, MS Harley 585 (discussed below).[43] The *galdor* seems to refer to the first passage of words in Irish (and also some Old English and Latin) that is heavily corrupted or deliberately obscured. An argument in favour of the latter is supported by the fact that these rituals against poison in *Bald's Leechbook* draw upon similar materials contained in the *Book of Cerne*, which also contains an acrostic poem (fol. 21r) that employs cryptographic devices to deliberately obscure its meaning.[44] The Christian, liturgical nature of this *galdor* is clear from its association with the singing of litanies and the Paternoster. It is evident that these Anglo-Saxon *galdru* are words of mysterious spiritual power that appear in different languages and alphabets, and that are used alongside other liturgical prayers and objects.

In the contents of Book III (fol. 110r), another ritual is identified as a *galdor* and this term is repeated in the main ritual itself. The ritual is against 'water-elf disease' and the description in the contents reads: 'Tacnu hu þu meaht ongitan hwæþer mon sie on wæter ælf adle and læcedom wiþ þam and gealdor on to singanne and þæt ilce mon mæg singan on wunda.'[45] This *galdor* is distinguished from a remedy ('læcedom') and marked off as a separate component of the ritual. The main text (fols. 125rv) also makes this distinction, as the 'læcedom' consists of a list of nineteen ingredients, after which the 'gealdor' is given:

---

[42] Jacqueline Borsje, 'A Spell Called *Éle*', in *Ulidia 3: Proceedings of the Third International Conference on the Ulster Cycle of Tales*, Gregory Toner and Séamus MacMathúna, eds (Berlin, 2013), pp. 193–212, pp. 204–6.

[43] Borsje, 'Spell Called *Éle*', p. 206. See also Pettit, *Anglo-Saxon Remedies*, Vol. II, pp. 22–9.

[44] For a discussion, see Brown, *Book of Cerne*, pp. 131–8.

[45] Cockayne, *Leechdoms*, Vol. II, p. 304; 'Signs for how you may know whether a man is in the water-elf disease, and a leechdom against it, and a *gealdor* to sing on it, and a man may also sing that on wounds.'

sing þis gealdor ofer þriwa. Ic benne awra[ð] betest beado wræda swa
benne ne burnon ne burston ne fundian ne feologan ne hoppetan ne wund
waco sian ne dolh diopian ac him self healde hale wæge ne ace þe þon ma
þe eorþan on eare ace. Sing þis manegum siþum eorþe þe on bere eallum
hire mihtum 7 mægenum. þas galdor mon mæg singan on wunde.[46]

Sing this *gealdor* over [it] three times: 'I have bound round the wounds
the best of war clasps, so the wounds neither burn nor burst, nor go
further nor spread nor throb; nor may the wounds be wicked, nor the
sore deepen, but may he himself hold on in a healthy way, nor ache you
more than the earth aches in ear (of corn).' Sing this many times: 'May
earth bear on you with all her might and strength.' A man may sing
these *galdor* over a wound.

The words of this sung *galdor* describe the performer as winding
healing power around the wounds so that they may not develop into
wicked wounds ('wund waco') and so that the individual may be
brought to health. It serves 'to bring out the natural potency of the
herbs' and it imitates the 'nec' formula often found in liturgies of
exorcism.[47] Although no explicitly Christian terminology is included
in this *galdor*, it combats the wicked effects of the disease and restores
physical and spiritual health to the sick subject.

The final appearance of *galdor* in this manuscript is found in a ritual
against joint pain in Book III ('liþwærce', fol. 116r). This entry is very
short and it opens with a simple instruction to 'sing VIIII siþum þis
gealdor' and spit on the site of the pain.[48] The *galdor* is then given and
it consists of three Latin phrases that describe the development of the
pain and God's healing power: 'malignus obligauit; angelus curauit;
dominus Saluauit'.[49] The text concludes with the statement 'him biþ
sona sel' to reinforce the *galdor*'s success.[50] Although this ritual is very
short, it is clear that this sung utterance conveys a message about the
evil origin of the pain (in the 'malignus'), the curative process by which
the pain is overcome (with the 'angelus'), and the source of restored
health (in 'dominus'). This simple progression reflects a typical Anglo-
Saxon spiritual interpretation of physical suffering because the minor
pain of joints is presented in terms of the cosmic battle between good
and evil.[51] The health of the individual that is at stake is spiritual as

---

[46] Cockayne, *Leechdoms*, Vol. II, pp. 350–2.
[47] See Jolly, *Popular Religion*, pp. 167–8. For examples of texts containing this
formula, see Chapter 3.
[48] Cockayne, *Leechdoms*, Vol. II, p. 322; 'sing this *gealdor* nine times'.
[49] Cockayne, *Leechdoms*, Vol. II, p. 322; 'The evil one tied, the angel cured, the Lord
saved.' For a comparison of this ritual with another from Harley 585 (fol. 183r),
see Olsan, 'Latin Charms', pp. 127–8.
[50] Cockayne, *Leechdoms*, Vol. II, p. 322; 'He will soon be well.'
[51] See Audrey L. Meaney, 'The Anglo-Saxon View of the Causes of Illness', in
Health, Disease and Healing in Medieval Culture, Sheila Campbell, Bert Hall, and

well as physical, and the *galdor* gives an eschatological meaning to the physical pain. The source of pain is evil (like the Fall), the medium of healing is divine (like the Incarnation, announced by an angel), and the source of restored health is in God (through the Second Coming). As it also facilitates this curative process, the *galdor* assumes the same role as the angel who cured the pain ('angelus curauit'), showing it to be a powerful Christian utterance that mediates between God and man and channels power from heaven to earth. This correlation of *galdor* with angelic power may be compared with the *galdrum* spoken by St Guthlac when he describes his angelic revelation to his servant in *Guthlac B*, as discussed in Chapter 1.

Bald's Leechbook and *Leechbook* III contain the largest number of ritual texts that refer to a *galdor* as a component of their performance. Because the first two books seem to have been composed some time before the surviving manuscript was written and *Leechbook* III was added, it is possible that these usages reflect an understanding of *galdor* that predates a redefinition of it by reformers at the Old Minster. However, *Leechbook* III also contains a ritual that uses a *galdor* and the manuscript was copied in Æthelwold's school, indicating that *galdor* was viewed as an important and powerful ritual performance consisting of divine mysteries and words of spiritual wisdom. At least some ecclesiastics from this late tenth-century monastic milieu approved of this practice when it was used in explicitly Christian contexts. In this manuscript, the term is intimately connected with Christian wisdom, prayers, exorcism, and the Eucharist, and it is uncontroversially used alongside liturgical prayers and objects. Some *galdru* conceal their divine utterances by employing ancient, foreign alphabets or by deliberately obscuring their language. This provides one explanation for the many condemnations of the term in non-ritual texts as these *galdru* were perceived to be powerful utterances that could be dangerous if they were used by unauthorised people. Their secret language might conceal the words of the ritual from those who should not try to use them, and it may have been the case that particular ecclesiastics were skilled in interpreting these *galdru* for their performance. As well as the manuscript's monastic origin, the presence of liturgical prayers and objects may indicate that these rituals could be performed only by priests who knew how to read and use them. The *galdru* often invoke the evangelists and other saints (Veronica and the litanies), one directly connects it with the Eucharist (in the chalice), and they sometimes contain Scriptural passages. They also exorcise evil forces

David Klausner, eds (London, 1992), pp. 12–33; Karen Jolly, 'Father God and Mother Earth: Nature Mysticism in the Anglo-Saxon World', in *The Medieval World of Nature: A Book of Essays*, Joyce E. Salisbury, ed. (New York, 1993), pp. 221–52.

that cause physical and spiritual suffering, and they mediate between God and men like the angels, and indeed priests. The manuscript often uses *galdor* with other Christian prayers, and liturgical elements consistently accompany its performance.

London, British Library, MS Harley 585

London, British Library, MS Harley 585 is similar to Royal 12 D. xvii as it is also a book of healing. It contains translations of the *Herbarium Apuleis* (fols. 1–66v), pseudo-Dioscorides' *De herbis femininis* and *Curae herbarum* (fols. 66v–101v), Sextus Placitus' *Liber medicinae ex animalibus* (fols. 106v–114v), and a collection of remedial texts and rituals commonly referred to as the *Lacnunga* (fols. 130r–193r).[52] The manuscript dates to the first quarter of the eleventh century on palaeographical grounds, but its place of origin remains unknown.[53] There are many textual correspondences between *Bald's Leechbook* and Harley 585, and it is possible that a common exemplar was used for both manuscripts.[54] Audrey Meaney also drew attention to similar textual parallels in other healing books that were written in Winchester in the late tenth and early eleventh centuries, indicating a Winchester origin for Harley 585.[55] Furthermore, Alger Doane highlighted the influence of a Winchester style in the manuscript's zoomorphic capitals, and Edward Pettit drew connections between the *Lacnunga* and a number of private prayer books for women containing Irish materials that were in Winchester by the eleventh century.[56] Stephanie Hollis believes that the *Lacnunga* was compiled from a number of earlier sources according to its corrupted texts and disordered organisation.[57] She also claims that four prayer books which were written in two south-western monasteries in the late eighth century influenced the collection, particularly its focus on poison.[58] It may be the case that Harley 585 was compiled in the eleventh century from a number of older exemplars that were available at

---

[52] See Ker, *Catalogue*, pp. 305–6.

[53] Doane, *Books of Prayers and Healing*, p. 26. See also Gneuss, *Handlist*, p. 75; Scragg, *Conspectus*, p. 53.

[54] See Audrey L. Meaney, 'Variant Versions of Old English Medical Remedies and the Compilation of *Bald's Leechbook*', *ASE*, 13 (1984), 235–68.

[55] Meaney, 'Compilation of *Bald's Leechbook*', pp. 258–64. The manuscripts are London, British Library, MSS Additional 34652, Cotton Galba A. xiv, and Cotton Otho B. xi. Cotton Galba A. xiv was mostly written at the Nunnaminster c. 1000.

[56] See Doane, *Books of Prayers and Healing*, pp. 26, 29; Pettit, *Anglo-Saxon Remedies*, Vol. I, pp. xxix–xxxii, li–liii, 135, 159–60. See also Doane, *Books of Prayers and Healing*, pp. 5, 15, 37, 49, 52.

[57] Hollis, 'Medical Writings', pp. 199, 201.

[58] Hollis, 'Medical Writings', p. 201. See also Patrick Sims-Williams, *Religion and Literature in Western England, 600–800* (Cambridge, 1990), pp. 273–327.

the Old Minster (also housing *Bald's Leechbook*'s and its exemplar) and the Nunnaminster (possibly housing the private prayer books).

It is clear that the compiler of Harley 585 had access to a range of materials from at least one well-resourced library in the early eleventh century. Given the manuscript's close connections with other books that were available in reforming minsters, it is likely that it was written in a monastery or nunnery that was associated with the Reform. Multiple scribal hands are evident in the manuscript, suggesting that a team of scribes worked on the collection; the main scribe wrote most of the manuscript (up to fol. 179r), and at least two scribes finished the collection and added in capitals and a contents for the *Herbarium*.[59] The range of materials that seem to have been gathered and the number of scribes that wrote the collection indicate that Harley 585 was a well-resourced and rather large project. The uses of *galdor* in this manuscript are akin to those in Royal 12 D. xvii, and this ritual practice was evidently still seen to be an important component of ancient healing wisdom by the time it was written. Slight differences between *Bald's Leechbook* and the *Lacnunga* indicate that more care was taken to distinguish the *galdor* from other ritual practices in Harley 585.

The *Lacnunga* of Harley 585 (fols. 130r–193r) contains four texts that instruct the singing of a *galdor*, and all appear in the first stage of scribal copying before folio 179r. Importantly, all of these texts appear in the main writing space of the manuscript, showing that they were conceived of as uncontroversial components of the collection as a whole by the compiler. The first appearance of *galdor* is found in a ritual against serpents ('wið wyrme', fol. 136v). Alger Doane and Edward Pettit interpret the text as a response to 'accidental ingestion of worms or poison' and 'infestation in unhygienic conditions by tapeworms, roundworms, and threadworms'.[60] L. B. Pinto believed that 'a kind of Platonic "ideal worm", i.e. the demon-worm' is common in medieval medical texts, and the rituals of this manuscript certainly associate worms and snakes with evil.[61] Victoria Thompson discusses the eschatological significance of the 'wyrm' in the *Lacnunga* and Anglo-Saxon culture more generally, arguing that particular ailments inflicted by reptiles often took on a religious dimension as the sickness reflected a spiritual punishment.[62] The *galdor* that works against serpents simultaneously drives out the source of evil that physically afflicts the patient

---

[59] Ker, *Catalogue*, pp. 305–6; Doane, *Books of Prayers and Healing*, p. 27.
[60] Doane, *Books of Prayers and Healing*, p. 30; Pettit, *Anglo-Saxon Remedies*, Vol. I, p. xxxiii.
[61] L. B. Pinto, 'Medical Science and Superstition: A Report on A Unique Medical Scroll of the Eleventh-Twelfth Century', *Manuscripta*, 17 (1973), 12–21, pp. 14–15.
[62] Victoria Thompson, *Dying and Death in Later Anglo-Saxon England* (Woodbridge, 2004), p. 93, see also pp. 132–69.

and restores spiritual health to the subject, cancelling out the sin that caused their punishment.

The ritual opens with instructions to sing a 'leoð' (song, poem) into the right ear if the afflicted subject is male, and into the left ear if they are female. The passage that follows this instruction is an obscure sequence with elements of Irish and Old English: 'Gonomil orgomil marbumil marbsai ramum tofeð tengo docuillo biran cuiðær cæfmiil scuiht cuillo scuiht cuib duill marbsiramum'.[63] The first three words of this *leoð* have been identified as an Irish formula meaning 'I slay the beast, I slaughter the beast, I kill the beast' that have parallels in ninth- and tenth-century Old High German and Old Saxon rituals.[64] As seen in Bede's *Historia Ecclesiastica* and *Bald's Leechbook*, the use of Irish in this ritual increases its efficacy as a repellent against serpents. Pettit offers a tentative translation of the whole passage, based on many different scholarly interpretations:

> I wound the animal, I hit the animal, I kill the animal. Kill the (?)persis-tent creature! Its tongue will fall out. I destroy the little spear with verse. Against the (?)dear-animal. (?)An ending. I destroy. (?)An ending (?to the) (?)dear-animal. Kill the (?)persistent creature![65]

As this sequence is very obscure and indecipherable in places, it may be that the original Irish was misunderstood by the scribe. However, even if this were the case the scribe may have still regarded the pres-ence of Irish in such rituals 'as a string of *uoces magicae*'.[66] As seen with *Bald's Leechbook*, the use of different languages in some *galdru* presents the reader with what Alderik Blom calls 'an obscure or downright incomprehensible code', but this may well have been the purpose of such techniques to prevent them from becoming easily known.[67]

This passage is immediately followed by an instruction to sing 'þis galdor' nine times with one Paternoster.[68] The entry that imme-diately follows this ritual opens with a prescription to sing this same *galdor* ('þis ylce galdor') to counteract penetrating serpents ('smeogan wyrme').[69] The *galdor* is therefore equated with a song ('leoð') that is

---

[63] Pettit, *Anglo-Saxon Remedies*, Vol. I, p. 14.

[64] Calvert S. Watkins, *How to Kill a Dragon: Aspects of Indo-European Poetics* (Oxford, 1995), pp. 522–3, 527.

[65] Pettit, *Anglo-Saxon Remedies*, Vol. II, p. 33. For an overview of the different interpretations of this text, see Vol. II, pp. 31–4.

[66] Alderik Blom, 'Linguae Sacrae in Ancient and Medieval Sources: An Anthropological Approach to Ritual Language', in *Multilingualism in the Graeco-Roman Worlds*, Alex Mullen and Patrick James, eds (Cambridge, 2012), pp. 124–40, p. 137.

[67] Blom, 'Linguae Sacrae', p. 137.

[68] Pettit, *Anglo-Saxon Remedies*, Vol. I, p. 15.

[69] Pettit, *Anglo-Saxon Remedies*, Vol. I, p. 16.

to be sung about the patient's head, and it consists of a formula that incorporates at least one different language, working alongside the Paternoster in driving out the hostile enemy and restoring spiritual health as it is uttered.

The second text that uses a *galdor* is a ritual prescription for a holy salve ('haligre sealf', fols. 146v–149r). It opens with an extensive list of ingredients required to make the salve before holy water is finally added. The concoction is then stirred with a stick inscribed with the names of the four evangelists, and a series of psalms, prayers, and litanies are then sung:

> ðu sing ofer ðas sealmas, 'Beati immaculati'…, ælcne ðriwa ofer, and 'Gloria in excelsis D(e)o', and 'Credo in D(eu)m Patrem', and letanias arime ofer, þ(æt) [i]s ðara haligra naman and 'D(eus) m(eu)s et pater', et 'In principio', and þ(æt) wyrmgealdor; and þis gealdor singe ofer.

> sing these psalms over it, 'Blessed are the undefiled'…, each one three times over it, and 'Glory to God in the Highest', and 'I believe in God the Father', and recite litanies over it, that is the names of the saints and 'My God and Father', and 'In the Beginning' and the 'worm'-incantation [*wyrmgealdor*]; and sing this incantation [*gealdor*] over it.[70]

These prayers complement the inscribed names of the evangelists, thus establishing a highly Christian and liturgical response to a wound.

Two types of *gealdor* accompany these liturgical prayers and are named as distinct ritual utterances. The 'wyrmgealdor' probably refers to the ritual against a 'wyrm' on folio 136v, particularly because it also identifies itself as a *galdor*. The second prescribed *galdor* follows the same (but much shorter) formula as the ritual against flying venom in *Bald's Leechbook*: 'Acre arcre arnem nona ærnem beoðor ærnem. nidren. arcun cunað ele harassan fidine'.[71] Borsje provides a literal translation of this passage:

> The urging of a claim
> Against gore
> Against poison *nona*
> Against poison they struck (?)
> Against the poison of a snake
> Against wounding with a *nath* 'poem' *éle* (*cunað* = *cu nath*: *co* 'with' + *nath* 'piece of verse')
> [Or:] Against wounding with another poem
> [Or:] Against wounding with the poem (*nath*) of a satire (*ail*) *harassan fidine*.[72]

[70] Pettit, *Anglo-Saxon Remedies*, Vol. I, pp. 32–3.
[71] Pettit, *Anglo-Saxon Remedies*, Vol. I, p. 32.
[72] Borsje, 'Spell Called *Éle*', p. 207.

Another version of this 'acre' formula is used in Harley 585, and it also appears in the earlier *Book of Cerne*, the *Book of Nunnaminster*, and the Irish *Liber Hymnorum*.[73] This formula evidently emerged from an Irish tradition, but only this ritual and the version in *Bald's Leechbook* identify it as *galdor*. The *Leechbook*'s version uses the formula against flying venom, whereas the *Lacnunga*'s salve ritual specifies that it protects against harmful utterances ('cunað'), indicating that this sequence could be adapted for different rituals.

The text then instructs that this *galdor* is to be sung nine times before the ingredients are blessed by a priest. Following this, a number of prayers are to be sung ('singe ðas orationis ofer') that are also found in rites of exorcism and liturgical blessings for the sick and for new fruit.[74] This ritual makes careful distinctions between the types of texts to be said and sung as it designates 'ðas sealmas', 'letanias', 'ðara haligran naman', two *galdru*, and 'orationis'. It is worth noting that Latin terms for liturgical prayers are combined with *galdor*, thus equating this type of ritual performance with mainstream liturgy and indicating that an authorised ecclesiastic was required to perform it. Unlike *Bald's Leechbook*, these *galdru* appear as distinct category terms in this list of prayers and they are included as separate but related ritual utterances.

The third text of Harley 585 that uses a *galdor* is commonly referred to as the *Nine Herbs Charm* (fols. 160r–163v). It is viewed as one of the most important examples of an Anglo-Saxon 'charm' with pre-Christian origins because of its mention of Woden alongside other 'heathen elements and botanical animism'.[75] However, as Audrey Meaney pointed out, it seems very improbable that Woden would have still been seen as a non-Christian deity by the time that this text was written.[76] Indeed, the mention of Woden is immediately followed by a reference to the crucified Christ ('þa wyrte gesceop witig Drihten, halig on heofonu(m), þa he hongode'), and the text concludes with a declaration of Christ's power over all poisons: '+ Crist stod ofer alde ængancundes'.[77] Rather than providing evidence of surviving

[73] See Brown, *Book of Cerne*, pp. 136–8, 152; Pettit, *Anglo-Saxon Remedies*, Vol. I, pp. xxix–xxxiv, Vol. II, pp. 22–4; Karen Jolly, 'Tapping the Power of the Cross: Who and for Whom?', in *The Place of the Cross in Anglo-Saxon England*, Catherine E. Karkov, Sarah Larratt Keefer, and Karen Louise Jolly, eds (Woodbridge, 2006), pp. 58–79, pp. 60–1. Jolly also notes later copies in Oxford, Bodleian Library, Bodley 163 (s. xi), and Cambridge, Gonville & Caius College, 379 (s. xii).

[74] Pettit, *Anglo-Saxon Remedies*, Vol. I, pp. 32–6.

[75] Pettit, *Anglo-Saxon Remedies*, Vol. II, p. 103. For an overview of scholarship on this texts, see Vol. II, pp. 99–100.

[76] Meaney, 'Woden in England', pp. 110, 114. See also Jolly, *Popular Religion*, pp. 127–8.

[77] '+ Christ (?)being of a unique nature [?(*or*) in a way that was unique], stood upon (?)disease [?(*or*) the ancient ones]', Pettit, *Anglo-Saxon Remedies*, Vol. I, pp. 66–7. Ferdinand Ohrt drew comparisons between this text and later traditions of

paganism in Anglo-Saxon England, this single surviving copy is found in a markedly Christian context.[78]

The ritual comprises a list of nine different types of herbs, with accompanying legends recounting their healing qualities. As there are no opening instructions for performance, the text reads like a practitioner's compendium of herbal lore that should be memorised. The legendary stories that recount the herbs' healing qualities aid in this task of memorisation, and they specify the illnesses that each herb successfully counteracts.[79] All of the herbs are useful in treatments for poison and infections ('attrum'), and others are particularly powerful against malicious demons ('wreceð heo wraðan'), venemous reptiles ('wið wyrm'), and bewitchment ('malscrunge').[80] These are all ailments that are identified elsewhere in other rituals, and the surrounding manuscript context highlights the obvious benefit that a practitioner would have in memorising this text. It is also worth remembering from Chapter 1 that *galdru* are condemned alongside these and other similar terms, indicating that certain types of *galdru* were understood to be evil if they were used by the wrong people.

Following this list of herbs, a recipe for a salve concludes the text. It instructs the practitioner to 'sing þæt galdor' on each of the prescribed herbs before they are blended, and to sing it again ('þæt ilce gealdor') into the patient's mouth, ears, and on their wound.[81] The *galdor* evidently refers to the list preceding this salve, suggesting that it was recited in a ritual summoning of the herbs' natural powers.[82] This *galdor* refers to the practitioner's knowledge of herbs and their understanding that their potency came from Christ, who has power over all poisons. In this context, *galdor* signifies words of healing wisdom that were to be sung over herbs in a Christian ritualistic way.

The final ritual of Harley 585 that uses a *galdor* is against a dwarf

belief that plants grew in Christ's blood at the foot of the cross, *'Herba, Gratia Plena': Die Legenden der älteren Segensprüche über den göttlichen Ursprung der Heil- und Zauberkräuter* (Helsinki, 1929), pp. 1–30. Willy L. Braekman also drew comparisons with Mark 16: 15–18, 'Notes on Old English Charms', *Neophilologus*, 64 (1980), 461–9.

[78] Similar arguments against surviving paganism in references to Woden have been made in studies of the Anglo-Saxon royal genealogies, see especially Kenneth Sisam, 'Anglo-Saxon Royal Genealogies', *Proceedings of the British Academy*, 39 (1953), 287–348; David Dumville, 'The Anglian Collection of Royal Genealogies and Regnal Lists', *ASE*, 5 (1976), 23–50; Richard North, *Heathen Gods in Old English Literature* (Cambridge, 1997), pp. 111–32.

[79] For other memorisation techniques employed in rituals, see Lea Olsan, 'Charms in Medieval Memory', in *Charms and Charming in Europe*, Roper, ed., pp. 59–88.

[80] Pettit, *Anglo-Saxon Remedies*, Vol. I, pp. 62–4.

[81] Pettit, *Anglo-Saxon Remedies*, Vol. I, p. 68.

[82] See Jolly, *Popular Religion*, p. 127. For the division of sections in this text as it appears in the manuscript, see Bredehoft, 'Boundaries Between Verse and Prose', p. 150.

('wið dweorh', fol. 167r). The affliction of a dwarf is enigmatic and may refer to nightmares or fever, but its sinister nature is evident.[83] The ritual opens with an instruction to write the names of the Seven Sleepers of Ephesus on communion wafers: 'man sceal niman VII lytle oflætan swylce man mid ofrað, and wri[t]an þas naman on ælcre oflætan: Maximian(us), Malchus, Iohannes, Martimianus, Dionisius, Constantinus, Serafion'.[84] There are other rituals against fever that invoke the Seven Sleepers, and there is one other example of inscribing these names on communion wafers in a twelfth-century medical manuscript from Rochester (London, British Library, MS Royal 12 E. xx).[85] The Christian, liturgical nature of this ritual is immediately made clear with the use of a Eucharistic object and the invocation of these saints from Christian legend.

The ritual then prescribes that a *galdor* is to be sung into each ear and above the patient's head: 'Þænne eft þ(æt) galdor þ(æt) heræfter cweð man sceal singan, ærest on þ(æt) wynstre eare, þænne on þæt swiðre eare, þænne [b]ufan þæs mannes moldan'.[86] Felix Grendon distinguished between these opening instructions, claiming that the inscription forms 'a Christian preface to the superstitious ritual', and that the *galdor* utterance is 'a characteristic Heathen spell'.[87] However, the close proximity of the vocal utterance and the written performance shows that the *galdor* cannot be separated from the inscription on the hosts, and that it is inextricably linked to the Eucharist.[88] Furthermore, the instruction concludes with a prescription to have a virgin hang one inscribed host about the patient's neck, thus completing a cruciform shape around the head as the *galdor* is sung in both ears and above the head. A fascinating recent discovery by John Hines

---

[83] See Nelson, 'Charm against Nightmare', pp. 17–18; David E. Gay, 'Anglo-Saxon Metrical Charm 3 Against a Dwarf: A Charm against Witch-Riding?', *Folklore*, 99 (1988), 174–7; B. R. Hutcheson, '*Wið Dweorh*: An Anglo-Saxon Remedy for Fever in its Cultural and Manuscript Setting', in *Secular Learning in Anglo-Saxon England: Exploring the Vernacular*, Lázló Sándor Chardonnens and Bryan Carella, eds (Amsterdam, 2012), pp. 175–202. See also Pettit, *Anglo-Saxon Remedies*, Vol. I, p. xxxiii; for further scholarship on this text, see Vol. II, pp. 172–6, 183.

[84] 'one must take seven little sacramental wafers such as one makes offertory with, and write these names on each wafer: Maximianus, Malchus, Iohannes, Martimianus, Dionisius, Constantinus, Serafion', Pettit, *Anglo-Saxon Remedies*, Vol. I, pp. 72–3.

[85] See Wilfrid Bonser, 'The Seven Sleepers of Ephesus in Anglo-Saxon and Later Recipes', *Folklore*, 56 (1945), 254–6; Tony Hunt, *Popular Medicine in Thirteenth-Century England* (Cambridge, 1990), p. 349.

[86] 'Then afterwards one must sing the incantation [*galdor*] that is related hereafter, first into the left ear, then into the right ear, then above the crown of the person's head', Pettit, *Anglo-Saxon Remedies*, Vol. I, pp. 72–3.

[87] Grendon, 'Anglo-Saxon Charms', p. 215.

[88] For the ritual's probable Christian origin in the second half of the tenth century, see Pettit, *Anglo-Saxon Remedies*, Vol. II, p. 184.

of a lead plaque, found near Fakenham in Norfolk, parallels this text very well. The plaque has runes inscribed on it that, when translated, read 'the dwarf is dead', and it has a punched hole in a rounded corner above the inscription.[89] Hines believes that this object could have been worn suspended on the person, in much the same way as the inscribed Eucharistic host in the Harley ritual. This object was probably made in the hope that the afflicted patient would survive and make a full recovery, suggesting that inscribed material objects were believed to be effective in counterattacking the evil influence of a dwarf. What is of particular interest here is that the Harley ritual uses both the verbal performance of the *galdor* and inscribed Eucharistic hosts, the most powerful material object available to a medical practitioner in a monastic setting. The ritual thus provides a more powerful and comprehensive treatment to drive out and ward off the sinister spirit. Research on this remarkable lead object has yet to be pursued, but, if it was meant to be hung around the neck of a suffering patient, a very close material parallel can be made with this *galdor* ritual.[90]

The words of this *galdor* open with a narrative account of an 'inspi-denwiht' that left its mark on the person's neck ('Leg[d]e þe his teage an sweoran').[91] The spirit is later referred to as a wild beast ('deores') and the mark of this creature is countered by the inscribed host that is hung around the neck.[92] The end of this sung narrative refers to the *galdor* as a special ritual practice that can be performed only by a skilled practitioner:

> Þa co(m) ingangan deores sweostar.
> Þa g(e)ændade heo, and aðas swor
> ðæt næfre þis ðæ(m) adlegan derian ne moste,
> ne þæm þe þis galdor begytan mihte,
> oððe þe þis galdor ongalan cuþe.
> Am(en). Fiað.

> Then came walking in the beast's sister.
> Then she interceded, and swore oaths
> That this (*i.e.* this beast) might never harm the sick person,

---

[89] John Hines, 'The Dwarf Is Dead', *British Archaeology*, 157 (2017), 52–7.

[90] For another example of an object to be hung around the neck in a ritual against dysentery from Harley 585 (fols. 184rv), see Storms, *Anglo-Saxon Magic*, pp. 274–5.

[91] 'It laid its reins [*teage* / 'mark'] on your neck', Pettit, *Anglo-Saxon Remedies*, Vol. I, pp. 72–5.

[92] Although the concept of a malevolent spirit in the form of a spider is Germanic in origin, the mark that this beast leaves on the subject's forehead may be an allusion to the apocalyptic sign of the beast that is forcibly marked on the heads of doomed sinners in Revelations 13: 16–17.

Nor the person who could obtain this incantation [*galdor*],
Or who knew how to recite this incantation [*galdor*].
Amen. Let it be done.[93]

This *galdor* forces the beast's sister ('deores sweostar') to submit and swear oaths to never harm the person again. The mark of the beast is overcome by a sacramental object and this *galdor* completes the spiritual protection by subduing its kin, concluding with 'Amen, fiat', as do other liturgical curses and sanctions from late Anglo-Saxon England.[94] Given that the ritual opens with an inscription on hosts that are used in conjunction with the *galdor*, the 'Amen' is not, as Grendon claims, 'tacked on at the end to save appearances'.[95] It is a fitting liturgical end to a Christian ritual that uses the *galdor* as part of a repertory of spiritual weapons with which to overcome demonic influence. The text also explicitly depicts the *galdor* as a ritual utterance that can be obtained and performed only by a skilful and knowledgeable person, indicating that other *galdru* could be performed only by those who knew how to read them.[96] This possibility helps to explain why obscure language features in many of these *galdru*, to prevent them from becoming easily known.

In a very similar way to Royal 12 D. xvii, Harley 585 contains ritual texts that use a *galdor* consisting of obscure language and liturgical texts and objects. This provides evidence that the *galdor* was viewed by at least some people as an important ritual practice in an eleventh-century minster, probably associated with the Reform and located in Winchester. In contrast to Royal 12 D. xvii, Harley 585 provides clearer distinctions between *galdor* and other vocal performances, indicating that it was understood as a separate type of ritual practice that could complement others used in the liturgy, such as psalms, prayers, and litanies.

London, British Library, MS Cotton Caligula A. vii

London, British Library, MS Cotton Caligula A. vii contains the C version of the *Heliand* and the *Æcerbot* field ritual, which prescribes

---

[93] Pettit, *Anglo-Saxon Remedies*, Vol. I, pp. 74–5.
[94] See Lester K. Little, *Benedictine Maledictions: Liturgical Cursing in Romanesque France* (Ithaca, NY, 1993), p. 57; Petra Hofmann, 'Infernal Imagery in Anglo-Saxon Charters', Unpublished Doctoral Thesis (University of St Andrew's, Scotland, 2008), pp. 47–9, 256–337.
[95] Grendon, 'Anglo-Saxon Charms', p. 215.
[96] An interesting comparison can be found between this statement and Revelations 14: 3 where God's elect sing a song that only they are able to discern, see *Biblia Sacra*, Vol. II, p. 1895.

the performance of a *galdor*. According to palaeographical evidence, *Heliand C* was written in the second half of the tenth century, and the *Æcerbot* was written in the early eleventh century.[97] Unlike Royal 12 D. xvii and Harley 585, this ritual was added to an earlier manuscript and it is therefore more difficult to draw conclusions about how the scribe of this text perceived *galdor*. However, the *Æcerbot* ritual is written on two distinct folios (like a booklet), and there are clues in this manuscript that the eleventh-century scribe read the *Heliand* around the time of writing. Close textual correspondences between these two texts also indicate that the *Æcerbot* was added to the *Heliand* by an Anglo-Saxon compiler, and this is further supported by a marginal note on folio 17r of the *Heliand* (beside the Annunciation scene) that was written by an eleventh-century scribe, who was probably the same scribe as the *Æcerbot*.[98]

The *Heliand* is an Old Saxon heroic rendering of the gospel story in verse, and the *Æcerbot* is an Old English agricultural ritual which uses a *galdor* to exorcise and heal an infertile field. *Heliand C* was copied in England by a single scribe from a lost exemplar, probably at Winchester.[99] Alger Doane and Rolf Bremmer suggest that the exemplar was originally given to Æthelwulf of Wessex in 856, whereas Malcolm Godden believes that it may have been recited at Alfred's court along with other biblical poetry that would have been known to Alfred's Frankish connections, such as his priest John the Old Saxon.[100] There is evidence to suggest that the *Heliand* inspired the composition or re-writing of the *Æcerbot* ritual. An eleventh-century marginal note appears on folio 17r of the *Heliand* and is written in a hand very

---

[97] Ker, *Catalogue*, p. 172; Doane, *Books of Prayers and Healing*, p. 1; Gneuss, *Handlist*, p. 61; Scragg, *Conspectus*, p. 34. The C version of the *Heliand* is printed in Eduard Sievers, ed., *Heliand* (Halle, 1878).

[98] See Ciaran Arthur, 'Ploughing through Cotton Caligula A. VII: Reading the Sacred Words of the *Heliand* and the *Æcerbot*', *RES*, 65 (2014), 1–17; 'Three Marginal Notes in London, British Library, MS Cotton Caligula A. vii', *N&Q*, 62 (2015), 211–17.

[99] See R. Priebsch, *The Heliand Manuscript: Cotton Caligula A VII in the British Museum* (Oxford, 1925), pp. 27–9; James E. Cathey, ed., *Hêliand: Text and Commentary* (Morgantown, 2002), p. 23; Malcolm Godden, 'Prologues and Epilogues in the Old English *Pastoral Care*, and their Carolingian Models', *JEGP*, 110 (2011), 441–73, p. 457. G. Ronald Murphy claims that it was copied in East Anglia, 'The Old Saxon *Heliand*', in *Perspectives on the Old Saxon Heliand: Introductory and Critical Essays, with an Edition of the Leipzig Fragment*, V. A. Pakis, ed. (Morgantown, 2010), pp. 34–62, pp. 35–6.

[100] Alger N. Doane, ed., *The Saxon Genesis: An Edition of the West Saxon Genesis B and the Old Saxon Vatican Genesis* (Madison, 1991), p. 53; Rolf Bremmer, 'Continental Germanic Influences', in *Companion to Anglo-Saxon Literature*, Pulsiano and Treharne, eds, pp. 375–87, pp. 383–4; Godden, 'Prologues and Epilogues', p. 457. The Old English poem *Genesis B* is also known to have circulated with the *Heliand* as witnessed by the ninth-century manuscript Rome, Vatican Library, MS Palatinus Latinus 1477.

similar to the *Æcerbot* scribe, reading 'be sancta marian'. The note draws attention to the Blessed Virgin Mary in the Annunciation scene, and there are close correspondences between the Annunciation and Marian elements in the *Æcerbot*.[101] The field ritual presents its *galdor* as an important Christian utterance that could simultaneously exorcise poison sown in the land and resurrect crops and the faith of the community.[102]

The *Æcerbot* spans two full folios at the end of the manuscript (fols. 176r–178r), and the term *galdor* appears only once in this text.[103] The ritual opens with instructions to cut sods from each corner of the field that has been made infertile by poison ('lyblace'). The first set of prescribed words that is to be uttered is taken from Genesis 1: 28 and is given in an inter-lexical translation:

> *Crescite,* wexe, *et multiplicamini,* and gemænigfealda,
> *et replete,* and gefylle, *terre,* þas eorðan. *In*
> *nominee patris et filii et spiritus sancti sit benedicti.*[104]

> *Crescite,* grow, *et multiplicamini,* and multiply, *et replete,* and fill, *terram,* the earth. *In nomine patris et filii et spiritus sancti sitis benedicti.*[105]

These words are God's command to Adam to multiply and they confirm man's supremacy over the earth and all of Creation. This biblical passage provides a central motif that is repeated throughout the entire ritual like a refrain. After these words are said for the first time, the sods are placed beneath an altar and four Masses are sung over them before the end of the day. Four wooden crosses bearing the names of the evangelists are then placed into the field and the names are recited as this is done, thus encompassing the land with the power of the gospels.[106] After the sods have been placed above the crosses, the *Crescite* passage is recited nine times with the Paternoster.

Following this, an instruction 'cweð þonne þas word' (then say these words) marks a lengthy passage that is to be uttered before the ploughing of the field:

> Eastweard ic stande, arena ic me bidde.
> Bidde ic ðone mæran domine, bidde ðone miclan drihten,
> bidde ic þone haligan heofonrices weard.

---

[101] Arthur, 'Three Marginal Notes', pp. 214–17.
[102] See Hill, '*Æcerbot* Charm'; John D. Niles, 'The Æcerbot Ritual in Context', in *Old English Literature in Context*, John D. Niles, ed. (Cambridge, 1980), pp. 44–56; Arthur, 'Ploughing through Cotton Caligula A. VII', pp. 10–11.
[103] No cognates of *galdor* appear in the Old Saxon *Heliand*.
[104] Storms, *Anglo-Saxon Magic*, p. 173.
[105] Translation from Jolly, *Popular Religion*, p. 7.
[106] Thomas D. Hill has drawn comparisons between this instruction and the *Kollektaneum Bedae*, Hill, 'Irish-Latin Analogue'.

Eorðan ic bidde and upheofon,
and ða soþan Sancta Marian,
and heofones meaht and heah reced,
þæt ic mote þis gealdor mid gife drihtnes
toðum ontynan, þurh trumne geþanc
acweccan þas wæstmas us to woruldnytte,
gefylle þas foldan mid fæste geleafan,
wlitigigan þas wancgturf.[107]

Eastwards I stand, for mercies I pray, I pray the great domine (lord), I
pray the powerful lord, I pray the holy guardian of heaven-kingdom,
earth I pray and sky and the true sancta (holy) Mary and heaven's might
and high hall, that I may this charm [*galdor*] by the gift of the lord open
with (my) teeth through firm thought, to call forth these plants for our
worldly use, to fill this land with firm belief, to beautify this grassy turf.[108]

The passage identifies the *galdor* as a ritual utterance that is capable of
resurrecting crops ('acweccan þas wæstmas'), filling the earth ('gefylle
þas foldan'), and replenishing fields ('wlitigigan þas wancgturf')
through God's grace ('mid gife drihtnes'). Its Christian nature is made
explicit in its emphasis on the need for faith ('þurh trumne geþanc'), its
focus on resurrection, and its invocation of God, Mary, and the whole
of heaven.

Following this utterance, the plough is blessed with holy water and
three sets of prescribed words are to be said as the field is ploughed.
These passages are also heavily dependent upon Christian references,
and one addresses Mother Earth in the following way:

Hal wes þu folde, fira modor,
beo þu growende on Godes fæþme,
fodre gefylled firum to nytte.[109]

Whole may you be (Be well) earth, mother of men! May you be growing
in God's embrace, with food filled for the needs of men.[110]

This address has parallels with the Archangel Gabriel's greeting to
the Virgin Mary at the Annunciation in *Heliand C*, near to where the
Æcerbot scribe made the marginal note ('be sancta marian'):

'Hel uuis thu, Maria' quathie, 'thu bist thinon herron lief,
uualdandi uuirðig, huand thu giuuit habs,
idis enstio ful. Thu scealt furi allon uuesan
uuibon giuuihid' (259–62).[111]

[107] Storms, *Anglo-Saxon Magic*, p. 174.
[108] Jolly, *Popular Religion*, p. 7.
[109] Storms, *Anglo-Saxon Magic*, p. 176.
[110] Jolly, *Popular Religion*, p. 8.
[111] Eduard Sievers, ed., *Heliand* (Halle, 1878), p. 22.

'Health be with you, Mary. The Lord is very fond of you. You are precious to the Ruler for your wisdom, woman full of grace. You are to be sanctified more than any other woman.'[112]

Mother Earth is addressed in the *Æcerbot* in similar fashion to Mary in the biblical poem, and the marginal note that draws attention to Mary's role in the *Heliand* strongly indicates that the scribe perceived Mother Earth as a Marian figure rather than a pre-Christian goddess, as critics have consistently claimed.[113] Towards the end of the ritual a bread offering is made when a loaf is placed into the earth – perhaps bread consecrated in the previous Masses – suggesting connections between the *galdor* and the Eucharist.[114] Finally, the ritual concludes with the triple repetition of the *Crescite* passage and the Paternoster.

Although the word *galdor* appears only once in the *Æcerbot* it occupies a central position just before the field is ploughed.[115] It is a declaration that Mother Earth's crops and the community's faith are resurrected, and it shares similarities with the angelic revelation of Mary's conception in the *Heliand*. The *galdor* reveals God's power and exorcises the poison that is in the earth, and it is accompanied by biblical passages, Masses, and invocations of the Christian deity and saints. Caligula A. vii demonstrates that *galdor* could be used to refer to words of power that were used in an overtly liturgical context.

Cambridge, Corpus Christi College, MS 41

The final manuscript that includes a reference to a *galdor* in a ritual context is Cambridge, Corpus Christi College, MS 41. This manuscript dates to the first quarter of the eleventh century on palaeographical grounds, and it was probably written in the south of England before it came into Leofric's possession in Exeter (1050–72).[116] The main text of this manuscript is the earliest full copy of the Old English version of

---

[112] G. Ronald Murphy, trans, *The Heliand: Saxon Gospel* (Oxford, 1992), p. 12. See also Arthur, 'Three Marginal Notes', pp. 214–17.

[113] See, for example, Audrey Duckert, 'Erce and other Possibly Keltic Elements in the Old English Charm for Unfruitful Land', *Names*, 20 (1972), 83–90; Rodrigues, *Verse Charms*, p. 33; Debby Banham, 'The Staff of Life: Cross and Blessings in Anglo-Saxon Cereal Production', in *Cross and Cruciform in the Anglo-Saxon World: Studies to Honor the Memory of Timothy Reuter*, Sarah Larratt Keefer, Karen Louise Jolly, and Catherine E. Karkov, eds (Morgantown, 2010), pp. 279–318, pp. 286–7.

[114] See Arthur, 'Ploughing through Caligula A. VII', pp. 13–16.

[115] On the centrality of *galdor* in this passage and its function as a marker of verse, see Bredehoft, 'Boundaries Between Verse and Prose', pp. 151–2.

[116] Ker, *Catalogue*, p. 45; Gneuss, *Handlist*, p. 31. See also Gameson, 'Origin of the Exeter Book', pp. 141–2.

Bede's *Ecclesiastical History*, and a single scribe later added a number of texts into the manuscript's margins. The fact that the rituals in this manuscript appear as later marginal additions makes conclusions about the scribe's understanding of *galdor* more speculative. It may have been the case that these texts were simply added into the margins to fill space, or that they were written down as they came to mind, or that the scribe copied them into whatever space he could find when he had access to different exemplars and wished to update materials for his community.[117] These possibilities raise the question of whether the *galdor* ritual was simply copied from an earlier exemplar of unknown origin, and this may say little about how the scribe understood this term. However, convincing arguments have been made that the scribe deliberately wrote the marginal texts in specific places in the manuscript to complement passages from Bede's *History* in the main writing space.[118] This would suggest that the scribe consciously chose to record the *galdor* ritual as a useful supplement to a passage in Bede (Book IV, Chapter 50) that might be of interest to the reader of the main text. It is therefore possible that the scribe viewed *galdor* as a powerful ritual performance that was completely compatible with other mainstream Christian texts.

The marginal additions include seven rituals that have been classified as 'charms', the *Solomon and Saturn I* verse dialogue, homilies, chants, and Mass texts.[119] Richard Pfaff believes that the marginal additions point to non-Reform materials, and observes that the texts from the Divine Office are for the secular form of Sunday matins rather than the Benedictine form.[120] However, Christopher Hohler and Robert Butler argued that Irish elements in some of the manuscript's marginal texts indicate that these were added in or near Glastonbury (where Irish monks also resided), possibly at the instruction of a reforming ecclesiastic.[121] Sarah Larratt Keefer and Karen Jolly believe that Corpus

---

[117] For these arguments, see Sarah Larratt Keefer, 'Margin as Archive: The Liturgical Marginalia of a Manuscript of the Old English Bede', *Traditio*, 51 (1996), 147–77; Thomas A. Bredehoft, 'Filling the Margins of CCCC 41: Textual Space and a Developing Archive', *RES*, 57 (2006), 721–32; Billett, *Divine Office*, pp. 220–51.

[118] See especially Lea Olsan, 'The Marginality of Charms in Medieval England', in *The Power of Words: Studies on Charms and Charming in Europe*, James Kapaló, Éva Pócs, and William Ryan, eds (Budapest, 2013), pp. 135–64, pp. 140–9.

[119] For the 'charms', see Raymond J. S. Grant, ed., *Cambridge, Corpus Christi College MS 41: The Loricas and the Missal* (Amsterdam, 1979), pp. 3, 5–22. There are many Irish parallels with the marginalia of this manuscript, in particular the *Solomon and Saturn* poem, see Charles D. Wright, *The Irish Tradition in Old English Literature* (Cambridge, 1993), pp. 237–42.

[120] Pfaff, *Liturgy in Medieval England*, p. 66. For the monastic office, see Milton McC. Gatch, 'The Office in Late Anglo-Saxon Monasticism', in *Learning and Literature in Anglo-Saxon England*, Michael Lapidge and Helmut Gneuss, eds (Cambridge, 1985), pp. 341–62.

[121] Christopher Hohler, 'Review of Raymond J. S. Grant, ed., *Cambridge, Corpus*

41 was likely to have been produced in a provincial scriptorium at a small religious house with a minimal library.[122] Most recently, Jesse Billett has argued that some pre-Gregorian chants in the manuscript's marginalia indicate that these were copied at an unreformed minster 'well outside the influence of Winchester'.[123] The marginal texts of this manuscript were probably written at a small minster in the south-west of England that lay beyond the influence of Æthelwold's school in Winchester, where *galdor* seems to have been undergoing redefinition as a dangerous spiritual practice. As the *galdor* ritual in this manuscript was copied alongside homilies and prayers for the Mass and Office, this scribe evidently considered this type of ritual to be entirely compatible with these liturgical materials as well as Bede's *History*.

The *Old English Bede* contains a condemnatory reference to *galdor*, and this appears in the same Book of Bede's *History* as the marginal *galdor* ritual. The term is listed among the many evil practices and heresies against which St Cuthbert fought:

> Forðon ðe monige ðone geleafan, þe hie hæfdon, mid unrihtum weorcum idledon, ond swylce eac manige in ða tid þæs myclan woles & moncwildes gymeleasedan ðæm gerynum þæs halgan geleafan, mid þæm hie gelærede wæron, & to ðæm dwoligendum læcedomum deofulgylda ofsetton & scyndon; swa swa hie þæt sende wite from God Scyppende þurh heora galdor oþþe lyfesne oððe þurh hwylce hwugu deogolnesse deofolcræftes bewerian mehton (IV, 27).[124]

> For many of them profaned the creed they held by wicked deeds and some of them too, in times of plague, would forget the sacred mysteries of the faith into which they had been initiated and take to the false remedies of idolatry, as though they could ward off a blow inflicted by God the Creator by means of incantations [*galdor*] or amulets or any other mysteries of devilish art.[125]

Christi College MS 41: the Loricas and the Missal (Amsterdam: Rodopi, 1979)', *Medium Aevum*, 49 (1980), 275–81; Butler, 'Early History of the Exeter Book', pp. 211–15. For further on the Irish presence in Glastonbury, see James P. Carley and Ann Dooley, 'An Early Irish Fragment of Isidore of Seville's *Etymologiae*', in *The Archaeology and History of Glastonbury Abbey: Essays in Honour of the Ninetieth Birthday of C. A. Ralegh Radford*, Lesley Abrams and James P. Carley, eds (Woodbridge, 1991), pp. 135–61.

[122] Keefer, 'Margin as Archive', p. 147; Jolly, 'Margins of Orthodoxy', p. 137. On the manuscript's use for teaching, see George Molyneaux, 'The *Old English Bede*: English Ideology or Christian Instruction?', *EHR*, 124 (2009), 1289–323. See also Sharon M. Rowley, 'Nostalgia and the Rhetoric of Lack: The Missing Exemplar of Corpus Christi College, Cambridge, Manuscript 41', in *Old English Literature in its Manuscript Context*, Lionarons, ed., pp. 11–35.

[123] Billett, *Divine Office*, p. 223, see also pp. 227–36.

[124] Miller, *Old English Version of Bede's Ecclesiastical History*, Vol. II, p. 362.

[125] Bede, *Ecclesiastical History*, p. 433.

In a similar way to other texts considered in Chapter 1, this condemnatory use of *galdor* presents the term as a dangerous ritual when it leads Christians astray. This passage associates *galdor* with other evils to condemn it as a harmful practice ('dwoligendum læcedomum deofulgylda', 'lyfesne', 'deogolnesse deofolcræftes'). This is one particular use of a *galdor* that is in complete opposition to the mysteries ('gerynum') of the Christian faith, and it is depicted as a false and useless attempt to avert God's just punishments.

The ritual that prescribes the performance of a *galdor* is commonly referred to as the *Journey Charm*; it appears in the margins of folios 350–353 alongside Book IV, Chapter 50 of the *Old English Bede*, which describes St Cuthbert setting out on a pastoral journey as a bishop.[126] The ritual immediately opens with the performer's description of drawing a protective circle before setting out on a journey:

> Ic me on þysse gyrde beluce and on godes helde bebeode wið þane sara sice, wið þane sara slege, wið þane grymma gryre, wið ðane micela egsa þe bið eghwam lað, and wið eal þæt lað þe in to land fare, syge gealdor ic begale, sigegyrd ic me wege wordsige and worcsige, se me dege.[127]

> I encircle myself with this rod and entrust myself to God's grace, against the sore stitch, against the sore bite, against the grim dread, against the great fear that is loathsome to everyone, and against all evil that enters the land. A victory charm [*syge gealdor*] I sing [*begale*], a victory rod I bear, word-victory, work-victory. May they avail me.[128]

In this opening declaration, the instrument which marks a perimeter around the performer has parallels with the power of the cross because it is referred to as a victory rod ('gyrde', 'sigegyrd').[129] The *galdor* is also presented as victorious through the compound 'syge-gealdor', and through this it is closely associated with other compounds describing the performer's words and deeds ('wordsige and worcsige') and the saints ('sigerofra').[130]

This particular focus on victorious words and deeds has close par-

---

[126] On the potential connections between this section of the *History* and the *Journey Charm*, see Katrin Rupp, 'The Anxiety of Writing: A Reading of the Old English *Journey Charm*', *Oral Tradition*, 23 (2008), 255–66, p. 263; Olsan, 'Marginality of Charms', pp. 145–9.

[127] Based on Jolly's transcription, 'Margins of Orthodoxy', p. 170.

[128] Rodrigues, *Verse Charms*, p. 157.

[129] On the meaning of this word see Heather Stuart, '"Ic me on þisse gyrde beluce": The Structure and Meaning of the Old English "Journey Charm"', *Medium Ævum*, 50 (1981), 259–73; Thomas D. Hill, 'The Rod of Protection and the Witches' Ride: Christian and Germanic Syncretism in Two Old English Metrical Charms', *JEGP*, 111 (2012), 145–68, pp. 152–3.

[130] See also Marie Nelson, '"Wordsige and Worcsige": Speech Acts in Three Old English Charms', *Language and Style*, 17 (1984), 57–66.

allels with the passage from Bede's *History* in the main writing space, which describes Cuthbert in the following way:

> ægheþer ge mid his singalum gebedum scylde, ge mid his halwendum moningum 7 larum to ðæm heofenlican cegde 7 laðode; 7 þætte swiðost gewunað halige lareowas gefultuman, swa hwæt swa he mid his worde lærde, he ær mid dædu*m* gefylde.

> he both shielded with his continual prayers and called and incited to heavenly things by his salutary warnings and teaching; and, what in general is the greatest aid to pious teachers, what he taught in word, he first fulfilled in deed.[131]

The opening of the ritual places emphasis on the protective and victorious power of words and deeds ('word-sige', 'worc-sige'), and it connects the rod which the performer carries and the *galdor* to these concepts through the same compounding ('sige-gyrd', 'syge gealdor'). Interestingly, St Cuthbert would have carried a staff as a bishop, he protects himself with continuous 'gebedum', and he is famed for fulfilling in deed ('mid dædu*m*') what he taught in word ('his worde'). The rationale for copying the ritual beside this passage in Bede's *History* is clear, and it may perhaps be the case that this ritual was recorded for use by an ecclesiastical authority, possibly even for a bishop going on his pastoral visitations. Whoever the intended reader may have been, the *galdor* reference occurs in an overtly Christian context in this manuscript, and the scribe clearly correlated this ritual text with a story concerning a pastoral journey made by St Cuthbert.

The Christian nature of this victory-*galdor* is further affirmed by the invocation of Old Testament patriarchs and New Testament saints, much like a litany, so that the individual may be protected from a range of hostile forces:

> moyses and iacob and davit and iosep and euan and annan and elizabet, saharie and ec marie modur Christes, and eac þæ gebroþru petrus and paulus and eac þusend þira engla clipige... biddu ealle bliðu mode þæt me beo hand ofer heafod matheus helm, marcus byrne leoht lifes rof, lucos min swurd scer(a)p and scir ecg, scyld Iohannes.[132]

> Moses and Jacob, and David and Joseph, and Eve and Anna and Elizabeth, Zacharias and also Mary, Christ's mother, and also the brothers, Peter and Paul, and also thousands of thy angels, I call on... In blithe mood I bid them all that Matthew be my helm, Mark my coat of mail, strong light of my life, Luke my sword, sharp and bright-edged, John my shield.[133]

---

[131] Miller, *Old English Version of Bede's Ecclesiastical History*, Vol. II, pp. 368–9.
[132] Jolly, 'Margins of Orthodoxy', p. 171.
[133] Rodrigues, *Verse Charms*, p. 157.

This passage is similar to Irish Christian *loricae* that adapt St Paul's *Letter to the Ephesians* (Eph. 6. 10–17), which describes the armour of God.[134] It also resonates with the description of Cuthbert shielding his people through continuous prayer ('his singalum gebedum scylde').[135] The *galdor* that is written in the first person is also referred to as an invocation ('clipige') and a form of prayer ('biddu'), and this is later repeated when God and the saints are called upon to protect the traveller ('bidde ic nu sigere godes miltse').[136]

The *galdor* of this ritual is therefore closely connected to Christian victory, litanies of saints, Scripture, and prayers to God. It has the power to overcome all evil that goes throughout the land ('eal þæt lað þe into land fare'), and it has the ability to summon the whole hosts of heaven so that the traveller may be protected. It is clear that *galdor* was considered an appropriate word to describe a powerful Christian utterance by this scribe in the early eleventh century.

Conclusions

The four manuscripts that use *galdor* in ritual texts reflect how a variety of Anglo-Saxons understood this term in the tenth and eleventh centuries. Two manuscripts that contain the most references to *galdor* incorporate this particular type of ritual performance into the main writing space, demonstrating that it was conceived of as an important component of a collection of healing texts. *Bald's Leechbook* was copied from an earlier exemplar in Æthelwold's Old Minster in Winchester when the term was perhaps restricted in meaning to denote a harmful spiritual practice. However, *galdor* also appears in *Leechbook* III, which was probably added when Books I and II were copied. Harley 585 was also compiled from exemplars that were housed in a minster associated with the Reform in Winchester in the early eleventh century, and the *Æcerbot* ritual in Caligula A. vii was also copied (if not composed) around this time, perhaps in a Winchester scriptorium. The evidence from these manuscripts indicates that *galdor* was at times uncontroversially associated with explicitly Christian concepts, prayers, Masses, and other liturgical rites in the very same minsters that were producing texts which condemn this term along with a range of threatening beliefs and practices. The marginal texts of Corpus 41 were copied from sources that were not influenced by Winchester productions, and the close correspondences between its *galdor* ritual and Bede's *History* indicate that the ritual's

---

[134] See Hill, 'Invocation of the Trinity'.
[135] Miller, *Old English Version of Bede's Ecclesiastical History*, Vol. II, p. 368.
[136] Jolly, 'Margins of Orthodoxy', p. 171.

scribe perceived this term as a powerful Christian formula that could summon divine protection.

The appearance of *galdor* in only twelve surviving rituals perhaps suggests that the word was deliberately avoided for its problematic connotations. Other ritual texts that label a verbal utterance as 'gebed' instead of 'galdor' may perhaps reflect such efforts to avoid the term around this time. A ritual against dysentery in Harley 585, for example, prescribes a 'gebed' that consists of obscure language (possibly Irish) when one may have expected to find an instruction to sing 'þis galdor'. This ritual appears on folios 185r–186v, and was therefore written by a different scribe to the main one, who wrote up to folio 179r. The notion that this second scribe omitted the word *galdor* and substituted it for the less problematic *gebed* is very speculative, particularly because there are four other appearances of this word in the collection. We will never know how common it was to prescribe a *galdor* in ritual texts prior to the Benedictine Reform, or to what extent this word was replaced in the process of copying. However, the origins of the manuscripts in which a *galdor* is prescribed provide important information about how the term was still used in the tenth and eleventh centuries to describe powerful Christian ritual performances. Certain ecclesiastics evidently viewed *galdor* as an appropriate component of Christian ritual practice, and they incorporated it into liturgical texts at a time when other authorities such as Ælfric and Wulfstan were condemning its use. It may be the case that many clergy considered *galdru* to be part of mainstream Christian observances if they were used in the right context by authorised ecclesiastics.

We have seen that the term *galdor* does not satisfactorily define an entire genre of 'charms', especially as it appears in only twelve ritual texts. When the word does appear in these rituals it refers to powerful formulas of spiritual wisdom and revelation that are used in conjunction with the liturgy. The obscure language of many of these *galdru* may conceal their meaning, and they seem to have required specialised skill and knowledge for their performance. This helps to explain why *galdor* was consistently forbidden by ecclesiastical authorities, as it could lead Christians astray if it was used by the wrong people. It therefore seems more appropriate to understand *galdor* as a component of Anglo-Saxon liturgical practice than it is to view this term as evidence of pre-Christian magic and paganism. The few surviving references to *galdor* in ritual contexts are in fact far removed from traditional understandings of 'charms', and this calls into question all of the other rituals that have been classified thus and included in this genre. Reconsidering the rituals' liturgical content and manuscript contexts reveals more information about how some Anglo-Saxons understood these texts, and what cultural and environmental concerns prompted scribes to write them down.

Part II

3

Ite Missa Est:
The Liturgical Nature of 'Charms'

> 'Ecclesiastical elements are found throughout the whole corpus of Anglo-Saxon medicine and magic. Paternosters accompany every conceivable medical process. Such elements are perhaps the least interesting of the factors in A[nglo-]S[axon] medicine, since they are known from many sources, are easily recognized, and still survive in folk-custom.'[1]

This view of Charles Singer epitomises the traditional scholarly approach to the liturgical elements of Anglo-Saxon 'charms', and – to use an idiom – it is an unsatisfactory way of avoiding the elephant in the room. The extent to which these rituals draw upon liturgical texts makes it difficult to maintain distinctions between 'charms' and liturgy. Many 'charms' incorporate formulas from liturgical *ordines*, most prescribe the use of liturgical objects and prayers (including the Eucharist, holy water, incense, psalms, the Paternoster, the Creed, and litanies), and some are explicitly to be performed by priests or in the church building.[2] Although some scholars have discussed possible liturgical sources for some of the 'charms', they have still tended to maintain distinctions between ritual genres.[3]

Some manuscripts that contain 'charms' also include texts which are uncontroversially associated with the liturgy. London, British Library, MS Cotton Tiberius A. iii, for example, contains Æthelwold's translation of the *Rule of Benedict*; London, British Library, MS Cotton Vitellius E. xviii contains calculations of liturgical feasts; London, British Library, MS Royal 4 A. xiv contains homilies and Jerome's *Commentary* on the Psalms; and the margins of Corpus 41 include homilies, chants for the clerical Office, and Mass prayers.[4] The evidence of such manuscripts

---

[1] Singer, 'Magic and Medicine', p. 351.
[2] On the importance of the church building in 'charms', see Ciaran Arthur, '*Ex Ecclesia*: Salvific Power beyond Sacred Space in Anglo-Saxon Charms', *Incantatio*, 3 (2013), 9–32.
[3] See Barkley, 'Liturgical Influences'; Jolly, *Popular Religion*, pp. 113–23. See also Hill, 'Irish-Latin Analogue'; '*Æcerbot* Charm'; 'Cosmological Cross'; Niles, '*Æcerbot* Ritual in Context'.
[4] For details of Cotton Tiberius A. iii, see Ker, *Catalogue*, pp. 240–7; Joseph McGowan, 'Four Unedited Prayers in London, Cotton Tiberius A. iii', *Medieval Studies*, 56 (1994), 189–216; Helmut Gneuss, 'Origin and Provenance of Anglo-Saxon Manuscripts: The Case of Cotton Tiberius A III', in *Of the Making of Books:*

demonstrates that some Anglo-Saxon compilers and scribes grouped 'charms' with other texts that were concerned with the liturgy, and they evidently did so without any obvious concern about the texts that modern scholars distinguish from mainstream liturgy. Roy Liuzza has written about such groupings in manuscripts that focus on devotions to the cross, and argues that 'charms' were included in these collections because they have the same focus and function as other liturgical prayers and devotions.[5] Liuzza proposes that scholars should focus on the specificity of the ritual's occasion and the extrinsic loci of authority for its performance rather than on constructed dichotomies like orthodoxy and heterodoxy or magic and religion.[6] As seen in the previous chapter, ritual texts that appear in the main writing space of a manuscript provide the best evidence of how their Anglo-Saxon scribe or compiler understood these practices at the time of writing. The arrangements of texts reflect how these scribes grouped different materials together, and there is often great overlap between liturgical texts and 'charm' rituals, showing that medieval distinctions between ritual genres were very different to modern ones. More care is needed when analysing rituals that appear in the margins of manuscripts as these could have been written down to simply fill blank spaces and they may not have any obvious connections with the texts of the main writing space. However, as seen with the *Journey Charm*, it is often possible to find connections between such texts, and these offer evidence of how marginal scribes understood ritual practices.

There was great diversity in the rituals practised in Anglo-Saxon England in the tenth and eleventh centuries, and in this period new liturgies were often created and other ones were revised and adapted.[7] Part 2 of this study reconsiders the manuscript sources in which

---

Medieval Manuscripts, their Scribes and Readers; Essays Presented to M. B. Parkes, P. R. Robinson and Rivkah Zim, eds (Aldershot, 1997), pp. 13–49; *Handlist*, pp. 67–8; Tracey-Anne Cooper, 'The Homilies of a Pragmatic Archbishop's Handbook in Context: Cotton Tiberius A. iii', *Anglo-Norman Studies*, 28 (2006), 47–65; *Monk-Bishops and the English Benedictine Reform Movement: Reading London, BL, Cotton Tiberius A. iii in Its Manuscript Context* (Turnhout, 2015). For details of Cotton Vitellius E. xviii, see Chapter 4. For details of Royal 4 A. xiv, see Ker, *Catalogue*, p. 320; Phillip Pulsiano, *Anglo-Saxon Manuscripts in Microfiche Facsimile, Vol. 4: Glossed Texts, Aldhelmiana, Psalms* (Binghamton, 1996), pp. 47–50; Gneuss, *Handlist*, p. 80. For details of Corpus 41, see Chapters 2 and 3.

[5] Roy Liuzza, 'Prayers and/or Charms Addressed to the Cross', in *Cross and Culture in Anglo-Saxon England: Studies in Honor of George Hardin Brown*, Karen Jolly, Catherine E. Karkov, and Sarah Larratt Keefer, eds (Morgantown, 2008), pp. 276–320.

[6] Liuzza emphasises the porosity between charms and liturgy but he maintains these category terms as opposite ends of an alternative spectrum, Liuzza, 'Prayers and/or Charms', pp. 322–3.

[7] See also Andrew Prescott, 'The Text of the Benedictional of St Æthelwold',

'charms' appear, and this chapter compares 'charms' with contemporary liturgical texts that were written in similar ecclesiastical centres. I argue that some, if not all, of the rituals that have been traditionally categorised as 'charms' are better considered as liturgical texts that are part of this ecclesiastical culture of diversity, innovation, and experimentation. The chapter takes case studies of 'charms' and liturgical rites and blessings that address similar socio-cultural concerns of healing, exorcism, marriage, politics, and travel. These themes are based loosely on the organisation of texts within benedictionals and pontificals to demonstrate how similar 'charms' are to other liturgical texts that were written for use by bishops and priests. As connections between 'charms' and agricultural blessings have been firmly established, I will postpone analysis of this common concern until the next chapter, which undertakes a case study of the *Vitellius Psalter*. Several 'charms' were written for use by local priests and lay people – particularly pregnant women – indicating that some functioned to encourage liturgical practice in the wider community. The thematic and textual similarities between 'charms' and liturgical texts demonstrate how difficult it is to sustain distinctions between these rituals.

Visiting the Sick

Sickness is possibly the most predominant concern of the so-called 'charm' rituals, and the majority of these healing texts are found in Royal 12 D. xvii and Harley 585 (discussed in Chapter 2).[8] Many of these rituals have close correspondences with liturgical texts associated with healing. For example, one 'charm' for healing internal and external sickness provides evidence of an attempt to extend liturgical practice beyond the church grounds. The *Heavenly Letter* is found in the main writing space of London, British Library, MS Cotton Caligula A. xv (+ BL Egerton 3314) (fol. 140r), which according to its annal entries was written between 1073 and 1076 in Christ Church, Canterbury (see

---

in *Bishop Æthelwold*, Yorke, ed., pp. 119–47; David Dumville, *Liturgy and the Ecclesiastical History of Late Anglo-Saxon England: Four Studies* (Woodbridge, 1992), p. 85; Jones, 'Chrism Mass', pp. 105–42; Gittos, *Liturgy, Architecture, and Sacred Places*, pp. 221–56; 'Researching the History of Rites', in *Understanding Medieval Liturgy: Essays in Interpretation*, Helen Gittos and Sarah Hamilton, eds (Farnham, 2015), pp. 13–37.

[8] See also Stanley Rubin, *Medieval English Medicine* (New York, 1974); Marilyn Deegan and Donald G. Scragg, eds, *Medicine in Early Medieval England: Four Papers* (Manchester, 1989); Donald G. Scragg, ed., *Superstition and Popular Medicine in Anglo-Saxon England* (Manchester, 1989); Cameron, *Anglo-Saxon Medicine*; Barbara Brennessel, M. Drout, and R. Gravel, 'A Reassessment of the Efficacy of Anglo-Saxon Medicine', *ASE*, 34 (2005), 183–95.

below).[9] The text claims that it was placed on the altar at St Peter's in Rome by an angel from heaven, and that its recitation is equivalent to praying the entire psalter: 'Se engel brohte þis gewrit of heofonum. 7 lede hit on uppan þes petrus weofud on rome. Se þe þis gebed singð on cyrcean þoṅ forstent hit him sealtera sealma.'[10] This would have obvious benefits to monks who were under the obligation of praying the Office, but it could also have encouraged lay devotion as it is presented as an equivalent to regulated prayer. This may also be indicated in the instruction to sing it each night before going to sleep: 'sing þis ylce gebed on niht ær þu to þinum reste ga'.[11]

A more remarkable claim of this text, however, concerns its equivalence to the Eucharist: 'And se þe hit singð æt his ende dæge þonne forstent hit him husel gang.'[12] As noted in Chapter 2, there are other rituals that use the Eucharist in their prescribed performances, but this text is unique in its claim that its recital is as efficacious as receiving the Eucharist on the death bed. If in emergency the dying person could not receive the Eucharist in the administration of Extreme Unction, the singing of these sacred words seems to have sufficed instead.[13] Following this statement, the text instructs that it can be effective against all unknown evil forces: 'wið æghwilcum uncuþum yfele ægðer gefleogendes gefarendes'.[14] If the evil is internal the words are to be sung over a drink, and if it is external they are to be sung over butter that is then used to anoint the body.[15]

Another 'charm' against elf-disease from the main writing space of *Leechbook* III (s. x$^{3/4}$, Old Minster, Winchester, fols. 123v–125v) uses

---

[9] See Ker, *Catalogue*, p. 173; Gneuss, *Handlist*, p. 74; Lapidge, *Anglo-Saxon Library*, p. 169; Roy Liuzza, *Anglo-Saxon Prognostics: An Edition and Translation of Texts from London, British Library MS Cotton Tiberius A iii* (Cambridge, 2010), pp. 9–12; Scragg, *Conspectus*, p. 35.

[10] 'The angel brought this letter from heaven, and laid it upon Peter's altar in Rome. He who sings prayer in church benefits by it as by the psalms of the psalter.' Transcriptions and translations of this text are my own.

[11] 'Sing this same prayer at night before you go to your bed.'

[12] 'And he who sings it at his end days (i.e. at his time of death) benefits by it as by the Eucharist.'

[13] Other records survive from eighth-century Irish traditions that use rites for healing and 'which are built around the communion service of the Mass'; Frederick S. Paxton, 'Anointing the Sick and the Dying in Christian Antiquity and the Early Medieval West', in *Health, Disease and Healing in Medieval Culture*, Sheila Campbell, Bert Hall, and David Klausner, eds (London, 1992), pp. 93–102, p. 95.

[14] 'against every unkown evil, both flying (ie. airborne) and death-causing (ie. terminal)'.

[15] 'Gif hit innon bið sing þis on wæter syle him drincan. sona him bið sel. Gif hit þonne utan si sing hit on fersce buteran. 7 smere mid þ(æt) lic. sona hī(m) kymð bot'; 'If it is internal, sing this over water and give it him to drink; he will soon be whole. If it is external, sing it on fresh butter and smear the body; he will soon come to health.'

a number of liturgical formulas with the administration of an herbal drink:

> Writ þis gewrit. Scriptum est rex regum et dominus dominantium. byrnice. beronice. lurlure. iehe. aius. aius. aius. *Sanctus. Sanctus. Sanctus.* dominus deus Sabaoth. amen. alleluiah. Sing þis ofer þam drence 7 þam gewrite. Deus omnipotens pater domini nostri iesu cristi. per Inpositionem huius scriptura expelle a famulo tuo .N. omnem impetum castalidum. de capite. de capillis. de cerebro. de fronte. de lingua. de sublingua. de guttore. de faucibus. de dentibus. de oculis. de naribus. de auribus. de manibus. de collo. de brachiis. de corde. de anima. de genibus. de coxis. de pedibus. de compaginibus. omnium membrorum intus et foris. amen. Wyrc þonne drenc… writ .III. crucem mid oleum infirmorum 7 cweð. pax tibi. Nim þonne *þæt* gewrit writ crucem mid ofer þam drince 7 sing þis þær ofer… wæt *þæt* gewrit on þam drence 7 writ crucem mid him on ælcum lime 7 cweð signum crucis xpi consu-eruate In uitam eternam. amen. Gif þe ne lyste hat hine selfne oððe swa gesubne swa he gesybbost hæbbe 7 senige swa he selost cunne. þes cræft mæg wiþ ælcre feondes costnunge (fols. 124v–125r).[16]

> Write this writing: 'It is written, King of kings and Lord of lords. byrnice, beronice, lurlure, iehe, aius, aius, aius, holy, holy, holy, Lord God of hosts. Amen, alleluia.' Sing this over the drink and the writing: 'God, omnipotent Father of our lord Jesus Christ, through the imposition of this writing expel from your servant (Name) all enemy attacks from the head, from the hair, from the brain, from the forehead, from the tongue, from the epiglottis, from the throat, from the gullet, from the teeth, from the eyes, from the nose, from the ears, from the hands, from the neck, from the arms, from the heart, from the soul, from the knees, from the hips, from the feet, from the joints, and all internal and external members. Amen.' Then work up a drink [of numerous herbs and holy water]… Write three crosses with oil of unction and say: 'peace be with you'. Then take the writing, write a cross with it over the drink and sing this over it… Wet the writing in the drink and write a cross with it on every limb and say: 'May the sign of the cross of Christ keep you for eternal life. Amen.' If you do not have instruction, order (the person) himself or as close a kinsman as he has and sign (the cross) as best he can. This practice is powerful against all the fiend's temptations.[17]

The sacred writing that is used in this ritual is composed of scriptural references, and contains the *Sanctus* of the Mass. Some of the words are difficult to interpret but there is an evident inclusion of Greek in the triple repetition of 'aius', which is probably supposed to be

---

[16] Cockayne, *Leechdoms*, Vol. II, pp. 348–50.

[17] Other similar instructions can be found in this manuscript, see Cockayne, *Leechdoms*, Vol. II, pp. 334–6, 344–6. See also Jolly, *Popular Religion*, pp. 154–60; Rolf Bremmer, 'Old English "Cross" Words', in *Cross and Cruciform in the Anglo-Saxon World*, Keefer, Jolly, and Karkov, eds, pp. 204–32, pp. 212–15.

'agios', the Greek equivalent to 'sanctus'. The words that precede this liturgical invocation have been interpreted as names of saints, particularly 'byrnice' and 'beronice' as 'Veronica', and 'iehe' as 'Yahweh' or 'Jesus'.[18] The word 'lurlure', however, is more obscure and has not been identified. This particular word could be deliberately obscured, as seen in other rituals in this manuscript that may use encryption, or it could refer to some spiritual entity that has since been forgotten. Whatever the meaning of these words, it is clear that the ritual opens with writing holy words and names before they are applied to the sick subject.

The ritual then prescribes the singing of a prayer listing no fewer than twenty-one body parts that are to be protected by the power of God. The blessing 'pax tibi' is then said as each limb is anointed with the oil of unction and the sign of the cross. Following this, the written text is dipped into the herbal drink and used to mark another sign of the cross on each limb, during which an invocation of Christ's cross is repeated.[19] Finally, the ritual explicitly states that the sick person or next of kin can perform the ritual if the performer does not know what to do ('Gif þe ne lyste'). This suggests that the ritual could be performed by any literate person, and this final instruction may indicate that it could have been used by a lay person.[20] It could also have been written for use in a monastic infirmary; the ritual allows for a monk who can read but not write, and in this context the sick monk may have known how to perform the ritual.

There are many liturgical texts concerned with healing, especially votive Masses and liturgical *ordines* for the infirm and dying. Visiting the sick was an important pastoral responsibility of monks, as stressed in the *Rule of Benedict* (Chapter 36).[21] Chapter Twelve of the *Regularis Concordia* also outlines the performance of a ritual involving the whole monastic community for a sick brother.[22] Prescriptions for this type of ceremony are found in other rites for visiting the sick as seen, for example, in Part A of the so-called *Leofric Missal* (Oxford, Bodleian Library, MS Bodley 579, written c. 860–920) that Nicholas Orchard believes was probably written for Plegmund, archbishop of Canterbury (890–923) by scribes trained on the Continent. *Leofric A* contains a number of Masses for the sick and dying (fols. 228r, 238r, 239r), as well as a full *Ordo ad uisitandum et unguendum et communicandum Infirmum*

---

[18] See Storms, *Anglo-Saxon Magic*, p. 233; Jolly, *Popular Religion*, p. 163.
[19] For other 'charm' rituals that invoke the sign of the cross and their liturgical analogues, see Liuzza, 'Prayers and/or Charms', pp. 318–20.
[20] For another example of this, see Cockayne, *Leechdoms*, Vol. I, p. 136. On lay uses of death-related rituals, see Thompson, *Dying and Death*, pp. 62–3.
[21] Logeman, *Rule of S. Benet*, pp. 67–8.
[22] See Symons, *Regularis Concordia*, p. 64.

(fols. 319r–324r).[23] Victoria Thompson has also discussed several later eleventh-century manuscripts that contain devotions for the sick and dying, including Oxford, Bodleian Library, MS Laud Misc. 482, the *Red Book of Darley* (Cambridge, Corpus Christi College, MS 422), and the *Lanalet Pontifical* (Rouen, Bibliothèque Municipale, MS A. 27 (368)).[24] Thompson suggests that penitential devotions which were to be said at the death bed originated in King Alfred's reign and gained popularity in the tenth and eleventh centuries.[25]

A later version of the rite for visiting the sick is found in a Mass for the sick in the *Missal of Robert of Jumièges* (Rouen, Bibliothèque Municipale, MS Y.6 (274), fols. 207r–212v).[26] This manuscript is an English Mass-book that was written sometime between 1014 and 1023, and it therefore post-dates the ritual for elf-disease in *Leechbook* III.[27] It was probably written for a monastic bishop at Ely or Peterborough before it came into the possession of Robert of Jumièges, bishop of London (1044) and archbishop of Canterbury (1051).[28] The *ordo* in this manuscript has Old English instructions and it also allows flexibility in who can perform the rite.[29] Like other *ordines* of this period, it opens with the asperging of a house with holy water before the priests enter

---

[23] Nicholas Orchard, ed., *The Leofric Missal, 1: Introduction, Collation Table, and Index; 2: Text*, 2 Vols., HBS, Vols. 113–14 (Woodbridge, 2002), Vol. II, pp. 343–4, 356, 358, 444–50. A similar *ordo* for the housebound sick is found in G. H. Doble, ed., *Pontificale Lanaletense (Bibliothèque de la Ville de Rouen A. 27. Cat. 368)*, HBS, Vol. 74 (London, 1937), pp. 131–9; Orchard, *Sacramentary of Ratoldus*, pp. 411–16. On the dating of *Leofric A*, see Orchard, *Leofric Missal*, Vol. I, pp. 10–13, 16–20.

[24] Thompson, *Dying and Death*, pp. 67–88. See also Helen Gittos, 'Is there any Evidence for the Liturgy of Parish Churches in Late Anglo-Saxon England? The Red Book of Darley and the Status of Old English', in *Pastoral Care in Late Anglo-Saxon England*, Tinti, ed., pp. 63–82, pp. 75–6.

[25] Thompson, *Dying and Death*, p. 67. See also Allen Frantzen, 'The Tradition of Penitentials in Anglo-Saxon England', *ASE*, 11 (1982), 23–56, pp. 49–52.

[26] On the Latin sources of this alternative rite, see Henry A. Wilson, ed., *The Missal of Robert of Jumièges*, HBS, Vol. 11 (London, 1896), pp. lxxi–lxxii.

[27] Wilson, *Missal of Robert*, pp. xxiv–xxvi; Gneuss, *Handlist*, p. 141; Brown, *Manuscripts*, p. 163; Gernot R. Wieland, 'A Survey of Latin Manuscripts', in *Working with Anglo-Saxon Manuscripts*, Gale R. Owen-Crocker, ed. (Exeter, 2009), p. 121; Scragg, *Conspectus*, p. 83. See also J. B. L. Tolhurst, 'An Examination of Two Anglo-Saxon Manuscripts of the Winchester School: The Missal of Robert of Jumièges, and the Benedictional of Aethelwold', *Archaeologia*, 83 (1933), 27–44.

[28] See Ker, *Catalogue*, p. 449; Dumville, *Liturgy and the Ecclesiastical History*, p. 87; M. Bradford Bedingfield, *The Dramatic Liturgy of Anglo-Saxon England* (Woodbridge, 2002), pp. 15–16. Dumville also offers an alternative possibility that it was copied from an exemplar from Ely or Peterborough at Christ Church, Canterbury, David Dumville, *English Caroline Script and Monastic History: Studies in Benedictinism, A.D. 950–1030* (Cambridge, 1993), pp. 118–19.

[29] For other manuscripts with similar vernacular instructions for this rite, see Gittos, 'Liturgy of Parish Churches', pp. 74–80.

and say 'pax huic domui' three times.[30] This resonates with the instruction to write three crosses with oil and say 'pax tibi' in the 'charm' for elf-disease. Following this, the interior of the house and the sick subject are to be sprinkled with water before penitential psalms are sung.[31] A prayer is then said that refers to the Roman Centurion who asked Christ to heal his servant (Matt. 8: 5–13), and a litany of the saints follows that includes Cuthbert, Guthlac, Brigid, Æthelthryth, Sexburg, and Wihtburg.[32] The elf-disease 'charm' similarly uses scriptural references and what seems to be a short litany in the text to be written down.

Another prayer then follows the litany in the *ordo*, and it petitions the God of Abraham, Isaac, and Jacob to drive out all hostile forces and grant the protection of His angels: 'expelle omnes inimici insidias. mitte ei domine angelum pacis qui hanc domum pace perpetua custodiat'.[33] The elf-disease 'charm' also drives out evil forces in the same way ('expelle a famulo tuo .N. omnem impetum castalidum').[34] The *ordo* then instructs that the sign of the cross is to be marked on the individual's body:

> Þonne wyrc se sacerd cristes rodetacen mid þan halig wætere 7 mid þam axun ofer his breost 7 onlecge hæran oððe wyllen 7 smirie hine mid þon haligan ele. 7 oðre betrynan þan syngan þa sealm(as) þe her gemearcode sint.[35]

> Then let the priest make the sign of the cross with the holy water, and with the ashes over his breast, and lay on the sackcloth or wool, and anoint him with the holy oil. And the others who are well should then sing those psalms that are noted here.

An antiphon and psalm are then given, and a series of alternative prayers are listed with further antiphons and psalms.[36] These stages of the *ordo* echo the marking of the sign of the cross with the holy oil and drink in the 'charm' for elf-disease.

Following this initial anointing, the *ordo* provides vernacular instructions outlining the parts of the body that are to be marked with the oil along with an accompanying prayer of anointing:

---

[30] Wilson, *Missal of Robert*, p. 287.
[31] For further comparisons between 'charms' and liturgical blessings of houses and rooms, see Wilson, *Missal of Robert*, pp. 277–9 and Storms, *Anglo-Saxon Magic*, pp. 202, 206.
[32] See Wilson, *Missal of Robert*, pp. 287–9.
[33] Wilson, *Missal of Robert*, pp. 289–90; 'Expel all the deceits of the Evil One, send him, Lord, an angel of peace who may guard this house in perpetual peace.'
[34] 'expel from your servant (Name) all enemy attacks'.
[35] Wilson, *Missal of Robert*, p. 290.
[36] Wilson, *Missal of Robert*, pp. 290–2.

Þonne se untrumne bið gesmyred on þam mold gewinde 7 on foran-
heafde. 7 on þan þunwengon. 7 on his nebbe. Þonne cweðe se sacerd
þis gebed.
Unguo te .N. oleo sancto in nomine patris et filii et spiritus sancti sicut
unxit samuel dauid regem et prophetam. ut non lateat in te spiritus
inmundus. neque in membris. neque in medullis. neque in nulla † com-
pagine membrorum. sed in te habitet uirtus Christi altissimi et spiritus
sancti. quatenus per huius operationem mysterii. et per hanc sacrati
olei unctionem atque nostrum deprecationem uirtute sanctae trinita-
tis medicatus siue sanatus pristinam et melioratam recipere merearis
sanitatem. per.[37]

When the sick person is anointed all around the top of the head, and on
the forehead, and on the temples, and on his nose, then let the priest say
this prayer:
'I anoint you, (Name), with holy oil in the name of the Father, and the
Son, and the Holy Spirit just as Samuel anointed David as king and
prophet; so that the unclean spirit does not lurk in you, neither in your
limbs, nor in your middle, nor in any of your limbs' joints, but may the
power of Christ the most high and the Holy Spirit dwell in you. Through
this work of mystery here, and through the unction of the consecrated
oil, and our prayer, by the power of the Holy Trinity, may you merit to
regain, be cured or be healed to former and better health.'

Once this prayer is said and the sick subject is paralleled with biblical
figures (through references to Samuel and David), all other bodily
extremities are then anointed. The bodily members are identified
by a vernacular instruction, and every prayer that is to be said over
each member is consistently identified as 'þis gebed'. The bodily
members are the eyes ('þa eagan'), ears ('earan innan 7 utan'), nose
('nosu fore wearde 7 innan'), lips ('weleras'), throat and heels ('hrace 7
spyran'), shoulders ('sculdru'), breast ('breost'), hands ('handa'), and
feet ('fet').[38] These body parts differ in order of appearance from the
elf-disease ritual, and the *ordo* instructs the priest to recite this list over
the sick person, whereas the 'charm' instructs that it is to be sung over
a drink. The ritual for elf-disease also identifies roughly double the
number of bodily members that are to be protected than those listed in
the *ordo*. However, the comprehensive anatomical protection of both
texts demonstrates a very close overlap in their content.

Following the anointing of each body part and towards the end of
the *ordo*, another prayer is to be said that reinforces the earlier petitions

---

[37] Wilson, *Missal of Robert*, p. 292. On the appearance of this 'neque' formula in
other ritual traditions, see Jolly, 'Magic, Miracle, and Popular Practice', p. 165;
Edina Bozóky, 'Medieval Narrative Charms', in *The Power of Words*, Kapalo,
Pócs, and Ryan, eds, pp. 101–16, p. 103.
[38] Wilson, *Missal of Robert*, pp. 292–3.

to drive out evil, restore health to the body and soul, and grant the sick subject remission of sins. Instructions then follow to consume both the bread and wine of the Eucharist, and to recite two more prayers: 'Onbyrie þonne godes lichaman 7 blodes þus cweðene… On þære fyllednysse þissere þenunge.'[39] After the final prayer, the priests pray silently over the sick person, but if there is a bishop present then he is to recite another prayer which is provided in the *ordo*: 'Þissun eallun þus gefylledon cweðum þa sacerdas þas gebedu ofer þone untruman swa fela swa þær beo synderlic. Gif þær þonne bisceop beo his þenung þæt bið.'[40] The *ordo*, the elf-disease 'charm', and the *Heavenly Letter* all demonstrate flexibility in their performance, showing how certain measures were taken to ensure that this pastoral duty of visiting the sick and dying could be carried out by bishops, priests, the sick patients themselves, or their related kin.

The significant number of overlaps in theme and content in the *ordo* and so-called 'charms' indicate that distinctions between their performances may not have been easily perceived, if at all. The *Heavenly Letter* shows how devotional rituals were perhaps used in cases of emergency when a dying person could not receive the Eucharist. As the elf-disease ritual predates the *ordo* in the *Missal of Robert of Jumièges*, it may even be the case that some of the so-called 'charms' influenced developments in some liturgical rites. These healing 'charms' have many features in common with liturgical texts and very close overlap in content. There is no evidence to suggest that they were perceived as belonging to different genres in late Anglo-Saxon and early Norman England.

Exorcism

Closely related to the pastoral concern of ministering to the sick is the theme of exorcism. There are two forms of liturgical rites relating to exorcism in extant Anglo-Saxon sources: that of exorcising people and things such as salt, water, oil, palms, and catechumens; and the ordination of an exorcist.[41] Karen Jolly has discussed in detail the con-

---

[39] Wilson, *Missal of Robert*, p. 294; 'Then consume God's body and blood, saying thus… Upon the fulfilment of this ministry (say then)'.

[40] Wilson, *Missal of Robert*, p. 294; 'This is all fulfilled (when) the priests say these prayers over the sick person with as many more (said) silently. If the bishop is there in his ministry, that is…'

[41] On the development of these rites, see Jones, 'Chrism Mass', pp. 108–9, 124; Florence Chave-Mahir, *L'exorcisme des possédés dans l'Église d'Occident (Xe–XIVe siècle)* (Turnhout, 2011). For versions of these rites see Orchard, *Leofric Missal*, Vol. II, pp. 394, 414–15, 434–55, 465–6; *Sacramentary of Ratoldus*, pp. 58–9, 147; D. H. Turner, ed., *The Claudius Pontificals (from Cotton MS Claudius A. iii in the*

nections between 'charm' rituals and rites for exorcising water and salt in the *Leofric Missal*, the *Durham Collectar*, and Corpus 41, and there is no need to redraw these comparisons here.[42] Some so-called 'charms' also have close correspondences with the rite for ordaining an exorcist. For example, in the *Benedictional of Robert* (Rouen, Bibliothèque Municipale, Y.7 (369), written in Winchester c. 975, fols. 135rv) the rite opens with the exorcist receiving a letter of authority from his bishop.[43] He is then ordered to memorise the document so that he may have power over the possessed, the baptised, and catechumens: 'Accipe et commenda memoriae. et habeto potestatem inponendi manum super inerguminum. siue baptizatum. siue caticuminum.'[44] The fact that the exorcist has to commit the document to memory indicates that exorcisms were perceived as powerful rites that must be closely guarded and known only to those who were authorised to perform them. The term 'inerguminum' (the possessed) is found mainly in Anglo-Saxon liturgical books, but it also appears outside of this context in Aldhelm's *Prosa de Virginitate*.[45] In Aldhelm's work the word is used to describe St Anatolia's cure of a man bound by demons, and it is glossed with the Old English word 'deouelseocne'.[46] The Latin word for possession was rendered as 'devil-sickness', and a number of 'charm' rituals directly attribute sicknesses to the devil.

The bishop gives the exorcist power over the possessed provided that he commits the written testimony of his ordination to memory. A blessing follows this opening instruction and it emphasises the exorcist's power over the demon and the many evils it brings: 'ut

---

British Museum), HBS, Vol. 97 (London, 1971), pp. 32, 45; Doble, *Pontificale Lanaletense*, pp. 7–9, 51, 81–2, 111–16, 123–5; Henry A. Wilson, ed., *The Benedictional of Archbishop Robert*, HBS, Vol. 24 (London, 1903), pp. 44, 116; *Missal of Robert*, pp. 94–6, 100, 275–6; H. M. J. Banting, ed., *Two Anglo-Saxon Pontificals: (The Egbert and Sidney Sussex Pontificals)*, HBS, Vol. 104 (London, 1989), pp. 19–20; Reginald M. Woolley, ed., *The Canterbury Benedictional (British Museum Harl. MS. 2892)*, HBS, Vol. 51 (London, 1917), pp. 23, 37, 134.

[42] Jolly, *Popular Religion*, pp. 116–22 166; 'Prayers from the Field', pp. 105–9, 122; 'Margins of Orthodoxy', pp. 163–4. See also Bremmer, 'Cross Words', pp. 212–15; Ursula Lenker, 'Signifying Christ in Anglo-Saxon England: Old English Terms for the Sign of the Cross', in *Cross and Cruciform in the Anglo-Saxon World*, Keefer, Jolly, and Karkov, eds, pp. 233–75, p. 273.

[43] For the origins of this manuscript see Nelson, *Politics and Ritual*, p. 369; Gneuss, *Handlist*, p. 141; Gittos, *Liturgy, Architecture, and Sacred Places*, pp. 280–1. A marginal note referring to other symbols of office of an exorcist can be found in the so-called *Sidney Sussex Pontifical*, see Banting, *Two Anglo-Saxon Pontificals*, pp. xli–xlii; Gittos, 'Liturgy of Parish Churches', pp. 76–7.

[44] Wilson, *Benedictional of Archbishop Robert*, p. 117; 'Accept (it) and commit (it) to memory, and hold power in setting (your) hands over the possessed, or the baptised, or catechumens.'

[45] See, for example, Orchard, *Sacramentary of Ratoldus*, pp. 416–19.

[46] Napier, *Old English Glosses*, pp. 82, 126. For a discussion of this passage, see Hall, *Elves in Anglo-Saxon England*, pp. 149–50.

sit spiritalis imperator ad abiciendos demones de corporibus obsessis cum omni nequitia eorum multiformi'.[47] The exorcist is presented as a master of spirits that manifest their demonic effects in the corporeal world. An alternative blessing that follows this also outlines the exorcist's ability to coerce demonic forces through his words and through the imposition of his hands: 'ut per inpositionem manum et officium oris eum eligere digneris ut imperium habeat spirituum inmundorum cohercendo et probabilis sit medicus eclesiae tuae gratia curarum uirtute confirmatus'.[48] The exorcist's mouth and hands are given spiritual power to command hostile forces, and he is depicted as a physician of the Church ('medicus eclesiae').

There are ten Anglo-Saxon 'charms' that identify the devil and use exorcism formulas which combine symbolic hand gestures with verbal commands to drive out evil. There are many more that claim to have power over the 'feond', 'ælfsidene' (elf-sickness), or other creatures associated with evil, and some personally address demons to maximise power over them.[49] Two of these ten 'charms' are in *Leechbook* III, and they specifically identify the devil and his evil effects in society: 'Wyrc sealfe wið ælfcynne and nihtgengan and þam mannum þe deofol mid hæmð' (fol. 123r); 'Wiþ deofle liþe drenc and ungemynde… Drenc wiþ deofles costnunga' (fol. 125v).[50] The first ritual is for a salve that draws out the evil influences of elves, night-walkers (maybe nightmares), and those who have had intercourse with the devil. The second ritual is for a drink that was used as a defence against evil states of mind ('ungemynde') and other general temptations ('costnunga').

Eight other 'charm' rituals employ exorcism formulas; most identify the 'diabolus', and they all follow similar formulaic imperative and subjunctive constructions:

(London, BL, MS Royal 2 A. xx; s. viii[1]-viii[med])
Adiuro te satanae diabulus aelfae. per deum unum ac verum. et per trementem diem iudicii ut refugiatur ab homine illo qui (h)abeat hunc a Cristo scriptum secum (fol. 45v).[51]

---

[47] Wilson, *Benedictional of Archbishop Robert*, p. 117; 'so that he may be the master of spirits to cast down demons dwelling in bodies with all of their many evil forms'.

[48] Wilson, *Benedictional of Archbishop Robert*, p. 117; 'so that through the imposition of hand and duty of mouth you may deem it worthy to choose him, so that he may have power to coerce unclean spirits, and may be an acceptable healer of the pains of your Church, confirmed by your powerful grace'.

[49] Jolly, 'Margins of Orthodoxy', pp. 166–7. See also Peter Dendle, 'The Demonological Landscape of the *Solomon and Saturn* Cycle', *ES*, 80 (1999), 281–92.

[50] Cockayne, *Leechdoms*, Vol. II, pp. 344, 352; 'Work a salve against elves and night-walkers and men with whom the devil has intercourse'; 'A sweet drink against the devil and mental disturbance… A drink against temptations of the devil.'

[51] Storms, *Anglo-Saxon Magic*, p. 294; 'I adjure you elf-demon of Satan, through the

(London, BL, MS Royal 12 D. xvii; s. x$^{3/4}$)
per Inpositionem huius scriptura expelle a famulo tuo .N. omnem
impetum castalidum (fol. 125r).[52]

(London, BL, MS Harley 585; s. x^{ex}/xi^1)
per impositionem manuum mearum refugiat inimicus diabolus… ut
non habeat potestatem diabolus (fol. 149r).[53]

ut del(e)as omnia opera diaboli. ab isto homine inuoco s(an)ctam trini-
tatem in admini(cu)lum meum (fol. 149r).[54]

Sane[n]tur animalia in orbe terre et ualitudine uexantur in nomine dei
patris et filii et spiritus s(an)c(t)i extinguatur [extingunt] diabolus per
inpositionem manuum [manum] nostrarum (fol. 182v).[55]

(Corpus 41; s. xi$^{1/4}$)
ut non habeant potestatem diabulus ab homine isto (fol. 272v).[56]

(Oxford, Bodleian, MS Junius 85; s. xi^{med})
Fuge diabolus, Christus te sequitur. Quando natus est Christus fugit
dolor (fol. 17v).[57]

(London, BL, MS Harley 464; s. xvii)
adjuro et obtestor vos diaboli, ut non habeatis ullam (fol. 177).[58]

All of these examples correspond closely with the role of the exorcist in
driving out demons from the corporeal world through his speech and
the imposition of his hands. The similarities between these formulas
are quite clear, and they all draw upon the key features of liturgical
exorcisms.

Very literal parallels can also be found between 'charms' and some

---

one true God, and through the fearful day of judgement, that (you) flee from
whoever may have this letter from Christ with him.'
[52] Cockayne, *Leechdoms*, Vol. II, p. 348; 'through the imposition of this writing
expel from your servant (Name) every attack of the elves'.
[53] Cockayne, *Leechdoms*, Vol. III, p. 26; 'through the imposition of my hands, may
the hostile demon flee… so that the demon may not have power'.
[54] Cockayne, *Leechdoms*, Vol. III, p. 26; 'so that you may remove all works of the
demon from that man, I invoke the Holy Trinity to come to my aid'.
[55] Cockayne, *Leechdoms*, Vol. III, p. 64; 'May the animals of the earth and distressed
by illness be healed in the name of the Father and the Son and the Holy Spirit,
may the demon be destroyed through the imposition of our hands.'
[56] Storms, *Anglo-Saxon Magic*, p. 285; 'so that the demon may not have power over
this man'. This formula is slightly corrupted as the noun 'diabolus' does not
agree with the plural subjunctive 'habeant'. This ritual opens with a quotation
from Psalm 117: 16–17.
[57] Storms, *Anglo-Saxon Magic*, p. 279; 'Flee demon, Christ pursues you. When
Christ was born, suffering fled.'
[58] Storms, *Anglo-Saxon Magic*, p. 276; 'I adjure and entreat you, demons, that you
may not have any [power].'

exorcism rites. For example, the 'charm' for animals that are vexed by demons in Harley 585 ('Sanetur animalia in orbe terre et ualitudine uexantur') is strikingly similar to a prayer in the earlier *Leofric Missal* (fol. 307v):

> ORATIONES SVPER EOS QVI A DAEMONIO VEXANTVR. Omnipotens sempiterne deus, pater domini nostri ihesu christi te supplices exoramus, impera diabolo qui hunc famulum tuum .ill. detinet, ut ab eo recedat et extinguatur per impositionem manuum nostrarum.[59]

> Prayers over those who are vexed by a demon. Omnipotent, everliving God, Father of our Lord Jesus Christ, we implore you, command the demon who possesses your servant (Name) here, so that it may depart from him, and may be driven away through the imposition of our hands.

Although this prayer refers to a person who is vexed by a demon, whereas the Harley ritual refers to animals, certain spellings are common to both texts ('uexantur', 'extinguatur', 'manuum'), and it is quite possible that the scribes of these 'charms' drew directly upon liturgical rites and prayers similar to that found in the *Leofric Missal*.[60] The close correspondences between 'charms' and exorcisms indicate that many 'charm' rituals were understood as liturgical rites of exorcism that were likely to have been performed by an authorised exorcist. Indeed, the similarities in the texts' language and formulaic commands suggest that Anglo-Saxon scribes did not distinguish between these exorcism rituals.

Marriage and Childbirth

Marital relations and childbirth are another theme common to 'charms' and liturgical texts. One so-called 'charm' against miscarriage that is found in the main writing space of Harley 585 (fols. 185rv) instructs that the woman should utter prescribed words over a dead man's grave, in bed with her lord, in front of the church's altar, at her dead child's grave, beside running water, and in a different house to the one she previously left. The ritual begins at the site of the grave where a mother confronts her grief over her previous miscarriage, and defies the forces of evil that threaten her fertility. After visiting the grave, she must then recite more words in the marital bed:

> and þon(ne) þ(æt) wif seo mid bearne and heo to hyre hlaforde on reste ga, þon(ne) cweþe heo:

[59] Orchard, *Leofric Missal*, Vol. II, p. 434.
[60] Jolly notes that these exorcisms from the *Leofric Missal* were censored in the twelfth century, Jolly, 'Father God and Mother Earth', p. 235.

'Up ic gonge, ofer þe stæppe
mid cwican cilde, nalæs mid cwe[l]endum,
mid fulborenum, nalæs mid fægan.'

And when the woman is with child and goes to her husband in his rest
(*or* bed), then let her say:
'Up I go, over you I step;
With a living child, not with a dying one,
With a child brought to full-term, not with a doomed (*i.e.* premature)
one.'[61]

The mother confidently declares that her actions will give her a 'cwican
cilde' (living child) and resurrect her fertility.

The mother is then instructed to go before a church altar to confirm
the conception in Christ's name:

and þon(ne) seo modor gefele þ(æt) þ(æt) bearn si cwic, ga þon(ne) to
cyrican, and þon(ne) heo toforan þan weofude cume cweþe þon(ne):
'Criste, ic sæde, þis gecyþed.'

And when the mother feels that the child is alive, then let her go to
church, and when she comes before the altar then let her say: '(?)To
Christ, I have said, this is made manifest.'[62]

To my knowledge, the only other 'charm' that prescribes a verbal utterance inside the church building is the *Heavenly Letter* from Caligula A.
xv (+ Egerton 3314), and this reference in the Harley ritual is highly
significant as it provides evidence of female ritual practice before an
altar.[63] The first two recitations at the grave and in the marital bed
anticipate this performance at the church where the mother's pregnancy is paralleled with Mary's conception and her child's life is correlated with Christ. Finally, the locations following the church safeguard
against the mother's past from being repeated by visiting her child's
grave, drinking running water from a stream (symbolic of constant
change), and returning to a different house.

The prescribed movements in this ritual have been understood
to be pagan in origin with the Christian interpolation of visiting the
church building.[64] However, a close parallel can be found between
these instructions and the biblical story of Elisha and the Shunammite
woman who lost her child (2 Kings 4: 29–37):

---

[61] Pettit, *Anglo-Saxon Remedies*, Vol. I, pp. 112–13.
[62] Pettit, *Anglo-Saxon Remedies*, Vol. I, pp. 112–13.
[63] On the significance of these two prescriptions, see Arthur, '*Ex Ecclesia*', pp. 27–8.
[64] See Marie Nelson, 'A Woman's Charm', *Studia Neophilologica*, 57 (1985), 3–8;
L. M. C. Weston, 'Women's Medicine, Women's Magic: The Old English
Metrical Childbirth Charms', *Modern Philology*, 92 (1995), 279–93; Paul Cavill,
Anglo-Saxon Christianity (London, 1999), p. 25.

et ille ait ad Giezi accinge lumbos tuos et tolle baculum meum in manu tua et vade si occurrerit tibi homo non salutes eum et si salutaverit te quispiam non respondeas illi et pones baculum meum super faciem pueri... ingressus est ergo Heliseus domum et ecce puer mortuus iacebat in lectulo eius ingressusque clusit ostium super se et puerum et oravit ad Dominum et ascendit et incubuit super puerum posuitque os suum super os eius et oculos suos super oculos eius et manus suas super manus eius et incurvavit se super eum et calefacta est caro pueri at ille reversus deambulavit in domo semel huc et illuc et ascendit et incubuit super eum et oscitavit puer septies aperuitque oculos et ille vocavit Giezi et dixit ei voca Sunamitin hanc quae vocata ingressa est ad eum qui ait tolle filium tuum venit illa et corruit ad pedes eius et adoravit super terram tulitque filium suum et egressa est.[65]

He said to Gehazi, 'Gird your loins and take my staff in your hand and go. If you meet anyone, do not greet him, and if anyone greets you, do not reply to him. And lay my staff on the face of the child'... When Elisha came into the house, he saw the child lying dead on his bed. So he went in and shut the door behind the two of them and prayed to the Lord. Then he went up and lay on the child, putting his mouth on his mouth, his eyes on his eyes, and his hands on his hands. And as he stretched himself upon him, the flesh of the child became warm. Then he got up again and walked once back and forth in the house, and went up and stretched himself upon him. The child yawned seven times, and the child opened his eyes. Then he summoned Gehazi and said, 'Call this Shunammite.' So he called her. And when she came to him, he said, 'Pick up your son.' She came and fell at his feet, bowing to the ground. Then she picked up her son and went out.

The instructions in the ritual against miscarriage resonate with this biblical story in several ways. Firstly, the mother in the ritual is twice ordered to not look back once she has visited certain sites, and Elisha orders his servant to not speak a word to anybody he meets on the way to the house.[66] Secondly, the mother of the ritual assumes a dominant position over her partner ('Up ic gonge, ofer þe stæppe'), and Elisha assumes a dominant posture by lying over the dead child. Thirdly, multiple movements between locations occur in both the ritual and the biblical story as the mother visits more than one grave and multiple houses and Elisha moves numerous times within the house and over the child. Finally, the mother is instructed to visit a different house to the one she initially leaves, and the Shunammite mother leaves the house in which her dead child was resurrected. There is no reason to assume that ritual actions like these are pagan in origin, and it is

---

[65] *Biblia Sacra*, Vol. I, p. 508.
[66] For similar instructions in other 'charm' rituals against theft, see Storms, *Anglo-Saxon Magic*, pp. 206–9.

likely that such biblical stories – which would have been read by the ecclesiastics who produced the manuscripts in question – provided inspiration for the composition of these Anglo-Saxon rituals.[67]

Another so-called 'charm' for childbirth is found in the main writing space of Oxford, Bodleian Library, MS Junius 85. This manuscript was written in the mid-eleventh century in the south-east of England (possibly Kent, according to palaeographical evidence) and it contains a series of homilies for specific occasions, including one by Ælfric and some copied from the *Blickling Homilies*.[68] On folios 17rv four Latin 'charms' with Old English titles appear between homilies written by the main scribe. These are for childbirth (*Wið wif bearneacenu*), a stitch (*Wið gestice*), an unknown swelling (*Wið uncuðum swyle*), and toothache (*Wið toðece*).[69] These rituals could be interpreted as offering useful responses to common ailments and pains, and they were evidently seen to be relevant to some of their surrounding didactic materials as they are included in the main writing space.

The childbirth ritual instructs the writing of prescribed words on unused wax before fastening them to the mother's right foot. These words invoke specific biblical figures including Elizabeth, John the Baptist, Christ, the Virgin Mary, and Lazarus:

> Wiþ wif bearn eacenu.
> Maria virgo peperit Christum, Elisabet sterelis peperit Iohannem baptistam. Adiuro te infans, si es masculus an femina, per Patrem et Filium et Spiritum sanctum, ut exeas et recedas, et ultra ei non noceas neque insipientiam illi facias. Amen.
> Videns dominus flentes sorores Lazari ad monumentum lacrimatus est coram Iudeis et clamabat: Lazari veni foras. Et prodiit ligatis manibus et pedibus qui fuerat quatriduanus mortuus.
> Writ ðis on wexe ðe næfre ne com to nanen wyrce, and bind under hire swiðran fot.[70]

> For a pregnant woman.
> The Virgin Mary gave birth to Christ, infertile Elizabeth gave birth to John the Baptist. I adjure you, infant, whether you are male or female,

---

[67] Indeed, there are seemingly odd but similar instructions in some liturgical *ordines*, like that of baptism in the *Red Book of Darley* where a priest blows over the child three times and signs the cross on its forehead, breast, and (uniquely) in the palm of its right hand, see Gittos, 'Liturgy of Parish Churches', pp. 71–3.

[68] See also Ker, *Catalogue*, pp. 409–11; Gneuss, *Handlist*, p. 101; Scragg, 'Old English Prose', pp. 68–9; *Conspectus*, p. 77; Jolly, 'Tapping the Power of the Cross', p. 76; Jonathan Wilcox, *Anglo-Saxon Manuscripts in Microfiche Facsimile, Vol. 17: Homilies by Ælfric and other Homilies*, A. N. Doane and M. T. Hussey, eds (Tempe, AZ, 2008), pp. 113–28.

[69] Cockayne, *Leechdoms*, Vol. I, pp. 392–4; Storms, *Anglo-Saxon Magic*, pp. 279, 283, 286.

[70] Storms, *Anglo-Saxon Magic*, p. 283.

through the Father and Son and Holy Spirit, that you come out and
come away, and no longer cause any harm or bother. Amen.
Seeing the sisters of Lazarus weeping at the tomb, the Lord wept before
the Jews and he cried out: 'Lazarus come forth'. And he who had been
dead for four days came out with hands and feet bound.
Write this on wax which has never been used before, and bind it under
her right foot.

These references to biblical events have clear associations with fertility and child-bearing as the Virgin Mary and the infertile Elizabeth
both conceived Christ and John the Baptist through divine assistance.
The woman's child is commanded to come forth immediately before
the story of Lazarus is recounted, thus correlating the unborn child
with this biblical narrative so that it is summoned from the mother's
womb in the same way that Lazarus was called forth from his tomb.
This ritual draws parallels between the wife's fertility and mothers
from the New Testament to overcome pregnancy problems with biblical power.

Victoria Thompson argues that such Anglo-Saxon 'charms' against
miscarriage 'attest to a culture of unregulated and quasi- or non-
liturgical activities around the grave'.[71] However, these rituals have
some close similarities with marriage blessings for brides and bride-
grooms that also invoke biblical characters and correlate the couple
with Adam and Eve, Tobias and the archangel Raphael, and Christ and
the Virgin Mary. For example, one of the blessings in the *Benedictional
of Robert* (s. x$^{3/4}$, Winchester, fols. 73v–74v) reads:

Benedictio sponsi et sponsae.
Omnipotens deus qui primos parentes nostros adam et euam sua uirtute
creauit suaque benedictione sanctificauit et in sua societate copulauit...
Quique ad preparandas tobiae et serrae nuptias raphaelum angelum
misit... Et qui unigentum filium suum dominum nostrum ihesum chris-
tum redemptorem mundi uoluit de uirgine nasci.[72]

Blessing of a husband and wife.
Almighty God, who created our first parents Adam and Eve by His
power, and sanctified them by blessing, and joined them in fellowship
with one another... And who sent the angel Raphael to prepare the marriage of Tobias and Sarah... And His only-begotten son our Lord Jesus
Christ, the Redeemer of the world, who willed to be born of the Virgin.

Such references are common in blessings for marriages. God is asked
to bless the spouses as He blessed the union of Adam and Eve, and the
reference to the first parents of man ('primos parentes') emphasises the

---

[71] Thompson, *Dying and Death*, p. 96.
[72] Wilson, *Benedictional of Archbishop Robert*, p. 55.

couple's role in having children.[73] The reference to Tobias and Sarah from the book of Tobit recalls an event when God brought the spouses together through the archangel Raphael.[74] Sarah's previous seven marriages had been cursed by a demon (Tobit 3: 8–10) until it was driven away by Raphael so that Tobias could marry her, thus restoring marital unity through angelic assistance. The blessing's final reference to the Incarnation shows the fulfilment of these prophetic narratives. Christ is the second Adam and Mary is the second Eve, and they restore the order of Creation that existed before the Fall. Through the message of the archangel Gabriel, Mary becomes the mother of God and assumes Eve's title of the mother of men as heaven and earth are united through Christ's conception. In this blessing, the husband and wife are thus placed in these biblical contexts of divine matrimony and childbirth.

The *Benedictional of Robert* also includes a nuptial Mass in which there is a blessing that invokes Sarah, Rebecca, and Rachel (fols. 173rv).[75] Sarah was the wife of Abraham who was unable to bear children before she conceived Isaac through God's assistance (Genesis 17: 16–22). Rebecca was the wife of Isaac and the mother of Esau and Jacob. She was also infertile and conceived her two sons through God's help (Genesis 25: 19–28). Rachel was the second wife of Jacob who had difficulty bearing children before she also gave birth to Joseph through divine assistance (Genesis 30: 23–4). All three women from Genesis are invoked for their roles as both mothers and wives. A similar invocation is made in a blessing for infertile women in the *Leofric Missal* (fol. 300r), which asks for the intercession of the Virgin Mary who did not refuse to give birth for the redemption of mankind.[76]

The liturgical blessings for spouses and mothers share very similar features with Anglo-Saxon 'charms' for childbirth. Biblical wives and mothers from Genesis, Tobit, and Luke are invoked for their marriages and miraculous conceptions, along with other narratives such as Lazarus' resurrection. The nuptial blessings sanctify the spouses by placing them in the context of biblical history, and the 'charm' rituals invoke divine assistance with fertility. The Harley 585 ritual for childbirth prescribes utterances for the mother to say in the marital bed, and it encourages her to return to the church building – possibly the same church in which she was married – to confirm the conception

---

[73] This is echoed in a ritual against labour pain in the margins of Corpus 41 that refers to God's command to Adam to fill the earth, and aligns the mother with Eve before her curse of labour pain, see Jolly, 'Margins of Orthodoxy', p. 169, note 137.

[74] Other liturgical blessings for fields also invoke the book of *Tobit*, see Jolly, 'Prayers from the Field', pp. 116–19, 138–40.

[75] Wilson, *Benedictional of Archbishop Robert*, pp. 150–1. Similar blessings also appear in Wilson, *Missal of Robert*, p. 270; Turner, *Claudius Pontificals*, pp. 72, 82.

[76] Orchard, *Leofric Missal*, Vol. II, p. 426.

before an altar. The ritual in Junius 85 instructs that the mother must carry an inscribed prayer that invokes biblical figures and contains a passage from the gospel, thus allowing her to transport words of Christian power to a number of different locations beyond the church. The female user would have been greatly empowered by the ability to perform such rituals in domestic, public, and sacred spaces, reflecting efforts to encourage lay participation in the liturgy.

Kings, Coronations, and Councils

One 'gibberish charm' and some Anglo-Saxon liturgical texts address contemporary political concerns. The 'charm' is found in the main writing space of Cotton Caligula A. xv (+ Egerton 3314) (fol. 140r) immediately after the *Heavenly Letter* (fol. 140r). One Anglo-Saxon scribe wrote the original part of this manuscript that includes computistical materials, calendrical tables, prognostications, and annals for the years 925 to 1073 (with a later entry in the same hand for 1076), providing a *terminus ante quem* of 1073 for the first stage of writing. The manuscript also contains later additions, including a copy of Ælfric's *De temporibus anni* (Chapters 4–11), a list of the archbishops of Canterbury, and further annal entries up to the year 1268.[77]

The so-called 'charm' in Caligula A. xv was written by the main scribe, and it claims to be able to win the favour of one's lord or king or council. A transcription and very tentative interpretation are as follows:

> Gif þu wille ga […] þi*n*um hla*forde* oþþe to kyninge / oþþe to oþrum menn oððe *to* gemote þonne bær þu þas / st*a*fas [ ]lc þæ[ ] þonne bið h[ ] þ[ ] liþa bli[ ] x x [ ] h .d.e.o.e. / o.o.e.e.e.laf.d.R.U.fi.ð.f.p.A.x.Box. Nux. In nomine / patris Rex.M.*per*.X.xix.xcs.xh.ih. + Deo.eo.deo.deeo. / Lafdruel.bepax.box.nux.bu. In nomine patris rex marie. / ihs xpe dus ms ihc. + Bonifi[ca?] senioribus. H. ubr[ini?]lur her / letus contra me. hee. larrhibus. excitatio pacis inter uiru*m* / & mulieru*m*. […] .A.B. & alfa tibi reddit / uota fructu Leta lita tota tauta uel tellus *uel* ade uirescit.

> If you wish to go to your lord or to the king or to other men or to a council, then carry these letters with you. [Each of these will] then be […] gracious [and pleasant]: 'x x [ ] h .d.e.o.e.o.o.e.e.e.laf.d.R.U.fi.ð.f.p .A.x.Box.Nux. In the name of the Father, King. M. through. X. xix. xcs.

---

[77] Ker, *Catalogue*, pp. 173–6; Gneuss, *Handlist*, pp. 61, 74. For an overview of this manuscript, see P. J. Willetts, 'A Reconstructed Astronomical Manuscript from Christ Church Library Canterbury', *British Museum Quarterly*, 30 (1965), 22–30. For a more thorough study of this manuscript, see Ciaran Arthur, 'The Gift of the Gab in Post-Conquest Canterbury: Mystical "Gibberish" in London, British Library, MS Cotton Caligula A. xv', *JEGP*, forthcoming.

xh. ih. + God. eo. God. deeo. Lafdruel. bepax. box. nux. bu. In the name
of the Father, King, Mary. Jesus Christ my God, Jesus Christ. + Make
virtuous elders. H. ubr[ ]lur her delight [read *laetus*] against me. hee.
larrhibus. Build peace among men and women. [...] Alpha. Beta. And
Alpha to you shall vows [be made] with delight. The court leet (?*Leta*)
give favourable omens [from *litare*], all tauta or even the earth or even
all that grows green.'[78]

From the very little commentary that has been given to this ritual,
it has been described as 'a cruciform shaped text' with 'angelically
derived stafas (letters) that contain and transmit virtue'.[79] Despite the
illegibility of some words in this ritual, its fragmentary instructions
make it clear that its user may gain the political favour of their supe-
riors. If it were used by a monk, their 'hlaforde' would be the abbot
or bishop, and the 'gemote' would possibly be a chapter meeting. If
it were used by a lay person, then their lord would be a nobleman or
even the king himself ('kyninge'), and the 'gemote' might be a shire
court or royal audience. If the manuscript was owned by the archbishop, his lord would be the pope or the king, and the meeting might
refer to the papal or king's council. There are some indications that
the manuscript was originally written for an archbishop's use, as the
annals focus heavily on the appointments and activities of archbishops
of Canterbury, and a list of archbishops was later added in the late
eleventh or early twelfth century.[80]

Some parts of the ritual's obscure passage can be interpreted, and it
clearly contains some Latin prayers and invocations. It also seems to
draw upon at least three languages and alphabets (Latin, Greek, and
Old English), reminding us of other such uses of exotic language in
Royal 12 D. xvii and Harley 585, as discussed in Chapter 2. Like other
'charm' rituals, these passages could be either heavily corrupted or
deliberately obscured. Certain vowels are grouped together, perhaps
in a way to indicate a chant performance, but some consonants are
combined in such a way that they cannot be vocalised, as seen in
the first sequence: 'd.e.o.e.o.o.e.e.e.laf.d.R.U.fi.ð.f.p.A.x.Box.Nux'.
Furthermore, letters from the English alphabet, such as eth ('ð'), appear
among Latin words like 'deo' and 'pax', perhaps indicating that different languages are involved in the same phrase. It is possible that these
passages are anagrammatic, and that the reader must rearrange the

---

[78] Transcription and translation my own. I have also indicated the separation
of lines within texts as they appear on the manuscript page because if letter
rearrangements are to be used then line spacing may be important. Other
interpretations of this text are printed in Cockayne, *Leechdoms*, Vol. III, p. 290;
Storms, *Anglo-Saxon Magic*, pp. 300–1; Jolly, 'Tapping the Power of the Cross',
p. 64.
[79] Jolly, 'Tapping the Power of the Cross', p. 64.
[80] See Gneuss, *Handlist*, p. 74.

letters in order to decipher the prayer. The presence of cross-markers beside these sequences also indicates that the letters form prayers that can be uttered with ritual gestures once they have been rearranged.

The fragmentary state of the ritual is due to erasures on the parchment, and this is the only place in the entire quire where erasures have been made. Specific parts of the text have been removed, perhaps because its 'stafas' were believed to be powerful enough to influence the highest authorities, and it certainly indicates heavy encryption. Despite the erasures, it is clear that the ritual invokes God ('deo'), Jesus Christ ('ihs xpe dus ms ihc'), Mary ('marie'), and a mysterious 'Lafdruel', which may be the name of an angel. The Lord and King of heaven is invoked in a ritual that is to influence earthly lords and kings, and Mary's invocation as Queen of heaven may parallel the earthly queen and her potential influence over the king. Finally, the passage concludes with what appears to be an encrypted reference to Psalm 64 in its wording 'A.B. & alfa tibi reddit uota fructu'. Psalm 64 (verses 2–5) describes vows made to God, God's forgiveness of sins, and the man who has won God's favour and earned a place in His courts:

> Te decet hymnus deus in syon *et tibi reddetur votum* in ierusalem. Exaudi orationem meam ad te omnis caro veniet. Verba iniquiorum prevaluerunt super nos et impietatibus nostris tu propitiaberis. Beatus quem elegisti et adsumpsisti inhabitabit in tabernaculis tuis (emphasis mine).[81]

> Praise is due to you in Sion, O God, and *to you vows shall be made* in Jerusalem. Hear my prayer, to you will come all flesh. The words of the wicked have prevailed over us, and you will forgive us our sins. Blessed is he whom you choose and bring close, he will dwell in your courts.

If the words 'tibi reddit uota fructu' indicate a reference to Psalm 64 ('et tibi reddetur votum in ierusalem'), logical connections can be made between the psalm and this text. It is a ritual to obtain favours from one's lord, king, or council, and this psalm describes the loyalty of God's subjects in their swearing of vows and their reward in gaining God's favour. God's chosen people are also permitted to dwell in the heavenly courts, and this would be highly applicable to a member of the king's or pope's council. Much more research needs to be undertaken about this ritual and its surrounding texts; the manuscript contains another obscure runic inscription (fols. 123v–124r), and it focuses on angelic languages and alphabets in the Pachomius legend (fols. 122v–123r) and in the *Heavenly Letter* (also fol. 140r).[82] Whatever the

---

[81] Harsley, *Eadwine's Canterbury Psalter*, pp. 106–7.
[82] For an interpretation of the runic inscription, see MacLeod and Mees, *Runic Amulets*, pp. 120–1. On the legend of Pachomius, see Chapters 4 and 5.

meaning of this obscure passage, the ritual as a whole claims to be effective in gaining favour during an audience with one's superior or at a council.[83]

The political concerns of this ritual may be reflected in the annals that were written by the same Anglo-Saxon scribe, and which contain an interesting omission for the year 1066:

> .mlxi. Her forð ferde godwine b*isceop* 7 wulfric abb*od*.
> .mlxvi. Her forð ferde eadward kyng. (7 her c*om* willelm)
> .mlxvii. Her on þison geare barn xpes (*Cristes*) cyrc*an*.
> .mlxx. On þison geare c*om* landfranc abb*od* 7 hine man halgode to bis-
> ceope to xpes (*Cristes*) cyrc*an*.

> [1061] Here Bishop Godwine and Abbot Wulfric died.
> [1066] Here King Edward died. {And here came William}
> [1067] Here in this year Christ Church was burnt.
> [1070] In this year Abbot Lanfranc came and he consecrated a man as bishop of Christ Church.[84]

The kings that are recorded by this scribe earlier in the annals include 'ægelred' (d. 1016), 'cnut' (r. 1017), 'harold' (d. 1040), 'harðacnut' (d. 1042), and 'eadweard' (r. 1043), as well as archbishops and other political figures like 'godwine eorl' (d. 1053). Following Edward the Confessor's death in 1066, the scribe records nothing about any other secular ruler (except, notably, Earl Wælþeof in 1076) and focuses exclusively on ecclesiastical authorities. The entry '7 her co(m) willehm' is added into the year 1066 by a later scribe in a distinctively Norman hand. This Norman scribe also wrote annals for the years 1085–1109 in English, and he evidently returned to complete the Anglo-Saxon scribe's previous entry.[85] What is interesting is that the Norman Conquest was overlooked until at least the year 1076, and this suggests a possible political context for the 'charm' to obtain favours that was written by the same Anglo-Saxon scribe.[86]

The final entry for 1076 that records the death of Wælþeof may reflect the political unrest during the first decade of William's reign, as Wælþeof rebelled against the Norman king, for which he was tried and executed. Lanfranc, archbishop of Canterbury and abbot of Christ Church (1070–89), was present during Wælþeof's trial, and there is a

---

[83] On the deliberate use of textual obscurity because of political concerns in earlier traditions, see Ziolkowski, 'Theories of Obscurity', pp. 138–41.

[84] Transcription and translation my own. An edited version of these annals can be found in Felix Liebermann, ed., *Ungedruckte Anglo-Normannische Geschichtsquellen: Herausgegeben* (London, 1879), pp. 1–8.

[85] All entries following the death of Anselm in 1109 are in Latin.

[86] For further examples of English scribes remaining silent about the conquests of foreign invaders, particularly in the earlier reign of Cnut, see Treharne, *Living through Conquest*, pp. 48–68, 91–121.

possibility that he knew of or owned this manuscript. Lanfranc also had political conflicts within the Church as he had to go to a papal council in Rome to solidify his primacy as archbishop of Canterbury following the archbishop of York's resistance.[87] It is plausible that a politically active (and perhaps troubled) ecclesiastic like Lanfranc would have had cause to use such potent spiritual weapons like the ritual to obtain favours in the aftermath of the Norman Conquest. This idea becomes even more seductive when one considers that this text has no surviving variant (therefore possibly a recent composition), that it was included in a manuscript which was commissioned for a high-ranking ecclesiastic residing in Canterbury, and that it was written down during the political upheavals of the 1070s.

Pontificals are liturgical books for bishops that often contain rites for the consecration of a king, and this would have been one of the most high-profile performances of an archbishop's career.[88] Cambridge, Corpus Christi College, MS 44 is a mid-eleventh-century pontifical that was produced in Canterbury sometime after 1012, as St Ælfheah appears in some litanies.[89] David Dumville places the manuscript in the middle quarters of the eleventh century according to its style of Anglo-Caroline miniscule, and Mildred Budny suggested that the manuscript was made at St Augustine's, Canterbury for either Stigand (archbishop 1052–70) or Lanfranc (archbishop 1070–89).[90] Percy Schramm thought that this particular version of the coronation rite was written for William the Conqueror on the basis of its distinctive phraseology, which he believed reflected William's own personal circumstances.[91] Neil Ker recorded the presence of some Old English glosses, which he believed are contemporary with the main text, and Helen Gittos suggests that these may indicate a production for Stigand.[92] The mid-eleventh-century dating indicates that, like Caligula A. xv (+ Egerton 3314), this particular manuscript was produced in Canterbury under high political tension around the time of the Norman Conquest.

---

[87] Janet Bately, ed., *The Anglo-Saxon Chronicle, A Collaborative Edition: Volume 3, MS A* (Cambridge, 1986), p. xxxix.

[88] For a discussion of particularly English adaptations of Continental coronation rites in the tenth century, see Hohler, 'Some Service Books', pp. 66–9.

[89] Ker, *Catalogue*, p. 46; Orchard, *Leofric Missal*, Vol. I, p. 141. See also Gneuss, *Handlist*, p. 31; Scragg, *Conspectus*, p. 4.

[90] Dumville, *Liturgy and the Ecclesiastical History*, p. 71; Mildred Budny, *Insular, Anglo-Saxon, and Early Anglo-Norman Manuscript Art at Corpus Christi College, Cambridge: An Illustrated Catalogue*, 2 Vols. (Kalamazoo, MI, 1997), Vol. I, pp. 676–9.

[91] Percy E. Schramm, *A History of the English Coronation* (Oxford, 1937), pp. 28–9. Janet Nelson disagrees with this view and believes that the rite in Corpus 44 was meant 'to generalise the suitability of the Second English Ordo', Janet Nelson, *Politics and Ritual in Early Medieval Europe* (London, 1989), p. 381.

[92] Ker, *Catalogue*, p. 46; Gittos, *Liturgy, Architecture, and Sacred Places*, p. 282.

Corpus 44's lengthy *ordo* (fols. 279–308) is the latest extant version of the second English recension of coronation rites that was likely imported from the Continent in the early tenth century.[93] George Garnett noted that eleventh-century versions of this rite stress Englishness, and he believed that these reflect the political motives of Harold Godwinson and William the Conqueror.[94] As 'the number of English allusions is considerably augmented in CCCC 44', this version seems to have been produced in a particularly sensitive environment around the time of the Conquest.[95] It opens with the king's promise to serve the bishops, Christ's Church, and all Christian people. This is followed by a responsory, a bishop's prayer over the king, an antiphon, and the archbishop's prayer of anointing which makes reference to Abraham, Moses, Joseph, David, and Solomon. These Old Testament patriarchs reflect particular qualities of leadership under God's protection: 'predicti abrahe fidelitate firmatus. moysi mansuetudine fretus. iosue fortitudine munitus. david humilitate exaltatus. atque salomonis sapientia decoratus'.[96] Following this explicit association of the king with biblical rulers in the hope that he will replicate their qualities, the archbishop's prayer then petitions for divine assistance so that the king may protect his people from all visible and invisible enemies:

> hic domine quaesumus totius regni anglo saxonum aecclesiam deinceps cum plebibus sibi commissis ita enutriat. ac doceat. muniat. et instruat. contraque omnes uisibiles et inuisibiles hostes idem potenter regaliterque tuae uirtutis regimine regat et defendat. ut in regale solium uidelicet anglorum uel saxonum tua gratia sublimatus.[97]

> We beseech you, Lord, that he may hereafter support all who reign over the Anglo-Saxon Church together with the people themselves. And may he instruct, protect, and marshal against all visible and invisible enemies, and may he mightily and royally lead and defend the same with your strength's guidance; so that on the royal throne, namely of the Angles or Saxons, he may be placed under your grace.

This emphasis on protection and guidance continues throughout the whole *ordo*, but what is of particular interest is the underlying political significance of the rite's focus on the Anglo-Saxon Church and

---

[93] See Turner, *Claudius Pontificals*, p. xxxiii; Nelson, *Politics and Ritual*, pp. 361–74.
[94] George Garnett, 'The Third Recension of the English Coronation *ordo*: The Manuscripts', *Haskins Society Journal*, 11 (1998), 43–72, p. 69.
[95] Garnett, 'Third Recension', p. 69.
[96] John W. Legg, ed., *Three Coronation Orders*, HBS, Vol. 19 (London, 1900), p. 55; 'The aforesaid Abraham with fixed loyalty, Moses with gentle confidence, Joseph with secure fortitude, David with exalted humility, and Solomon adorned with wisdom.' All translations from this text are my own.
[97] Legg, *Three Coronation Orders*, p. 55. The *Sacramentary of Ratoldus* identifies the 'albionis ecclesiam', Orchard, *Sacramentary of Ratoldus*, p. 49.

people. Explicit mention is made of the Angles and Saxons, and this is again repeated at the very end of the rite: 'Sicque tua protectione anglisaxonicum cum fac regere populum. sicut salomonem fecisti regnum obtinere pacificum. ut post cursum uite huius percipiat iugiter regna celorum. Amen'.[98] This final emphasis on the Anglo-Saxon people is not found in the earlier coronation rites of the *Sacramentary of Ratoldus* (Canterbury? c. 950, fols. 27v–29v), the *Pontifical of Egbert* (Paris, Bibliothèque Nationale, MS. Lat. 10575, possibly Worcester, s. x^{mid}–x^{ex}, fols. 130v–138v), the *Benedictional of Robert* (Winchester, s. x^{ex}, fols. 162r–170v), and the *Claudius Pontifical II* (London, British Library, MS Cotton Claudius A. iii, s. xi, fols. 9v–18v).[99] On the other hand, the later twelfth-century *ordo* in *Claudius Pontifical III* (fols. 19r–29v) from Canterbury (probably Christ Church) contains no reference to the Anglo-Saxon Church or people at all, indicating that this particular emphasis was dropped after Norman rule was firmly established.[100]

This minor detail that is found in Corpus 44 indicates an important social and historical context for the *ordo* in mid-eleventh-century Canterbury. Assuming that a similar (if not the same) *ordo* was used in coronations around this time, this added emphasis on the king's obligation to guide and protect the Anglo-Saxon Church and people carries political significance. If the subject of this coronation was Edward the Confessor (r. 1042–66), who was raised in exile in Normandy, faced local opposition from Earl Godwin, and appointed many Normans to court, his loyalty to the English populace would have been stressed. Edward was succeeded by his brother-in-law Harold Godwinson, who was not of royal blood, and this emphasis would have also served to remind Harold of his duties to the Church as well as to the people. If the king was William the Conqueror (r. 1066–87), he would have been left in no doubt about his spiritual as well as political obligations to his new subjects. Archbishop Stigand, who may have owned Corpus 44, was present at the consecrations of both Harold and William. Finally, if the rite was conducted by Lanfranc in the coronation of William Rufus in 1087, there are implications about the continued identities of the Anglo-Saxon people and Church under Norman occupation.[101] The

---

[98] Legg, *Three Coronation Orders*, p. 61; 'And thus with your protection establish rule of the Anglo-Saxon people, just as you made Solomon sustain peaceful kingship. So that, after the course of this life, the kingdoms of the heavens may be continuously gained. Amen.'

[99] The blessings read 'Da ei a tuo spiramine (cum mansuetudine ita) regere populum, sicut salomonem fecisti regnum obtinere (/optinere) pacificum'; Orchard, *Sacramentary of Ratoldus*, p. 55; Banting, *Two Anglo-Saxon Pontificals*, p. 110; Wilson, *Benedictional of Archbishop Robert*, pp. 146–7; Turner, *Claudius Pontificals*, p. 94. See also Gittos, *Liturgy, Architecture, and Sacred Places*, pp. 43–4, 280–1.

[100] See Turner, *Claudius Pontificals*, pp. vi, 115–22; Gneuss, *Handlist*, p. 62.

[101] See especially Nelson, *Politics and Ritual*, pp. 380–3; Garnett, 'Third Recension', p. 69.

politically sensitive details of this coronation *ordo* from mid-eleventh-century Canterbury quite possibly reflect the same preoccupations of the so-called 'charm' for political favours in Caligula A. xv (+ Egerton 3314). The 'charm' contains Latin invocations and what appears to be 'encrypted references to psalms', and more liturgical formulas or passages may be concealed in its obscure, possibly anagrammatic writing. Rather than dismissing such a text as corrupted to the point of being nonsensical, we could be better informed about its possible meanings and uses when it is compared with contemporary liturgical rites.

Other related blessings for councils over which the king usually presided may also reflect contemporary political concerns. The *Canterbury Benedictional* (London, British Library, MS Harley 2892) contains one of these blessings. This manuscript was written after 1023, according to a blessing for the feast of St Ælfheah's translation, and possibly as late as 1052 on the basis of its style of Anglo-Caroline miniscule, making it contemporary with Corpus 44.[102] The *Benedictional*'s blessing petitions God to grant charity to the members of the council, to deliver them from their sins, and to make them faithful until the Second Coming:

> Christus dei filius qui est initium et finis. complementum uobis tribuat caritatis. *Amen.*
> Et qui nos ad expletionem huius fecit peruenire concilii. absolutos uos efficiat ab omni contagion[e] delicti. *Amen.*
> Ab omni reatu liberiores effecti. absoluti etiam per donum spiritus sancti. felici redditu uestrarum sedium cubilia repetatis illesi. *Amen.*
> Semper proficiat cura uestra. ut quando iudex uenerit. euigilet fides uestra. uigilantie premium de domino receptura. *Amen.*[103]

> May Christ, the Son of God who is the beginning and end, grant you the fullness of charity. Amen.
> And may he who brought us to completion of this council absolve you from every taint of sin. Amen.
> May you be made free from all guilt and also absolved through the gift of the Holy Spirit, may you regain your rest by the happy return to your thrones. Amen.
> May your care be always productive so that, when the Judge will come, your faith may remain active, ready to receive the reward of vigilance from the Lord. Amen.

This blessing is also found in earlier liturgical books that would have had different political contexts surrounding their production.[104] In

---

[102] Dumville, *Liturgy and the Ecclesiastical History*, pp. 79–80; Alicia Corrêa, ed., *The Durham Collectar*, HBS, Vol. 107 (London, 1997), pp. 108–9; Gittos, *Liturgy, Architecture, and Sacred Places*, pp. 281–2.
[103] Woolley, *Canterbury Benedictional*, p. 124.
[104] See Wilson, *Benedictional of Archbishop Robert*, p. 153; Banting, *Two Anglo-Saxon Pontificals*, pp. 106–7.

the context of the *Canterbury Benedictional* in mid-eleventh-century Canterbury, the blessing's focus on the members' absolution from sin and removal of guilt may be interpreted as a reminder of their loyalty to the king, whom they may not have previously supported in his claim to the throne. The blessing reinforces the need for unity among the king's council and for reconciliation of hostilities between its members. Elaine Treharne has highlighted that this emphasis on unity and the king's obligation to the Church is found in earlier prayers that were written by Wulfstan following Cnut's coronation.[105] The subtle phraseology of liturgical rites and blessings may have carried significant political weight during the succession claims of the mid-eleventh century.

The coronation rite of Corpus 44 and the liturgical blessing of councils in the *Canterbury Benedictional* were written in Canterbury during a period of rising political tension. The preoccupations of the so-called 'charm' in Caligula A. xv (+ Egerton 3314) are very likely a reflection of the climactic outcome of earlier political upheavals. The coronation *ordo* declares the king's sovereignty over the native populace and reminds him of his duties to the Church and people, and the blessing for the king's council subtly imposes an obligation to the king on the members of the council. The ritual to obtain favours from one's lord or king or council uses obscure words of power to influence political circumstances and figures, in much the same way as other liturgical texts that compel high-ranking authorities to maintain political stability. Given the origins of these three manuscripts in mid- to late eleventh-century Canterbury and the political environments in which they were likely to have been produced, it is more beneficial to read the 'charm' for political favours alongside contemporary liturgical texts than it is to distinguish it from other ritual practices.

Travellers (Pro iter agentibus)

There are many liturgical blessings and votive Masses associated with travelling, and it is also given special attention in the *Rule of Benedict*.[106] The most obvious example of an Old English ritual for travel is the marginal 'Journey Charm' of Corpus 41 (added s. xi$^{1/4}$, SW Eng, possibly Glastonbury). As discussed in Chapter 2, this ritual begins

---

[105] Treharne, *Living through Conquest*, pp. 54–68.
[106] Orchard, *Leofric Missal*, Vol. II, pp. 24, 41–3, 335–6; *Sacramentary of Ratoldus*, pp. 399–400; Woolley, *Canterbury Benedictional*, p. 126; Wilson, *Missal of Robert*, p. 260; *Benedictional of Archbishop Robert*, p. 55; Banting, *Two Anglo-Saxon Pontificals*, pp. 105–6; Doble, *Pontificale Lanaletense*, p. 109; Turner, *Claudius Pontificals*, p. 27. For travel in Chapters 50 and 67 of the *Rule of Benedict*, see Logeman, *Rule of S. Benet*, pp. 86, 113.

with the performer drawing a protective circle with a victory-rod ('sigegyrd') and reciting a victory-*galdor* ('syge gealdor'). This ritual utterance invokes a number of biblical figures to protect the traveller, including angels ('þusend þira engla', 'soðfæstra engla', 'eall engla blæd'), Old Testament figures ('abrame 7 isace', 'moyses 7 iacob 7 dauit 7 iosep', 'euan', 'saharie'), and New Testament saints ('annan 7 elizabet', 'marie', 'petrus 7 paulus', the four evangelists).[107] This 'charm' has been interpreted as an allegory of life's journey as well as a practical spiritual defence.[108] Its literal meaning reinforces the power of Christianity against all hostile forces, and its eschatological meaning serves to edify its audience about their spiritual journey through life. The ritual was written in the margins beside a passage describing St Cuthbert preparing for his pastoral journey as bishop in the Old English version of Bede's *Historia Ecclesiastica* (see Chapter 2). It seems plausible that the 'Journey Charm' provided a nervous ecclesiastic with an excellent spiritual defence before setting out on his (assumedly dangerous) pastoral mission.

The physical and spiritual dangers that the traveller faces in the journey ritual are reflected in liturgies for those on a journey.[109] For example, when the *Leofric Missal* was at Exeter in the mid-eleventh century (*Leofric C*), a lengthy Mass for travellers was added (fols. 28v–30v).[110] It is likely that the *Leofric Missal* was brought to Exeter with Corpus 41 by Leofric (bishop of Exeter 1050–72), as both manuscripts contain an *ex-dono* inscription.[111] The first reading of this Mass for travellers (fols. 28v–29r) is taken from Genesis 24: 7, which describes Abraham's request to his servant to find a wife for his son Isaac from his own people:

> LECTIO LIBRI GENESIS. *IN DIEBVS ILLIS*. Locutus est dominus ad Abraham dicens. Dominus deus cęli qui tulit me de domo patris mei, e terra natiuitatis meę. Qui locutus est mihi, et iurauit dicens. Semini tuo dabo terram hanc, ipse mittet angelum suum coram te.[112]

> Reading from the book of Genesis. In those days; the Lord spoke to Abraham saying: 'The Lord God of heaven, who took me from my

---

[107] Transcriptions from Jolly, 'Margins of Orthodoxy', p. 171. For a discussion of the potential dangers faced by the traveller, see Wilfrid Bonser, 'Anglo-Saxon Laws Relating to Theft', *Folklore*, 57 (1946), 7–11; Hill, 'Rod of Protection', pp. 145–68.

[108] Rupp, 'The Anxiety of Writing', p. 255. See also Stuart, 'Old English "Journey Charm"', pp. 268–9.

[109] See also Hill, 'Rod of Protection', p. 155.

[110] See Orchard, *Leofric Missal*, Vol. I, pp. 206–34; Scragg, *Conspectus*, pp. 69–70. Another Mass blessing for travellers (fol. 16r) was added when the manuscript was in Canterbury (*Leofric B*), see Orchard, *Leofric Missal*, Vol. II, p. 24.

[111] Lapidge, *Anglo-Saxon Library*, p. 56.

[112] Orchard, *Leofric Missal*, Vol. II, p. 41.

father's house, from the land of my birth, who spoke to me, and swore (to me) saying: "To your seed I will give this land"; He will send His angel into your presence.'

The chapter from Genesis is suitable for travellers, as it describes an angel's protection of Abraham as he enters his new land. Abraham and Isaac are also invoked in Corpus 41's journey ritual, and the traveller calls upon the angels for protection: 'abrame 7 isace 7 swilce men… 7 eac þusend þira engla clipige to are wið eallum feondum'.[113] The Gradual and Preface of the Mass also reiterate the traveller's protection by angelic hosts:

> GRADVALE. Angelis suis deus mandauit de te ut custodian[t] te in omnibus uiis tuis…
> PREFATIO […] Quatinus angelorum tuorum presidio fultus et inter-cession[e] sanctorum munitus, a cunctis aduersitatibus tua miseratione defensus.[114]

> Gradual. The Lord has commanded his angels concerning you, to guard you in all your ways…
> Preface. […] In so far as [he] is helped by the guidance of your angels, and protected by the intercession of the saints, he is defended from all adversities by your mercy.

This prayer for protection against danger resonates strongly with the petition for protection against all evils in the journey ritual of Corpus 41 ('simbli gehaleþe wið eallum feondum'; 'wið þa laþan se me lyfes eht').[115]

The gospel reading of this votive Mass in *Leofric C* (fol. 29r) is Matthew 10: 7–15, which describes Jesus sending his disciples out to preach, forbidding them to take anything with them and instructing them to bless any house in which they are made welcome.[116] Thomas Hill has noted strong comparisons between this specific gospel passage and the journey ritual of Corpus 41.[117] Although the Corpus ritual was added into the margins and it predates the additional texts of *Leofric C*, it may be the case that scribes in Exeter – where the votive Mass for

---

[113] 'Abraham and Isaac and such men… and also a thousand of the angels, I call to my help against all foes', Jolly, 'Margins of Orthodoxy', p. 171.

[114] Orchard, *Leofric Missal*, Vol. II, pp. 42, 43.

[115] 'ever secure against all foes'; 'protected from the evil one who seeks my life', Jolly, 'Margins of Orthodoxy', pp. 171–2. On the importance of angels in other marginal texts in Corpus 41, see Richard F. Johnson, 'Archangel in the Margins: St. Michael in the Homilies of Cambridge, Corpus Christi College 41', *Traditio*, 53 (1998), 63–91. Blessings for travellers in the *Egbert Pontifical* refer to the Book of Tobit, which also involves angelic assistance, see Banting, *Two Anglo-Saxon Pontificals*, pp. 133–4.

[116] Orchard, *Leofric Missal*, Vol. II, p. 42.

[117] Hill, 'Rod of Protection', pp. 150–3.

travellers was written – were aware of the close connections between this gospel narrative and rituals for travel. It may even be the case that the scribes of *Leofric C* knew of the journey ritual (or other versions of it) after Corpus 41 was brought to Exeter.

Other correspondences can be found between the so-called 'charm' and the readings from the votive Mass. For example, the Corpus ritual concludes with a desire for peace in foreign lands under the protection of God and the angels. This echoes the first reading of the Mass that narrates God's promise to Abraham of angelic protection on his journey to new lands, and the gospel passage that tells of Jesus' instruction to bless the houses in which the disciples are made welcome:

> bidde ic nu {sigere godes miltse} god siðfæt godne smylte 7 lihte wind wereþum… gehaleþe wið eallum feondum freond ic gemete wid þæt ic on þis ælmihgian on his frið wunian mote belocun wið þa laþan se me lyfes eht on engla bla blaed gestaþelod 7 inna halre hand hofna rices blæd þa hwile þe ic on þis life wunian mote amen.

> I pray for good favour from the God of victory, for a good voyage, a calm and light wind to the shores… Ever secure against all foes, I meet with friends, that I may live in the peace of the Almighty, protected from the evil one who seeks my life, established in the glory of the angels, and in the holy hand, the glory of the kingdom of heaven, as long as I may live in this life. Amen.[118]

There are many connections between liturgical blessings and this ritual for travellers, and they draw upon common biblical motifs. Further comparisons can be made with other 'charms' that are related to travel, such as those against stitches and sprains that may occur whilst travelling, and amuletic rituals that protect those moving between locations.[119] All of these texts served the dual purpose of securing immediate protection for a literal journey and placing the traveller in the context of salvation history. The biblical motifs and invocations of the 'Journey Charm' are also found in liturgies for travellers, and the close connections between these texts indicate that the ritual in Corpus 41 was perceived as a liturgical prayer for those on a journey. Indeed, the scribes of *Leofric C* may not have viewed texts like the ritual from Corpus 41 as anything other than a liturgical text.

Observations

These common themes and scriptural references demonstrate that so-called 'charms' and liturgical texts were written to respond to similar

---

[118] Jolly, 'Margins of Orthodoxy', pp. 171–2.
[119] See Storms, *Anglo-Saxon Magic*, pp. 248–51, 284, 286.

remedial, spiritual, conjugal, political, and socio-cultural concerns. A large number of healing 'charms' use formulas and objects from liturgical *ordines* for visiting the sick, and some offer liturgical devotions for lay people in times of emergency. These rituals also frequently draw upon liturgical rites of exorcism to respond to spiritual sickness. Other rituals for childbirth use similar biblical motifs to nuptial blessings, and provide a pregnant mother with ritual practices in different locations including the marriage bed and at a church altar. One 'charm' that attempts to win the favour of political authorities was written in Canterbury in the aftermath of the Norman Conquest, and contemporary coronation rites and liturgical blessings reflect similar political tensions. Finally, a lengthy votive Mass for travellers was written when the so-called 'Journey Charm' was in Exeter in the mid-eleventh century, and both texts use the same biblical references to protect those on a journey. The significant overlaps in the rituals' content indicate that 'charms' offered liturgical responses to particular needs within ecclesiastical and lay environments. Cross-comparisons of these texts show that it is difficult to maintain distinctions between 'charms' and liturgical texts: they appear in similar manuscripts, they draw upon the same ideas, and they sometimes use the same sacred objects and liturgical formulas. Indeed, there is no evidence to suggest that Anglo-Saxon scribes distinguished between what we traditionally call 'liturgy' and 'charms'.

Conclusions

In addition to these overlaps in theme and content, manuscripts containing 'charms' provide further evidence that these texts were perceived as components of the liturgy. Some of these rituals were written in manuscripts that were possibly used as study books in a monastery, indicating that they were useful for monastic training (e.g. London, BL, MSS Cotton Faustina A. x, added s. xii[1], unknown origin; Cotton Tiberius A. iii, s. xi[med], Christ Church, Canterbury).[120] Others appear alongside homilies, saints' lives, Patristic writings, biblical commentaries, and calculations of liturgical feasts, suggesting that they often complemented hagiography, biblical exegesis, and computus (e.g. Cambridge, Corpus Christi College, MS 367, added s. xii[2], Worcester; London, BL, MS Royal 4 A. xiv, added s. xii, Worcester; Oxford, St John's College, MS 17, c. 1110, Thorney Abbey).[121] Some

---

[120] For details of Faustina A. x, see Chapter 5. For details of Tiberius A. iii, see note 4.

[121] For details of Corpus 367, see Ker, *Catalogue*, p. 110; Gneuss, *Handlist*, p. 37; Jolly, 'Tapping the Power of the Cross', p. 77; Scragg, *Conspectus*, p. 15. For details of Royal 4 A. xiv, see note 4. For details of St John's College 17, see Chapter 4.

'charms' were probably used for private devotional practices in a convent (e.g. London, BL, MS Royal 2 A. xx, 818 × 830, Worcester, with additional s. xii 'charms'), and at least one other manuscript also indicates that some scribes of these rituals were inspired by texts that expounded the gospels (e.g. London, BL, MS Cotton Caligula A. vii, s. xi[1], Winchester?).[122]

The thematic overlaps considered in this chapter show how it is better to consider 'charms' as liturgical texts that are part of an innovative, experimental, and diverse ecclesiastical culture in the tenth and eleventh centuries. Some rituals appear to be devotional, like the *Heavenly Letter* that is to be sung every night before bed, and some indicate solo performance, like the childbirth rituals. However, many have very strong correspondences with formal liturgical rites that would have been more public in performance, such as visiting the sick, exorcism, or rogationtide processions (see Chapter 4). Rituals that have been classified as 'charms' are, in essence, liturgical texts for public or private performances. Some were to be performed by ecclesiastics and have such close overlap with mainstream liturgies that it is unhelpful to draw categorical distinctions between them. Others were written for lay people and provided them with 'para-liturgical' devotions and ritual responses to some very individual concerns. Whether formal liturgies or para-liturgical practices, public or private, these texts have little to do with modern understandings of a 'charm' and its connotations of magic and paganism, or at best heterodox Christianity.

To return briefly to the quotation by Charles Singer at the beginning of this chapter, these rituals are saturated with liturgy; and to use another idiom, it is better to give up the ghost and refer to these texts as liturgical. Reading the rituals as components of new and experimental liturgies allows us to overcome and dismantle the restrictive category of 'charms' with all of its associated terminology that disregards their rich liturgical nature. Even the most enigmatic references that are found in these texts can be better understood by considering their liturgical sources that are often found in the rituals' surrounding materials. It is therefore of paramount importance to now resituate these rituals in their manuscript contexts, which reflect the ecclesiastical environments in which they were produced.

---

[122] For details of Royal 2 A. xx, see Ker, *Catalogue*, pp. 317–18; Jennifer Morrish, 'Dated and Datable Manuscripts Copied in England During the Ninth Century: A Preliminary List' *Mediaeval Studies*, 50 (1988), 512–38; Sims-Williams, *Religion and Literature*, pp. 273–327; Doane, *Books of Prayers and Healing*, pp. 52–9; Gneuss, *Handlist*, p. 79; Michelle P. Brown, 'Female Book Ownership and Production in Anglo-Saxon England: The Evidence of the Ninth-Century Prayerbooks', in *Lexis and Texts in Early English: Studies Presented to Jane Roberts*, C. J. Kay and L. M. Sylvester, eds (Amsterdam, 2001), pp. 45–63; Jolly, 'Tapping the Power of the Cross', p. 76. For details of Caligula A. vii, see Chapter 2.

4

Crops and Robbers:
A Case Study of the *Vitellius Psalter*

'they were concerned with transmitting and concealing the sacred, the wisdom inaccessible to those unable to decode it... [and] secrets open only to those who are able to discover and then apply their codes, in order to disclose their mysteries'.[1]

Having demonstrated that it is more beneficial to consider 'charms' as part of diverse, mainstream ecclesiastical traditions, it is now important to consider how these rituals appear in their manuscripts. Editors of the 'charms' extracted texts from a large number of manuscripts for their editions. The rituals have therefore been isolated from their manuscript contexts, and their many connections with surrounding texts in the manuscripts have been overlooked. Reading these rituals alongside other texts in their manuscripts uncovers intertextual relationships that exist between diverse materials. This approach challenges modern distinctions between textual genres because it exposes (sometimes surprising or obscure) connections between different types of texts that were made by medieval scribes and compilers. In order to understand how Anglo-Saxon scribes viewed these rituals, it is necessary to resituate the 'charms' in their respective manuscript contexts.

Some scholars have already conducted case studies of these rituals in their surrounding manuscript contexts. Stephanie Hollis analysed four manuscripts containing different versions of three cattle-theft 'charms' (in Cambridge, Corpus Christi College, MSS 41, 383; London, British Library, MS Cotton Tiberius A. iii; and Rochester, Cathedral Library, MS A.3.5).[2] Lea Olsan has provided an overview of how some 'charms' are copied in manuscripts, and suggested that they were first recorded as marginalia before they were included in the main body of the manuscript page.[3] Rebecca Fisher has also investigated some 'charms' in the *Royal Prayerbook* (London, BL, Royal 2 A. xx), and argued that they are closely related to surrounding devotional materials for a

---

[1] Rafal Boryslawski, 'The Elements of Anglo-Saxon Wisdom Poetry in the *Exeter Book* Riddles', *Studia Anglica Posnaniensia*, 38 (2002), 35–47, pp. 36, 38.
[2] Stephanie Hollis, 'Old English "Cattle-Theft Charms": Manuscript Contexts and Social Uses', *Anglia*, 115 (1997), 139–64.
[3] Olsan, 'Inscription of Charms'; 'Marginality of Charms'.

female religious community in the early ninth century.[4] Other studies of *Bald's Leechbook*, Harley 585, and Corpus 41 have highlighted correspondences between 'charms' and their surrounding texts.[5] However, all of these studies maintain that 'charms' form a distinct genre that was differentiated from other ritual practices by Anglo-Saxon scribes. Some scholars have challenged such distinctions in individual case studies of manuscripts. In her study of Corpus 41, Karen Jolly argues that all of its marginal texts were perceived to belong to the same genre by the single scribe.[6] Roy Liuzza also produced a very good study of the relationships between 'charms' and devotional prayers to the cross in Cotton Tiberius A. iii and related manuscripts, and he highlighted the porosity between these religious texts.[7] Such approaches need to be extended to the many other manuscripts that have been plundered for editions of 'charms' because they focus on how Anglo-Saxon scribes understood these rituals instead of how 'charms' should be classified by modern editors.[8] When 'charms' are analysed in their manuscript contexts, it becomes difficult to uphold distinctions between these and other liturgical or para-liturgical texts.

As emphasised in previous chapters, texts that appear in the main writing space of a manuscript often best reflect how a scribe or compiler perceived them as part of the collection as a whole. Discussing the full range of contents in a manuscript that was written by multiple scribes poses risks, as some contain later additions and quires were often rearranged over time. This calls into question whether later scribes paid close attention (if any) to the original materials within the manuscript or booklet at the time of writing. The journey ritual in Corpus 41 offers an interesting example of how a later scribe did indeed pay attention to the main text of the manuscript, choosing to deliberately record this text beside descriptions of St Cuthbert's pastoral journeys in Bede's *Historia Ecclesiastica*. However, to avoid such complications for the sake of this study, I will consider one manuscript that contains

---

[4] Fisher, 'Texts in Context'.

[5] See Linda Voigts, 'Anglo-Saxon Plant Remedies and the Anglo Saxons', *Isis*, 70 (1979), 250–69; Grant, *Loricas and the Missal*; Meaney, 'Compilation of Bald's *Leechbook*'; Malcolm L. Cameron, 'Bald's *Leechbook*'; 'Anglo-Saxon Medicine and Magic', *ASE*, 17 (1988), 191–215; 'Cultural Interactions'; Keefer, 'Margins as Archive'; Nokes, 'Compilers of *Bald's Leechbook*'; Bredehoft, 'Filling the Margins of CCCC 41', pp. 721–32.

[6] Jolly, 'Margins of Orthodoxy', p. 144.

[7] Liuzza, 'Prayers and/or Charms'.

[8] See also Phillip Pulsiano, 'The Prefatory Matter of London, British Library, Cotton Vitellius E. xviii', in *Manuscripts and Their Heritage*, Pulsiano and Treharne, eds, pp. 85–116, p. 104; Graham Caie, 'Codicological Clues: Reading Old English Christian Poetry in its Manuscript Context', in *The Christian Tradition in Anglo-Saxon England: Approaches to Current Scholarship and Teaching*, Paul Cavill, ed. (Cambridge, 2004), pp. 3–14.

a collection of liturgical materials including 'charms' and that was written by a single scribe in mid-eleventh-century Winchester.

This chapter takes a case study of the *Vitellius Psalter* (London, British Library, MS Cotton Vitellius E. xviii) that has been used in editions of 'charms', and it reconsiders its rituals in their wider manuscript context. One scribe wrote all of the psalter's prefatory texts and Old English glosses to the psalms, and the close connections that exist between these texts demonstrate that this scribe did not distinguish between 'charms' and liturgy. The rituals in the prefatory matter of this manuscript form an important component to a holistic collection of materials concerned with the cosmos, liturgy, hidden divine knowledge, and textual obscurity.

The Vitellius Psalter

The *Vitellius Psalter* is a glossed Gallican psalter with a prefatory collection of computistical texts, prognostications, agricultural rituals, and exercises in secret writing. Several of its agricultural rituals have been extracted from its manuscript context and categorised as 'charms', despite the fact that the psalm glosses and all of the prefatory texts are written in one scribal hand. The manuscript was written between 1060 and 1087 according to a cross marking that is found in an Easter table (fol. 13v), which was likely to have been made by the original scribe.[9] Phillip Pulsiano suggested a more accurate dating of 1062 on the basis of another marker that 'appears to be original' in the same column of the Easter table.[10] In the final text of the prefatory collection, the name 'Ælfwine' is concealed in an exercise in encryption, indicating that the manuscript was copied in the New Minster, Winchester from an exemplar dating to Ælfwine's abbacy in this monastery between 1031/2 and 1057.[11] There are also strong connections between the *Vitellius Psalter* and Ælfwine's personal *Prayerbook* (London, BL, MSS Cotton Titus D. xxvi/ii) that was written while he was still dean at the New Minster, Winchester (1023 × 1031), providing further evi-

---

[9] Karl Wildhagen, *Das Kalendarium der Handschrift Vitellius E XVIII (Brit. Mus.): Ein Beitrag zur Chronologie und Hagiologie Altenglands* (Halle, 1921), pp. 117–18.

[10] Pulsiano, 'Prefatory Matter', pp. 102–3. For other descriptions of this manuscript, see Ker, *Catalogue*, pp. 298–301; Pusliano, *Psalters I*, pp. 50–6; Gneuss, *Handlist*, p. 73; Jolly, 'Tapping the Power of the Cross', pp. 63, 77; Chardonnens, *Anglo-Saxon Prognostics*, pp. 37–8; Liuzza, *Anglo-Saxon Prognostics*, pp. 14–15; Gneuss and Lapidge, *Bibliographical Handlist*, pp. 334–5.

[11] See Phillip Pulsiano, 'Abbot Ælfwine and the Date of the Vitellius Psalter', *ANQ*, 11 (1998), 3–12; Catherine E. Karkov, 'Abbot Ælfwine and the Sign of the Cross', in *Cross and Cruciform in the Anglo-Saxon World*, Keefer, Jolly, and Karkov, eds, pp. 103–32, pp. 103–4.

dence that the psalter's prefatory texts originated in Ælfwine's New Minster.[12]

As the *Vitellius Psalter* was written in the second half of the eleventh century, it is possible that the materials of the prefatory collection were added at this time to an original exemplar which contained the Latin psalter and Old English gloss. This possibility would suggest that the psalter and gloss can be associated with Ælfwine's school and that the additional prefatory texts were not originally integral to the manuscript's exemplar. However, the final text that contains a cryptogram of Ælfwine's name indicates that at least some, if not all, of these additional materials were also composed during Ælfwine's abbacy. The Vitellius scribe may have copied an already complete collection of computus, prognostics, rituals, and ciphers, or he or she may have gathered and copied different materials from Ælfwine's school that were perceived to be useful for a glossed psalter. It is clear that at least one Anglo-Saxon ecclesiastic saw important connections between the 'charm' rituals, the other prefatory texts, and the manuscript as a whole. A more daring claim would be that the close intertextual links between these materials and the attribution of one text to Ælfwine's authorship together indicate that other texts in this collection were also composed by Ælfwine. It is impossible to say with confidence that the psalter's so-called 'charms' were originally written by this abbot, but their thematic overlap with surrounding diagrams, astronomical calculations, and encryptions make it tempting to speculate on Ælfwine's involvement in their compilation or composition.

The Scope of the Prefatory Collection

The *Vitellius Psalter* was badly damaged in the Cottonian fire of 1731 and its opening two folios are now lost.[13] The prefatory collection is found on folios 2r–16v, and it is primarily concerned with the divine ordering of the cosmos and the Easter season. Computistical calculations of Easter dominate the first eleven folios of the collection; this information is then used in predictions of lunar movements and favourable times of the year for environmental and medical issues.

---

[12] Ælfwine's name is also found in a private prayer and a miniature of the crucifixion in his *Prayerbook*, see Beate Günzel, ed., *Ælfwine's Prayerbook: London, British Library, Cotton Titus D. xxvi + xxvii*, HBS, Vol. 108 (London, 1993), p. 187; Karkov, 'Abbot Ælfwine', p. 128. The *Prayerbook* was divided into two manuscripts by Sir Robert Cotton.

[13] From the mid-nineteenth century the foliation was rearranged a number of times until it was rebound in 1954 with what is now believed to be its correct foliation; see Ker, *Catalogue*, p. 299; Pulsiano, *Psalters I*, p. 50; 'Prefatory Matter', pp. 106–7, 116.

The series of rituals extends these prognostications and offers a range of spiritual responses to some of the predicted concerns. Finally, an encrypted riddle and an exercise for secret writing conclude the collection. These prefatory texts share many features and serve similar purposes, and the overlap in their thematic content demonstrates a coherent and cohesive investigation into cosmological signs, symbology, astronomy, and liturgy. Computistical calculations are common in medieval psalters, and they were fundamental for the ordering of the liturgical year and monastic life. As well as providing practical guides and points of reference, these numerical calculations indicate the spiritual environment in which they were used, where intellectual investigations are united with liturgical feasts, celebrations, and times for ritual performance.[14]

Prognostications follow these computistical calculations and they predict the most opportune times in the year for blood-letting and childbirth.[15] One particular prognostic for childbirth in the psalter is a translation of a Latin text found in *Ælfwine's Prayerbook*, but it makes a significant addition:

> [Titus D. xxvi, fols. 4rv]
> Tres dies sunt in anno cum totidem noctibus, ut fertur, in quibus mulier numquam nascitur, et uir qui natus fuerit in ipsis numquam corpus illius putredine soluetur usque ad diem iudicii, id est nouissimus de thebet et duo primi de sabath.[16]

> [Vitellius E. xviii, fol. 15r]
> [Þ]ry dagas syndon on twelf monðum mid þrim ni[ht]um o[n þam ne bið] nan wif accened ac swa hwilc wæpman swa on ðam dagum ace[ned bið ne] forealdað his lichama næfre on eorðan ær domes dæge, þæt is an [ðæra] daga on æfteweardan decembre 7 tweigen on foreweardan ia[nuarii]; *feawma manna syndon þe þas dagas cunnon.* (Emphasis mine)[17]

The psalter's prognostication presents knowledge of the cosmos as a rare secret that is known to only few learned men. This element

---

[14] See Jolly, 'Tapping the Power of the Cross', p. 63.

[15] On the impact of the lunar movements on blood and birth, see Tory Vandeventer Pearman, *Women and Disability in Medieval Literature* (New York, 2010), esp. pp. 108–9; Sophie Page, *Astrology in Medieval Manuscripts* (Toronto, 2002), pp. 54–60.

[16] Günzel, *Ælfwine's Prayerbook*, p. 145; 'There are three days in the year with the same number of nights, that is held, in which no woman is born, and the man who is born in them will never decay in body until the Day of Judgement, that is the last of Tebet (Hebrew month of approximately December) and the first two of Sabat (Hebrew month of approximately January).' Translation my own.

[17] Pulsiano, 'Prefatory Matter', p. 101; 'There are three days in twelve months with three nights on which no woman is born but the man who is born in these days, his body will never grow old on the earth before Judgement Day, that is one of the days following December and two before January; *there are few men who know of these days.*' Translation my own.

of secret knowledge resonates strongly with the ensuing enigmatic rituals and encrypted texts in the prefatory collection.[18]

The six ritual texts that follow the prognostics on folios 15v–16r offer a range of spiritual responses to agricultural concerns. A number of these rituals have been categorised as 'charms', although editors and commentators differ in opinion about which rituals belong to this genre.[19] Two of them have been consistently labelled as 'charms' because they employ obscure diagrams and 'gibberish' writing, but Jolly has noted that all of the rituals relate to the preceding computus and prognostics through their references to particular times of the year.[20] Indeed, two prognosticatory diagrams bookend this series of rituals, and two exercises in secret writing conclude the collection on folio 16v. The diagrams and ciphered texts perhaps provide clues about how these obscure rituals were understood as encrypted spiritual responses to specific agricultural concerns. The prefatory material of the *Vitellius Psalter* is a coherent collection of texts that seek to decode the signs of the cosmos, predict astronomical movements and effects, overcome agricultural problems, and re-conceal knowledge in secret writing.

The Rituals in Context

The order of the manuscript is as follows (* denotes texts that have been classified as 'charms'):

Fols. 2r–13r – calendar; feast limits; Easter tables; calculations for Septuagesima, Lent, and Easter.

Fols. 13r–15r – prognostications for blood-letting and childbirth; first Apuleian Sphere.

Fol. 15v – ritual instructions for protecting bees*; *Columcille's Circle*; theft diagram*; ritual for sick cattle and sheep*.

Fols. 15v–16r – livestock ritual*.

---

[18] This emphasis on secrecy is also found in versions of this prognostic in the *Red Book of Darley* (Corpus 422, fol. 49, c. 1061) and Caligula A. xv (+ Egerton 3314) (fol. 131r, c. 1073), which are contemporary with the *Vitellius Psalter* (c. 1062), see Chardonnens, *Anglo-Saxon Prognostics*, pp. 6, 232–3. There are further close textual correspondences between prognostications found in manuscripts from the New Minster, Winchester and Christ Church, Canterbury (including Tiberius A. iii, xi[med]), see Liuzza, *Anglo-Saxon Prognostics*, pp. 3–25.

[19] Cockayne printed eight texts from this manuscript, Grendon edited two, and Storms edited three; Cockayne, *Leechdoms*, Vol. I, pp. 386–9, Vol. III, pp. 290–1; Grendon, 'Anglo-Saxon Charms', pp. 204–7; Storms, *Anglo-Saxon Magic*, pp. 287, 309–11. For different classifications by commentators, see Ker, *Catalogue*, p. 300; Pulsiano, 'Prefatory Matter', pp. 89–90; Jolly, 'Tapping the Power of the Cross', pp. 66–7; Liuzza, *Anglo-Saxon Prognostics*, p. 14; Banham, 'Staff of Life', p. 314.

[20] Jolly, 'Tapping the Power of the Cross', pp. 66–7.

Fol. 16r – barn ritual*; second Apuleian Sphere.
Fol. 16v – encrypted riddle; exercise in secret writing.
Fols. 18r–131r – Gallican version of the psalms with continuous Old
   English gloss.
Fols. 131v–146v – canticles; prayers; litany; lections.[21]

In order to understand the intimate connections between the so-called
'charms' and their surrounding materials, it is important to analyse
each ritual on folios 15v–16r in order of appearance. I include discussions of the final texts of the collection because these are closely related
to the agricultural rituals. As there has been very little commentary
on this manuscript, the following analyses do not provide definitive
solutions to the obscure, and often fragmentary, rituals that it contains.
However, they do offer a number of alternative interpretations of these
texts according to their wider manuscript context.

Protection of bees

The first legible entry on folio 15v has lost its opening lines due to fire
damage but it is clear that it is a ritual for protecting bees against theft.
The fragmentary text reads: '[s?]e mæder cið on þinre hyfe þonne ne
aspond̄ nan man þine beon ne hi ma[n] ne mæg forstelan þa hwile þe
se cið on þære hyfe bið'.[22] These instructions appear on lines 6–8 of
the main writing space, and it is impossible to tell whether this was
the first text of the folio (see fig. 1). The fragmentary instructions make
it clear that a madder shoot ('mæder cið') should be placed inside the
beehive to prevent the bees from being stolen. The madder plant has
small, yellowish-white flowers that grow in clusters with red stalks;
perhaps the idea was that placing a plant with attractive flowers inside
the hive would minimise the need for the bees to travel far to find
other pollinating plants.

   The movement of bees from one property to another was a socio-
economic concern in Anglo-Saxon England, as Lori Ann Garner and
Kayla Miller have discussed in the context of a bee-ritual against a
swarm from Corpus 41. They argue that ritual practices for calming
a swarm would have been legally binding as the original owner
publically laid claim to the bees.[23] Placing a madder plant inside the
beehive could have been another preventative measure against the

---

[21] For a more detailed manuscript description, see Pulsiano, *Psalters I*, pp. 51–5.

[22] '(When the?) madder shoot (is) in your hive, thereafter no man would be lured
to your bees, nor is he able to steal them while that plant is in the hive'. All
transcriptions and translations from this manuscript are my own.

[23] Lori Ann Garner and Kayla M. Miller, '"A Swarm in July": Beekeeping
Perspectives on the Old English *Wið Ymbe* Charm', *Oral Tradition*, 26 (2011),
355–76, pp. 371–2.

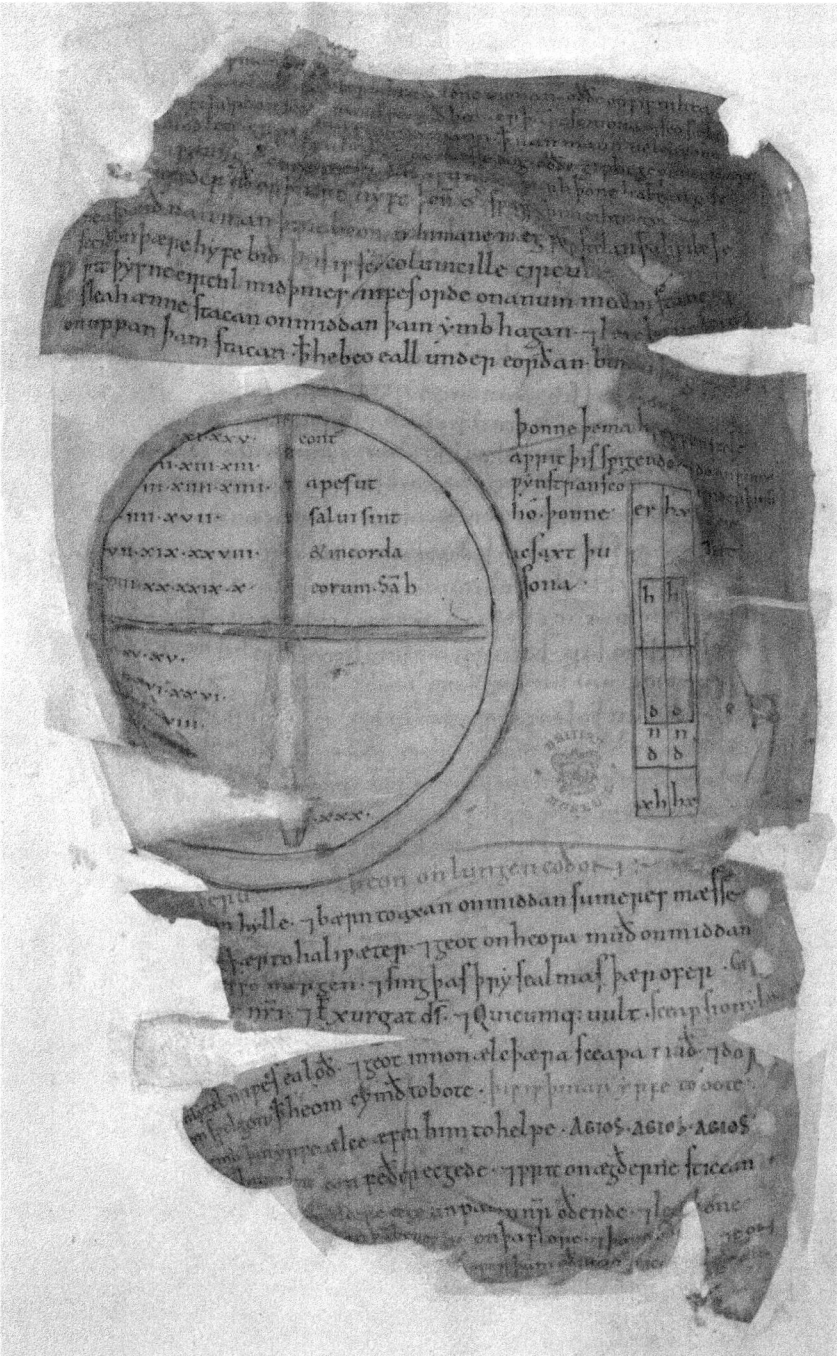

Figure 1: London, British Library, MS Cotton Vitellius E. xviii, fol. 15v
© The British Library Board

bees swarming onto somebody else's land, which would result in a legal forfeit of the livestock and their 'theft' ('forstelan'). The ritual that is now lost due to fire damage may have had multiple meanings, but some thematic connections between this instruction and its surrounding texts can be gleaned through its focus on loss of property, bees, and a remedy for livestock.

Columcille's Circle

The bee-ritual is immediately followed by *Columcille's Circle*, which is a diagram containing an inscription and instructions for its use. This text was described as a 'gibberish charm' in Felix Grendon's and Godfrid Storms' editions because of its obscure inscription.[24] St Columcille, or Columba (d. 597), was an Irish saint who founded Iona Abbey and who was renowned for his influence on agriculture.[25] In this ritual, a circle was to be inscribed on stone and placed in the centre of a beehive, and its instructions read:

> Þis is s(an)c(t)e columcille circul :- Writ þysne circul mid þinnes cnifes orde on anum mealan stan 7 sleah ænne stacan on middan þam ymbha-gan 7 lete þane stan on uppan þam stacan þæt he beo eall under eorðan butan þam gewritenan.

> This is Saint Columcille's Circle: Write this circle with your knife's edge on a malmstone, and thrust a stake in the middle of the beehive, and lay the stone above the stake so that it may be all under the earth except for the writing.

Like the madder plant, this circle was also to be placed inside the hive to protect the bees, and the two rituals may have been used together. The type of stone that is to be inscribed is probably malmstone, a chalky type that is easy to engrave.[26] These instructions are immediately followed by a template of the circle that is to be inscribed (fig. 1).

The inscription on the stone circle is divided into four quadrants with encompassing inner and outer circles. The use of a cruciform shape within this circle parallels other diagrams and ritual instructions in the prefatory collection.[27] Furthermore, the numbers that appear in

---

[24] Grendon, 'Anglo-Saxon Charms', pp. 115, 204; Storms, *Anglo-Saxon Magic*, pp. 297, 309–11.

[25] On the life of Columba, see Adamnán, *Life of St Columba*, Richard Sharpe, ed. and trans (London, 1995). For the Columcille legend and its relevance to this ritual, see Martha Dana Rust, 'The Art of Beekeeping Meets the Arts of Grammar: A Gloss of "Columcille's Circle"', *PQ*, 78 (1999), 359–87, pp. 363–4.

[26] See Storms, *Anglo-Saxon Magic*, p. 309; Jolly, 'Tapping the Power of the Cross', p. 78.

[27] See also Jolly, 'Tapping the Power of the Cross', p. 67.

the upper left, lower left, and lower right quadrants of the circle replicate those found in the two Apuleian Spheres of Life and Death. The upper right quadrant contains an abbreviated formula concerning the bees: 'cont apes ut salui sint & incorda eorum. Sā h'.[28] Pulsiano argues that this inscription 'seems rather to be a rubric to a charm, itself illuminated by the cryptic *S ā h'*.[29] Martha Rust, however, argues that the abbreviation stands for 'scribam hanc', and believes that the inscription glosses a passage from Jeremiah 31: 33, which contains the phrase 'et in corde eorum scribam eam' (and in their hearts I will write it [God's law]). Rust argues that this phrase would have reminded a monastic community of God's promise to write His law in their hearts.[30] Earlier traditions of figurative poetry and enigmata, which were likely to have been brought to England in the late seventh century, also have spiritual texts written inside and around diagram structures.[31] Aldhelm (d. 709) and Boniface (d. 754) used these forms of poetry to encourage their readers to discern spiritual meanings beyond the text, and these may have provided a source of inspiration for diagrams like *Columcille's Circle*. Enigmatic abbreviations are also a feature of Carolingian glosses that use Greek to deliberately conceal the meaning of a text and to highlight the obscurity of language and spiritual knowledge.[32] The abbreviated inscription of *Columcille's Circle* seems to follow these hermeneutic practices of deliberately obscuring knowledge by encoding a scriptural reference in an image.

The prefatory collection contains other obscure writing, which supports Rust's view that the diagram requires the decoding of language and the discernment of spiritual meaning. It includes unconventional abbreviations in glosses to the psalms,[33] numerical equivalents for lunar letters in the second Apuleian Sphere (fol. 16r), obscure letter arrangements in the theft diagram to the right of this ritual, and vowel substitution in the concluding cryptograms. All of these texts require the reader to use letters in various ways to discern spiritual meaning, calculate predictions, and conceal knowledge.

Columcille's Circle is evidently not just a grammatical exercise to be fathomed in the middle of a beehive, nor was it expected to be a gloss

---

[28] 'For bees so that they may be well and in their hearts. Sā h.'
[29] Pulsiano, 'Prefatory Matter', p. 94.
[30] Rust, 'Art of Beekeeping', p. 376.
[31] David A. E. Pelteret, 'A Cross and an Acrostic: Boniface's Prefatory Poem to his *Ars grammatica'*, in *Cross and Cruciform in the Anglo-Saxon World*, Keefer, Jolly, and Karkov, eds, pp. 53–102, pp. 58, 81–2. See also Chapter 5.
[32] Sinead O'Sullivan, 'The Sacred and the Obscure: Greek and the Carolingian Reception of Martianus Capella', *Journal of Medieval Latin*, 22 (2012), 67–94, p. 82; Teeuwen, 'Carolingian Scholarship', pp. 29–47.
[33] See James L. Rosier, ed., *The Vitellius Psalter: Edited from British Museum MS Cotton Vitellius E. xviii* (Ithaca, NY, 1962), pp. xx–xxi.

to be discerned by bees. Rust believes that the inscription to be written in stone reflects its symbolic meaning of inscribing God's law into the hearts of the bees and the monastic community.[34] She also argues that the obscure abbreviation highlights the ability of the *ars grammatica* to signify God's Word and mystical presence.[35] If Rust's interpretation is correct, *Columcille's Circle* establishes a connection between the bees, the beekeeper, the monastic community, and God's Law and Word. As no other version of this ritual survives, *Columcille's Circle* is a unique diagram which brings together several traditions for a particular agricultural concern. Its obscure language adds to its uniqueness and relates to the surrounding texts that focus on spiritual mystery and secret writing.

While much has been discussed about the inscription and purpose of the ritual, little has been said about where the abbreviated prayer appears in the diagram. As mentioned, the numbers used replicate those in the Apuleian Spheres on folios 14v and 16r. Phillip Pulsiano argued that *Columcille's Circle* reflects 'a corrupt conflation of texts' during the process of copying, but the same scribe evidently planned the writing space to accommodate this diagram between two other Spheres.[36] Rust also says that its numerals 'attest to the communicative power of the circle' but she does not explain how they do so.[37] The two Spheres in Vitellius E. xviii are divided only into upper and lower halves but other Spheres and charts attributed to Apuleius are divided into four quadrants like *Columcille's Circle*, indicating that the place-ment of the obscure inscription in the upper right quadrant reflects a deliberate manipulation of these diagrams for a particular agricultural concern.[38] The Sphere of Life and Death was used to diagnose illness according to the lunar cycle, the particular day of the week, and the numerical equivalence of a subject's name. When these values were obtained, a calculation was made and the numerical result was put back into the diagram to determine whether the subject would suffer or be in good health at that particular time. The values in the right side of the Sphere signify a short illness and those on the left signify a prolonged illness. If the value fell into the upper quadrants the patient would live, whereas the lower quadrants signify their death. The inscription in *Columcille's Circle* appears in the upper right quadrant of the diagram, the place in the Sphere that would signify a short illness and survival. The formula's appearance in this section con-nects the bees to the best possible outcome of the Sphere, that predicts

---

[34] Rust, 'Art of Beekeeping', p. 377.
[35] Rust, 'Art of Beekeeping', p. 378.
[36] Pulsiano, 'Prefatory Matter', p. 94.
[37] Rust, 'Art of Beekeeping', pp. 374–5.
[38] For these other Spheres, see Chardonnens, *Anglo-Saxon Prognostics*, pp. 195–222.

their survival after a short-term illness. *Columcille's Circle* is a carefully composed ritual that relates to this wider prognosticative tradition. Indeed, as the Sphere of Life and Death was used simply as a numerical chart, the *Columcille* ritual can be seen as a unique experimental development of this prognostication. This unusual diagram shows a scribe gathering material from astronomical traditions, and its position in the manuscript reflects an awareness of the thematic progression from computus and prognostics to a practical use of such knowledge for the livestock of a monastery.

The safe-guarding of livestock and their produce was very important in monasteries, and apiaries were particularly significant. Honey was a valuable resource with medicinal properties, and it was used to make mead. The wax harvested from the bees was also vital for the production of candles.[39] The *Exultet* that was sung in the liturgical procession on Holy Saturday associates the bee with the Virgin Mary; and Ambrose, Aldhelm, and Ælfric (among others) depicted the bee as a figure of the Virgin and the Church.[40] The reproduction of bees and the increase of the colony would have symbolically reflected the growth of the Church. The religious significance of the bees' produce for monastic life is also extensive. The *Regularis Concordia*, for instance, compares the updating of monastic customs to 'honey [that] is gathered by bees from all manner of wild flowers and collected into one hive'.[41] The cells of honeycomb were also likened to monastic cells, and the bee provided a model for the monk's life in its celibacy, continuous labour, and service to others.[42] Seen in this context, the protection and well-being of bees was also symbolic of the monastic community's health. *Columcille's Circle* offers protection for the bee colony through the power of God's Law and through the intercession of this Irish saint, but it also affirms that the spiritual sickness of the monastic community will be neither fatal nor prolonged. This ritual is an intricate component of the prefatory collection, as it combines astronomical calculations, predictions of revived health, and an encrypted prayer for the physical and spiritual protection of livestock and the monastic community.

---

[39] See Austin E. Fife, 'Christian Swarm Charms from the Ninth to the Nineteenth Centuries', *Journal of American Folklore*, 77 (1964), 154–59, p. 154; Gittos, *Liturgy, Architecture, and Sacred Places*, pp. 264, 266.

[40] Augustine Cassiday, 'St Aldhelm's Bees (*De Uirginitate Prosa*, cc. iv–vi): Some Observations on a Literary Tradition', *ASE*, 33 (2004), 1–22.

[41] 'quaeque ex dignis eorum moribus honesta colligentes, uti apes fauum nectaris diuersis pratorum floribus in uno alueario', Symons, *Regularis Concordia*, p. 3.

[42] See Debra Hassig, *Medieval Bestiaries: Text, Image, Ideology* (Cambridge, 1995), pp. 52–61.

Theft Diagram

The diagram to recover stolen property that is copied next to *Columcille's Circle* also uses obscure epigraphy, and it too was described as a 'gibberish charm' by Felix Grendon and Godfrid Storms.[43] Its instructions read: 'Þonne þema[n] hwet forstele awrit þis swigende 7 do on þinne wynstran scó under þinum hó þonne geacsaxt þu hit sona.'[44] The diagram accompanying these instructions is rectangular and contains a number of cruciform shapes that are layered within its rectangular frame (see fig. 1). Certain letters are placed in every corner within the diagram, and the letters *h*, *x*, *n*, and *d* all mirror each other, with the exception of *er* in the top left corner.

Felix Grendon believed that the theft diagram contains 'mysterious letters and numbers [that] are the magic symbols in spells', and which are 'not in verbal form'.[45] The meaning behind these letters may never be recovered but it is likely that they encrypt their meaning like the *Columcille* abbreviation and the ciphered exercises at the end of the collection. Some of these letters may stand for the Greek delta (δ), eta (η), and chi (χ), and *xh* may be a conflated acronym of the Greek 'Xp' ('Christ') and Roman 'ih' ('Jesus'), but this does not seem very plausible. Rearrangements of these letters offer very tentative conclusions and they do not convincingly account for why they appear in specific places in the diagram. Karen Jolly has argued that 'the cruciform lines dividing the rectangle have spatial significance, and perhaps the letters refer to the cardinal directions or symbols associated with them'.[46] It would make sense to use the cardinal directions in a compass-like diagram to locate stolen property. Other Anglo-Saxon prognostics, for instance, use the cardinal directions to predict agricultural disasters, and some of these are found in *Ælfwine's Prayerbook* (Titus D. xxvi, fols. 9v–10v).[47] However, there is no apparent correlation between the names of the winds and the letters of the theft diagram.

It is likely that this diagram's cruciform shapes have spiritual significance and represent Christ's cross. The invocation of the cross is made explicit in other Anglo-Saxon theft rituals.[48] Theft is also an important theme in the gospel accounts of the Passion, as Christ is crucified

---

[43] Grendon, 'Anglo-Saxon Charms', pp. 115, 206; Storms, *Anglo-Saxon Magic*, pp. 297, 311.

[44] 'When a man steals from you, write this silently and place (it) in your left shoe under your heel, then you will soon find out (about it).'

[45] Grendon, 'Anglo-Saxon Charms', pp. 115, 135.

[46] Jolly, 'Tapping the Power', p. 68, note 31.

[47] See Chardonnens, *Anglo-Saxon Prognostics*, pp. 247–69.

[48] See Storms, *Anglo-Saxon Magic*, pp. 202–6; Phillip Pulsiano, 'British Library, Cotton Tiberius A. iii, fol. 59rv: An Unrecorded Charm in the Form of an Address to the Cross', *ANQ*, 4 (1991), 3–5; Liuzza, 'Prayers and/or Charms'.

between two thieves, one of whom repents and is redeemed (Luke 23: 42). The repentant thief is referred to in liturgies for Good Friday, as seen, for example, in *Leofric A* (s. ix^ex / x^in, Canterbury, fol. 107v), where a collect refers to the thief's salvation: 'Deus a quo et iudas reatus sui poenam et confessionis suae latro premium sumpsit'.[49] A text on the names of the crucified thieves is also found in London, BL, MS Cotton Tiberius A. iii (xi^med, Christ Church, Canterbury), which has many correspondences with the *Vitellius Psalter* and *Ælfwine's Prayerbook* and was probably copied from a Winchester exemplar.[50] Ælfwine had a deeply personal devotion to the cross, and he firmly associated himself with the crucifixion by inscribing his name above a crucifixion miniature in his *Prayerbook*.[51] As Ælfwine was probably involved in the compilation of the *Vitellius Psalter*'s exemplar, it is likely that this theft ritual is linked to similar devotions to the cross.

The diagram was to be placed in the left shoe and carried by the owner of the stolen property, and it is therefore designed as an amuletic device.[52] Another amuletic ritual in *Ælfwine's Prayerbook* (Titus D. xxvi, fols. 3rv) claims to be measured by the same length of Christ's body and the cross:

> De mensium saluatoris: Haec figura sedecies multiplicata perficit mensuram Domini nostri Iesu Christi corporis et est assumpta a ligno pretioso dominice. Crux Christi de .iiii. lignis facta est, qui uocantur cipressus et cedrus et pinus et buxus. Sed buxus non fuit in cruce, nisi tabula de illo ligno super frontem Christi fuerat, in qua conscriptum Iudei illud titulum habuerunt: 'Hic est rex Iudeorum.'[53]

> The measurements of the Saviour: This multiplied figure completes sixteen measures of the body of our Lord Jesus Christ, and it was adopted by the precious wood of the Lord. The cross of Christ was made from four types of wood, which are called cypress and cedar and pine and box-wood. But box-wood did not exist in the cross, unless the plank from that wood was above Christ's head, on which the Jews had written that title: 'This is the king of the Jews.'

This text originally appeared after a collection of prayers to the cross and prognostications similar to those found in the *Vitellius*

---

[49] Orchard, *Leofric Missal*, Vol. II, p. 166; 'O God, from whom both Judas received the penalty of his crime, and the robber (received) the reward of his confession'.

[50] See Gneuss, *Handlist*, p. 67; Chardonnens, *Anglo-Saxon Prognostics*, pp. 53–9; Liuzza, *Anglo-Saxon Prognostics*, pp. 3–15. The thief also has an important role as a witness to the Resurrection in the *Gospel of Nicodemus*, which was well known in Anglo-Saxon England, see Michael Swanton, *Anglo-Saxon Prose* (London, 1975), pp. 139–57; Lenker, 'Signifying Christ', pp. 259–61.

[51] See Karkov, 'Abbot Ælfwine', pp. 106–7. See also Barbara Raw, *Trinity and Incarnation in Anglo-Saxon Art and Thought* (Cambridge, 2006), pp. 143–86.

[52] Jolly, 'Tapping the power of the Cross', p. 68.

[53] Günzel, *Ælfwine's Prayerbook*, p. 144.

Psalter.[54] *Ælfwine's Prayerbook* also concludes with a ritual for finding a thief (Titus D. xxvi, fol. 79v), a transcription of which reads:

> Pro furto
> si habes aliquam rem perditam. Scribe has litteras in carta uirgine . & pone subtus capud tuum in nocte dum dormis & uideliis eum qui tibi abstulit
> T. R. N. I. e. ʒ ę □ ⊦ e ⊦ ʐ m R. iii² y ⊦ c A ii ⊦ c ⊦ c z ɟ E ʒ oᶠ g′ F iiii.

> For theft.
> If you have lost anything, write these letters on virgin parchment, and put it underneath your head at night while you sleep, and you will see him who steals from you.
> T. R. N. I. e. ʒ ę □ ⊦ e ⊦ ʐ m R. iii² y ⊦ c A ii ⊦ c ⊦ c z ɟ E ʒ oᶠ g′ F iiii.

Phillip Pulsiano claimed that this theft ritual contains 'magical and meaningless letters', and Beate Günzel believes that it was 'used by illiterate scribes'.[55] However, the letter sequence appears to be a heavily encrypted phrase with a range of graphemes from no fewer than three different alphabets.[56] The letters may reflect certain features of the crucifixion, as the Roman capitals 'R N I' indicate a reverse reading of 'INRI' ('Iesus Nazarenus Rex Iudeorum') or, alternatively, the first four letters together may signify 'Trinitas'. The number four also appears at the end of the sequence, perhaps reflecting the four corners of the cross or the four types of wood used in the crucifixion. Given that many textual overlaps exist between *Ælfwine's Prayerbook* and the *Vitellius Psalter*, the theft diagram could be an amulet that depicts the cross of Christ with deliberately ciphered phrases. In a similar way to other obscure writing in Anglo-Saxon texts – like the use of runes in riddles and wisdom poems – the letters require the reader to discern meaning beyond the immediate image.[57] The letters of these two theft rituals in

---

[54] See Liuzza, 'Prayers and/or Charms', pp. 286–7; Karkov, 'Abbot Ælfwine', pp. 123–5.

[55] Pulsiano, 'Prefatory Matter', p. 102; Günzel, *Ælfwine's Prayerbook*, p. 78.

[56] Some graphemes closely resemble those found in an alphabet list on folio 5v of Oxford, St John's College, MS 17 (c. 1110, Thorney Abbey), see Faith Wallis, *The Calendar and the Cloister: Oxford, St John's College, MS 17* (Montreal, 2007): <http://digital.library.mcgill.ca/ms-17> accessed 26 September 2017. Although later in date, there are some textual correspondences between this manuscript and *Ælfwine's Prayerbook* and Caligula A. xv. On the dating and location of St John's 17, see Charles Singer, 'A Review of the Medical Literature of the Dark Ages, With a New Text of About 1110', *Proceedings of the Royal Society of Medicine*, 10 (1917), 107–60, p. 138; Neil R. Ker, 'Two Notes on MS Ashmole 328 (*Byrhtferth's Manual*)', *Medium Ævum*, 4 (1935), 16–19; *Catalogue*, p. 435; Cyril Hart, 'The Ramsey *Computus*', *EHR*, 85 (1970), 29–44, pp. 31–4; Peter S. Baker, 'Byrhtferth's *Enchiridion* and the Computus in Oxford, St John's College 17', *ASE*, 10 (1981), 123–42, p. 125.

[57] See especially Birkett, 'Runes and *Revelatio*'; Jill Hamilton Clements, 'Reading,

Ælfwine's Prayerbook and the *Vitellius Psalter* simultaneously conceal meaning through semantic negation and reveal the thief or the location of hidden property.

There may also be a liturgical significance to this theft ritual. For instance, Greek letters and markings were made in a cruciform shape on the Paschal candle at the Easter vigil to signify Christ's title as Alpha and Omega and his holy wounds.[58] The markings of the theft diagram are likewise inscribed around cruciform shapes and they are placed at each of their corners. The arrangement of letters around a cruciform shape is also a feature of an Anglo-Saxon church dedication rite, which underwent significant revisions in Canterbury around the same time as the production of the *Vitellius Psalter*.[59] The revised rites open with the bishop's silent entrance into the church before he was to write two full alphabets diagonally across the floor.[60] A prayer then connects the letters to the tablets of the Ten Commandments (Exodus 3: 5) and Jacob's ladder to heaven (Genesis 28: 10–17): 'et uerba legis tue. in tabulis cordium eorum misericordiae tuae digito asscribe… hic scala pacis et caritatis assurgat'.[61] The bishop's silent entrance and the writing of mystical letters in a cruciform shape resonate with the theft diagram's instructions, and may correspond with the inscription of an obscure scriptural passage in the quadrants of *Columcille's Circle*. Liturgical practices of alphabetic writing may have inspired the construction of the theft diagram, and they provide a more plausible source of inspiration than 'magical' or meaningless letters.

Another possible explanation of the letters is that they may be linked to lunar calculations. Numerical equivalents for letters are used in the two Apuleian Spheres, a table of lunar letters is found on folio 13v of this manuscript, and several manuscripts that have correspondences with the *Vitellius Psalter* also contain different lunar tables.[62] In other manuscripts, some tables provide numerical values for the English

---

Writing and Resurrection: Cynewulf's Runes as a Figure of the Body', *ASE*, 43 (2014), 133–54.

[58] The earliest record of the alpha and omega being marked on the Paschal candle is found in a tenth-century gradual from León, see Orchard, *Sacramentary of Ratoldus*, p. clxiv.

[59] See Gittos, *Liturgy, Architecture, and Sacred Places*, pp. 229–36; 'Liturgy of Canterbury Cathedral', p. 45. For an earlier version of this rite from the *Romano-Germanic Pontifical* tradition, see Brian V. Repsher, ed. and trans, *The Rite of Church Dedication in the Early Medieval Era* (Lewiston, NY, 1998), pp. 145–6, 176.

[60] For a discussion of this rite and St Andrew's cross, see Dáibhí Ó Cróinín, *Early Irish History and Chronology* (Dublin, 2003), pp. 293–4.

[61] 'and write the words of your law on the tablets of their hearts with the finger of your mercy… here let the ladder of peace and truth rise up'; transcriptions and translations from Gittos, *Liturgy, Architecture, and Sacred Places*, p. 234.

[62] Such manuscripts include *Leofric A* (s. ix / x), Titus D. xxvi/ii (s. xi[1]), Caligula A. xv (s. xi[ex]), and Oxford, St John's College, MS 17 (c. 1110, Thorney Abbey).

and Roman alphabets, as seen in Byrhtferth of Ramsey's *Enchiridion*. Byrhtferth expounds the spiritual significance of certain numbers – the number three, for instance, is said to represent the Holy Trinity – and it may be the case that these letters signify important numerical values and combinations.[63] Exploring the numerical significance of letters in the diagram poses a very complex task that would be fraught with speculation, and it would require a full, specialised inquiry so I will not attempt to provide further possibilities here. Even if the correct numerical significance of these letter combinations is discovered, some reasoning must be found for their values and positioning in the diagram. For the purposes of the present study, the surrounding manuscript context of the theft ritual indicates that the letters must have significance beyond their cruciform layout.

Although only some scribes or monks may have known the significance of these shapes and letters, the manuscript context of the prefatory matter exposes some major concerns that are likely to be deeply involved in this ritual. The diagram relates to the widespread use of numerology in other Anglo-Saxon texts and to inscriptions of letters around cruciform shapes in other liturgical rituals.

For Sick Cattle and Sheep

Directly below *Columcille's Circle* and the theft diagram is a ritual for cattle with lung disease. This text evidently continues the theme of agricultural protection and healing, and it is intimately connected to its surrounding rituals. The text opens with a set of instructions to burn something to ash on midsummer's day so that it may be used as a remedy (fig. 1):

> hryþeru beon on lungen coðon :-
> […] ton hylle . 7 bærn to axan on middan sumeres mæsse [dæg . do] þærto hali wæter . 7 geot on heora muð on middan [sumeres mæ]sse mergen . 7 sing þas þry sealmas þær ofer . [Deus misereatu]r nostri 7 Exurgat dominus [read deus] 7 Quicumque uult.

> (If) cattle […] are with (disease) of the lungs:
> […] (to the hill?), and burn to ash on midsummer's mass-day. Then put holy water on it, and pour in their mouths on midsummer's mass-morning. And sing these three psalms over (it): *May God have mercy on us* [Psalm 66], and *Arise lord* [Psalm 67], and *Whosoever wishes* [Athanasian creed].

The object to be burnt to ash is unknown but it clearly had a connection with treating lung problems or cattle. Another remedy for cattle with

---

[63] See Byrhtferth, *Enchiridion*, pp. 202–5.

lung disease in the *Lacnunga* of Harley 585 instructs the grinding of a local plant before holy water is added for an oral treatment: 'Wyþ lungenadle hriðerum: þa wyrt on wordigum [read worðigum] (heo bið gelic hundes micgean ðære wyrte) þær wexeð blaco bergean eal swa micele swa oðre pysbeana, gecnuca; do in haligwæter; do þon(ne) on muð þæm hryþerum'.[64] The plant is also later burnt with incense, fennel, cotton, and hassuck. It may be the madder plant, which is also prescribed in the ritual for bees at the top of the folio, because it is elsewhere used in treatments for lung diseases in the *Herbarium Apuleis* of Harley 585 and Book II of *Bald's Leechbook*.[65] The specification to burn something to ashes at midsummer also reflects the earlier calendrical concerns of the prefatory collection, and corresponds with ensuing rituals that identify similar times of the year in the grain harvest and Lammas day.

Cattle are prone to respiratory diseases after pasturing in warm, humid conditions, and this was most likely to occur around midsummer.[66] Placing ashes in the cattle's mouth may have had the practical value of making the animal cough to release any excess mucus in the lungs. The prescriptions of holy water and ashes, and singing psalms and the Athanasian Creed add a spiritual dimension to the ritual and reflect its penitential focus. For instance, ashes, holy water, and the same penitential psalms are used in the rite for visiting the sick, as seen in Chapter 3.[67] The first psalm reference is legible only by the word 'nostri' but Phillip Pulsiano interprets this as a reference to Psalm 66 (*Deus misereatur nostri*), which is a harvest song.[68] This is most likely to be the case, given that the incipit to Psalm 67 (*Exurgat deus*) immediately follows.[69] The relevance of Psalm 66 for an agricultural ritual is evident; the sick cattle are to become as fruitful as the bounty of the harvest: 'terra dedit fructum suum. Benedicat nos deus deus noster benedicat nos deus et metuant eum omnes fines terrę.'[70] The *Regularis Concordia*

---

[64] 'For lung disease in cattle: the plant [(?)grows] in homesteads [*or* on roads] (it is like the plant 'dog's piss' [*i.e.* (?)hound's tongue] (?)where black berries grow as big as other (?)peas, pound; put into holy water, then put in the mouth of the cattle', Pettit, *Anglo-Saxon Remedies*, Vol. I, pp. 96–7. See also Vol. II, p. 264.

[65] See Cockayne, *Leechdoms*, Vol. I, p. 154; Vol. II, p. 268. The plant also had fertilising qualities, see C. P. Biggam, ed., *From Earth to Art: The Many Aspects of the Plant World in Anglo-Saxon England* (Amsterdam, 2003), pp. 233–7.

[66] See Richard F. Keeler and Anthony T. Tu, eds, *Handbook of Natural Toxins, Vol. I: Plant and Fungal Toxins* (New York, 1983), p. 87; Hany Elsheikha and Jon S. Patterson, *Vetinary Parasitology* (Boca Raton, FL, 2013), p. 201.

[67] See also Wilson, *Missal of Robert*, p. 287.

[68] Pulsiano, 'Prefatory Matter', p. 93.

[69] Pulsiano, 'Prefatory Matter', pp. 89, 93, 110. Cockayne transcribed this as the beginning of Psalm 122 (*Miserere nostri*), although this is not the psalm's incipit, Cockayne, *Leechdoms*, Vol. I, p. 388.

[70] 'eorðan he sealde wæstm heora bletsa us god god ure bletsa us god 7 ondrædan hine ealle endas eorðan', Rosier, *Vitellius Psalter*, p. 154; 'the earth yielded its

instructs the singing of this psalm during the distribution of ashes and before the liturgical procession on Ash Wednesday.[71] The *Canterbury Benedictional* also prescribes the singing of this psalm during the Ash Wednesday procession, and it was also used in the Mass on Tuesday of Holy Week and Maundy Thursday.[72] The singing of Psalm 66 and the use of burnt ashes evoke a penitential response to this agricultural problem; the cattle's bodily sickness was caused by the spiritual sickness of the monastic community, and this is countered with penance.

The second psalm (*Exurgat deus*) contrasts with the first as it is a song of triumph over God's enemies, and it contains a number of references that resonate with the ritual. Firstly, the psalm describes how God's enemies are driven away and melted like wax: 'sicut deficit fumus deficiant sicut fluit cera a facię ignis sic pereant peccatores a facię dei'.[73] In the same way, the hostile forces causing the cattle's illness and the community's spiritual sickness are driven away, and melted like wax. Secondly, God rains down blessings on all his people and creatures: 'Pluuiam uoluntariam segregabis deus hereditate tuę et infirmata est tu uero perfecisti eam. Animalia tua habitabunt in ea parasti in dulcedine tua pauperi deus.'[74] Psalm 67 petitions God to bless the sick cattle and the monastic community. Thirdly, it acknowledges God as saving His people from death, thus resonating with the ritual's curing of diseased cattle and the community's salvation from spiritual death: 'Deus noster deus saluos faciendi et domini domini exitus mortis'.[75] Finally, the psalm metaphorically refers to Egypt as a beast of the reeds, and a herd of bulls among innocent calves: 'Increpa feras harundinis congregatio taurorum in uaccis populorum.'[76] The

---

harvest. May God bless us, may our God bless us, and may all the ends of the earth revere him.'

[71] Symons, *Regularis Concordia*, p. 32. See also Ælfric, *Ælfric's Letter to the Monks of Eynsham*, Christopher A. Jones, ed. and trans (Cambridge, 1998), pp. 122–3.

[72] Woolley, *Canterbury Benedictional*, p. 17; Orchard, *Leofric Missal*, Vol II, pp. 161, 164.

[73] 'swaswa teorade smic hy geteoriað swaswa flewð weax of ansyne fyres swa forwurðað synfulle fram ansyne godes', Rosier, *Vitellius Psalter*, p. 154; 'as smoke is blown away may they be blown away, as wax melts before the face of the fire may the wicked disappear before the face of God'.

[74] 'ren wilsumne: syndrast god yrfewerdnesse þin 7 geuntrumod is þu soðlice fulfremedest him. nytenu þine eardiað on þam þu gearwadest on swetnesse þinre þearfan god', Rosier, *Vitellius Psalter*, pp. 155–6; 'You, God, will shed abundant rain on your heritage, and you restored it in your truth as it was weakened. Your flock lived in it, and you, God, provided for the poor in your goodness.'

[75] 'god ure god halne to donne 7 driht drihten utgang deaðes', Rosier, *Vitellius Psalter*, p. 157; 'our God is a saving God, and to God, the Lord (belongs) escape from death'.

[76] 'þu þrea wildeor hreodes gemot gaderung fearra on cuum folca', Rosier, *Vitellius Psalter*, p. 158; 'Rebuke the beasts of the reed, the herd of bulls among the calves of the people.'

sinful beasts of Egypt that attack innocent calves are humbled before God in the psalm, and in this ritual the hostile forces that threaten the innocent cattle are made subservient to God's will.

Unlike the *Deus misereatur nostri* that was used on Ash Wednesday and during Holy Week, the *Exurgat deus* was used in Masses for Pentecost Sunday and the Wednesday within the Octave of Pentecost.[77] The triumphant psalm declares the success of the first penitential petition to God to bless the land, livestock, and community. These psalms are also prescribed because they mark key stages of Lent and Eastertide, thus framing the most significant liturgical solemnities, and resonating with the earlier focus on Easter in the computistical calculations. Finally, the prescription to recite the Athanasian Creed confirms the power of God, the biblical events of the Easter season, and the renewed faith of the community:

> Quicumque vult salvus esse, ante omnia opus est, ut teneat catholicam fidem... Qui passus est pro salute nostra, descendit ad infernos, tertia die resurrexit a mortuis. Ascendit ad caelos, sedet ad dexteram Dei Patris omnipotentis... Haec est fides catholica, quam nisi quisque fideliter firmiterque crediderit, salvus esse non poterit.[78]

> Whosoever wishes to be saved, before all things the labour is that he may hold the Catholic faith... He who died for our salvation, he descended to hell, the third day he rose from the dead. He ascended into the heavens, he sits on the right of Almighty God the Father... This is the Catholic faith, which unless everybody believes faithfully and firmly, one is not able to be saved.

The psalms and Creed were carefully chosen for their relevance to this ritual, and possibly for their significance in the liturgical year.

The text that immediately follows the ritual for cattle with lung disease is a remedy for sheep. This has been edited as a separate 'charm' but it closely follows the prescriptions for treating cattle, and may be better thought of as an extension of its preceding text (see fig. 1).[79] The opening words for this ritual read: '[Gif] sceap si on ylon [nima]n lytel niwes ealoð 7 geot innon ælc þæra sceapa muð 7 do þæt [...]r swelgon þæt heom cymð to bot.'[80] The instruction to

---

[77] See Orchard, *Leofric Missal*, Vol. II, pp. 200, 202.

[78] Ferdinand Holthausen, 'Eine ae Interlinearversion des athanasischen Glaubensbekenntnisse', *Englische Studien*, 75 (1942–43), 6–8.

[79] Cockayne, *Leechdoms*, Vol. I, pp. 388–9.

[80] 'If sheep are ailing, take a little new ale and pour it into each of the sheep's mouths, and do that [...] swallow (so) that it provides a remedy for them.' The words preceding 'swelgon' are interpreted by Jolly as 'hi hraðor', allowing the translation 'make them swallow it quickly', Jolly, 'Tapping the Power of the Cross', p. 78.

put new ale into the sheep's mouth echoes the earlier prescription to put ashes into the mouths of the cattle. The new ale indicates a certain time of the year, and Karen Jolly suggests that it is 'a summer application when ale would be newly made after the grain harvest (e.g. August?)'.[81] This would make sense following the reference to midsummer in the preceding text, and it indicates that this oral treatment for sheep is an extension of the cattle ritual. The proximity and overlap of these two texts implies that the same psalms and Creed would also be sung around the sheep. Assuming these were also sung, the animal's physical ailment and the community's spiritual sickness are once again reflected in Psalm 66 (*Deus misereatur nostri*), and their renewed physical and spiritual health is reflected in Psalm 67 (*Exurgat deus*).

Livestock Ritual

The text following the ritual for cattle and sheep has also been described as a 'charm' by some scholars, but Karen Jolly has drawn comparisons between this ritual and liturgical processions at cemetery dedications and Rogationtide.[82] The text is marked off from others, as its opening words are rubricated in red ink and it begins: 'Þis is þinan yrfe to bote: [...] ymb þin yrfe ælce æfen him to helpe. ΑGIOS. ΑGIOS. ΑGIOS.'[83] This text closely corresponds to the previous rituals that focus on the health and protection of livestock through practical and spiritual means. The prescription also designates a time for performance, as it is to be sung every evening around one's cattle, probably after Vespers. Other 'charm' rituals also prescribe the singing of the 'agios', as seen in the ritual against elf-sickness in *Bald's Leechbook* which draws heavily on the rite for visiting the sick (discussed in Chapter 3). Another ritual from Harley 585 prescribes the singing of a number of liturgical prayers around livestock.[84] This feature of moving around one's livestock is also a feature of rogation processions before the Ascension: 'We sculon... Cristes rodetacen forðeran and his þa halige godspell and oðre halignessa, mid þam we sceolon bletsian ure þa eorðlican speda, þæt synd æceras and wudu and ure ceap.'[85]

---

[81] Jolly, 'Tapping the Power of the Cross', p. 67.
[82] Jolly, 'Tapping the Power of the Cross', pp. 68, 78. See also Gittos, *Liturgy, Architecture, and Sacred Places*, pp. 103–45. It is categorised as a 'charm' by Cockayne, *Leechdoms*, Vol. I, pp. 386–7; Storms, *Anglo-Saxon Magic*, p. 287; Ker, *Catalogue*, p. 300; Pulsiano, 'Prefatory Matter', p. 89.
[83] 'This is a remedy for your cattle [...] around your cattle every evening to help them. Holy. Holy. Holy.'
[84] See Pettit, *Anglo-Saxon Remedies*, Vol. I, pp. 96–7.
[85] 'We ought to... carry forth the sign of Christ's cross and his holy gospels and other holy things, with which we must bless our worldly riches, that is fields

The livestock ritual indicates that processions may have occurred on a daily basis during the summer around the monastery grounds in eleventh-century Winchester.[86]

The spiritual significance of this ritual is found in the biblical source for the *Agios* (*Sanctus*) and its liturgical usage. The *Sanctus* is a composite of the seraphic hymn from Isaiah 6: 3 and the cries of praise at Christ's entry into Jerusalem in Matthew 21: 9. Singing the hymn around the animals invokes God's divine presence among the livestock, as the hymn is used in the Mass immediately before the transformation of the bread and wine into Christ's body and blood. The gospel account of Christ's entry into Jerusalem was recited during Palm Sunday processions that passed between ecclesiastical buildings and through public spaces, and this resonates with the previous ritual for cattle and sheep that uses a psalm from this period of Lent.[87] This simple ritual instruction to sing the *Agios* around cattle each evening uses a liturgical prayer to protect the community's livestock, and it has close correspondences with its surrounding materials.

Barn Ritual

The line following the final 'Agios' of the livestock ritual is missing through fire damage, and the next legible words begin with 'lange sticcan feðerecgede'. These words have been edited as a continuation of the previous text but they are probably the opening instructions for a related but different ritual.[88] The text runs from the bottom of folio 15v to line 8 of folio 16r (see figs. 1 and 2):

> […] lange sticcan feðerecgede . 7 writ on ægðerne sticcan […] ælcere ecge an pater noster oð ende 7 leg[e] þone […]an þam berene on þa flore . 7 þone oðerne on […] ofer þam oðrum stic[c]an . [Fol. 16r] þæt þær si rode tacen on . 7 nim o[f] ðam gehalgedan hlafe þe man halgie on hlafmæssedæg feower snæda . 7 gecryme on þa feower hyrna [.] þæs berenes . Þis is þeo bletsung þærto . Vt surices garbas non noceant has preces super garbas dicis et non dicto eos suspendis hierosolimam ciuitate . ubi surices nec habitent nec habent potestatem . nec grana colligent . nec triticum congaudent . Þis is seo oðer bletsung . Domine deus omnipotens qui fecisti cẹlum et terram . tu benedicis fructum istum in nomine patris et filii et spiritus sancti . amen . 7 Pater noster.

and woods and our cattle'; Joyce Bazire and James E. Cross, eds and trans, *Eleven Old English Rogationtide Homilies* (Toronto, 1982), p. 112.

[86] On processions within monastic precincts in Anglo-Saxon England, see Gittos, *Liturgy, Architecture, and Sacred Places*, pp. 95–145.

[87] See Symons, *Regularis Concordia*, pp. 34–5; Ælfric, *Letter to Monks of Eynsham*, pp. 124–5. See also Gittos, *Liturgy, Architecture, and Sacred Places*, p. 124.

[88] Cockayne, *Leechdoms*, Vol. I, p. 386; Vol. II, p. 290; Storms, *Anglo-Saxon Magic*, p. 287.

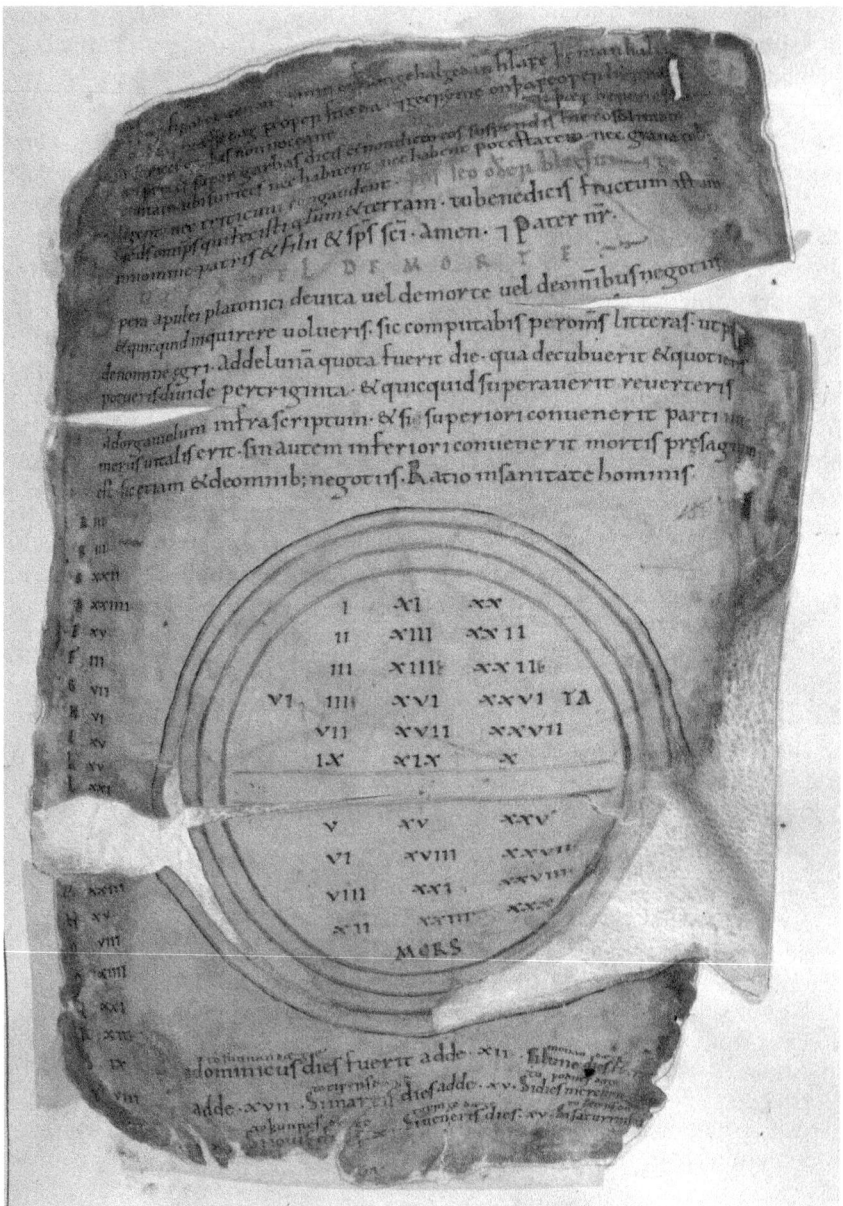

Figure 2: London, British Library, MS Cotton Vitellius E. xviii, fol. 16r
© The British Library Board

[…] long four-edged sticks, and write on each edge of every stick one Paternoster to the end, and lay the (stick) on the floor of the barn, and the other on (top) above the other stick. [Fol. 16r] that there is the sign of the cross on (it). And take four pieces from the hallowed bread which man hallows on Lammas day, and crumble in the four corners of the barn. This is the blessing for that: So that mice may not harm plant sheaves, say this prayer above the sheaves 'and I do not say you hang them in the city of Jerusalem, where mice may not live nor have power, nor gather seeds, nor rejoice with wheat'. This is the other blessing: 'Almighty Lord and God, who made the havens and the earth, you bless this fruit in the name of the Father and of the Son and of the Holy Spirit. Amen.' And Paternoster.

These instructions make it clear that sticks are to be inscribed with the Paternoster and placed on the floor of a barn in a cruciform shape ('rode tacen'). An interesting parallel with this prescription is found in the eleventh-century *Æcerbot* field ritual in London, BL, MS Cotton Caligula A. vii, also probably from Winchester (see Chapter 2). In the *Æcerbot*, four sticks are inscribed with the names of the evangelists and placed into each corner of the field to drive out evil from the land and resurrect crops by the power of the gospels. The rite for consecrating a cemetery also uses crosses to demarcate the cemetery with spiritual power.[89] The *Æcerbot* and cemetery rite offer parallels for this barn ritual, and indicate that certain liturgical practices could be adapted for different occasions.

The reference to Lammas day (1 August) also indicates a similar time of year for performance as the earlier references to midsummer and the time when new ale is made.[90] The Lammas bread was blessed as the first fruits of the grain harvest, and the ritual instructs that it was to be crumbled in four corners of the building, thus forming a cruciform shape inside the barn. The first blessing that follows this instruction is obscure, but it is apparent that it is a prayer over plant sheaves ('has preces super garbas') to protect them from the influence of mice ('surices').[91] The prayer states that the sheaves are not to be hung in the city of Jerusalem ('et non dicto eos suspendis hierosolimam ciuitate'). As Christ was hung on the cross in Jerusalem, the crops must not be killed by the power of rodents ('nec habitent nec habent potestatem'). This reference to the events in Jerusalem in Holy Week resonates with the song of Christ's entry into Jerusalem in the previous ritual, and with the penitential psalm from Ash Wednesday and Holy Week that is used in the ritual for cattle and sheep. Its reference to theft

---

[89] See Gittos, *Liturgy, Architecture, and Sacred Places*, p. 49. See also Helen Foxhall Forbes, *Heaven and Earth in Anglo-Saxon England: Theology and Society in An Age of Faith* (Farnham, 2013), pp. 273–8, 294–332. The writing of holy names on sticks may have been inspired by Ezekiel 37: 15–20.

[90] See Jolly, 'Tapping the Power of the Cross', p. 69; Banham, 'Staff of Life', pp. 299–300.

[91] Cambridge, Gonville and Caius College, MS 385 (s. xiii) also contains a ritual to protect a barn from rats, see Jolly, 'Prayers from the Field', p. 110.

of crops by mice also relates to earlier rituals that protect bees from theft and locate stolen goods. The prayer then makes reference to the gathering of wheat ('nec grana colligent . nec triticum congaudent'). This is probably an allusion to the parable of the darnel seed that is sown among the wheat by the devil to ruin the harvest (Matthew 13: 24–30). The darnel is gathered in a separate bundle and burnt, whereas the wheat is gathered in a barn (Matthew 13: 30). Similar language from Matthew's gospel is found in this prayer, as the wheat is referred to as 'triticum', the produce is 'herba et fructum', and the darnel is 'zizania' that is gathered ('colligent') and burnt.[92] The gospel passage is highly relevant to this ritual that counters the power of hostile forces which attack crops. The second prayer is much shorter and simply petitions the Creator of heaven and earth to bless the produce in the name of the Trinity ('qui fecisti cęlum et terram tu benedicis fructum istum'), and this formula is commonly found in liturgical blessings for palms and new fruit.[93]

The two prayers of this barn ritual have close liturgical analogues. The first blends an allusion to Christ's Passion with a gospel passage, and the second employs a liturgical formula from Mass blessings. This text is a unique ritual that uses liturgical prayers, readings, and objects, and it is closely related to the previous texts in the collection. It continues the rituals chronologically (from midsummer to Lammas), it marks the physical space of a barn with a cruciform shape, and it instructs the recital of liturgical prayers inside an agricultural enclosure.

Sphere of Life and Death

Immediately following this barn procession is an introduction to the second Sphere of Life and Death (identified as the Sphere of Apuleius, 'Spera Apulei'), with the diagram drawn beneath it (see fig. 2).[94] The diagram is akin to the first Sphere on folio 14v and, as mentioned, it has parallels with *Columcille's Circle* on folio 15v.[95] This Sphere, like

---

[92] This passage from Matthew is also the gospel reading for Septuagesima Sunday, see Orchard, *Leofric Missal*, Vol. II, p. 122.

[93] See Wilson, *Missal of Robert*, pp. 279–82; Turner, *Claudius Pontificals*, pp. 63–5; Orchard, *Leofric Missal*, Vol. II, pp. 416–20. See also Jolly, 'Prayers from the Field', pp. 96, 107–8.

[94] For a transcription of this introduction, see Chardonnens, *Anglo-Saxon Prognostics*, p. 195.

[95] Facsimiles of the two Spheres are printed in Chardonnens, *Anglo-Saxon Prognostics*, pp. 196, 216. Other similar prognosticatory diagrams are found in London, BL, MSS Harley 3667 (fol. 4v), Cotton Tiberius C. i (fol. 7v), Cotton Tiberius C. vi (fol. 6r), Cotton Caligula A. xv (fol. 125v), Arundel 155 (fol. 9v); *Leofric A* (fol. 50r); Oxford, St John's College, MS 17 (fol. 8r). See also Linda Voigts, 'The Latin Verse and Middle English Prose Texts on the Sphere of Life and Death in Harley 3719', *The Chaucer Review*, 21 (1986), 291–305; Roy M. Liuzza,

the first, was used to determine the outcome of an illness by lunar calculations, and it relates to the computistical calculations and lunar prognostications found earlier in the prefatory collection. Like other rituals in this collection, this prognosticatory diagram was used to calculate the spiritual health or sickness of the monastic community as well as the health or sickness of humans, livestock, and crops.

A prose introduction explains how to use the diagram, and numerical values for letters are provided beside the Sphere. The substitution of letters for numbers resonates with the ensuing texts that explain how to encrypt writing. Indeed, another (incomplete) prognosticatory Sphere – the Sphere of Petosiris – from Oxford, St John's College, MS 17 (c. 1110, Thorney Abbey, fol. 8r) includes Greek labels and cryptographic writing.[96] This manuscript also contains other cryptograms that use the same system of vowel substitution as the final texts of the *Vitellius Psalter*'s prefatory collection, indicating that some prognosticatory diagrams were sometimes closely related to ciphered writing and obscure language. The Apuleian Sphere is an appropriate addition to the collection, as it links the previous calculations and encrypted rituals to the final texts about secret writing.

Encrypted Riddle

The final folio (16v) of this prefatory collection begins with an encrypted riddle that is followed by an explanation of secret writing (fig. 3). These texts are designed to educate the reader in composing and deciphering secret messages, and they provide entertaining exercises in textual concealment. The encryptions follow a simple substitution of vowels for their following consonants, and this system was used by Boniface, Dunstan, and Carolingian writers.[97] On folios 17rv, three later scribes added prayers using the same code, indicating that these exercises

'The Sphere of Life and Death: Time, Medicine, and the Visual Imagination', in *Latin Learning and English Lore: Studies in Anglo-Saxon Literature for Michael Lapidge*, Katherine O'Brien O'Keeffe and Andy Orchard, eds (Toronto, 2005), pp. 28–52.

[96] For a digitisation of this manuscript and an excellent, extensive commentary, see Wallis, *The Calendar and the Cloister*: <http://digital.library.mcgill.ca/ms-17> accessed 26 September 2017. See also Chardonnens, *Anglo-Saxon Prognostics*, pp. 31, 221–2. Another Sphere of Apuleius that is found in Caligula A. xv (fol. 125v) also uses Greek letters.

[97] See Wilhelm Levison, *England and the Continent in the Eighth Century: The Ford Lectures* (Oxford, 1943), p. 292; and Chapter 5. It is also found in *Riddle* 36 of the Exeter Book, and in Hrabanus Maurus' *De Laudibus Sanctae Crucis* (Cambridge, Trinity College, MS B.16.3, fol. 1r), see Simon Keynes, *Anglo-Saxon Manuscripts in Trinity College*, OEN Subsidia Series, Vol. 18 (Binghamton, 1992), p. 13; Gerhard F. Strasser, 'Ninth-Century Figural Poetry and Medieval Easter Tables – Possible Inspirations for the Square Tables of Trithemius and Vigenère?', *Cryptologia*, 34 (2009), 22–6.

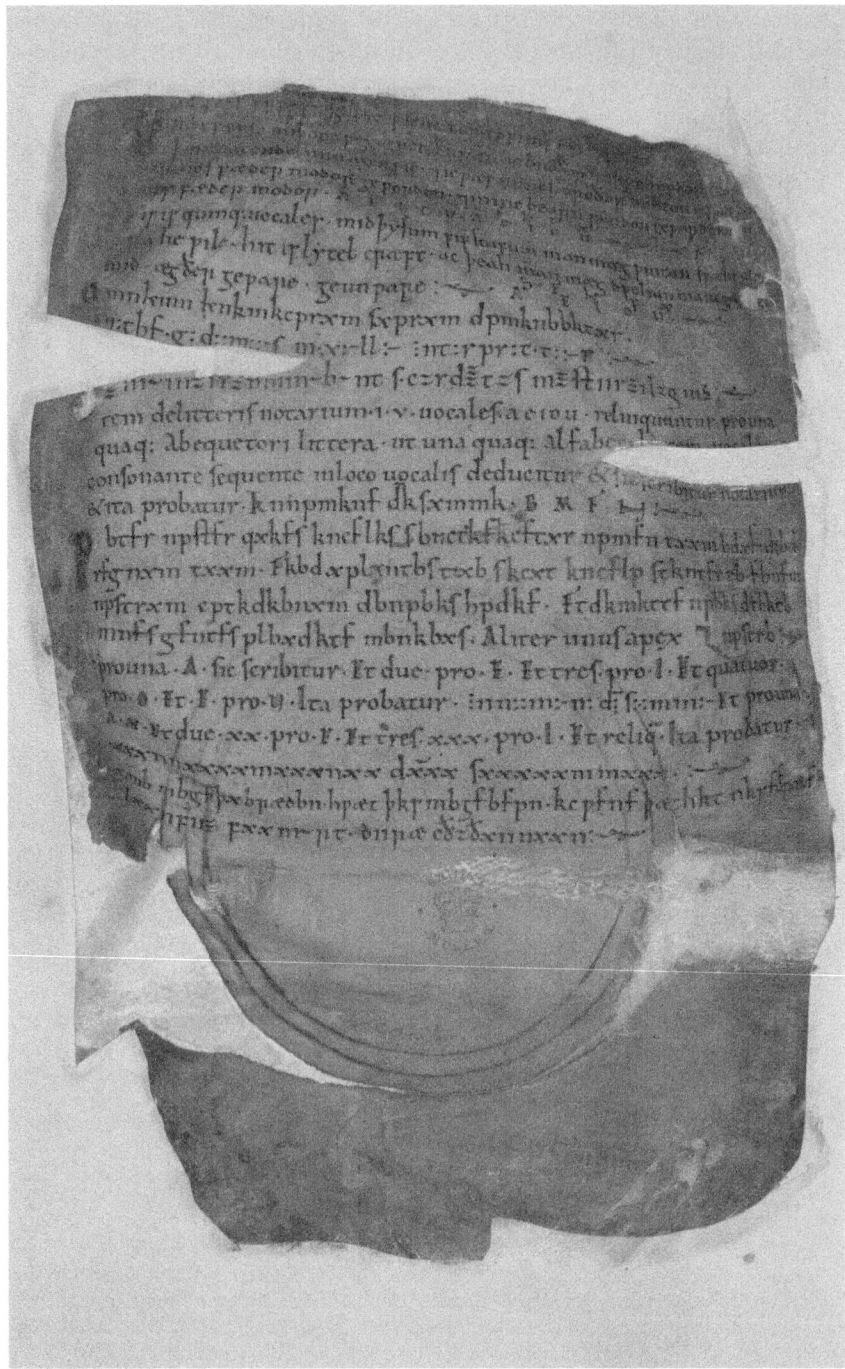

Figure 3: London, British Library, MS Cotton Vitellius E. xviii, fol. 16v
© The British Library Board

were still being read after the Anglo-Saxon period.[98] The encrypted riddle in the *Vitellius Psalter* reads:

> Nys þks frfgfn sy:llkc þknc to rædfnnf. Þu þe færst on þone weg gret ðu minne broðor minre modor ceorl þone acende min agen wif . 7 ic wæs mines broðor dohtor . 7 ic eom mines fæder modor . geworden . 7 mine bearn syndon geworden [m]ines fæder modor.[99]

> This question is not a strange thing to explain. When you go by the way, greet my brother, my mother's husband then it begot my own wife. And I was my brother's daughter, and I am become my father's mother, and my sons are become my father's mother.

The opening line is encrypted, and when deciphered it reads 'Nys þis fregen syellic þinc to rædenne'. The riddle that follows is 'a kinship riddle' and a solution of 'hound and hind' has recently been proposed.[100] In its monastic context, the riddle can be interpreted in a spiritual way, as all human relationships are relinquished to become a member of the religious community. The monks are brothers, they are all sons of God, and the ordained monks are fathers. This also applies to nuns, as all are sisters, they are brides of Christ, and they are subordinate to an abbess or Mother Superior.

The ciphered sentence acts as a title for the riddle, indicating that the task of solving it is not difficult. However, the phrase can also stand alone as a riddle in its own right as the reader must decipher its meaning before solving the kinship riddle. It must be remembered that the explanation for how to use this form of encryption comes *after* this text, and so the reader is immediately challenged with decoding this sentence before it is explained below. The system of vowel substitution is relatively simple and its appearance at the top of the folio indicates that the reader is confronted with a different type of enigmatic text as they turn the page after reading the rituals and the second Sphere of Life and Death. The riddle's appearance at the end of this collection

---

[98] For incipits of these texts, see Pulsiano, *Psalters I*, p. 53.

[99] See also Max Förster, 'Ein altenglisches Prosa-Rätsel', *Archiv für das Studium der neueren Sprachen und Literaturen*, 115 (1905), 392–3, p. 392. Another version of this riddle is also found in a mid-eleventh-century hand in Oxford, Bodleian Library, MS Bodley 572 (fol. 40r). This manuscript originated in Wales at the end of the tenth century, and it was later brought to the New Minster, Winchester, where the riddle was added, see Gneuss, *Handlist*, p. 95; Liuzza, *Anglo-Saxon Prognostics*, p. 15. This version reads 'A^b E^f I^k O^p V^x: c:.:nn· n:.s m·g· ð:.: aræd·n hwæt þ:·s m·g: b:on kc w:n: þ(æt) h:·t nis n· :ð ræd: Is ðks frfgfn sfllkc þknge to rædfnf', transcription my own. When deciphered this reads 'cunna nis magað ðu arædan hwæt þis mage beon ic wene þæt hit nis ne eð ræde. Is ðis fregen sellic þinge to rædene'.

[100] See R. D. Fulk and Christopher M. Cain, eds, *A History of Old English Literature*, 2nd edn (Malden, MA, 2005), p. 347; Niles, *Enigmatic Poems*, pp. 98–9; Murphy, *Exeter Book Riddles*, p. 10.

of calculations, predictions, and rituals indicates a spiritual function of encrypted writing and hidden knowledge that must be discerned. This is developed in the final text of the prefatory collection, which provides examples from religious texts to explain how to use this strategy of textual concealment.

Explanation of Secret Writing

The text that immediately follows the riddle begins with a short introduction in Old English:

> A. E. I. O. U. a^b e^f i^k o^p u^x – Ðis is quinque uocales . mid þysum fif stafum man mæg writan swa hwæt swa he wile . hit is lytel cræft . ac þeah man mæg dwelian manega [m]en mid . ægðer ge ware . ge unware :-.

> A. E. I. O. U. a^b e^f i^k o^p u^x – This is the five vowel [system]. With these five letters a man is able to write that which he wishes. It is a small skill, but he may deceive many men, both the enlightened and the ignorant.

This form of encryption offered a practical way to communicate in secret. It would have been useful in a monastery, as it would have provided a monk under the vow of silence with an alternative method of communication. This system would have helped to conceal messages so that they would not be easy for others to read if they were intercepted, whether they were learned or unlearned ('ægðer ge ware . ge unware'). This type of text also reflects the intellectual forms of entertainment of learned monks who wished to record clever ways of manipulating language and deceiving ('dwelian') a reader.

The examples that follow this introduction begin with a simple demonstration of how to substitute letters but they become increasingly more complex as multiple different methods of encryption are introduced. Punctuation marks, dots, horizontal and vertical lines, and the letter 'x' are all used to mark the vowels; 'a' has one dot or line or 'x', 'e' has two, 'i' has three, 'o' has four, and 'u' has five. All of the examples are in Latin with the exception of the final exercise, which contains a complex anagram in the vernacular.[101] Among the Latin examples are two references to the Psalms: 'Omnium inimicorum suorum dominabitur' (He will rule over all his enemies, Psalm 9: 26); 'Omnes gentes plaudite manibus' (All people clap your hands, Psalm 46: 2). The use of psalm references in these exercises is not surprising in a glossed psalter, although this is the only manuscript containing this text. The first reference is interesting because Psalm 9 describes a deceitful enemy who misleads with his tongue ('sub lingua eius

---

[101] For solutions to these exercises, see Pulsiano, 'Prefatory Matter', pp. 97–9.

labor et dolor', 9: 28).[102] The reference indicates that such misleading enemies will be overcome by God's help, and this example may playfully refer to this exercise in language manipulation as a misleading and laborious task that must be overcome like God's enemies. The second psalm reference contrasts with the first as it calls on the faithful to clap their hands in joy, and Phillip Pulsiano believed that this might be a playful applauding of the reader for having thus far successfully deciphered the text.[103] The other Latin examples include a phrase from Origen's homily for Palm Sunday that explains the meaning of the town Betheage ('Betheage domus maxilli interpretatur'),[104] a comment on the mysteries of the Law ('Quia in ea ruminabant sacerdotes misteria legis'),[105] the Paternoster, and the name of God ('in nomine dei summi').[106] The increasingly complicated examples are taken from an exegetical text (Origen's homily), Scripture (the Paternoster), and commentaries on divine mysteries and the unknowable name of God.

The final exercise is the most complex as it includes an encrypted anagram in the vernacular, and it reads 'Ælxxnfıı≡ fxxm-rt dıræ cð·=ðxıınxxn:-'. Phillip Pulsiano provided the solution to this example by transliterating it as 'Æluunfei emuuart deræ cðeðuenen' and rearranging the letters to read 'Ælfuuine me uurat . ræde ðu ðe cenne (Ælfwine wrote me. Read you who might be able)'.[107] Although it is rare to discover the identity of medieval authors, this text conceals a name in the most difficult cryptogram of the manuscript that also employs a complex anagram.[108] The solution to this final example identifies an ecclesiastical authority called Ælfwine who actively engaged with the composition of encrypted texts. While this name was common and no doubt there were many men called Ælfwine in Winchester at this time, there are other ciphers that use the same

---

[102] 'under tungan his gewinn 7 sar', Rosier, *Vitellius Psalter*, p. 17; 'under his tongue are labour and pain'.

[103] Pulsiano, 'Prefatory Matter', p. 98.

[104] 'Betheage is interpreted as the house of jawbones', see M. F. Toal, ed., *The Sunday Sermons of the Great Fathers*, 4 Vols. (San Francisco, 2000), Vol. II, pp. 159, 168.

[105] 'Because in it the priests were ruminating on the mysteries of the Law'. I do not know of any source for this reference.

[106] 'In the name of God the most high'.

[107] Pulsiano, 'Prefatory Matter', pp. 99–100, 102. Another Anglo-Saxon formula that is similar reads 'Wulfwi me wrat', see Gameson, *The Scribe Speaks?*, p. 18.

[108] Anagrammatic writing is also a feature of *Riddles* 19 and 75 of the *Exeter Book* that use runic letters, and Cynewulf's encrypted signatures have been viewed in a similar way, see Lois Bragg, 'Runes and Readers: In and Around "The Husband's Message"', *Studia Neophilologica*, 71 (1999), 34–50, p. 38; Birkett, 'Runes and *Revelatio*', pp. 774–8; Clements, 'Cynewulf's Runes', pp. 148–54. Formulaic inscriptions of proprietorship that utilise Roman and runic script are also found in many engraved objects from Anglo-Saxon England, see Ramey, 'Writing Speaks', pp. 342–3.

code in the personal *Prayerbook* of Ælfwine, abbot of the New Minster (1031/2). Folio 13v of Titus D. xxvii contains a cryptogram of the name Ælsinus who was a scribe that worked under Abbot Ælfwine and one of three scribes who wrote his *Prayerbook* ('{lsknxs mf scrkpskt', 'Ælsinus me scripsit'). Ælsinus was also the main scribe of the *Liber Vitae* (London, British Library, MS Stowe 944) that was composed after 1031 when Ælfwine became abbot of the New Minster.[109] It is of course an assumption that the Ælfwine named in the *Vitellius Psalter* cryptogram is the same person as the owner of *Ælfwine's Prayerbook*. However, the kind of person who was capable of composing such learned texts and who would have owned a glossed psalter (with very close textual correspondences with *Ælfwine's Prayerbook*) suggests that this is a plausible assumption.

The *Vitellius Psalter* was produced after *Ælfwine's Prayerbook*, indicating that the original version of this text was contained in the *Psalter*'s exemplar. Its probable authorship, however, raises the further possibility that Ælfwine may have been involved in the composition of other texts in the prefatory collection. Ælfwine's interest in language manipulation and textual concealment is evident in his personal *Prayerbook*, and this offers an interesting source of inspiration for the obscure language in the *Psalter*'s other rituals. This final text of the prefatory collection complements the preceding materials that decode and utilise the signs of the cosmos. The divine ordering of the world is initially deciphered, predictions of cosmological movements are then made, the rituals harness spiritual power through liturgical prayers and obscure signs and letters, and this exercise engages with secret language to simultaneously conceal and reveal Scriptural and exegetical knowledge.

Conclusions

When the texts of the prefatory collection are read as a whole, it becomes clear that the *Vitellius Psalter* is a liturgical book that seeks to decode and predict God's will in the heavenly movements, to anticipate agricultural problems and offer liturgical responses to them, and to re-conceal spiritual knowledge by encrypting language. This manuscript reveals that scribes from the monastic school at the New Minster, Winchester used signs and language in particular ways to discern divine mysteries, to harness spiritual power, and to re-conceal knowledge. When considered in their manuscript contexts, it is clear

---

[109] See Simon Keynes, ed., *The Liber Vitae of the New Minster and Hyde Abbey Winchester: British Library Stowe 944*, EEMF, Vol. 26 (Copenhagen, 1996), pp. 111–13; Günzel, *Ælfwine's Prayerbook*, p. 3.

that the texts from the *Vitellius Psalter* which have been traditionally categorised as 'charms' form part of a coherent unit within this liturgical book. There is no reason to think that contemporaries would have seen them as different to other kinds of useful knowledge or that they distinguished them from other rituals which developed from mainstream liturgical practices. As some texts in the *Vitellius Psalter* have been described as 'gibberish charms', this manuscript opens a new and fascinating approach to obscure language and writing in ritual texts. The production of 'gibberish' texts in intellectual and ecclesiastical environments indicates that their obscurity is perhaps a deliberate strategy of textual concealment.

Part III

5

In the Beginning Was the Letter:
The Cosmological Power of 'Gibberish'

'Like their ancient predecessors, learned Anglo-Saxons perceived in writing the ability to make knowledge secret by transposing one thing into another. This secrecy might be created by using encryption, by jumbling or substituting letters.'[1]

The final part of this book engages with the phenomenon of so-called 'gibberish' writing, which features consistently in rituals that have been categorised as 'charms'. The *Vitellius Psalter* reveals an interest in obscure writing in late Anglo-Saxon monasteries, in this case specifically the New Minster, Winchester. The text in this manuscript that explains how to encrypt language explicitly states that letters can be manipulated to communicate in secret ('mid þysum fif stafum man mæg writan swa hwæt swa he wile'),[2] and its rituals seem to use letters and language in such a way as to conceal meaning. *Ælfwine's Prayerbook* also contains a number of texts with obscure letter combinations, particularly the ritual against theft that instructs the writing of 'has litteras' from at least three different alphabets. We have also encountered a comparable use of letters in the 'charm' to obtain favours in Caligula A. xv, which was discussed in Chapter 3. This ritual claims that specific 'stafas' have the power to influence important political authorities ('Gif þu wille ga[…] þ[in]um hla[forde] oþþ[e] to kyninge oþþe to oþrum menn oððe [t]o gemote þonne bær þu þas stafas').[3]

In Chapter 2 we also saw that rituals containing a *galdor* or *gebed* often use obscure words and phrases from several languages. In *Bald's Leechbook*, for example, a ritual for spring fever prescribes a *galdor*, two 'godcund gebed' (divine prayers) that use the runic and Roman alphabets, and the writing of Greek letters in silence ('sceal mon swigende þis writan').[4] Other rituals in this manuscript prescribe the

---

[1] Edward Christie, 'By Means of a Secret Alphabet: Dangerous Letters and the Semantics of *Gebregdstafas* (*Solomon and Saturn I*, Line 2b)', *Modern Philology*, 109 (2011), 145–70, p. 169.

[2] 'With these five letters a man is able to write that which he wishes'.

[3] 'If you wish to go to your lord or to the king or to another man or to a council, then carry these letters with you.'

[4] Cockayne, *Leechdoms*, Vol. II, p. 140.

writing of 'greciscum stafum' for a *galdor* against elf-sickness, and the singing of an obscure Irish *galdor* ('Acræ ærcræ ærnem') against flying venom.[5] Two rituals against worms in the *Lacnunga* of Harley 585 also provide obscure Irish, English, and Latin words and phrases for their *galdru* (beginning 'Gonomil orgomil marbumil' and 'Acre arcre arnem', respectively).[6] These texts combine individual 'stafas' to signify powerful ritual performances. There may have been a delib-erate element of secrecy and concealment deployed in these rituals, indicating that they were understood to be too powerful to become common knowledge.

The obscure language of these and other rituals has often been described as 'gibberish', and it has been interpreted as evidence of the unlearned, folk nature and oral transmission of 'charms'. Building on the manuscript contexts already discussed in previous chapters, I argue that it makes far more sense to read these rituals in the context of learned, Patristic traditions that were interested in alphabets, letters, numerology, obscurity, and textual concealment. This chapter provides an overview of how 'gibberish' has been used to classify a significant proportion of the 'charms' corpus, and it considers examples of texts that have been classified in this way. It then outlines philosophical approaches to language in late Anglo-Saxon England, and argues that this is the context in which 'gibberish' rituals were perceived. There is much work yet to be done to better understand these texts, and reading them in this context could help to uncover information that may be hidden in their secret language.[7]

'Gibberish' in Anglo-Saxon Rituals

In his 1909 edition of Anglo-Saxon 'charms', Felix Grendon claimed that a large proportion of these texts are characterised by their use of 'powerful names or magical formulas composed of senseless words'.[8] He suggested that these apparent meaningless, jumbled words may have been corrupted from classical sources, but concluded that 'since gibberish spells have been found among peoples widely different in race, it may fairly be argued that English spells arose among the English themselves'.[9] Grendon therefore created a large sub-category

[5] Cockayne, *Leechdoms*, Vol. II, pp. 138, 112.
[6] Pettit, *Anglo-Saxon Remedies*, Vol. I, pp. 14, 32.
[7] I am currently conducting a project on this topic entitled 'Obscurity and Textual Concealment in Early Medieval England' (2017–20), funded by the Leverhulme Trust.
[8] Grendon, 'Anglo-Saxon Charms', p. 114.
[9] Grendon, 'Anglo-Saxon Charms', p. 124.

of 'gibberish charms', which he believed reflected a distinctively English, heathen tradition:

> These conjurations, unlike the preceding ones, are crude, formless pieces, destitute of literary merit. Their distinguishing feature is a meaningless formula composed of a jumble of more or less obscure words. Occasionally a Greek, Latin, Hebrew, Gaelic, or Anglo-Saxon word appears, and a few words seem to have had their origin in one or other of those languages; but the derivation of a majority of the words is not ascertainable… [in some 'charms'] the formula consists, not of meaningless words strung together, but of unintelligible collocations of liturgical Latin. As a rule, the ceremonies prescribed are of Heathen ancestry.[10]

Grendon selected ritual texts from three manuscripts for their use of 'gibberish' (London, British Library, MSS Cotton Faustina A. x; Harley 585; Royal 12 D. xvii), and he also associated rituals in Caligula A. xv and the *Vitellius Psalter* with this sub-category.[11] Grendon thought that the letters in these rituals are 'formless pieces', but it may be the case that they were not meant to be readily accessible to the reader; prior knowledge of deliberately obscured language and foreign alphabets would have been required to understand and use their 'unintelligible collocations'.

Consider, for example, the language that is used in three rituals from Harley 585 for toothache, a dwarf, and theft that led Grendon to classify them as 'gibberish charms':

Wið Toðece (fol. 135v)
Sing ðis wið toðece, syððan sunne beo on setle, swiðe oft: 'Caio laio quaque, uoaque ofer sæloficia sleah manna wyrm'. Nemne her þone man and his fæder, cweð þonne: 'Lilumenne, aceð þæt ofer eall þonne alið; coliað, þonne hit on eorðan hatost byrneð; finit, amen.'[12]

Wið Dweorh (fol. 164v)
Writ ðis ondlang ða earmas wiþ dweorh: + t + w A and gnid cyleðenigean on ealað. Sanctus Macutus, sancte Victorici.
Writ ðis ondlang ða earmas wiþ dweorh: + t + p + N + w + t + m + M + w A and gnid cyleðenigean on ealað. Sanctus Macutus, sancte Victorici.[13]

[10] Grendon, 'Anglo-Saxon Charms', pp. 124, 127.
[11] See Grendon, 'Anglo-Saxon Charms', pp. 116, 168–73, 202–7, 210, 217–19, 233–51.
[12] Grendon, 'Anglo-Saxon Charms', p. 170; 'Sing this against toothache very often, when the sun sets: "Caio laio, uoaque over sæloficia the man struck the serpent". Here name the man and his father, say then: "Lilumenne, it aches over all the (?) loss (read 'lost tooth'?); it cools, then it burns hottest on earth; finit, amen".'
[13] Grendon, 'Anglo-Saxon Charms', p. 210; 'Write this along the arms against a dwarf: + t + w A and crumble calendine into ale. Saint Macutus, Saint Victoricus.

Wið Þeofentum (fol. 178r)

Wið Þeofentum: Luben luben niga efið efið niga fel ceid fel, delf cumer fel orcgaei cuefor dard, giug farig fidig delou delupih.[14]

These 'gibberish' texts show that a number of languages were used in such formulas. The ritual for toothache shows elements of Old English ('sleah manna wyrm'), phonetic Greek ('Caio laio'), and Latin ('quaque', 'finit'). The ritual against a dwarf abbreviates names or words or phrases with single letters, and it separates each with markers for the sign of the cross. The theft ritual also seems to use obscure Irish with Anglo-Saxon letters (namely 'ð'). Grendon classed many more texts as 'gibberish charms' according to their similar uses of language and alphabets.[15]

In the second main corpus of Anglo-Saxon 'charms', Godfrid Storms described how 'the mystification of a foreign tongue' appealed to English scribes in the copying of ritual texts.[16] He also maintained that 'gibberish' is one of the main criteria that can be used to identify 'charms':

> [Against tooth-ache] This and the next twenty formulas may be called 'gibberish or jingle charms', because the contents have become incomprehensible for the most part. The reason lies in the introduction of foreign elements whose meaning soon became unknown, with the result that the words gradually developed into unintelligible, meaningless sounds.[17]

Storms greatly added to Grendon's collection of 'gibberish' rituals, as he included twenty-one out of eighty-six texts in this category. They are taken from nine of the twenty-three manuscripts that Storms used for his edition, demonstrating that 'gibberish' constitutes a significant proportion of his corpus of 'charms'.[18]

Examples of texts that Storms classified as 'gibberish charms' include rituals against a dwarf, black blains, and fever:

> Write this along the arms against a dwarf: + t + p + N + w + t + m + M + w A and crumble calendine into ale. Saint Macutus, Saint Victoricus.'

[14] Grendon, 'Anglo-Saxon Charms', p. 168; 'Against theft: Luben luben niga efið efið niga fel ceid fel, delf cumer fel orcgaei cuefor dard, giug farig fidig delou delupih.'

[15] See, for example, Grendon, 'Anglo-Saxon Charms', pp. 113–16.

[16] Storms, *Anglo-Saxon Magic*, p. 1.

[17] Storms, *Anglo-Saxon Magic*, p. 297. See also pp. 5, 38, 119, 271.

[18] The manuscripts are: Cambridge, Corpus Christi College, MS 367 (fol. 52r); Cambridge, Gonville & Caius College, MS 379 (fol. 49r); Caligula A. xv (fols. 129r, 140r); Faustina A. x (fol. 116r); the *Vitellius Psalter* (fol. 15v); Harley 585 (fols. 135r–137r, 178rv, 182rv, 185v–186v); Royal 12 D. xvii (fols. 20rv, 43rv); Oxford, Bodleian Library, MS Auct. 7-3-6 (fols. 1, 2v); and Oxford, Bodleian Library, MS Junius 163 (fol. 227), see Storms, *Anglo-Saxon Magic*, pp. viii, 297–311.

Wiþ Dworh (Oxford, Bodleian Library, MS Auct. F. 3. 6, fol. 2v, s. xi)
and thebal guttatim aurum et thus de. + albra Iesus. + alabra Iesus +
Galabra Iesus. +
Wið þone dworh. on. III. oflætan writ: THEBAL GUTTA.[19]

Black Blains (Oxford, Bodleian Library, MS Bodley 163, fol. 227, s. xi[med])
Tigað. Tigað. Tigað. calicet ac locluel sedes adclocles arcre encrcre
erernem Nonabaioth arcum cunat arcum arcua fligata soh wiþni necutes
cuterii rafaf þegal uflen binchni. arta. arta. arta. tuxuncula. tuxuncula.
tuxuncula.
Querite et invenietis. pulsate et aperietur vobis. Crux Matheus. crux
Marcus. crux Lucas. crux Iohannes. Adiuro te pestiferum virus per
patrem et filium et spiritum sanctum. ut amplius non noceas neque
crescas sed arescas. Amen.[20]

Wiþ Gedrif (London, British Library, MS Cotton Caligula A. xv, fol. 129r,
c. 1073)
Wið gedrif . + In nomine domini nostri Iesu Christi. tera. tera. tera. testis.
contera. taberna. gise. ges. maude. leis. bois. eis. andies. mandies. moab.
lib. lebes.
Dominus deus adiutor sit illi. illi. eax. filiax. artifex. Amen.[21]

In the same way as Grendon, Storms classed these and other rituals
as 'gibberish' according to their use of obscure languages and foreign

---

[19] Storms, *Anglo-Saxon Magic*, p. 305; 'and thebal (?) drop by drop gold and frank-
incense de. + albra Iesus. + alabra Iesus + Galabra Iesus. + Against the dwarf,
write on three Eucharistic hosts: Thebal (?) drop.' For details of this manuscript, see Ker, *Catalogue*, pp. 354–5; Gameson, 'Origin of the Exeter Book',
p. 150; Gneuss, *Handlist*, p. 90; Wieland, 'Latin Manuscripts', p. 148; Lapidge,
Anglo-Saxon Library, pp. 140, 328–30; Jolly, 'Tapping the Power of the Cross',
pp. 60, 76.

[20] Storms, *Anglo-Saxon Magic*, p. 302; 'Tigað. Tigað. Tigað. calicet ac locluel sedes
adclocles arcre encrcre erernem Nonabaioth arcum cunat arcum arcua fligata
soh wiþni necutes cuterii rafaf þegal uflen binchni. arta. arta. arta. tuxuncula.
tuxuncula. tuxuncula. Seek and you will find. Knock and it will be opened to
you. Cross Matthew. Cross Mark. Cross Luke. Cross John. I command you,
pestilent virus, through the Father and Son and Holy Spirit, so that you no
longer injure nor multiply but wither. Amen.' A later version of this ritual
survives in a twelfth-century medical collection in Cambridge, Gonville and
Caius College, MS 379, which also contains a work on the simple virtues of
medicine, the *Liber de compendio Salerni*, Matthaeus Platearius' work on medicine, as well as many other recipes for particular ailments. The 'thigat' formula
in this manuscript is immediately followed by an alternative ritual that invokes
the cross in Latin, see Storms, *Anglo-Saxon Magic*, p. 294. See also M. R. James, *A
Descriptive Catalogue of the Manuscripts in the Library of Gonville and Caius College*,
2 Vols. (Cambridge, 1907–8), Vol. II, pp. 430–3; Jolly, 'Tapping the Power of the
Cross', p. 77.

[21] Storms, *Anglo-Saxon Magic*, p. 300; 'Against fever: + In the name of our Lord
Jesus Christ. tera. tera. tera. testis. contera. taberna. gise. ges. maude. leis. bois.
eis. andies. mandies. moab. lib. lebes. May the Lord God be a helper for him.
eax. filiax. artifex. Amen.'

alphabets. The ritual against a dwarf uses Latin ('aurum et thus') and what appears to be Hebrew ('thebal'), and it includes markers for the sign of the cross. It was written along with other 'nonsense charms' against nosebleed by an eleventh-century scribe on a flyleaf of a manuscript containing poetry by Prudentius (with added glosses in Old English and Latin), and verses on the *Passion of St Romanus*.[22] When the obscure language of this ritual is considered with the manuscript's texts, it is possible that the scribe of this ritual had read the manuscript and was interested in mystical languages and Christian poetry. The ritual for black blains uses Latin and apparent Irish, and it was added in the mid-eleventh century to an early eleventh-century manuscript containing Bede's *Historia Ecclesiastica*, Æthelwulf's *De abbatibus*, and excerpts from Jerome and Orosius.[23] Other mid-eleventh-century additions to this part of the manuscript include glosses to Bede's *Historia* (fols. 66r, 111v, 112r, 154r) and a West-Saxon version of *Cædmon's Hymn*.[24] The surrounding context for this 'gibberish charm' suggests that the scribe of this ritual was perhaps interested in exotic languages, the Cædmon legend, and Patristic writings.[25] Finally, the ritual against fever from Caligula A. xv is part of a short series of texts for healing that form part of a larger collection concerned with mystical language. As seen in Chapter 3, this part of the manuscript was written by one scribe from Christ Church Cathedral, Canterbury. The manuscript

---

[22] Ker, *Catalogue*, pp. 354–5. See also Lapidge, *Anglo-Saxon Library*, pp. 140, 328–30; Scragg, 'Old English Prose', pp. 68–9; *Conspectus*, p. 77; Mary Swan and Owen Robertson, 'The Production and Use of English Manuscripts 1060 to 1220': <http://www.le.ac.uk/english/em1060to1220> accessed 26 September 2017.

[23] See Ker, *Catalogue*, p. 358; Katherine O'Brien O'Keeffe, *Visible Song: Transitional Literacy in Old English Verse* (Cambridge, 1990), pp. 30–7; Gneuss, *Handlist*, p. 92; Daniel Paul O'Donnell, *Cædmon's Hymn: A Multi-Media Study, Edition, and Archive* (Cambridge, 2005), p. 81; Lapidge, *Anglo-Saxon Library*, pp. 143–7, 295, 323; Jolly, 'Tapping the Power of the Cross', pp. 60, 76; Gneuss and Lapidge, *Bibliographical Handlist*, pp. 439–40.

[24] O'Brien O'Keeffe, *Visible Song*, pp. 30–7; Owen Robertson, 'The Production and Use of English Manuscripts 1060 to 1220': <http://www.le.ac.uk/english/em1060to1220> accessed 26 September 2017. A Latin-Old English glossary was later added when the manuscript was at Peterborough in the early twelfth century.

[25] Another example of this intellectual preoccupation can be found in the twelfth-century manuscript Cambridge, Queen's College, MS 7, which contains Adalbert's *Speculum Gregorii* and his commentary on Gregory the Great's exegetical work *On the Song of Songs*. A Latin ritual for fever that appears in this manuscript (fol. 142v) has the title 'Exorcismus ad Febres expellendas', and it includes phonetic spellings of Greek and Aramaic words, see Thomas Hartwell Horne, *A Catalogue of the Library of the College of St. Margaret and St. Bernard, Commonly Called Queen's College in the University of Cambridge*, 2 Vols. (London, 1827), Vol. II, pp. 999–1000; M. R. James, *A Descriptive Catalogue of the Western Manuscripts in the Library of Queen's College, Cambridge* (Cambridge, 1905), pp. 7–8; Storms, *Anglo-Saxon Magic*, pp. 295–6.

context surrounding this fever ritual indicates that ecclesiastics from high-status minsters like Canterbury Cathedral were interested in – if not able to read – obscure language in these ritual texts. Despite these possibilities, Storms followed Grendon in claiming that such rituals form a distinctive type of 'charm' because they incorporate foreign elements that were misunderstood by their scribes. According to these editors, meaningless, garbled sounds replaced heathen formulas and were recorded because their mysterious epigraphic appearance was appealing.

These views of Grendon and Storms have led scholars to continue to say that nonsensical 'gibberish' is a defining characteristic of 'charms'. Paul Cavill, for example, believes that it was used to console superstitious patients:

> Charms are the literature of desperation. Ideas from any source, which might give hope to the suffering, found a place. Other charms have strings of 'magical' gobbledegook, meaningless syllables, bits of Latin, instructions on ritual actions such as culling herbs at dawn, crossing rivers and keeping silent – anything to enhance the air of mystery and lend authority to the charmer. These things apparently co-existed with a predominantly Christian world view. Sometimes Christian mumbo-jumbo has replaced heathen elements.[26]

According to Cavill, sick subjects and poorly educated monks turned to mysterious languages that they could not understand simply to aid their belief in a reality beyond their immediate suffering.

Despite arguments that 'gibberish' writing developed from the corrupt copying of misunderstood texts, Leslie Arnovick has claimed that it was not perceived to be entirely nonsensical by Anglo-Saxon performers and audiences. Indeed, she believes that the more unintelligible words and phrases are, the more this would have added to their linguistic efficacy, and that the technical fluency of the performer in pronouncing these formulas would have reflected their competence and gained the audience's trust.[27] Arnovick acknowledges the likelihood of scribal error and corruption of source texts but argues that this would not have been of great concern to the performer and audience,

---

[26] Cavill, *Anglo-Saxon Christianity*, p. 25. For similar arguments, see George Hardin Brown, 'Solving the "Solve" Riddle in B. L. MS Harley 585', *Viator*, 18 (1987), 45–51; R. A. Banks, 'The Uses of Liturgy in the Magic, Medicine, and Poetry of the Anglo-Saxons', in *The Timeless and the Temporal: Writings in Honour of John Chalker by Friends and Colleagues*, Elizabeth Maslen, ed. (Exeter, 1993), pp. 19–40, p. 29; Rosanne Hebing, 'The Textual Tradition of Heavenly Letter Charms in Anglo-Saxon Manuscripts', in *Secular Learning in Anglo-Saxon England*, Chardonnens and Carella, eds, pp. 203–22, p. 207; Olsan, 'Marginality of Charms', pp. 136–7.

[27] Arnovick, *Written Reliquaries*, p. 42. See also Jolly, *Popular Religion*, pp. 117–18.

as the words prescribed on the manuscript page would have represented the healer's script for performance, whatever their meaning.[28] Furthermore, she argues that the modern perception of such language being nonsensical does not take into account the spiritual audience it addresses. Arnovick usefully proposes an alternative reading of 'gibberish' as 'spirit code', a language that would have made sense and been understood by spirits, much like speaking in tongues.[29] The vocalisation of obscure formulas, she claims, would have also mystified an Anglo-Saxon audience who believed that the authorised performer knew how to harness spiritual power through this linguistic medium, although she does not explain how formulas which cannot be vocalised would have been performed.[30] Arnovick's counter-arguments credit Anglo-Saxon scribes and compilers with logical reasons for deliberately including particular types of obscure texts in important manuscript collections. They were not simply (mis)copied arbitrarily because of their superstitious appeal, they functioned to effectively communicate with the spiritual world, and they elevated the ritual performance through their unintelligibility. However, Arnovick's view that 'gibberish' was understood to be a 'spirit code' that could simultaneously coerce demons and mystify an illiterate Anglo-Saxon audience does not convincingly account for the linguistic capabilities of highly educated scribes who were at the very least bilingual and also interested exotic alphabets and language manipulation.

Building upon Arnovick's argument that there is much more to obscure language in ritual texts than nonsensical and meaningless 'gibberish', I propose that, rather than reflecting a language which could only be understood by spirits and which mystified illiterate Anglo-Saxon audiences (neither of which can be proved), obscure writing in rituals reflects the censorship of these powerful texts that were performed only by those who knew how to read and decipher them. In other words, 'gibberish' writing may reflect more about the composers and authorised performers of these rituals than it does about the effects it had on human and spiritual audiences. It is of course possible that Anglo-Saxon scribes confused and corrupted letters and alphabets during the copying of texts; it is well known that even the highest-quality manuscript productions contain grammatical and linguistic errors. However, such rigid conclusions about scribal error and the complete misunderstanding of source materials do not convincingly explain the production of these rituals in learned ecclesiastical environments. It may also be the case that 'gibberish' was perceived by church officials as a mystifying but not fully comprehendible language

---

[28] Arnovick, *Written Reliquaries*, p. 30.
[29] Arnovick, *Written Reliquaries*, pp. 33, 58–9.
[30] Arnovick, *Written Reliquaries*, pp. 35–6, 57–8.

that could summon great spiritual power, in similar fashion to how the illiterate laity may have perceived Latin. Some texts may indeed reflect this attitude but, in some cases, it does not seem convincing that highly educated churchmen saw this type of ritual language as mystical 'hocus pocus' (in the original sense of this corrupted phrase). There is evidence to suggest that high-ranking ecclesiastics may have at least known of or owned some of these manuscripts, and they had years of training both in England and abroad, with knowledge of multiple languages. Furthermore, impenetrably obscure words, phrases, and passages that required knowledge of foreign languages are most often found in particular types of texts and manuscript collections that were written to deliberately challenge their readers or prevent unauthorised people from accessing them.[31] Even if some (or many) obscure texts are corrupted, attempts should be made to make sense of their strange letter combinations, phonetic spellings, incomplete references, and possible ciphered systems; and this requires scholars to entertain the possibility that the writing is far from nonsensical.

The manuscript contexts surrounding 'gibberish' rituals show that many were written in monastic schools at a time when ecclesiastics were interested in language manipulation and obscurity, and when the study of vernacular and foreign languages was intensified. It is worth remembering that grecisms and neologisms were developed in English monasteries like Christ Church, Canterbury (under Oda) and the Old Minster, Winchester (under Æthelwold), and that there was great traffic between English and Continental monasteries at this time. It may be that some texts were deliberately obscured in the process of copying from an exemplar, or it may also be the case that they were composed at the time of writing (where no variants of a text survive). Ælfwine's probable involvement in the composition of ciphers reminds us of how some learned Anglo-Saxons were interested in manipulating language, and the ritual for favours in Caligula A. xv demonstrates that obscure texts were also of interest to important, politically influential ecclesiastics in Canterbury. As will be seen in this chapter, it makes more sense to understand 'gibberish' writing in the context of intellectual engagements with classical and early medieval philosophies of language, language study, and textual concealment.

Gibberish in other Anglo-Saxon Writings

'Gibberish' writing is also found in other Anglo-Saxon texts, and studies of obscure language in wisdom poems, riddles, and scribal

---

[31] For a similar argument, see Pelteret, 'Cross and an Acrostic', p. 63.

signatures can inform our understanding of this phenomenon in ritual texts. Lois Bragg proposes that the runic sequence in the *Husband's Message* is alliterating gibberish that was used as 'a kind of stage prop appropriate to his [the poet's] legendary setting'.[32] Bragg also believes that the scholar's inability to interpret such writings demonstrates how Anglo-Saxon scribes and readers must not have been able to understand them either:

> When we recall the frequency of errors that Moltke has reported and consider that modern runologists, armed with comprehensive, edited collections of inscriptions recovered with recently developed technology, cannot make head nor tail of most of the inscriptions, it is unlikely that post-Alfredian Anglo-Saxons could read them. Perhaps, finding the inscriptions illegible, they assumed that they were cryptographic.[33]

Bragg takes a traditional approach to obscure writing in Anglo-Saxon texts, and believes that it provides evidence of scribal error and textual corruption. However, the modern reader's inability to understand these writings is no basis to claim that they are nonsensical.

Tom Birkett's recent work on runic letters in riddles and wisdom poems has opened fascinating interpretations of how these graphemes were used to uncover as well as conceal hidden meanings in texts. Indeed, he highlights the literary contexts in which runes are associated with unlocking hidden meanings, whereby the rune itself becomes a key to the correct interpretation of the enigmatic text.[34] He also discusses the spiritual significance of runes in challenging the reader to discern meaning beyond the literal sense of the text, much like exegetical reading practices.[35] Jill Clements argues that Cynewulf's runic signatures add an eschatological dimension to wisdom poems that end with his colophon. She convincingly argues that the physical separation of the runic letters that spell Cynewulf's name reflects the fragmentation of his human body into its most elemental or anatomical state.[36] Like Cynewulfian signatures, other riddles and wisdom poems incorporate runic writing to enhance their enigmatic nature, and the graphemes force the reader to look for meaning beyond the immediate, literal sense of the text. These texts reflect an interest in letter manipulation, alphabet substitution, and encryption that were used in different Christian literary traditions. Objects, concepts, and letters are given multiple meanings, and it is likely that different alphabets and

---

[32] Bragg, 'Runes and Readers', p. 40.
[33] Bragg, 'Runes and Readers', p. 45.
[34] Birkett, 'Runes and *Revelatio*', pp. 774–5. 776. See also Tom Birkett, *Reading the Runes in Old English and Old Norse Poetry* (Abingdon, 2017).
[35] Birkett, 'Runes and *Revelatio*', p. 776.
[36] Clements, 'Reading, Writing and Resurrection', pp. 138, 149, 153.

languages are used in rituals to deliberately obfuscate their meaning in a similar fashion.

In addition to this role of graphemes in concealing information and encoding knowledge, letters were also believed to possess apotropaic power. A poetic version of the *Solomon and Saturn* dialogue, contained in Corpus 41, depicts the letters of the Paternoster as engaging the devil in military combat which, when vocalised, become animated warriors for Solomon.[37] A prose version of this text also contains a passage that describes Mercury as the inventor of letters, and scholars have interpreted this as a reference to Woden's creation of the alphabet.[38] Rolf Bremmer disputes this and highlights the many possible transmissions of the Mercury legend from classical sources.[39] Patristic and classical traditions about the origins of language are also likely to have influenced other Anglo-Saxon writings that harness the cosmological power of letters and alphabets.

Other combinations of graphemes are also found in non-manuscript sources from England. The coffin of St Cuthbert, for example, contains an inscription that combines Roman and runic letters which spell the names of seven angels.[40] Leslie Webster believes that such word play and encryptions which utilise parallel scripts arose out of Christian traditions in Anglo-Saxon England.[41] The twelfth-century Bridekirk font

---

[37] See especially Marie Nelson, 'King Solomon's Magic: The Power of a Written Text', *Oral Tradition*, 5 (1990), 20–36, p. 29; O'Brien O'Keeffe, *Visible Song*, pp. 47–76; Andy Orchard, 'The Word Made Flesh: Christianity and Oral Culture in Anglo-Saxon Verse', *Oral Tradition*, 24 (2009), 293–318; Tom Birkett, 'Unlocking Runes? Reading Anglo-Saxon Runic Abbreviations in Their Immediate Literary Context', *Futhark*, 5 (2015), 91–114, pp. 108–12.

[38] J. S. Ryan, 'Othin in England: Evidence from the Poetry for a Cult of Woden in Anglo-Saxon England', *Folklore*, 73–4 (1962–3), 460–80, p. 476; H. R. Ellis Davidson, *Gods and Myths of Northern Europe* (Harmondsworth, 1964), p. 141; Edward O. G. Turville-Petre, *Myth and Religion of the North* (London, 1964), p. 71. On the prose version of this text more generally, see John Hermann, 'The Pater Noster Battle Sequence in *Solomon and Saturn* and the *Psychomachia* of Prudentius', *Neuphilologische Mitteilungen*, 77 (1976), 206–10; Thomas D. Hill, 'The Devil's Forms and the Pater Noster's Powers: The Prose Solomon and Saturn *Pater Noster* Dialogue', *SP*, 85 (1988), 164–76; Dendle, 'Demonological Landscape'.

[39] Rolf Bremmer, 'Mercury-Hermes and Woden-Odin as Inventors of Alphabets: A Neglected Parallel', in *Old English Runes and their Continental Background*, Alfred Bammesberger, ed. (Heidelberg, 1991), pp. 409–19.

[40] See Ernst Kitzinger, 'The Coffin-Reliquary', in *The Relics of St. Cuthbert*, C. F. Battiscombe, ed. (Oxford, 1956), pp. 202–307; J. M. Cronyn and C. V. Horie, 'The Anglo-Saxon Coffin: Further Investigations', and R. I. Page, 'Roman and Runic on St Cuthbert's Coffin', in *St Cuthbert, his Cult and his Community to A.D. 1200*, Gerald Bonner, David W. Rollason, and Clare Stancliffe, eds (Woodbridge, 1995), pp. 247–56 and pp. 257–65.

[41] Leslie Webster, 'The Iconographic Programme of the Franks Casket', in *Northumbria's Golden Age*, Jane Hawkes and Susan Mills, eds (Stroud, 1999), pp. 227–46, pp. 227–8.

from Cumbria has a Middle English couplet carved in Scandinavian runes, and reads 'Rikarþ:he:me:iwr[o]kte:7:to:þis:me:rÐ:ʒer:**:me:br okte' ('Rikarþ wrought me, and to this [ʒer:**] brought me').[42] The inscription identifies those responsible for making the font, and their names are encoded and fastened to this liturgical object in a similar way to the cryptograms of the *Vitellius Psalter* and *Ælfwine's Prayerbook*. Encrypted inscriptions abound in early medieval objects,[43] and there is good evidence that some scribes of manuscripts also consciously used distinctively obscure forms of writing from a range of different alphabets to conceal the meaning of a text. Even if the meanings of these texts were known only to a small group or community, there was likely to be a specific purpose behind their seemingly erroneous content. Such writings have in fact been successful (for now) in concealing their secrets, much to the bemusement (and delight) of scholars.

The surviving Anglo-Saxon manuscripts that contain obscure writing were written in minsters where signs, symbols, and letters were used to interpret astronomical movements, and where ritual responses to cosmological events were carefully composed. Language played a crucial role in decoding the cosmos and encoding spiritual mysteries, and some English writers were directly influenced by Patristic philosophies in their understanding of how letters functioned in the ordering of the universe. It is therefore better to read Anglo-Saxon 'gibberish' writing according to learned, Christian traditions that engaged with the origin of languages, exotic alphabets, letter manipulation, numerology, and secret writing.

Anglo-Saxon Philosophies of Language

There is a wealth of evidence to suggest that leading English ecclesiastics had a keen interest in language's role in the creation of the world and in the transmission of divine mysteries. They drew upon writings from Late Antiquity and Carolingian Europe that provide explanations for the origins of language and the mystical obscurity of Scripture.[44] Many classical and early medieval texts provide interesting justifica-

---

[42] See R. I. Page, *An Introduction to English Runes*, 2nd edn (Woodbridge, 1999), pp. 207–8. Page suggests that the sequence 'ʒer:**' could be another personal name of one who commissioned or embellished the font.

[43] See Leslie Webster, 'Visual Literacy in a Protoliterate Age', in *Literacy in Medieval and Early Modern Scandinavian Culture*, P. Hermann, ed. (Odense, 2005), pp. 21–46; 'Encrypted Visions: Style and Sense in the Anglo-Saxon Minor Arts AD 400–900', in *Anglo-Saxon Styles*, Catherine E. Karkov and George Hardin Brown, eds (Albany, NY, 2012), pp. 11–30.

[44] On the importance of obscurity in medieval hermeneutics, see O'Sullivan, 'The Sacred and the Obscure', p. 70; Stephenson, *The Politics of Language*, pp. 14, 19.

tions for unconventional uses of language and symbols. Three core issues from these writings can inform Anglo-Saxon textual obscurity: the biblical accounts of the fall of the Tower of Babel and Pentecost are used to interpret the spiritual origin and nature of human languages; the individual letter is presented as the principal foundation of the art of grammar, which is essential for the translation of Scripture and biblical exegesis; and once languages are broken down into their smallest components they can be manipulated for secret communication. All of these ideas were developed by English theologians, and they inform our understanding of 'gibberish' writing in ritual texts.

A number of works by Jerome, Augustine, and Isidore of Seville (among many others) were well known in important Anglo-Saxon minsters.[45] By the late seventh century, the school of Theodore and Hadrian at Canterbury probably had copies of works by Jerome and Augustine, as well as all twenty books of Isidore's *Etymologies*.[46] These and other Patristic writings influenced important English authors including Aldhelm, Boniface, Bede, and later Ælfric and Byrhtferth of Ramsey. These theologians offer different perspectives on how language transmits knowledge and encodes divine secrets, and their insights provide an important philosophical context for Anglo-Saxon textual obscurity.

Jerome and Augustine

St Jerome (c. 347–419/20) is famous for his comprehensive translation of the Bible into the Latin vulgate from Greek and Hebrew (begun in 391, completed in 406). Ten years before this work was complete, Jerome wrote a letter to the Roman senator Pammachius in defence of his Latin translation of a Greek document. The letter reveals a number of important issues of language usage in biblical exegesis that continued throughout the medieval period, and Helen Gittos has argued

---

[45] See Peter Hunter Blair, *The World of Bede* (Cambridge, 1970), p. 292; Gneuss, 'Study of Language', pp. 8–9, 11–12; *Handlist*, pp. 153–5, 168–9; Lapidge, *Anglo-Saxon Library*, pp. 148, 217, 271, 315. See also Richard Marsden, 'Ælfric as Translator: The Old English Prose *Genesis*', *Anglia*, 109 (1991), 319–58, p. 324; Robert Stanton, *The Culture of Translation in Anglo-Saxon England* (Cambridge, 2002), pp. 77, 135–7; Christopher M. Cain, 'Sacred Words, Anglo-Saxon Piety, and the Origins of the *Epistola Salvatoris* in London, British Library, Royal 2.A.xx', *JEGP*, 108 (2009), 168–89, pp. 182–4.

[46] See Bernhard Bischoff and Michael Lapidge, *Biblical Commentaries from the Canterbury School of Theodore and Hadrian* (Cambridge, 1994), pp. 202–5, 275–96; Isidore of Seville, *The Etymologies of Isidore of Seville*, Stephen Barney, W. J. Lewis, J. A. Beach, Oliver Berghof, eds and trans (Cambridge, 2006), pp. 24–6; David W. Porter, 'Isidore's *Etymologiae* at the School of Canterbury', *ASE*, 43 (2014), 7–44.

that it is very likely that it was known to Ælfric.[47] In this work, Jerome described how every individual word is sacred in Scripture:

> ego enim non solum fateor, sed libera uoce profiteer me in interpretatione Graecorum absque scripturis sanctis, ubi et uerborum ordo mysterium est, non uerbum e uerbo, sed sensum exprimere de sensu… si non licet uerbum transferre pro uerbo, sacrilegium est uel celasse uel ignorasse mysterium.[48]

> Now I not only admit but freely announce that in translating the Greek – except of course in the case of Holy Scripture, where even the syntax contains a mystery – I render, not word for word, but sense for sense… Why, is it not forbidden to substitute one word for another? It is sacrilegious to conceal or disregard a mystery of God.[49]

Translating Scripture from Hebrew and Greek for exegesis was a dangerous venture in Jerome's day as, without official approval, it exposed the translator to charges of heresy.[50] However, Jerome also provided no fewer than fourteen examples of misquotations and incorrect references in the gospels to align his own sense-for-sense translations with the writings of the apostles: 'sed absit hoc de pedisequo Christi dicere, cui curae fuit non uerba et syllabas aucupari, sed sententias dogmatum ponere'.[51] In his letter, Jerome also wrote that the most difficult part of translating a text is accurately reflecting 'ipsum … uernaculum linguae genus'.[52] The fine balance between a correct literal translation and a rendering of sense became the principal concern of later translators, and this proved particularly important in Scriptural exegesis.[53]

In his preface to the Book of Kings, Jerome advised that the reader of his Latin translation should return to the original Hebrew of Scripture in order to understand the true meaning of a word or passage: 'If you

---

[47] Gittos, 'Audience of Old English', pp. 243–4.
[48] Jerome, 'Ad Pammachium de optimo genere interpretani', in *Sancti Eusebii Hieronymi Epistulae*, Isidorus Hilberg, ed., CSEL, Vol. 54, rev edn (Vienna, 1996), pp. 503–26, pp. 508, 516.
[49] Jerome, 'Letter to Pammachius', Paul Carroll, trans, in *Western Translation Theory: From Herodotus to Neitzsche*, Douglas Robinson, ed. (Manchester, 1997), pp. 23–30, pp. 25, 27.
[50] See especially Andrew Cain, *The Letters of Jerome: Asceticism, Biblical Exegesis, and the Construction of Christian Authority in Late Antiquity* (Oxford, 2009), pp. 168–96.
[51] Jerome, 'Ad Pammachium', p. 513; 'Far be it from Jerome, however, to speak like this about a follower of the Christ. The truth is that Matthew made it his business to formulate dogmas rather than scurry after words and syllables,' Jerome, 'Letter to Pammachius', p. 27.
[52] Jerome, 'Ad Pammachium', p. 510; 'the peculiar vernacular marrow of the language itself', Jerome, 'Letter to Pammachius', p. 26.
[53] See especially Rita Copeland, *Rhetoric, Hermeneutics, and Translation in the Middle Ages: Academic Traditions and Vernacular Texts* (Cambridge, 1991), pp. 37–62.

are incredulous… read the Greek and Latin manuscripts and compare them with these poor efforts of mine, and wherever you see they disagree, ask some Hebrew.'[54] He believed that the sacred mysteries of Scripture are contained in the original language of Hebrew, which should be consulted for correct theological interpretation.

Jerome offered another interesting insight into language's role in the transmission of divine mysteries. He translated the monastic *Rule of Pachomius* into Latin from Greek, which according to the legend was dictated to Pachomius by an angel. In his preface to the *Rule*, Jerome stated how Pachomius communicated with his bishops through a secret alphabet following his angelic visitation: 'angelus linguae mysticae scientiam dederit, ut scriberent sibi et loquerentur per alfabetum spiritale'.[55] This mystical alphabet came directly from heaven and allowed Pachomius to converse with his fellow ecclesiastics about spiritual matters. Another account of Pachomius' secret language is found in Gennadius's continuation of Jerome's work *De uiris illustribus*: 'In quibus alphabetum mysticis tectum sacramentis, velut humanae consuetudinis excendentem intelligentiam, clausit solis credo eorum gratiae vel meritis manifestum.'[56] Jerome introduced the Pachomius story into the Latin-speaking world, and with it a legend about a divine alphabet that was given to ecclesiastical authorities directly from heaven for secret communication. As seen in Chapter 4, the Pachomius legend was known in Anglo-Saxon England and images of this story appear in Caligula A. xv, which contains the *Heavenly Letter* (that also claims to have been delivered by an angel) and the ritual to obtain political favours with 'gibberish' writing. Jerome emphasised the need to read the original languages of Scripture to understand spiritual mysteries, and he wrote about the divine origin of a mystical alphabet for spiritual discourse. Some of Jerome's works were available in Anglo-Saxon England, and it is possible that they influenced obscure writings in other texts which use Hebrew, Greek, and Latin, and which claim to have come from heaven.

---

[54] Quoted in Bruce R. O'Brien, *Reversing Babel: Translation among the English during an Age of Conquests, c. 800 to c. 1200* (Newark, D.E., 2011), p. 24.

[55] Amand Boon, ed., *Pachomiana Latina: Règle et épîtres de S. Pachôme, épître de S. Théodore et 'Liber' de S. Orsiesius* (Louvain, 1932), p. 9; 'the angel gave knowledge of mystical speech so that they themselves might write and speak through a spiritual alphabet'.

[56] Ernest Cushing Richardson, ed., *Hieronymus liber de viris inlustribus: Gennadius liber de viris inlustribus* (Leipzig, 1896), pp. 63–4; 'He wrote letters also to the associated bishops of his district, in an alphabet concealed by mystic sacraments so as to surpass customary human knowledge and only manifest to those of special grace,' Ernest Cushing Richardson, trans, *A Select Library of Nicene and Post-Nicene Fathers of the Christian Church, Second Series, Vol. 3: Theodoret, Jerome, Gennadius, and Rufinus: Historical Writings* (Edinburgh, 1892, repr. 1979), p. 387. See also Christie, 'Secret Alphabet', p. 166.

St Augustine (354–430) was a contemporary of Jerome, and his writings had possibly the greatest influence on Western Christianity. Augustine touched on many issues about translation, particularly concerning faithful renderings of Scriptural texts. In his *De Doctrina Christiana*, Augustine distinguished between human language and divine signs in Scripture:

> signa sunt, quae sibi quaeque viventia invicem dant ad demonstrandos, quantum possunt, motus animi sui, vel sensa, aut intellecta quaeli-bet. Nec ulla causa est nobis significandi, id est signi dandi, nisi ad depromendum et trajiciendum in alterius animum id quod animo gerit is qui signum dat. Horum igitur signorum genus, quantum ad homines attinet, considerare atque tractare statuimus; quia et signa divinitus data, quae in Scripturis sanctis continentur, per homines nobis indicata sunt, qui ea conscripserunt.[57]

> signs are those which living things give to each other, in order to show, to the best of their ability, the emotions of their minds, or anything that they have felt or learnt. There is no reason for us to signify something (that is, to give a sign) except to express and transmit to another's mind what is in the mind of the person who gives the sign. It is this category of signs – to the extent that it applies to humans – that I have decided to examine and discuss, because even the divinely given signs contained in the holy scriptures have been communicated to us by the human beings who wrote them (II, 3).[58]

Augustine's statement that the divine signs of Scripture were written down by men has an important implication for the origin of language. The literal meaning of the Bible reflects its human transmission through writing, but divine mysteries are to be found in the signs themselves.

In the same work, Augustine associated ambiguous language with the Fall and the building of the Tower of Babel, when the one language spoken by humans was divided because of man's pride:

> Ista igitur signa non potuerunt communia esse omnibus gentibus, peccato quodam dissensionis humanae, cum ad se quisque principa-tum rapit. Cujus superbiae signum est erecta illa turris in coelum, ubi homines impii non solum animos, sed etiam voces dissonas habere mer-uerunt. Ex quo factum est ut etiam Scriptura divina, qua tantis morbis humanarum voluntatum subvenitur, ab una lingua profecta, qua oppor-tune potuit per orbem terrarum disseminari, per varias interpretum linguas longe lateque diffusa innotesceret gentibus ad salutem: quam

---

[57] Augustinus Hipponensis, *S. Aurelii Augustini Hipponensis Episcopi De Doctrina Christiana Libri Quatuor*, PL, Vol. 34 (1865), col. 0037.

[58] Augustine, *De Doctrina Christiana*, R. P. H. Green, trans (Oxford, 1995), pp. 57, 59. An eleventh-century Anglo-Saxon copy of this text is found in Salisbury, Cathedral Library, MS 106, see Gneuss, *Handlist*, p. 110.

legentes nihil aliud appetunt quam cogitationes voluntatemque illorum a quibus conscripta est, invenire, et per illas voluntatem Dei, secundum quam tales homines locutos credimus.[59]

These signs could not be shared by all nations, because of the sin of human disunity by which each one sought hegemony for itself. This pride is signified by the famous tower raised towards heaven at the time when wicked men justly received incompatible languages to match their incompatible minds. Consequently even divine scripture, by which assistance is provided for the many serious disorders of the human will, after starting off in one language, in which it could have conveniently been spread throughout the world, was circulated far and wide in the various languages of translators and became known in this way to the Gentiles for their salvation. The aim of its readers is simply to find out the thoughts and wishes of those by whom it was written down and, through them, the will of God, which we believe these men followed as they spoke (II, 4–5).[60]

According to Augustine, the Tower of Babel symbolised the division of language and the breakdown of communication between nations because of the sin of pride. However, Augustine also pointed out that this division of language allowed the conversion of the Gentiles after Pentecost, and that readers of the Bible constantly seek to understand God's will through different human languages.

Later in this work Augustine, like Jerome, offered a straightforward solution to the correct interpretation of Scripture:

Contra ignota signa propria magnum remedium est linguarum cognitio. Et latinae quidem linguae homines, quos nunc instruendos suscepimus, duabus aliis ad Scripturarum divinarum cognitionem opus habent, hebraea scilicet et graeca; ut ad exemplaria praecedentia recurratur, si quam dubitationem attulerit latinorum interpretum infinita varietas.[61]

An important antidote to the ignorance of literal signs is the knowledge of languages. Users of the Latin language – and it is these that I have now undertaken to instruct – need two others, Hebrew and Greek, for an understanding of the divine scriptures, so that recourse may be had to the original versions if any uncertainty arises from the infinite variety of Latin translators (II, 11).[62]

According to Augustine, the task of the biblical exegete is to adhere to the languages in which Scripture was written. While Augustine maintained the prominence of Hebrew and Greek as the principal languages of Scripture, he followed Jerome in advocating the use of

---

[59] Augustine, *De Doctrina Christiana Libri Quatuor*, col. 0038.
[60] Augustine, *De Doctrina Christiana*, Green, trans, p. 61.
[61] Augustine, *De Doctrina Christiana Libri Quatuor*, col. 0042.
[62] Augustine, *De Doctrina Christiana*, Green, trans, p. 61.

vernacular Latin for spiritual edification. As long as biblical scholars had knowledge of Scripture's original languages, their interpretations and translations in their own language would be useful in revealing divine mysteries. Indeed, Augustine praised the obscure nature of Scripture as it gives the exegete a sense of fulfilment when interpretations can be made: 'Quae quanto magis translatis verbis videntur operiri, tanto magis cum fuerint aperta dulcescunt'.[63] Jan Ziolkowski has argued that Augustine unintentionally opened the door to imitative practices of obscure writing in later centuries through his enthusiastic embrace of obscurity for exegesis.[64] It seems very plausible that Anglo-Saxon theologians attempted no less than their late antique and early medieval predecessors to imitate Scriptural obscurity by concealing the meaning of texts.

Jerome's and Augustine's views of the correct interpretations of divine mysteries by returning to the languages of Scripture have correspondences with the appearance of Greek and Hebrew in 'gibberish' rituals. In Harley 585, for example, one ritual against dysentery claims to have been brought by an angel from heaven, and it instructs the writing of a passage containing Hebrew, Greek, and Latin words:

> Þysne pistol se ængel brohte to Rome, þa hy wæran mid utsihte micclum geswæncte. Writ þis on swa langum bocfelle þæt hit mæge befon utan þæt heafod…
>
> Ranmigan. adonai. eltheos. mur. O ineffabile. Omiginan. midanmian. misane. dimas. mode. mida. memagartern. Orta min. sigmone. beronice. irritas. venas. quasi dulaþ. fervor. fruxantis. sanguinis. siccatur. fla. fracta. frigula. mirgui. etsihdon. segulta. frautantur. in arno. midoninis. abar vetho. sydone multo. saccula. pp pppp sother sother.
>
> Miserere mei deus deus mihi deus mi.
>
> A Ω N Y Alleluiah. Alleluiah.[65]

> The angel brought this letter to Rome, when they were greatly afflicted with dysentery. Write this on parchment so long that it can surround the head… etc.

The passage that was apparently delivered by the angel contains some evident Latin ('Miserere mei deus deus mihi deus mi'), Hebrew ('adonai'), and Greek ('A Ω N Y', an abbreviation of the Hebrew 'adonai'). Interestingly, Leslie Arnovick suggests that the phrase

---

[63] Augustine, *De Doctrina Christiana Libri Quatuor*, col. 0096; 'Indeed, the more opaque they seem, because of their use of metaphor, the greater the reader's pleasure when the meaning becomes clear', Augustine, *De Doctrina Christiana*, Green, trans, p. 217.

[64] Ziolkowski, 'Theories of Obscurity', pp. 152–3. See also Augustine, *De Civitate Dei*, Bernard Dombart and Alphonsus Kalb, eds, 5th edn, 2 Vols. (Stuttgart, 1981), 11. 19, Vol. I, p. 486.

[65] Storms, *Anglo-Saxon Magic*, p. 274.

'O ineffabile' in this passage may be a self-reflexive and subversive comment on the limitations of human language in conveying spiritual mysteries.[66]

There are other rituals that use Hebrew and Greek words which also appear to be very corrupted.[67] However, Carolingian scribes deliberately used Graecisms and Hebraisms to gloss texts in Latin (see below), and these Anglo-Saxon passages may also use Hebrew and Greek to deliberately obfuscate the rituals' spiritual meaning.[68] Greek letters are also frequently found in Anglo-Saxon texts, diagrams, and illuminations as abbreviations of spiritual names and titles.[69] Furthermore, Pádraic Moran has recently demonstrated that Irish scribes studied Greek and Hebrew from the evidence of glossed manuscripts dating from as early as the seventh century.[70] As seen in Chapter 2, there are strong Irish influences in Anglo-Saxon rituals that contain obscure language, and there is a possibility that Greek and Hebrew words from Irish manuscripts may have led to the inclusion of these alphabets when the texts were written in England.[71] The study of Greek was also promoted during Æthelwold's rule at the Old Minster, indicating the intellectual pursuits of ecclesiastics in high-status minsters from the later tenth century.

Jerome and Augustine recommended that the biblical scholar should return to the original languages of Scripture to uncover its divine mysteries, and Augustine emphasised that languages were divided after the fall of Babel. On the other hand, Anglo-Saxon rituals that use Greek and Hebrew letters bring together the languages of Scripture, and sometimes explicitly present the 'gibberish' amalgamation as divine writing that was transmitted from heaven itself. The incomprehensible language of this 'gibberish' relates to the theological interpretation of linguistic division; the combination of Hebrew, Greek, and Latin (among other languages) may be an attempt to reconstruct the original language of mankind before the building of the Tower of Babel, and it may encode spiritual mysteries in this composite form.

---

[66] Arnovick, *Written Reliquaries*, p. 59.

[67] See, for example, Storms, *Anglo-Saxon Magic*, pp. 268, 282, 291, 294–6, 302.

[68] See Ziolkowski, 'Theories of Obscurity', pp. 116–20; O'Sullivan, 'The Sacred and the Obscure', p. 82.

[69] For an example, see Chardonnens, *Anglo-Saxon Prognostics*, pp. 221–2.

[70] Pádraic Moran, 'Hebrew in Early Irish Glossaries', *Cambrian Medieval Celtic Studies*, 60 (2010), 1–21; 'A Living Speech? The Pronunciation of Greek in Early Medieval Ireland', *Ériu*, 61 (2011), 29–57.

[71] On the presence of Irish monks at Alfred's court in Winchester, see Nicole Guenther Discenza, 'Writing the Mother Tongue in the Shadow of Babel', in *Conceptualizing Multilingualism*, Tyler, ed., pp. 33–55, pp. 36–7.

Isidore of Seville

The *Etymologies* of Isidore of Seville (c. 560–636) was a highly influential work in early medieval Europe. In the first book of the *Etymologies*,
Isidore stated that the art of grammar is constructed by the letters of
the alphabet. These letters form every word and sign, and their power
to communicate meaning endures throughout time:

> De litteris communibus. Primordia grammaticae artis litterae communes
> existent, quas librarii et calculatores sequuntur. Quarum disciplina velut
> quaedam grammaticae artis infantia est… Litterae autem sunt indices
> rerum, signa verborum, quibus tanta vis est, ut nobis dicta absentium
> sine voce loquantur. (Verba enim per oculos non per aures introducunt).[72]

> The common letters of the alphabet are the primary elements of the art
> of grammar, and are used by scribes and accountants. The teaching of
> these letters is, as it were, the infancy of grammar… Indeed, letters are
> tokens of things, the signs of words, and they have so much force that
> the utterances of those who are absent speak to us without a voice, (for
> they present words through the eyes, not through the ears).[73]

According to Isidore, the letter has a transcendental significance in
the history of mankind.[74] Following this discussion, he elaborated on
language's role in the creation of the world before man was made:

> Cuiusmodi autem lingua locutus est Deus in principio mundi, dum
> diceret: 'Fiat lux', inveniri difficile est. Nondum enim errant linguae.
> Item qua lingua insonuit postea exterioribus hominum auribus, maxime
> ad primum hominem loquens… Loquitur autem Deus hominibus non
> per substantiam invisibilem, sed per creaturam corporalem, per quam
> etiam et hominibus apparere voluit, quando locutus est.[75]

> It is hard to determine what sort of language God spoke at the beginning
> of the world, when he said (Genesis 1:3) 'Be light made', for there were
> not yet any languages. Or again, it is hard to know with what language
> he spoke afterwards to the outer ears of humans, especially as he spoke
> to the first man… God speaks to humans not through an invisible sub-
> stance, but through a bodily creature, through which he even wished to
> appear to humans when he spoke.[76]

While letters transcend generations and preserve memory, Isidore
viewed language as a vehicle only for human communication. In this

---

[72] Isidore of Seville, *Etymologiarum sive Originum*, W. M. Lindsay, ed., 2 Vols.
(Oxford, 1911), Vol. I, I, 3, 1.
[73] Isidore, *Etymologies*, p. 39.
[74] See also O'Brien O'Keeffe, *Visible Song*, pp. 51–2.
[75] Isidore, *Etymologiarum*, Vol. I, IX, 1, 11–12.
[76] Isidore, *Etymologies*, p. 192. See also Stanton, *Culture of Translation*, p. 68.

interpretation of Genesis, he argued that God created the world by speaking through His creation rather than through a literal linguistic act, as God is beyond the rules of grammar.

Isidore followed Augustine in stating that Hebrew was the original language that was spoken by all nations before the building of the Tower of Babel, after which language was divided on account of man's sinful pride. Among these diverse languages were Greek and Latin, and Isidore maintained that these have divine significance because of their ability to communicate God's mysteries:

> Linguarum diversitas exorta est in aedificatione turris post diluvium. Nam priusquam superbia turris illius in diversos signorum sonos humanam divideret societatem, una omnium nationum lingua fuit, quae Hebraea vocatur; quam Patriarchae et Prophetae usi sunt non solum in sermonibus suis, verum etiam in litteris sacris... Tres sunt autem linguae sacrae: Hebraea, Graeca, Latina, quae toto orbe maxime excellunt. His enim tribus linguis super crucem Domini a Pilato fuit causa eius scripta. Unde et propter obscuritatem sanctarum Scripturarum harum trium linguarum cognitio necessaria est, ut ad alteram recurratur dum siquam dubitationem nominis vel interpretationis sermo unius linguae adtulerit.[77]

> The diversity of languages arose with the building of the Tower after the Flood, for before the pride of that Tower divided human society, so that there arose a diversity of meaningful sounds, there was one language for all nations, which is called Hebrew. The patriarchs and prophets used this language not only in their speech, but also in the sacred writings... There are three sacred languages – Hebrew, Greek, and Latin – which are preeminent throughout the world. On the cross of the Lord the charge laid against him was written at Pilate's command in these three languages (John 19: 20). Hence – and because of the obscurity of the Sacred Scriptures – a knowledge of these three languages is necessary, so that, whenever the wording of one of the languages presents any doubt about a name or an interpretation, recourse may be had to another language.[78]

According to Isidore, if any of these three principal languages fails to reveal Scriptural meaning, the biblical scholar should consult the other two languages to understand the passage. Divine mysteries are conveyed through Hebrew, Greek, and Latin but these human languages have limitations, which is why Scripture remains obscure.

Following Augustine, Isidore elsewhere commented on the value of Scripture's obscurity: 'Ideo in libris sanctis quaedam obscura, quaedam aperta reperiuntur, ut intellectus lectoris et studium augeatur. Nam

---

[77] Isidore, *Etymologiarum*, Vol. I, IX, 1, 1, 3.
[78] Isidore, *Etymologies*, p. 191.

si cuncta paterent, statim intellecta vilescerent.'[79] He also followed Jerome in arguing that Scripture can and should be translated into the vernacular because of the inherent capacity of all languages to convey divine truths.[80] Isidore established a spiritual significance for languages and letters that influenced later Anglo-Saxon writers; God does not speak in human language but He speaks through His creation, and His Word can be discerned by understanding the created world. This requires an interpretative skill that is also needed to understand the divine mysteries of Scripture.

A number of scholars have argued that the use of biblical languages in 'charms' adds to their 'sense of magic and mystery', and that the power associated with Scripture adds to their efficacy.[81] However, as seen with the ritual against dysentery in Harley 585, there may be a more theological reasoning for the appearances of these languages in such texts. Most of the 'gibberish' rituals contain vernacular instructions before obscure words and phrases from different languages are provided. The three languages of Scripture – Hebrew, Greek, and Latin – are frequently found in combination but they also appear with Irish and Old English. One ritual against black blains in Harley 585, for example, instructs the singing of a *gebed* that appears to include a number of these languages:

> Sing ðis gebed on ða blacan blegene VIIII syþðan ærest Pater noster.
> Tigað tigað tigað calicet. aclu cluel sedes adclocles. acre earcre arnem. nonabiuð ær ærnem niðren arcum cunað arcum arctua fligara uflen binchi cutern. nicuparam raf afðegal uflen arta. arta. arta trauncula. trauncula.
> Querite et invenietis. Adiuro te per Patrem et Filium et Spiritum sanctum, non amplius crescas sed arescas. Super aspidem et basilliscum ambulabis et conculcabis leonem et draconem. Crux Matheus crux Marcus crux Lucas crux Iohannes.[82]

> Sing this prayer on the black blains nine times before the Paternoster:
> Tigað tigað tigað calicet. aclu cluel sedes adclocles. acre earcre arnem. nonabiuð ær ærnem niðren arcum cunað arcum arctua fligara uflen

---

[79] Isidore, *Sententiae*, I, 18, PL, Vol. 83 (1862), col. 576C-577A; 'Some things in Holy Scripture are clear, others obscure, in order to increase the understanding and diligence of the reader. For if everything were immediately comprehensible, it would be cheapened,' translation from Vivien Law, *Wisdom, Authority and Grammar in the Seventh Century: Decoding Virgilius Maro Grammaticus* (Cambridge, 1995), p. 94.

[80] For further discussion of this, see Stanton, *Culture of Translation*, p. 68.

[81] Fisher (Writing Charms), p. 145. See also Vaughan-Sterling, 'Metrical Charms', pp. 192–3; Jolly, *Popular Religion*, p. 119; Claire Jones, '"Efficacy Phrases" in Medieval English Medical Manuscripts', *Neophilologische Mitteilungen*, 99 (1998), 199–210; Tornaghi, 'Language of Magic', pp. 445–6.

[82] Storms, *Anglo-Saxon Magic*, p. 301.

binchi cutern. nicuparam raf afðegal uflen arta. arta. arta trauncula. trauncula.

Seek and you will find. I command you through the Father and Son and Holy Spirit, may you no longer multiply but wither. Upon the asp and the basilisks you will tread and you will trample the lion and the dragon. Cross Matthew. Cross Mark. Cross Luke. Cross John.

In this passage there is evidence of Irish (in the 'acre' formula), Old English ('niðren'), Latin ('Adiuro te per Patrem'), and apparent Hebrew ('nonabiuð', elsewhere 'Nonabaioth'). Another version of this ritual was added to a manuscript containing excerpts from Patristic writings by Jerome and Orosius (Oxford, Bodleian Library, MS Bodley 163, discussed above on pages 173–4). Some *galdru* and *gebed* in *Bald's Leechbook* also consist of Greek letters ('greciscum stafum') and what appear to be Hebrew names ('Tiecon. leleloth'; 'HAMMANŷEL . BPONice . NOŷepTAŷEPΓ').[83]

It seems that scribes of these rituals included phonetic spellings of exotic words and phrases, reflecting an engagement with foreign languages that were believed to have spiritual power. It is also possible that they were deliberately brought together to reconstruct a homogenous language with theological significance.[84] Furthermore, the passages of such rituals look like an attempt to imitate Scriptural obscurity, which according to Augustine and Isidore increases the diligence of theologians and encourages exegetical readings. Some 'gibberish charms' use Scriptural as well as vernacular languages to form powerful ritual performances that conceal – and through doing so also reveal – divine mysteries.

Bede

Isidore's philosophy of language had a major influence on language study in Anglo-Saxon England. A number of other sources also seem to have been influential from the late seventh century in England, including grammatical works by Donatus, Priscian, Martianus Capella, and Cassiodorus.[85] The study of grammar was of fundamental importance to a monk's education, and it formed the basis of their training in liturgical observances, knowledge of Scripture, and biblical exegesis.

---

[83] Cockayne, *Leechdoms*, Vol. II, pp. 138, 140.

[84] A modern parallel for this interest would be the attempts to reconstruct Indo-European by philologists.

[85] Gneuss, 'Study of Language', pp. 6–10. Significant libraries that held such works were in Canterbury, York, Jarrow, Wearmouth, Malmesbury, and Nursling (Hants.), among others, see Helmut Gneuss, 'Anglo-Saxon Libraries from the Conversion to the Benedictine Reform', *Settimane di studio del Centro italiano di studi sull' alto medioevo*, 32 (1984), 643–88; Lapidge, *Anglo-Saxon Library*, pp. 31–44, 63–90, 275–342.

Bede had access to several Latin grammars in his monastery at Jarrow (between c. 682 and his death in 735), and he had knowledge of works by Jerome, Augustine, and Isidore.[86]

In his commentary on Genesis, Bede followed Augustine and Isidore in associating the Tower of Babel with the division of human languages: 'Merito confusum est labium in dispersionem, quia male conjuraverat in locutionem nefariam: ablata est potestas linguae superbis princip-ibus, ne in contemptum Dei subditos possent quae coeperant mala docere.'[87] Bede, however, added to this linguistic history by claiming that the language of each nation was given as a gift from God after the fall of Babel:

> Constat Adam in ea lingua, qua totum genus humanum usque ad con-structionem turris, in qua linguae divisae sunt, loquebatur, animantibus terrae et volatilibus coeli nomen imposuisse. Caeterum in dejectione turris, cum Deus suam cuique genti propriam atque diversam tribueret linguam, tunc eis credendus est etiam animantium vocabula quomodo et rerum caeterarum juxta suam cuique distinxisse loquelam: quamvis etiam non latet homines postea plurimis, quae sive nova forte occurre-runt rebus, haec animantibus per singulas gentes juxta suum placitum indidisse vocabula, et nunc etiam indere solere.[88]

> Notice that Adam named the animals of the earth and the birds of heaven in that language which the whole human race spoke up to the building of the tower at which time languages were divided. But in casting down the tower, when God assigned to each people its own separate lan-guage, he must also be supposed at that time to have specified for them the names of the animals as also of other things, for each according to their own language – although it is also no secret that men afterwards throughout the different peoples gave names at their own pleasure to many things, both to innovations that by chance occurred and to living things, and even now are accustomed to do so.[89]

---

[86] See also Roger Ray, 'Bede's Vera Lex Historiae', *Speculum*, 55 (1980), 1–21; Mark Amsler, *Etymology and Grammatical Discourse in Late Antiquity and the Early Middle Ages* (Amsterdam, 1989), pp. 184–7; A. H. Merrills, *History and Geography in Late Antiquity* (Cambridge, 2005), pp. 244–5.

[87] Bede, *Hexaemeron, sive libri quatuor in principium Genesis, usque ad nativitatem Isaac et electionem Ismaelis*, PL, Vol. 91 (1862), col. 0126A; 'Language was deservedly cast into confusion, because it had wickedly combined into impious speech. The power of language was taken from the proud rulers lest in contempt of God they might be able to teach their subjects the evils that they had begun,' Bede, *On Genesis*, Calvin B. Kendall, trans (Liverpool, 2008), p. 231.

[88] Bede, *Hexaemeron*, col. 0050C–0050D.

[89] Bede, *On Genesis*, p. 121. On Bede's engagement with the Hebrew language, particularly in his *Commentary on Genesis*, see Damian Fleming, '*Hebraeam scire linguam*: Bede's Rhetoric of the Hebrew Truth' in *Imagining the Jew: Jewishness in Anglo-Saxon Literature and Culture*, Samantha Zacher, ed. (Toronto, 2016), pp. 63–78.

This passage strongly indicates that Bede developed the philosophies of Augustine and Isidore, and followed Jerome in claiming that all vernacular languages have a divine origin.[90] Furthermore, Irina Dumitrescu has convincingly argued that Bede's *Historia Ecclesiastica* is structured on key episodes that describe linguistic healing miracles and the liberation of vernacular language.[91] Bede uses such episodes to integrate the English language into biblical history and to include this vernacular within a Pentecostal unity of languages following their division after Babel.

Bede arrived at the same conclusions as earlier writers about the use of vernacular languages for biblical study, and he also seems to have advocated their use in the liturgy. Cuthbert's *Epistola de obitu Bedae* says that he was translating the gospel of John into English on his deathbed,[92] and scholars have viewed his homage to Cædmon's poetry as his own statement that the English language was capable of communicating divine mysteries.[93] Indeed, Bede viewed the exegete's ability to interpret Scripture as a key tool for evangelisation and the re-enactment of the oratorical office, as argued by Rita Copeland.[94] Within this programme of vernacular exegesis, Bede saw all languages and their individual components as divinely inspired instruments for spiritual communication, discernment, evangelisation, and worship. Similar views of the divine nature of all languages are perhaps reflected in several Anglo-Saxon rituals that combine English and Irish with Scriptural languages, and in some that prescribe the recital of the opening of the Prologue to John's gospel ('In principio erat verbum').[95] The writing of two alphabets diagonally across the floor of a church in dedication rites also indicates that language was perceived to be the foundation of the Christian faith in other Anglo-Saxon liturgical practices.[96]

In addition to the revealing of divine mysteries through Scriptural and vernacular languages, Bede also described how letters of

---

[90] Bede also knew of the Pachomius legend through the writings of Cyril of Alexandria, see Bede, *The Reckoning of Time*, Faith Wallis, trans (Liverpool, 1999), p. 118.

[91] Irina A. Dumitrescu, 'Bede's Liberation Philology: Releasing the English Tongue', *PMLA*, 128 (2013), 40–56. See also Robert Stanton, 'Linguistic Fragmentation and Redemption before King Alfred', *The Yearbook of English Studies*, 36 (2006), 12–26, pp. 20–3.

[92] Cuthbert, 'Epistola de obitu Bedae', in *Ecclesiastical History*, Colgrave and Mynors, eds and trans, pp. 580–7, pp. 583–3.

[93] See especially Bruce Holsinger, 'The Parable of Cædmon's *Hymn*: Liturgical Invention and Literary Tradition', *JEGP*, 106 (2007), 149–75; Gittos, 'Audience of Old English', pp. 260–6.

[94] Copeland, *Rhetoric, Hermeneutics, and Translation*, p. 60.

[95] See Storms, *Anglo-Saxon Magic*, pp. 232, 236, 258, 292,

[96] See Repsher, *Rite of Church Dedication*, pp. 145–6, and Chapter 4.

different alphabets can be manipulated to conceal meaning. In his *De Temporum Ratione*, he described the substitution of letters for numerical values:

> Potest autem et de ipso quem praenotavi computo quaedam manualis loquela, tam ingenii exercendi quam ludi agenda gratia figurari; qua literis quis singillatim expressis verba, quae hisdem literis contineantur, alteri qui hanc quoque noverit industriam, tametsi procul posito, legenda atque intellegenda contradat, vel necessaria quaeque per haec occultis innuendo significans vel imperitos quosque quasi divinando deludens… Potest et ita scribe, si causa secretior exigat. Sed haec graecorum computo literisque facilius disci simul atque agi possunt, qui non, ut latini, paucis hisdemque geminatis suos numeros solent experimere literis… Qui et ideo mox numerous digitis significare didicerint, nulla interstante mora, literas quoque partier hisdem praefigere sciunt.[97]

> From the kind of computation I have just described, one can represent a sort of manual language, whether for the sake of exercising one's wits, or as a game. By this means one can, by forming one letter at a time, transmit the words contained by those letters to another person who knows this procedure, so that he can read and understand that even at a distance. Thus one may either signify necessary information by secret imitation, or else fool the uninitiated as if by magic… It can be written down in this manner, if greater secrecy is demanded. But this can be more easily learned and manipulated using the letters and numbers of the Greeks, who do not, like the Latins, express numbers by a few letters and their duplicate forms… Thus whoever has learned to signify numbers with his fingers knows without hesitation how to shape letters with them as well.[98]

Bede's comparison of this form of secretive communication to a 'game' that may mislead the uninitiated resonates with later Anglo-Saxon encrypted riddles and wisdom poems that function to entertain, challenge, and edify their audiences. This description also provides evidence of the deliberate concealment of meaning for the censorship of texts. Faith Wallis has discussed how similar strategies of concealment were used by the elite in Bede's time, where ecclesiastics carried official documents that contained encryptions of their identity through the so-called 'litterae formatae'.[99] These cryptograms could be solved according to the *computus Graecorum*, which revealed the identity of the sender, recipient, place of origin, and date for the ecclesiastic's authorised visit. These forms of letter manipulation and substitution

---

[97] Bede, *Bedae Opera De Temporibus*, Charles W. Jones, ed. (Cambridge, MA, 1943), p. 181.
[98] Bede, *Reckoning of Time*, pp. 11–12. On Bede's knowledge of the so-called 'Sirmond manuscript' from Ireland, see Wallis' commentary on pp. 260–1.
[99] Bede, *Reckoning of Time*, p. 262.

strongly resonate with other ciphered texts from later Anglo-Saxon England, and they inform our understanding of obscure letter combinations in ritual texts from this period.

Bede's 'manual language' gained greater secrecy when it was written down and when it included letters from other alphabets. Many of the 'gibberish' phrases in Anglo-Saxon rituals are to be written down – sometimes in silence – and they demonstrate the use of more than one language or alphabet. As seen in the Sphere of Life and Death in the *Vitellius Psalter*, letters were also substituted with numbers so that calculations could be made to determine the length and severity of illness. The enigmatic letters of the psalter's theft diagram may also have numerical significance, and the system of vowel substitution demonstrates a form of language manipulation that strongly parallels Bede's secretive sign language. Other Anglo-Saxon rituals also indicate that letters could be manipulated into different shapes to signify their meaning. For example, the theft ritual at the end of *Ælfwine's Prayerbook* (discussed in Chapter 4) uses at least three different alphabets in a passage that may have required rearrangement in a cruciform shape, especially as the ritual invokes the power of the cross.[100] Letter rearrangement is also a key feature of a childbirth ritual containing the 'Sator' formula that is found in Corpus 41 (fol. 329), which is written much like an acrostic poem.[101]

Bede's philosophy of language and knowledge of secret communication provide another interesting and convincing context in which to understand obscure writing in later Anglo-Saxon texts. According to Bede, all languages are capable of communicating God's Word and unlocking divine secrets through exegesis. Conversely, they could also obscure meaning and conceal information. As Bede believed in the divine origin of languages, their individual components could therefore be manipulated, recombined, and substituted to imitate the secretive and mysterious nature of God's Word.

Continental Influences

Ideas about the origin of language, the art of grammar, and the manipulation of letters were significantly developed by early medieval writers. This gave rise to the production of texts like acrostics, telestics, figural poetry, chronograms, and cryptograms in Latin traditions that imitated Scriptural obscurity and challenged readers to discern

---

[100] Günzel, *Ælfwine's Prayerbook*, p. 144. See also See Jolly, 'Tapping the Power of the Cross', p. 64.

[101] See Storms, *Anglo-Saxon Magic*, p. 281. O'Brien O'Keeffe has argued that this formula informs us of the scribe's use of letters in the manuscript's other marginal texts, O'Brien O'Keeffe, *Visible Song*, p. 70.

their hidden meaning.[102] The works of Virgilius Maro Grammaticus, for instance, provide perhaps the most comprehensive techniques of textual concealment that were being developed to deliberately protect the wisdom of the sages.[103] These included anagrammatic writing, unconventional abbreviation, the combination of languages to form new words, numerical substitution, and expansion or subtraction of words and sentences.[104] Complex acrostic poetry probably reached Theodore's school at Canterbury in the late seventh century, and it was continued in the literary works of Aldhelm (d. 709) and Boniface (d. 754).[105] Their figurative poetry used arrangements of words and phrases for devotional purposes that required the reader to discern the meanings of both images and texts.[106] The 'gibberish' sequences in Anglo-Saxon rituals also demand interpretation from the performer, and their letters may require rearrangement from a linear structure to reveal their meaning.

Aldhelm also assigned spiritual and cosmological significance to individual graphemes in his *Elementum* riddle, which depicts letters as principal components of the world as they 'are born from iron, and by iron return to death' ('Nascimur ex ferro rursus ferro moribundae').[107] Edward Christie has described this riddle as a depiction of the divine nature of individual letters as they have elemental significance in a causal chain of existence.[108] Aldhelm was evidently influenced by Patristic interpretations of the origin of language and the art of grammar, and he portrayed individual letters as foundational components of language, grammar, and the cosmos.

Boniface was directly influenced by Aldhelm's work and he also composed a number of figurative poems.[109] In his letter to Sigeberht,

---

[102] See especially Ziolkowski, 'Theories of Obscurity', pp. 130–45. As Ziolkowski pointed out, later tendencies to imitate the obscurity of Scripture is ironically what Augustine warned against, see pp. 151–2.

[103] Ziolkowski, 'Theories of Obscurity', pp. 134, 142.

[104] Law, *Wisdom, Authority and Grammar*, pp. 83–96.

[105] See Pelteret, 'Cross and an Acrostic', pp. 56–68, 87–102; Michael Lapidge, 'Aldhelm's Latin Poetry and Old English Verse', *Comparative Literature*, 31 (1979), 209–31. See also Vivien Law, *Grammar and Grammarians in the Early Middle Ages* (London, 1997), pp. 92–101, 169–97.

[106] See Copeland, *Rhetoric, Hermeneutics, and Translation*, p. 60; Pelteret, 'Cross and an Acrostic', pp. 57–8, 82. David Howlett has also proposed that meaning is encoded in the structure and numerology of Anglo-Saxon charters, see David Howlett, *Sealed from Within: Self-Authenticating Insular Charters* (Dublin, 1999).

[107] Aldhelm, *Aldhelm: The Prose Works*, Michael Lapidge and Michael Herren, eds and trans (Cambridge, 1979), p. 76. See also O'Brien O'Keeffe, *Visible Song*, p. 53.

[108] Edward Christie, 'The Image of the Letter: From the Anglo-Saxons to the Electronic Beowulf', *Culture, Theory and Critique*, 44 (2003), 129–50, p. 133.

[109] See Andy Orchard, *The Poetic Art of Aldhelm* (Cambridge, 1994), pp. 21–8; 'Old Sources, New Resources: Finding the Right Formula for Boniface', *ASE*, 30 (2001), 15–38. See also Lapidge, 'Hermeneutic Style', pp. 73–6.

Boniface stated that the study of grammar is fundamental to spiritual understanding:

> peritia grammaticae artis in sacrosancto scrutinio laborantibus ad sub-tiliorem intellectum, qui frequenter in sacris scripturis inseritur, ualde utilis esse… Hunc autem circulum in scemate noui ac ueteris instru-menti figurari non nescias.

> knowledge of the art of grammar is extremely useful to those who are toiling over their sacred studies to find the subtler meaning which is often concealed in the Holy Scriptures… You should not be unaware that this circle represents an image of the Old and New Testament.[110]

Boniface followed Patristic writers in connecting the study of lan-guage to knowledge of Scriptural mysteries, and he used language and images in symbolic ways to represent the Bible and imitate the obscurity of God's Word in his own figurative poetry.

Boniface is also said to have introduced cryptography to the Continent from England.[111] Two copies of a text that was probably composed by Hrabanus Maurus survive in an eleventh-century manu-script from Vienna and a twelfth-century manuscript from Heidelberg, and this text ascribes authorship of the vowel substitution system to Boniface (all square brackets indicate twelfth-century variations of the text):

A E I O V

: … · :: :·:

·NC·P·T V…RS:·: B::N·:C·· :RCH·…P·SC::P· GL::R·::S·Q:·:… M:RT·R·S·
Genus vero huius descriptionis, tam quod supra cum punctis V et vocal-ibus quam subtus cum aliis vocalibus quam solitum est informatum continetur, fertur quod sanctus Bonifacius archiepiscopus ac martyr, de [ab] Angulsaxis veniens, hoc antecessoribus nostris demonstraret [demonstrarit]. Quod tamen non ab illo inprimis coeptum est, sed ab antiquis istius modi usus crevisse comperimus.
kbrxs xpp fprtks tkrp knstbr sbffkrp brchktenens scrkptpr [brchktfnfns scptrp rfgnk xt dfcxs bxrk].[112]

A E I O V

: … · :: :·:

Incipit versus Bonifacii archiepiscopi gloriosique martiris.
(Here begins the verse of Boniface, archbishop and glorious martyr).

---

110 Text and translation from Law, *Grammar and Grammarians*, pp. 172, 174–5.
111 See also Rolf Bremmer, 'The Anglo-Saxon Continental Mission and the Transfer of Encyclopaedic Knowledge', in *Foundations of Learning*, Bremmer and Dekker, eds, pp. 19–50.
112 Transcription from Levison, *England and the Continent*, pp. 291–2. Also printed in Hrabanus Maurus, *B. Rabani Mauri Fuldensis Abbatis et Moguntini Archiepiscopi: Omnia Opera*, PL, Vol. 112 (1852), col. 1581–2.

Truly this type of description that is used, which is above with five dots and vowels, and with the other vowels beneath, contains information, it is held that the holy archbishop and martyr Boniface, coming (all the way) from the Anglo-Saxons, showed this to our ancestors. This, however, was not first begun by him, but we learn this kind of practice came into being from the ancients.

Karus Christo fortis tiro instar saffiro architenens scriptor [sceptro regni ut decus auri].

(Beloved of Christ, mighty soldier, image of sapphire, archer, writer [with the sceptre of the kingdom as ornament of gold]).

This system of vowel substitution is evident in a range of other Continental writings. It appears in a manuscript dating to about 800 from Heidenheim, where the name of an Anglo-Saxon nun (Hugeburc) is concealed in a highly complex cryptogram.[113] This cryptogram appears between the saints' lives of Wynnebald and Willibald, two contemporaries and companions of Boniface. It also appears in a letter that was sent to Dunstan from Fleury after 974, and it is used extensively in tenth- and eleventh-century Old High German and Latin glosses of Prudentius' *Psychomachia* that draw heavily on Isidore and Bede.[114] An English manuscript (Cambridge, Trinity College, MS B.16.3) that was carefully copied from a Carolingian exemplar in about 930 also contains this form of ciphered writing (fol. 1r).[115] The system of vowel substitution spread throughout Europe after Boniface introduced cryptography to the Continent, and the presence of different letters, medial points, and crosses in 'gibberish' rituals suggests that a number of different substitutions may be involved in their obscure formulas.

Hrabanus Maurus' works were well known in Anglo-Saxon England. Hrabanus was a Frankish monk who studied under Alcuin before he became abbot of Fulda (822–42) and archbishop of Mainz (847–56), and he had many connections with England.[116] In addition

---

[113] Transcribed in Levison, *England and the Continent*, p. 294. See also Lapidge, 'Hermeneutic Style', pp. 73–4.

[114] See Levison, *England and the Continent*, pp. 293–4; Sinead O'Sullivan, *Early Medieval Glosses on Prudentius' Psychomachia: The Weitz Tradition* (Leiden, 2004), pp. 38–40, 46–8, 56–8, 73–4.

[115] William Schipper, 'Hrabanus Maurus in Anglo-Saxon England: *In honorem sanctae crucis*', in *Early Medieval Studies in Memory of Patrick Wormald*, Stephen D. Baxter, Catherine Karkov, Janet L. Nelson, and David Pelteret, eds (Farnham, 2009), pp. 283–300, pp. 285–6.

[116] On Hrabanus' influence in England, see Charles W. Jones, 'A Legend of St. Pachomius', *Speculum*, 18 (1943), 198–210, pp. 198–200; Michael Lapidge, 'Dunstan and Hrabanus Maurus: zur Hs. Bodleian Auctarium F.4.32', *Anglia*, 96 (1978), 136–48; Els Rose, *Ritual Memory: The Apocryphal Acts and Liturgical Commemoration in the Early Medieval West (c. 500–1215)* (Leiden, 2009), pp. 57–77. See also Law, *Grammar and Grammarians*, pp. 137, 232.

to his knowledge of vowel substitution, Hrabanus was also interested in the origins of languages and alphabets. In his *De inventione litterarum*, he recorded the Hebrew letters that Moses discovered, Greek and Latin alphabets, and a strange alphabet of combined Hebrew and Greek attributed to Aethicus Ister and Jerome:

> Litteras etiam Æthici philosophi cosmographi natione Scythica, nobili prosapia, invenimus, quas venerabilis Hieronymus presbyter ad nos usque cum suis dictis explanando perduxit, quia magnifice ipsius scientiam atque industriam duxit: ideo et ejus litteras maluit promulgare.[117]

> We find also the letters of the philosopher and cosmographer Æthicus of the nation of Scythia, of noble stock, which the respected priest Jerome brought down to us through exposition in his own words, because he drew magnificently on his [Æthicus'] knowledge and industry; so he chose to to make his works known.

Hrabanus included the runic alphabet among the scripts said to have come from Moses, and he also used different alphabets to form symbols and monograms of biblical names.[118] An interesting parallel to Hrabanus' claim can be found in a miniature of the crucifixion from an eleventh-century psalter from Hastières (Munich, Bayerische Staatsbibliothek, Clm 13067, fol. 17v). In John's gospel, Pilate is said to have written an inscription above Christ's cross in Hebrew, Greek, and Latin (John 19: 19–22), but in the psalter's miniature the inscription contains Latin, Greek, and runic letters.[119] This raises many questions about the increasing theological value given to vernacular languages as Anglo-Saxon runes are used to substitute Hebrew, *the* Scriptural language most venerated by Patristic writers.

Hrabanus' experimental uses of alphabets reflect his keen interest in the spiritual origins of language, and the formation of divine words and names through the manipulation of letters. The conflation of Greek and Hebrew letters indicates that Hrabanus may have attempted to reconstruct the original language that was spoken by humans before the building of the Tower of Babel. It also closely parallels the combination of these languages in Anglo-Saxon 'gibberish' rituals, which often abbreviate biblical names and Scriptural references.[120]

---

[117] Hrabanus Maurus, *Omnia Opera*, col. 1579–80.

[118] Hrabanus Maurus, *Omnia Opera*, col. 1581–4.

[119] See Sabrina Longland, 'Pilate Answered: What I have Written I Have Written', *The Metropolitan Museum of Art Bulletin*, 26 (1968), 410–29, pp. 420–1; Birkett, *Reading the Runes*, pp. 14–15. I would like to thank Tom Birkett for bringing this to my attention.

[120] Hrabanus' student Lupus of Ferrières followed in his tutor's footsteps by creating his own set of signs for correcting manuscript errors, which became a widespread practice in Carolingian monasteries, see Teeuwen, 'Carolingian Scholarship', pp. 29–31, 33–7, 45–6.

Many exotic alphabets are also recorded side by side in Continental manuscripts dating from the eighth to tenth centuries. Alessandro Zironi identifies sixteen Carolingian manuscripts that contain Greek, Latin, Hebrew, Chaldaic, Gothic, and runic alphabets, as well as the alphabet ascribed to Aethicus Ister, and he believes that these were copied out of cryptographic interests or antiquarian curiosities.[121] By the second half of the ninth century, more complex forms of writing were also being developed. The manipulation of letters according to Greek numerology that was outlined by Bede is found throughout John Scottus Eriugena's (d. 877) glosses of Martianus Capella's grammatical work *De nuptiis Philologiae et Mercurii*.[122] In his *Periphyseon*, Eriugena also claimed that while God is beyond all human knowledge, symbols, letters, and language are embodiments of the human mind that reflects God's divine Creation.[123] Eriugena believed that letters and symbols are components of the created world, and his philosophy connected human language to a divine cause.

Abbo of Fleury (945–1004) was also interested in alphabetic writing, and he had considerable influence in Anglo-Saxon England. Shortly after Ramsey Abbey was founded in 969, Abbo visited the English monastery, from 986 to 988.[124] At this time Abbo was a deacon and he held the position of *armarius* in Fleury, which meant that he was in charge of the monastery's school, library, and archives.[125] From the vast resources that were available in Fleury, Abbo brought many manuscripts with him to England, including works by Bede, Hrabanus Maurus, Helperic of Auxerre, Macrobius, Dionysius Exiguus, Isidore

---

[121] Zironi, 'Marginal Alphabets'. See also René Derolez, 'Ogam, "Egyptian", "African" and "Gothic" Alphabets: some Remarks in Connection with Codex Bernensis 207', *Scriptorium* 5.1 (1951), 3–19; *Runica Manuscripta: The English Tradition* (Brugge, 1954), pp. 52–73, 90–4, 120–37, 174–92, 217–19; Bernhard Bischoff, *Mittelalterliche Studien, Ausgewählte Aufsätze zur Schriftkunde und Literaturgeschichte*, 3 Vols. (Stuttgart, 1966–81), Vol. II, pp. 34–51; Vol. III, pp. 73–111, 120–48; Walter Berschin, 'Elements in Medieval Latin Manuscripts', in *Sacred Nectar of the Greeks: the Study of Greek in the West in the Early Middle Ages*, M. W. Herren, ed. (London, 1988), pp. 85–104.

[122] O'Sullivan, 'The Sacred and the Obscure', pp. 84, 88. For Eriugena's other glosses, see John J. Contreni, 'The Biblical Glosses of Haimo of Auxerre and John Scottus Eriugena', *Speculum*, 51 (1976), 411–34.

[123] John Scottus Eriugena, *Periphyseon (De Diuisione Naturae), Liber Primus*, I. P. Sheldon-Williams, ed. and trans, 3 Vols. (Dublin, 1968), Vol. I, p. 191. See also Donald F. Duclow, 'Divine Nothingness and Self-Creation in John Scotus Eriugena', *Journal of Religion*, 57 (1977), 109–23.

[124] See Cyril Hart, 'The Foundation of Ramsey Abbey', *Revue Bénédictine*, 104 (1994), 295–327; Elizabeth Dachowski, *First Among Abbots: The Career of Abbo of Fleury* (Washington, 2008), pp. 269–71.

[125] Marco Mostert, *The Political Theology of Abbo of Fleury: A Study of the Ideas about Society and Law of the Tenth-Century Monastic Reform Movement* (Hilversum, 1987), pp. 32–40; Janneke Raaijmakers, *The Making of the Monastic Community at Fulda, c. 744–c. 900* (Cambridge, 2012), pp. 189–90.

of Seville, Jerome, and Martianus Capella.[126] Although Abbo's visit to Ramsey was brief, it had a lasting impact on English monastic training and study. Abbo also established important contacts with leading ecclesiastical reformers during and after his trip to England. After his arrival he was ordained by Oswald, archbishop of York (972–92) and bishop of Worcester (961–92), and he developed close friendships with Dunstan, archbishop of Canterbury (960–78), and Wulfric, abbot of St Augustine's, Canterbury (c. 1044–c. 1060).[127] Abbo's most famous pupil was Byrhterth of Ramsey, and Ælfric was heavily influenced by his hagiographical works.[128] Abbo evidently had connections with some of the most influential ecclesiastics of late Anglo-Saxon England, and his teaching and writings were held in the highest regard.

Abbo's grammatical treatise *Quaestiones grammaticales* provides information about his teaching at Ramsey.[129] In this text, Abbo closely compares the runic and Latin alphabets, and Marco Mostert has shown that other manuscripts from Fleury – that were probably owned by Abbo – also contain transliterations of runic, Greek, and Latin graphemes. Furthermore, unconventional runes used in this text also appear in some notes that were written by Byrhtferth of Ramsey, providing evidence that Abbo taught his pupils about the substitution of different alphabets and their origins.[130] Abbo's interests echo Hrabanus' earlier combinations of graphemes and parallel the use of runic, Roman, Greek, and Hebrew letters in Anglo-Saxon 'gibberish' rituals. Abbo also composed acrostic poems in honour of his close friend Dunstan, who also tried his hand at figurative poetry.[131] One manuscript that contains an acrostic poem by Abbo testifies to his direct impact on Anglo-Saxon thought and education. Oxford, St John's College, MS 17 also contains a table with the Roman, Greek, Hebrew, and runic alphabets recorded side by side with numerical values for each letter, and this is found on the same folio as cryptographic exercises and prognosticatory diagrams (fol. 5v).[132] Finally, some of Abbo's astronomical

---

[126] Hart, 'Byrhtferth and his Manual', p. 96. See also Gneuss, 'Study of Language', pp. 11–12.

[127] See Mostert, *Abbo of Fleury*, pp. 40–1; 'Relations between Fleury and England', in *England and the Continent in the Tenth Century: Studies in Honour of Wilhelm Levison (1876–1947)*, David Rollason, Conrad Leyser, and Hannah Williams, eds (Turnhout, 2010), pp. 185–208, p. 191.

[128] See Ciaran Arthur, 'Giving the Head's Up in Ælfric's *Passio Sancti Edmundi*: Postural Representations of the Old English Saint', *PQ*, 92 (2013), 315–34.

[129] Abbo of Fleury, *Quaestiones grammaticales*, A. Guerreau-Jalabert, ed. (Paris, 1982).

[130] Mostert, 'Fleury and England', pp. 192–3.

[131] See Scott Gwara, 'Three Acrostic Poems by Abbo of Fleury', *Journal of Medieval Latin*, 2 (1992), 203–35, pp. 215–26; Michael Lapidge, *Anglo-Latin Literature 900–1066* (London, 1993), pp. 151–6.

[132] Wallis, *The Calendar and the Cloister*: <http://digital.library.mcgill.ca/ms-17> accessed 26 September 2017.

and cosmographical works also survive, and Byrhtferth was greatly indebted to his teaching for the composition of the *Enchiridion*, which emphasises the cosmological significance of language (see below).[133]

There was evidently a close connection between studies of language and grammar and the interest in language manipulation in Anglo-Saxon England. There is considerable evidence for early medieval systems of encryption, and encrypted texts survive in Anglo-Saxon manuscripts from the tenth century. Michael Lapidge has claimed that by the close of this century, English monasteries surpassed those in Continental Europe in their use of hermeneutics in monastic training.[134] The study of language in early medieval England was significantly influenced by Patristic philosophy, the *Ars grammatica*, and an increase in experimentation with writing systems. Two of the most prolific English writers of the late tenth and early eleventh centuries drew directly upon these traditions to develop their own philosophies of language that emphasise the cosmological power of letters.

Ælfric

In the last decade of the tenth century, Ælfric (d. circa 1010) wrote his own *Grammar* to educate monks in both English and Latin, and he drew upon works by Donatus and Priscian for this work.[135] However, as Joyce Hill has argued, Ælfric did not seek to imitate the complex features of his Latin sources, and he used the vernacular to outline key principles of grammar, hermeneutics, and language study in simple terms.[136] Ælfric stated in the preface to his first series of *Homilies* that he translated his works into English not because of any confidence in obscure words ('nec obscura posuimus uerba') but to correct the errors of the unlearned ('simplicem Anglicam').[137] He also acknowledged a wide range of sources for his *Homilies*, including works by Augustine, Jerome, Bede, Gregory the Great, Smaragdus, and Haymo.[138] Ælfric was influenced by prolific Latin writers but he deliberately chose to present his material in simple vernacular writing to edify his English audiences and, as Helen Gittos has recently argued, to present English

---

[133] See R. B. Thomson, 'Two Astronomical Tractates of Abbo of Fleury', in *The Light of Nature: Essays in the History and Philosophy of Science Presented to A. C. Crombie*, J. D. North and J. J. Roche, eds (Dordrecht, 1985), pp. 113–33; 'Further Astronomical Material of Abbo of Fleury', *Mediaeval Studies*, 20 (1988), 671–3.

[134] Lapidge, 'Hermeneutic Style', p. 76.

[135] Thomas N. Hall, 'Ælfric as Pedagogue', in *Companion to Ælfric*, Magennis and Swan, eds, pp. 193–216, p. 200.

[136] Hill, 'Life and Works', pp. 48–9. See also Lapidge, 'Hermeneutic Style', p. 101; Law, *Grammar and Grammarians*, pp. 200–24.

[137] Ælfric, *Catholic Homilies*, Clemoes, ed., p. 173.

[138] 'Augustinum. Ypponiensem. Hieronimum. Bedam. Gregorium. Smaragdum, et aliquando Hægmonem', Ælfric, *Catholic Homilies*, Clemoes, ed., p. 173.

as equal to the traditional languages of exegetical study.[139] In this regard, Ælfric followed earlier authorities in their advocation of the vernacular, and his continuation of Patristic traditions is evident in his *Grammar*, which engages with the spiritual significance of language.

In the *Grammar*'s preface, Ælfric stated that 'God ought not to be subject to rules of grammar' ('nec deus arti grammaticae subiciendus est').[140] He immediately aligned his position with Isidore's in claiming that God's Word can never be fully conveyed in human language, and there are Isidorean influences elsewhere in the *Grammar*.[141] Ælfric gave this work the title of *De Arte Grammatica Anglice* – the English people's own *Ars grammatica* – and it begins with a discussion of the alphabet, and the division of books into sentences, words, and letters:

> Littera is stæf on englisc and is se læsta dæl on bocum and untodæledlic. We todælað þa boc to cwydum and syððan ða cwydas to dælum, eft ða dælas to stæfgefegum and syððan þa stæfgefegu to stafum.[142]

> 'Littera' is 'stave' in English and it is the smallest part in a book and it is indivisible. We divide the book into sentences, and then those sentences into words, again those words into syllables, and then those syllables into staves.

The 'stæf' or letter is the smallest component of language upon which words, phrases, and books are constructed. Letters are evidently important for the formation of holy writings and Scripture; everything is signified through letter combinations: 'butan ðam stæfum ne mæg nan word beon awriten'.[143] Ælfric also provided three characteristics of every letter in its name, shape, and power: 'ælc stæf hæfð þreo ðing: Nomen, Figura, Potestas, þæt is, nama and hiw and miht'.[144] The name of the letter is how it is known in the alphabet, its 'hiw' is how it is shaped, and its might is how it functions between other letters ('miht, hwæt he mæge betwux oðrum stafum').[145] The letter gains power or might when it forms words through its interaction with other letters.

Ælfric based this opening chapter of the *Grammar* on Priscian's *Excerptiones*, which comments on the similarity of the letter with the primary elements of the world: 'Littere autem etiam elementorum uocabulo nuncupantur ad similitudinem elementorum mundi.'[146]

---

[139] Gittos, 'Audience of Old English', p. 264.

[140] Ælfric, *Grammatik*, p. 2.

[141] See Ælfric, *Grammatik*, p. 293.

[142] Ælfric, *Grammatik*, pp. 4–5.

[143] Ælfric, *Grammatik*, p. 5; 'without those staves no word may be written'.

[144] Ælfric, *Grammatik*, p. 5; 'each letter has three things: "Nomen", "Figura", "Potestas", that is, name, shape, and might'.

[145] Ælfric, *Grammatik*, p. 5; 'might, what it is able (to do) between other letters'.

[146] 'Yet again, letters are called after the words "elements" because of similarity with the natural elements,' David W. Porter, ed. and trans, *Excerptiones*

The individual letter assumes the same cosmological significance as the elements, and it occupies a central position in the Creation story. Interestingly, Ælfric omitted this statement by Priscian, indicating that he was perhaps more reserved in explicitly connecting the creation of the world with language. His description of Creation in *De Temporibus Anni* closely follows the account in Genesis, and he does not labour any point about language's role in the division of the world into smaller components:

> Witodlice ða ða se ælmihtiga scyppend þisne middaneard gesceop þa cwæð he gewurðe leoht and leoht wæs ðærrihte geworden. Ða geseah God þæt þæt leoht wæs god and todælde þæt leoht fram ðam þeostrum and het þæt leoht dæg and ða þeostru niht... On ðam oðrum dæge gesceop God heofonan seo þe is gehaten firmamentum seo is gesewenlic and lichamlic.[147]

> Indeed when the Almighty Creator made this middle-world He then said 'let there be light', and light was immediately made. Then God saw that the light was good, and He divided that light from the darkness and called that light 'day' and the darkness 'night'... On the next day God made heaven that is called the firmament which is visible and bodily.

God 'spoke' ('þa cwæð he') when He divided the world ('todælde') into different parts, He named these different components ('het', 'gehaten'), and He gave them visible, bodily form ('gesewenlice and lichamlic'). However, Ælfric was careful not to compromise his view that God is beyond the rules of grammar and human language, and he simply reiterated the Genesis account. Like Isidore, Ælfric included language among the components of the created world but he did not explicitly engage with the question of whether God literally used language to perform His creative act, or what the nature of this language was if He did.

In his homily for Pentecost Sunday, Ælfric also followed Patristic interpretations of the division of languages following the fall of the Tower of Babel:

> Þa wæs an gereord on eallum mancynne. 7 þæt weorc wæs begunnen ongean Godes willan; God eac for þi hi tostencte: swa þ(æt) he forgeaf ælcum þæra wyrhtena seltcuð gereord: 7 heora nan ne cuðe oþres spræce tocnawan... Nu eft on þysum dæge þurh ðæs halgan gastes tocyme wurdon ealle gereord geanlæhte 7 geþwære: for þan ðe eall se halga heap cristes hiredes wæs sprecende mid eallum gereordum 7 eac þæt wunderlicor wæs: þa ða heora án bodode mid anre spræce. ælcum

---

de Prisciano: The Source for Ælfric's Latin-Old English Grammar (Rochester, NY, 2002), pp. 44–5.

[147] Ælfric, *Ælfric's De Temporibus Anni*, Heinrich Henel, ed., EETS Original Series, Vol. 213 (London, 1970), p. 2.

wæs geþuht þe ða bodunge gehyrde swilce he spræce mid his gereorde: wæron hi ebreisce oððe grecisce oððe romanisce. oððe egyptisce. oððe swa hwilcere þeode swa hi wæron þe ða lare gehyrdon.[148]

There was one language among all mankind, and that work [the tower] was begun against God's will. Therefore God drove them apart, so that he gave to each of the builders an unknown language, and not one of them knew how to understand the other's speech... Now also on this day, through the coming of the Holy Spirit, all languages were united and reconciled; because all the holy company of Christ's flock was speaking in all languages; and, furthermore, it was more wonderful when one of them preached in one language, it seemed to everyone, when that preaching was heard, as if he spoke in his language, whether it was Hebrew, or Greek, or Latin, or Egyptian, or of whatever people they were who heard that teaching.

Like earlier Patristic writers, Ælfric claimed that human language was originally united before the building of Babel, and that it was divided as a result of sin.[149] This breakdown in communication was overcome at Pentecost when the Holy Spirit gave the apostles the gift of tongues (or 'glossolalia'), and they preached to peoples of all languages. However, Ælfric also questioned the nature of this miracle as a linguistic act.[150] According to Ælfric, the Holy Spirit granted translinguistic understanding to those who listened to the apostles' preaching, thus overcoming the inability to comprehend different languages following the fall of Babel. The diverse languages that were unanimously understood are not presented as God-given gifts; rather, the Holy Spirit granted the people mutual understanding. This subtle point reiterates Ælfric's view that human languages do not have a divine origin, and that God is beyond the rules of grammar.

Ælfric maintained that God transcends the rules of grammar but, following Jerome, Augustine, and Isidore, he also claimed that language is a medium that is capable of communicating divine mysteries. In his homily for mid-Lent Sunday, he stated that God's Word is manifested in many divine signs in the created world, including writing. Scripture is full of hidden signs concerning Christ that were revealed after the Incarnation:

oft gehwa gesihð fægere stafas awritene. þonne heraþ he þone writere 7 þa stafas 7 nat hwæt hi mænað; Se ðe cann þæra stafa gescead. he heraþ

---

[148] Ælfric, *Catholic Homilies*, Clemoes, ed., pp. 358–9.

[149] On Ælfric's engagement with the Hebrew language, see Damian Fleming, 'Hebrew Words and English Identity in Educational Texts of Ælfric and Byrhtferth', in *Latinity and Identity in Anglo-Saxon England*, Rebecca Stephenson and Emily Thornbury, eds (Toronto, 2016), pp. 138–57.

[150] See Kees Dekker, 'Pentecost and Linguistic Self-Consciousness in Anglo-Saxon England: Bede and Ælfric', *JEGP*, 104 (2005), 345–72, p. 359.

heora fægernysse. 7 ræt þa stafas. 7 understent hwæt hi gemænað… Nis nah genoh þ(æt) ðu stafas scawie. buton þu hi eac ræde. 7 þ(æt) andgit understande… þa bec wæron awritene be criste ac þ(æt) gastlice andgit wæs ðam folce digle oð þ(æt) crist sylf com to mannum 7 geopenade þæra boca diglnysse: æfter gastlicum andgite.[151]

> Often someone sees lovely letters written then praises the writer and the letters, and not know what they mean. He who knows how to understand those letters praises their loveliness, and reads the letters, and understands what they mean… it is not enough that you behold letters without also reading them and understanding their sense… These books were written concerning Christ, but the spiritual sense was hidden from the people, until Christ himself came to men, and opened the books' secrets, according to the spiritual sense.

For Ælfric, the secrets of the Bible are hidden in its many letters, and although God cannot be subjected to the rules of grammar, divine mysteries are to be found in the powerful letter combinations of Scripture. After God created the world, the one language that was spoken among humans was divided after the building of the Tower of Babel, and divine mysteries were concealed from that time until the Incarnation. Christ manifested God's own Word in visible form, he spoke in human language, and he revealed the secrets of the Bible that were then preached to every nation after Pentecost. Ælfric believed that, following Pentecost, divine truths can be understood in any language, and that the diversity of language can be overcome through the same evangelising power given by the Holy Spirit.[152]

One ritual that has been classed as a 'gibberish charm' is found in the composite manuscript London, British Library, Cotton Faustina A. x. Part A of this manuscript (s. xi[2], SE England?) contains a copy of Ælfric's *Glossary* and *Grammar*, and Part B (s. xii[1], unknown origin) contains Æthelwold's translation of the *Rule of Benedict*, the only surviving version of Edgar's *Establishment of the Monasteries,* and a Latin and Anglo-Norman wordlist.[153] Folios 115v–116r of Part B were originally blank and some 'charms' were added by a scribe with similar

---

[151] Ælfric, *Catholic Homilies*, Clemoes, ed., pp. 277–8. See also Jolly, 'Magic, Miracle, and Popular Practice', p. 170.

[152] On Ælfric's possible fostering of the vernacular in liturgical rites, see Gittos, 'Liturgy of Parish Churches', pp. 81–2.

[153] Ker, *Catalogue*, pp. 193–4; Elaine M. Treharne, 'The Dates and Origins of Three Twelfth-Century Old English Manuscripts', in *Manuscripts and their Heritage*, Pulsiano and Treharne, eds, pp. 227–53, pp. 232–3; Alger N. Doane, *Anglo-Saxon Manuscripts in Microfiche Facsimile, Vol. 15: Grammars / Handlist of Manuscripts*, A. N. Doane and M. T. Hussey, eds (Tempe, AZ, 2007), pp. 4–6; López, 'Monastic Learning'. See also Orietta Da Rold and Mary Swann, 'The Production and Use of English Manuscripts 1060 to 1220': <http://www.le.ac.uk/english/em1060to1220> accessed 26 September 2017.

handwriting to Æthelwold's *Rule* in the twelfth century, including two eyesalve recipes, a 'nonsense charm' against dysentery, and two Latin rituals against fever (*Contra frigora* and *Contra febres*).[154] The dysentery ritual reads:

> Þis man sceal singan nigon syþon wiþ utsiht on hrerenbræden æg þry dagas: + Ecce dol gola ne dit dudum bethe cunda bræthe cunda. ele-cunda ele uahge macte me erenum. ortha fuetha la ta uis leti unda. noeuis terre dulge doþ. Paternoster oþ ende. And cweþ symle æt þam drore huic. ð(æt) is.[155]

> A man should sing this nine times against dysentery on a lightly boiled egg for three days: + 'Ecce dol gola ne dit dudum bethe cunda bræthe cunda. elecunda ele uahge macte me erenum. ortha fuetha la ta uis leti unda. noeuis terre dulge doþ'. Then the Our Father to its end. And say continuously at that: 'drore huic', that is.

Neil Ker believed that Part B of this manuscript was added to Part A in the early twelfth century, according to twelfth-century additions in Part B.[156] The manuscript context of this ritual in Part B could therefore indicate that its 'gibberish' may be informed by the surrounding texts concerned with language and translation. It uses Latin ('Ecce', 'noeuis terre'), Old English ('doþ'), and other unidentifiable words ('dol gola') alongside the Paternoster. If Part A was together with Part B when this ritual was added, then its 'gibberish' may have perhaps been informed by some of Ælfric's understandings of language: its individual letters are found in strange combinations which may have increased their might; its blending of multiple languages may be an attempt to over-come the division of language after Babel, and it may even be an attempt to replicate the reunification of language ('glossolalia') after Pentecost. Furthermore, Ælfric's claims that God is not bound by the rules of grammar and that spiritual mysteries are concealed in the letters of Scripture may parallel the ritual's ungrammatical form and obscure writing.

Ælfric's views on language reflect some Anglo-Saxon understand-ings of how language reveals and conceals divine mysteries, and these help us to understand how 'gibberish' may have been inspired by Patristic traditions. We can see, for instance, how some Anglo-Saxon texts use letters and words in ways that reflect Ælfric's three charac-teristics of a letter's name, shape, and might. The name ('nama') of a letter is an important feature of some riddling texts that require the

---

[154] Ker, *Catalogue*, pp. 194–5.
[155] Storms, *Anglo-Saxon Magic*, p. 307. For the other 'charms', see Ker, *Catalogue*, p. 195. An earlier version of the ritual against *utsiht* is found in Harley 585 (fols. 185v–186r).
[156] Ker, *Catalogue*, p. 196.

reader to know what each rune is called in order to solve the puzzle, as seen in the *Husband's Message*.[157] The shape ('hiw') of letters is also an important feature of the *Solomon and Saturn* dialogue, whereby certain runes have offensive, apotropaic capabilities in their attack against the devil.[158] Finally, the might ('miht') of every letter is increased when it functions between other letters, and this may help to explain why some ritual texts use different graphemes from multiple alphabets to increase the power of their concealed words and phrases. Ælfric's descriptions of Babel and Pentecost also have implications for how 'gibberish' could have been perceived by other ecclesiastics. The rituals' obscure writing may represent a pre-Babel homogenous language that can be understood only if the performer is inspired by the Holy Spirit, in the same way that the disciples overcame the multiplicity of languages at Pentecost. Finally, Ælfric described how divine secrets were kept hidden in the letters of Scripture until they were revealed by Christ, and the rituals' obscurity seems to conceal divine meaning that can be revealed only by Christian authorities.

Byrhtferth of Ramsey

Byrhtferth of Ramsey (c. 970–c. 1020) was a contemporary of Ælfric and a pupil of Abbo of Fleury. He was influenced by Oswald and Abbo and, like Ælfric, he promulgated the use of the vernacular in his most famous computistical work, the *Enchiridion*.[159] In the preface to this work, Byrhtferth presents his computus within the familiar framework of the principal languages of Scripture and ancient knowledge, but he also says: 'Her onginð gerimcræft æfter Ledenwarum and æfter Grecum and Iudeiscum and Egiptiscum and Engliscum þeodum'.[160] English is presented as equal to the languages of Scripture and capable of conveying ancient knowledge.[161] In a similar but more explicit way to Ælfric, Byrhtferth used English for the same purposes as the languages of Scripture: to instruct God's chosen people in spiritual mysteries in their own tongue.

---

[157] See Birkett, 'Runes and *Revelatio*'.
[158] See Hermann, 'Pater Noster Battle Sequence'; Hill, 'The Devil's Forms'.
[159] See Byrhtferth, *Byrhtferth of Ramsey: The Lives of St Oswald and St Ecgwine*, Michael Lapidge, ed. and trans (Oxford, 2009), pp. 1–204. See also Heinrich Henel, 'Notes on Byrhtferth's *Manual*', *JEGP*, 41 (1942), 427–43; Baker, 'Byrhtferth's *Enchiridion*'. On the dating of the *Enchiridion*, see Hart, 'Ramsey *Computus*'; 'Byrhtferth and his Manual', pp. 95–109; Stephenson, 'Scapegoating the Secular Clergy', p. 103.
[160] 'Here begins the computus of the Romans and the Greeks and the Hebrews and Egyptians, as well as of the English'; 'Incipit compotus Latinorum ac Grecorum Hebreorumque et Egiptiorum, necnon et Anglorum', Byrhtferth, *Enchiridion*, pp. 2–3.
[161] See Gittos, 'Audience of Old English', p. 264.

There are other sections of the *Enchiridion* that cast much light on Byrhtferth's understanding of how languages and letters convey spiritual mysteries. In Book II, for instance, he discusses the division of the created world into its foundational components:

> Fif untodælednyssa hiw synt. An bið on lichaman, oðer on þære sunnan, þridde on þam gebede, þæt ys on boclicum cræfte. Se læsta dæl on þam stæfgefege ys littera. Þonne we sumne dæl todælað on þære spræce oððe on þam gebede, þonne todælon we ærest þa syllabas… and syððan þæt stæfgefeg on þam stafum. Se stæf ne mæg beon todæled. (II, 3)

> There are five kinds of atom. One is in the body, the second in the sun, the third in speech [*gebede*] – that is, in the discipline of writing. The smallest division in the syllable is the letter [*littera*]. When we divide a certain part in speech [*spræce*] or in prayer [*gebede*], then we first divide the syllables… and afterward we divide the syllable into letters [*stafum*]. The letters [*stæf*] cannot be divided.[162]

The first thing to note about this passage is the range of vocabulary employed by Byrhtferth. He uses the words 'gebede' and 'spræce' for speech, 'syllabas' and 'stæfgefege' for syllable, and 'littera' and 'stæf' for letter. Peter Baker and Michael Lapidge have argued that this section of the *Enchiridion* is ultimately derived from sections of Hrabanus Maurus's *Liber de Computo*, and that he probably also consulted Isidore's *Etymologies* or Donatus' *Ars maior*.[163] However, Byrhtferth significantly developed Hrabanus' section on the division of language, which simply states that 'Atomos est in oratione littera' ('the atom is a letter in speech').[164]

Byrhtferth refers to speech as 'gebede' and 'spræce', and the dual meanings of these words are reflected in the translation by Baker and Lapidge, where 'gebede' is rendered as both 'speech' and 'prayer'.[165] Byrhtferth's deliberate obfuscation of speech and prayer as one of the principal components of the world is also evident in his prayer to the Holy Spirit, which introduces his reckoning of Easter:

> Oratio patris Byrhtferði:
> Spiritus alme, ueni. Sine te non diceris umquam;
> Munera da lingue, qui das (in) munere linguas.
> Cum nu, halig gast. Butan þe ne bis(t) þu gewurðod;
> Gyf þine gyfe þære tungan, þe þu gyfst gyfe on gereorde.

---

[162] Byrhtferth, *Enchiridion*, pp. 110–11.
[163] Baker, 'Byrhtferth's *Enchiridion*', pp. 136–7; Byrhtferth, *Enchiridion*, p. 306.
[164] See Baker, 'Byrhtferth's *Enchiridion*', p. 136. A lengthy marginal note quoting Hrabanus' *Liber de Computo* in Oxford, St John's College, MS 17 (fol. 15v) closely parallels this passage of the *Enchiridion*, see Byrhtferth, *Enchiridion*, pp. 389–90.
[165] See also Lapidge, 'Hermeneutic Style', p. 90.

Father Byrhtferth's prayer:
Come, Holy Spirit: without your support your name cannot even be
   pronounced;
Grant the gifts of speech, you who give the gift of tongues.
Come now, Holy Spirit! Without you, you cannot be honoured.
Give your gift to the tongue, to which you give a gift of speech.[166]

Unlike Ælfric, who stressed that the Holy Spirit's gift at Pentecost was
the ability to *understand* many languages, Byrhtferth directly associated
the Holy Spirit with the gift of speech ('qui das (in) munere linguas',
'þine gyfe þære tungan'). Speech must come from the Holy Spirit
for it to be reciprocated in prayer and worship ('gewurðod'), and in
this context 'gebed' can be rendered as divine speech. Byrhtferth presents the 'gebed' as one of the major constituent parts of the cosmos.
Where Ælfric described the book as the greatest combination of letters
in which divine secrets are kept, Byrhtferth described the 'gebed' as
the greatest formation of letters ('stafas') by which God can be both
revealed and honoured.

When the 'gebed' (or divine speech) is divided into its smallest
components, we are left with the 'stæf' (or letter). In Book III of the
Enchiridion, Byrhtferth discusses the numerical significance of letters
that can be used for the calculation of Easter. As letters and numbers are
anatomical components of the world, they can be interchanged and substituted, and Byrhtferth describes this phenomenon as a mystery that he
will explain to rustic priests: 'Heræfter we wyllað geopenian uplendis-
cum preostum þæra stafena gerena… and syððan heora todælednyssa
we willað gekyðan on þa wisan þe þa boceras habbað and healdað' (III,
3).[167] The letters of the alphabet are mysterious ('gerena') in their varied
functions, and this is elsewhere reinforced by Byrhtferth's account
of the legend of Pachomius. Byrhtferth was evidently influenced by
Jerome's account of this legend, and he elaborated on the mysterious
nature of the letters that Pachomius received from the angel:

Nu we habbað þæne Easterlice circul rihtlice amearcod and þa gerena þe
him to gebyriað be dæle onem him awriten, nu gerist hyt to swutelianne
mid ealre heortan meagolnysse hwanon he com and hwa hine gesette…
'Him sona of heofena mihte com unasecgendlic myrhð, engla sum mid
blisse, se þas word geypte and þæne abbod gegladode and þas uers
him mid gyldenum stafum awritene on þam handum betæhte, þe þus
wæron on his spræce gedihte: None Aprilis norunt quinos eall to þam
ende.' Nu we hig willað mid trahtnunge her geglengan and rihtlice
heora gerena kyrtenum preostum gecyðan (III, 2).

---

[166] Byrhtferth, *Enchiridion*, pp. 136–7.
[167] 'Now we will reveal to rustic priests the mysteries of the letters… and afterwards we will show their divisions in the manner that writers have and hold',
   Byrhtferth, *Enchiridion*, pp. 184–5.

Now that we have correctly written out the Easter cycle and alongside it written some of the mysteries [*gerena*] that belong to it, it is fitting to expound with wholehearted earnestness where it came from and who established it... 'Immediately there came to him from the might of the heavens inexpressible joy, and a certain angel, with bliss, who disclosed these words and gladdened the abbot and delivered into his hands these verses, written with golden letters [*gyldenum stafum*], which were composed thus in his language [*spræce*]: The nones of April know five regulars all the way to the end.' Now we will adorn them here with a commentary and accurately explain their mysteries [*gerena*] to comely priests.[168]

Byrhtferth claimed to know both the correct dating of Easter and all of the mysteries ('gerena') that belong to it.[169] By recounting the divine origin of this liturgical calculation, Byrhtferth lent authority to his computistical knowledge of heavenly mysteries and justified his use of the vernacular in revealing them. Unlike Jerome's account, where the angelic alphabet was secretive and known only to Pachomius and his friends, Byrhtferth stated that the angel's golden letters ('gyldenum stafum') were in Pachomius' own language (i.e. Egyptian). He continued this vernacular transmission of spiritual knowledge to clergymen in the letters of his own work ('rihtlice heora gerena kyrtenum preostum gecyðan'). According to Byrhtferth, new combinations of letters are made in heaven for the discernment of the cosmos and the correct instruction of God's people.

The letters of any language and alphabet have power to discern and convey spiritual mysteries. At the end of Book III of the *Enchiridion*, Byrhtferth also included a number of tables containing numerical values of letters in the Greek and Hebrew alphabets: 'Ebreiscra abecede we willað geswutelian and Grecisra. and þæt getæl þæra stafena we þencað to cyðanne, forþon we witon þæt hyt mæg fremian' (III, 3).[170] As seen with Bede's explanation of manual language, numerical values of letters were useful in calculating dates and substituting letters in secret communication. The previous chapter considered the possibility that tables such as these may have influenced some Anglo-Saxon rituals with obscure letter combinations, like the theft diagram in the *Vitellius Psalter*. It is clear that Byrhtferth assigned spiritual and numerical significance to individual letters regardless of the language or alphabet to which they belong. Every 'stæf' has a spiritual value,

---

[168] Byrhtferth, *Enchiridion*, pp. 138–9.

[169] It is also worth remembering that *galdor* is often connected to *ryne* in poems from the Exeter and Vercelli Books, see Chapter 1.

[170] 'we will expound the Hebrew and Greek alphabets. And we intend to make known the numerical value of the letters, for we know that it may be of use,' Byrhtferth, *Enchiridion*, pp. 186–7.

and it is the atom upon which all languages, prayers, and divine speech are constructed.

Byrhtferth gave special attention to prayer or speech ('gebed') as one of the five foundational elements of the world that is divided into the smallest component of the 'stæf'. These terms are frequently found in 'gibberish' rituals, as seen in the ritual for elf-sickness in *Bald's Leechbook* that uses Greek 'stafum' for a *galdor*: 'Wiþ ælcre yfelre leodrunan 7 wið ælfsidenne þis gewrit him þis greciscum stafum: ++ A ++ O + yºHρBγM +++++ BερρNN | κNεTTAN |'.[171] In Caligula A. xv, the *Heavenly Letter* that was brought by an angel to Rome provides a 'gebed' that is said to have equivalent power to the Eucharist, and the ritual to obtain political favours that follows this prescribes the writing of divine 'stafas'.[172] A detailed illustration of the Pachomius legend also accompanied these two rituals in this manuscript collection. Scriptural languages as well as Irish and English are used in the 'gebed' of other rituals from *Bald's Leechbook*, Harley 585, and Corpus 41.[173] A ritual for nosebleed that uses powerful letters which are associated with Christ's cross appears in a manuscript that contains a lot of Byrhtferth's work as well as cosmological diagrams and cryptograms. The ritual is written on folio 175r of Oxford, St John's College, MS 17 (c. 1110), and it instructs the marking of a prayer from the Greek liturgy in a cruciform shape on the forehead.[174] This cruciform prayer is part of a medicinal collection (fols. 175v–177v) that appears after a series of texts concerned with grammar (fols. 159v–175r).[175] The divine prayers (or 'gebed') of such rituals are encoded in their obscure letters (or 'stafas') that are composed from several alphabets and languages.

Observations

Patristic philosophies of language had a fundamental influence on how Anglo-Saxon theologians understood the spiritual significance of languages and letters. Key biblical events were used to conceptualise the origin, nature, and capabilities of human languages. Beliefs in the divine origin of languages were, however, divided as some

---

[171] Jolly, *Popular Religion*, p. 149; 'Against every evil sorceress and against elf-sickness (write) for him this writing in Greek letters: ++ A ++ O + yºHρBγM +++++ BερρNN | κNεTTAN |'. See also Cockayne, *Leechdoms*, Vol. II, pp. 138–40 and Chapter 2.

[172] Storms, *Anglo-Saxon Magic*, pp. 272, 300.

[173] Grendon, 'Anglo-Saxon Charms', pp. 184, 224; Storms, *Anglo-Saxon Magic*, pp. 234, 258, 266, 301, 308.

[174] Storms, *Anglo-Saxon Magic*, p. 291; Wallis, *The Calendar and the Cloister*: <http://digital.library.mcgill.ca/ms-17> accessed 26 September 2017.

[175] The ritual has correspondences with the acrostic poem of Abbo that is found in the same manuscript on folio 3r (mentioned above).

thought that this was a gift given directly to man by God, while others thought that God does not literally use language as He is beyond the rules of grammar. Despite this tricky theological point, Patristic writers maintained that language has the capacity to convey divine mysteries. Importantly, this was not limited to the principal Scriptural languages of Hebrew, Greek, and Latin; other vernaculars were also considered capable of transmitting the Word of God. These theological interpretations of language were enthusiastically developed by Anglo-Saxon and Carolingian ecclesiastics, and they offer a context within which to understand obscurity in medieval texts. Anglo-Saxon 'gibberish' rituals use alphabets and letters in ways that relate to these philosophical interpretations; several different languages – including vernaculars – often appear in combination, indicating an attempt to reconstruct the original language that was spoken by mankind before the fall of the Tower of Babel and the disciples' gift of tongues (or 'glossolalia') after Pentecost. Individual 'stafas' are prescribed for the performance of divine *galdru* and *gebed*, and they take on cosmological significance as principal elements of the universe. Finally, other rituals seem to employ different systems of encryption to conceal their spiritual meaning through letter manipulation, substitution, and rearrangement.

Conclusions

'Gibberish' has been used as a defining characteristic of Anglo-Saxon 'charms' in traditional scholarship, and obscure words and phrases have been viewed as evidence of scribal confusion and the deliberate obfuscation of heathen formulas. This view does not take into account complex philosophies of language that were being read and written by English theologians. Obscure writing in Anglo-Saxon texts has much in common with philosophical traditions that assigned great spiritual and cosmological significance to individual letters. Many of the manuscripts containing obscure rituals were written in monasteries where these Patristic works would probably have been available, and where language and grammar were studied. From this philosophical basis, English writers developed interesting ways of revealing and concealing spiritual mysteries in a wide range of literary outputs including riddles, wisdom poetry, exercises in encryption, inscriptions, and ritual texts, as Bruce O'Brien observes:

> Grammarians in England began their description of language with its smallest component – its litterae 'letters' – beyond which it could not be divided… Language, then, was something that could be broken down into its smallest parts to be examined and manipulated. The English

showed particular interest in such smallest parts, collecting codes and alphabets, some used to represent numbers, some used to write contemporary languages, others representing no known language.[176]

Building upon O'Brien's summary, Anglo-Saxon 'gibberish' writing is directly related to these intellectual engagements with language, and it reflects a long tradition of ideas about how the world was created, how it is sustained by language, and how divine speech can be formed by many different letters and alphabets.

The final part of this study has offered one alternative way of reading a significant proportion of texts that are included in editions of 'charms'. For instance, rituals that contain obscure writing comprise roughly one quarter of the texts in Storms' edition and they are taken from nearly one half of the manuscripts that he used. Furthermore, there are immediate correspondences between ritual *galdru* and strategies of textual concealment, strongly suggesting that the very concept at the heart of the 'charms' genre is intricately bound up with Christian theology and philosophy. Reading 'gibberish' rituals as encrypted texts has the potential to transform our understanding of late Anglo-Saxon ritual practice, and it offers exciting possibilities for deciphering their divine secrets.

---

[176] O'Brien, *Reversing Babel*, p. 25.

Conclusion

Anglo-Saxon 'charms' have been consistently understood as remnants of heathen religion or heterodox blends of Christianity and paganism. These texts have been extracted from their manuscript sources and often studied in isolation from them. There are significant problems with this approach as the concept of the 'charm' did not enter the English language until after the Anglo-Saxon period, and this calls into question how the manuscripts' scribes and readers understood these rituals. As the Christian nature of 'charms' is crucial to understanding these texts, it is necessary to re-evaluate them as rituals that were embedded in the ecclesiastical culture of late Anglo-Saxon England, in places such as the Old and New Minsters, Winchester and Canterbury Cathedral.

This book has critiqued three core issues that lie at the heart of the genre of Anglo-Saxon 'charms'. By reconsidering the meanings of *galdor*, the manuscript contexts that surround these rituals, and the learned nature of 'gibberish' writing, we can understand more about how early English scribes and ecclesiastics viewed these rituals as powerful Christian practices. While I have not considered every 'charm' in the corpus, I have examined a representative selection of texts from this 'genre' that are found in a range of manuscripts. I argue that scholars should abandon the concept of 'charms' in Anglo-Saxon England – with all of its connotations of paganism, superstition, and heterodox Christianity – and discuss them as they were viewed by the scribes and ecclesiastics who wrote them down. These texts are Christian rituals that developed from learned traditions and that were components of new liturgies for the sick, the possessed, travellers, political leaders, monastic communities, and lay people. They frequently incorporate prayers, formulas, and objects from other liturgies, and many seem to employ complex strategies of textual concealment, indicating that only highly skilled ecclesiastics could read and perform them. Over the course of this book, it has become apparent that these rituals are not vestiges of paganism that were clumsily miscopied, manipulated, or assimilated into heterodox Christian practices; they are deeply integrated in early medieval Christian liturgy, theology, and philosophy.

Part one of this study exposed the different meanings of *galdor*, which is often translated as 'charm'. This word appears in a wide

215

range of texts and it is predominantly used to signify a dangerous and unauthorised ritual practice. The evidence from the corpus of Old English indicates that efforts were made in the tenth and eleventh centuries to restrict meanings of this particular word to warn lay people and catechumens of performing unauthorised rituals, and I suggest that the noun seems to have undergone redefinition in Æthelwold's school in Winchester. Despite traditional scholarly opinion, *galdor* also appears in non-condemnatory ways in mainstream Christian texts that use the term to signify ancient knowledge, Christian wisdom, spiritual discernment, and divine revelation. These texts may reflect meanings of *galdor* before it was predominantly associated with forbidden practices, because they are found primarily in the Exeter and Vercelli Books, which were copied from exemplars predating the Reform. From the few times that *galdor* is used in these ways, the term has very clear connections with important Christian concepts. In some cases it is given explicit liturgical significance as a way of venerating the apostles and martyrs, and even as a medium through which a Eucharistic object reveals a spiritual mystery.

Chapter 2 focused on the only twelve surviving rituals that instruct a reader to write or recite a *galdor*, which are found in four manuscripts that were written in the late tenth and eleventh centuries. In these rituals, *galdor* is often closely associated with liturgical prayers, litanies, Masses, the Eucharist, and 'gibberish' writing. These manuscripts provide crucial evidence that it was understood by some ecclesiastics in high-status minsters as a powerful Christian ritual that was compatible with the sacraments and obscure, sacred language. Part one argued that *galdor* did not signify 'charm' in Anglo-Saxon England and that it was often used to denote ancient Christian wisdom and revelation.

Part two of the study engaged with the manuscript contexts of 'charms' because these texts have been consistently discussed in isolation from their manuscript sources and regrouped according to the criteria of modern editors. As seen in Chapter 3, liturgical elements are present in many 'charms', and close comparisons can be made between these ritual texts and contemporary liturgical rites. I argue that it is often hard to maintain distinctions between 'charms' and liturgy because of the many close correspondences that exist between these scripts for ritual performances. Given the manuscript contexts in which these rituals are found and the minsters in which they were written, it makes sense to read 'charms' as part of diverse Anglo-Saxon liturgical practices from a range of ecclesiastical centres.

Chapter 4 demonstrated that 'charm' rituals were incorporated into larger collections of medical, religious, astronomical, agricultural, and educational materials. They were written in Canterbury, Winchester, Worcester, Exeter, and Ramsey (among other places), reflecting the diversity of spiritual practices in high-status minsters. The *Vitellius Psalter* provides a good example of the close intertextual relationships that exist between these rituals and their surrounding texts. Its prefatory collection includes computistical calculations, astronomical predictions, agricultural rituals, and exercises in secret writing. The encrypted name of Ælfwine in the final text of the psalter's prefatory matter may also provide rare evidence for the identity of a composer of these 'charms' and his interest in obscure language. Cross-comparisons can be made between the psalter and other manuscripts from Canterbury and Winchester, and these expose interesting information about experimentations with liturgical practices in late Anglo-Saxon monasteries. Part two of this study argued that the manuscript contexts of 'charms' reveal how English scribes understood these rituals, and that there is no evidence to suggest that great distinctions (if any) were made between 'charms' and other liturgical rites.

The *Vitellius Psalter* reveals Ælfwine's interest in secret writing, and it is likely that the obscure rituals in this manuscript also contain complex encryptions. Part three of this study critiqued the phenomenon of 'gibberish' language in Anglo-Saxon rituals. Rather than providing evidence of deliberately corrupted heathen formulas or scribal misunderstandings of source materials, I have argued that Patristic and early medieval philosophies of language provide a convincing source of inspiration for complex strategies of textual concealment, from which 'gibberish' writing emerged. The final chapter delineated that 'gibberish' is used in many ritual texts, especially those that prescribe a *galdor* or *gebed*, to deliberately obscure meaning and prevent them from becoming easily known. This is a logical interpretation when one considers the efforts that reformers made to condemn certain types of ritual practices because they were dangerous if they were performed by unauthorised people. The close connections between some *galdru* and the Eucharist and the concealment of their prescribed words in obscure language suggest that these rituals could be performed as liturgical rites only by highly trained priests. Other rites and devotional poems also use letters in obscure ways to graphically encode spiritual meaning. In light of these parallels, an alternative theory can be posited that these highly enigmatic rituals emerged from early medieval scholarly predilections of textual concealment.

The study as a whole has argued that it is unhelpful to classify all of these ritual texts as 'charms', especially when this genre is defined by a very difficult Old English word that does not appear in most of these texts, and which seems to have been understood in different ways by learned Anglo-Saxon clergy themselves. All of these rituals should be approached with great caution and discussed in their manuscript contexts as case studies with due attention given to their own individual ecclesiastical environments. This book challenges the idea that there was any such thing as a 'charm' in Anglo-Saxon England, and it aims to offer a stepping-stone from this unconvincing traditional genre towards a plethora of new, exciting research for liturgy and secret writing in early medieval England and beyond.

Bibliography

Primary Sources

Abbo of Fleury, *Quaestiones grammaticales*, A. Guerreau-Jalabert, ed. (Paris, 1982).

Adamnán, *Life of St Columba*, Richard Sharpe, ed. and trans (London, 1995).

Ælfric, *Ælfrics Grammatik und Glossar*, Julius Zupitza, ed. (Berlin, 1880).

—— *Ælfric's Lives of Saints*, Walter W. Skeat, ed. and trans, 2 Vols., EETS Original Series, Vols. 76, 82, 94, 114 (London, 1881–1891).

—— *Die Hirtenbriefe Ælfrics in Altenglischer und Lateinischer Fassung*, Bernhard Fehr, ed. and trans, 2 Vols. (Hamburg, 1914).

—— *Ælfric's De Temporibus Anni*, Heinrich Henel, ed., EETS Original Series, Vol. 213 (London, 1970).

—— *Ælfric's Catholic Homilies: The Second Series*, Malcolm Godden, ed., EETS Supplementary Series, Vol. 5 (London, 1979).

—— *Ælfric's Catholic Homilies: The First Series, Text*, Peter Clemoes, ed., EETS Supplementary Series, Vol. 17 (Oxford, 1997).

—— *Ælfric's Letter to the Monks of Eynsham*, Christopher A. Jones, ed. and trans (Cambridge, 1998).

—— *The Old English Heptateuch and Ælfric's Libellus de Veteri Testamento et Novo*, Richard Marsden, ed., EETS Original Series, Vol. 330 (London, 2008).

Ælfwine's Prayerbook: London, British Library, Cotton Titus D. xxvi + xxvii, Beate Günzel, ed., HBS, Vol. 108 (London, 1993).

Aldhelm, *Aldhelm: The Prose Works*, Michael Lapidge and Michael Herren, eds and trans (Cambridge, 1979).

Andreas: An Edition, Richard North and Michael D. J. Bintley, eds, Exeter Medieval Texts and Studies (Liverpool, 2016).

Anglo-Saxon Chronicle, A Collaborative Edition: Volume 3, MS A, Janet Bately, ed. (Cambridge, 1986).

Anglo-Saxon Prognostics: An Edition and Translation of Texts from London, British Library MS Cotton Tiberius A iii, Roy Liuzza, ed. (Cambridge, 2010).

Anglo-Saxon Prognostics, 900–1100: Study and Texts, Lázló Sándor Chardonnens, ed. and trans (Leiden, 2007).

Anglo-Saxon Riddles of the Exeter Book, Paull F. Baum, trans (Durham, NC, 1963).

Augustine, *S. Aurelii Augustini Hipponensis Episcopi De Doctrina Christiana Libri Quatuor*, PL, Vol. 34 (1865).

—— *De Civitate Dei*, Bernard Dombart and Alphonsus Kalb, eds, 5th edn, 2 Vols. (Stuttgart, 1981).

—— *De Doctrina Christiana*, R. P. H. Green, ed. and trans (Oxford, 1995).

Bald's Leechbook: British Museum Royal Manuscript 12.D.xvii, Charles E. Wright, ed. and trans (Copenhagen, 1955).

Bede, *Hexaemeron, sive libri quatuor in principium Genesis, usque ad nativitatem Isaac et electionem Ismaelis*, PL, Vol. 91 (1850).

—— *Bedae Opera De Temporibus*, Charles W. Jones, ed. (Cambridge, MA, 1943).

—— *Ecclesiastical History of the English People*, Bertram Colgrave and R. A. B. Mynors, eds and trans, Oxford Medieval Texts (Oxford, 1969).

—— *The Reckoning of Time*, Faith Wallis, trans (Liverpool, 1999).

—— *On Genesis*, Calvin B. Kendall, trans (Liverpool, 2008).

Benedictine Office: An Old English Text, James M. Ure, ed. (Edinburgh, 1957).

Benedictional of Archbishop Robert, Henry A. Wilson, ed., HBS, Vol. 24 (London, 1903).

Beowulf, Charles L. Wrenn, ed., 2nd edn (London, 1958).

Beowulf, Michael Alexander, trans (Harmondsworth, 1973).

Biblia Sacra: iuxta Vulgatam versionem, Bonifatio Fischer, Iohanne Gribomont, H. F. D. Sparks, W. Thiele, et al, eds, 2 Vols. (Stuttgart, 1969).

Blickling Homilies: Edition and Translation, Richard J. Kelly, ed. and trans (London, 2003).

Boethius, *The Old English Boethius: An Edition of the Old English Versions of Boethius'* De Consolatione Philosophiae, Malcolm Godden and Susan Irvine, eds and trans, 2 Vols. (Oxford, 2009).

Bradley, S. A. J., trans, *Anglo-Saxon Poetry* (London, 1982).

Byrhtferth of Ramsey, *Byrhtferth's Enchiridion*, Peter S. Baker and Michael Lapidge, eds and trans, EETS Supplementary Series, Vol. 15 (Oxford, 1995).

—— *Byrhtferth of Ramsey: The Lives of St Oswald and St Ecgwine*, Michael Lapidge, ed. and trans (Oxford, 2009).

Cambridge, Corpus Christi College MS 41: The Loricas and the Missal, Raymond J. S. Grant, ed. (Amsterdam, 1979).

Canterbury Benedictional (British Museum Harl. MS. 2892), Reginald M. Woolley, ed., HBS, Vol. 51 (London, 1917).

Claudius Pontificals (from Cotton MS Claudius A. iii in the British Museum), D. H. Turner, ed., HBS, Vol. 97 (London, 1971).

Cockayne, Thomas Oswald, ed. and trans, *Leechdoms, Wortcunning, and Starcraft of Early England: Being a Collection of Documents, for the Most Part Never Before Printed, Illustrating the History of Science in this Country Before the Norman Conquest*, 3 Vols. (London, 1864–66).

Cynewulf's Elene, Pamela O. E. Gradon, ed. (London, 1958).

Dobbie, Elliot Van Kirk, ed., *Anglo-Saxon Minor Poems*, ASPR, Vol. 6 (New York, 1942).

Durham Collectar, Alicia Corrêa, ed., HBS, Vol. 107 (London, 1997).

Eadwine's Canterbury Psalter, Fred Harsley, ed., EETS Original Series, Vol. 92 (London, 1889).

'An Edition and Codicological Study of CCCC MS. 214', W. C. Hale, ed., Unpublished Doctoral Thesis (University of Pennsylvania, USA, 1978).

An Eighth-Century Latin-Anglo-Saxon Glossary: Preserved in the Library of Corpus Christi College, Cambridge (MS No. 144), J. H. Hessels, ed. (Cambridge, 1890).

Eleven Old English Rogationtide Homilies, Joyce Bazire and James E. Cross, eds and trans (Toronto, 1982).

Exeter Anthology of Old English Poetry: An Edition of Exeter Dean and Chapter MS 3501, Benjamin J. Muir, ed., 2 Vols. (Exeter, 1994).

Exeter Book, George Philip Krapp and Elliot Van Kirk Dobbie, eds, ASPR, Vol. 3 (New York, 1936).

Exeter Book of Old English Poetry, R. W. Chambers, Max Förster, and Robin Fowler, eds (London, 1933).

Felix, *Felix's Life of Saint Guthlac*, Bertram Colgrave, ed. and trans (Cambridge, 1956).

Förster, Max, ed., 'Vom Fortleben antiker Sammellunare im Englischen und in anderen Volkssprachen', *Anglia*, 67 (1944), 1–171.

Glossar zum Vespasian-Psalter und den Hymnen, Conrad Grimm, ed. (Heidelberg, 1906).

Grattan, George H. G. and Charles J. Singer, eds and trans, *Anglo-Saxon Magic and Medicine* (London, 1952).

Grendon, Felix, 'The Anglo-Saxon Charms', *Journal of American Folk-Lore*, 22 (1909), 105–237.

Hall, Joseph, ed., *Selections from Early Middle English 1130–1250*, 2 Vols. (Oxford, 1920).

Harley Latin-Old English Glossary, R. T. Oliphant, ed. (The Hague, 1966).

Heht, H., ed., *Bischof Waerferths von Worcester Üebersetzung der Dialoge Gregors des Grossen* (Leipzig, 1900).

Heliand, Eduard Sievers, ed. (Halle, 1878).

Hêliand: Text and Commentary, James E. Cathey, ed. (Morgantown, 2002).

Hrabanus Maurus, *B. Rabani Mauri Fuldensis Abbatis et Moguntini Archiepiscopi: Omnia Opera*, PL, Vol. 112 (1852).

Isidore of Seville, *Sententiae*, I, 18, PL, Vol. 83 (1862).

—— *Etymologiarum sive Originum*, W. M. Lindsay, ed., 2 Vols. (Oxford, 1911).

—— *The Etymologies of Isidore of Seville*, Stephen Barney, W. J. Lewis, J. A. Beach, Oliver Berghof, eds and trans (Cambridge, 2006).

Jente, Richard, ed., *Die Mythologischen Ausdrücke im Altenglischen Wortschatz* (Heidelberg, 1921).

Jerome, *Pachomiana Latina: Règle et épîtres de S. Pachôme, épître de S. Théodore et 'Liber' de S. Orsiesius*, Amand Boon, ed. (Louvain, 1932).

—— 'Ad Pammachium de optimo genere interpretani', in *Sancti Eusebii Hieronymi Epistulae*, Isidorus Hilberg, ed., CSEL, Vol. 54, rev edn (Vienna, 1996), pp. 503–26.

—— 'Letter to Pammachius', Paul Carroll, trans, in *Western Translation Theory: From Herodotus to Neitzsche*, Douglas Robinson, ed. (Manchester, 1997), pp. 23–30.

John Scottus Eriugena, *Periphyseon (De Diuisione Naturae), Liber Primus*, I. P. Sheldon-Williams, ed. and trans, 3 Vols. (Dublin, 1968).

Junius-Psalter: Die Interlinear-Glosse der Handschrift Junius 27 der Bodleiana zu Oxford, Eduard Brenner, ed. (Heidelberg, 1909).

Lambeth-Psalter: Eine Altenglische Interlinearversion des Psalters in der HS. 427 der Erzbischöflichen Lambeth Palace Library, U. Lindelöf, ed., 2 Vols. (Helsingfors, 1909–14).

'Latin-Old English Glossary in MS. Cleopatra A. III', W. G. Stryker, ed., Unpublished Doctoral Thesis (Stanford University, USA, 1951).

Laws of the Earliest English Kings, F. L. Attenborough, ed. and trans (Cambridge, 1922).

Leofric Missal, 1: Introduction, Collation Table, and Index; 2: Text, Nicholas Orchard, ed., 2 Vols., HBS, Vols. 113–14 (Woodbridge, 2002).

Leonhardi, Günther, ed., *Kleinere angelsächsische Denkmäler I*, Bibliothek der Angelsächsischen Prosa, Vol. 6 (Hamburg, 1905).

Liber Vitae of the New Minster and Hyde Abbey, Winchester, British Library Stowe 944, Simon Keynes, ed. and trans, EEMF, Vol. 26 (Copenhagen, 1996).

Liebermann, Felix, ed., *Ungedruckte Anglo-Normannische Geschichtsquellen: Herausgegeben* (London, 1879).

—— *Die Gesetze der Angelsachsen*, 3 Vols. (Halle, 1903).

—— *Die Gesetze der Angelsachsen: Herausgegeben im Auftrage der Savigny-Stiftung*, 2 Vols. (Halle, 1916).

Liuzza, Roy, ed., *Old English Poetry: An Anthology* (Ontario, 2014).

'Minor Latin-Old English Glossaries in MS. Cotton Cleopatra A. III', J. J. Quinn, ed., Unpublished Doctoral Thesis (Stanford University, USA, 1956).

Missal of Robert of Jumièges, Henry A. Wilson, ed., HBS, Vol. 11 (London, 1896).

Old English Glosses, Arthur S. Napier, ed. (Oxford, 1900).

Old English Glosses: A Collection, Herbert Dean Meritt, ed. (Oxford, 1945).

Old English Glosses of MS. Brussels, Royal Library, 1650 (Aldhelm's De Laudibus Virginitatis*)*, Louis Goosens, ed. (Brussels, 1974).

Old English Martyrology: Edition, Translation and Commentary, Christine Rauer, ed. and trans (Cambridge, 2013).

Old English Version of Bede's Ecclesiastical History of the English People, Thomas Miller, ed., 2 Vols., EETS Original Series, Vols. 95–6, 110–11 (London, 1890–91, 1898).

Paris Psalter and the Meters of Boethius, George Philip Krapp, ed., ASPR, Vol. 5 (New York, 1932).

Pettit, Edward, ed. and trans, *Anglo-Saxon Remedies, Charms, and Prayers from British Library MS Harley 585: The Lacnunga: Introduction, Text, Translation, and Appendices*, 2 Vols. (Lewiston, NY, 2001).

Pontificale Lanaletense (Bibliothèque de la Ville de Rouen A. 27. Cat. 368), G. H. Doble, ed., HBS, Vol. 74 (London, 1937).

Porter, David W., ed. and trans, *Excerptiones de Prisciano: The Source for Ælfric's Latin-Old English Grammar* (Cambridge, 2002).

Prayerbook of Aedeluald the Bishop Commonly Called the Book of Cerne: Edited from the MS in the University Library, Cambridge with Introduction and Notes, A. B. Kuypers, ed. (Cambridge, 1902).

Raith, J., ed., *Die alternglische Version des Halitgar'schen Bussbuches* (Hamburg, 1933).

Regius-Psalter: Eine Interlinearversion in HS. Royal 2 B. 5 des Brit. Mus., Fritz Roeder, ed. (Halle, 1904).

Regularis Concordia: Monastic Agreement of the Monks and Nuns of the English Nation, Thomas Symons, ed. and trans (New York, 1953).

Repsher, Brian V., ed. and trans, *The Rite of Church Dedication in the Early Medieval Era* (Lewiston, NY, 1998).

Richardson, Ernest Cushing, ed., *Hieronymus liber de viris inlustribus: Gennadius liber de viris inlustribus* (Leipzig, 1896).

—— *A Select Library of Nicene and Post-Nicene Fathers of the Christian Church, Second Series, Vol. 3: Theodoret, Jerome, Gennadius, and Rufinus: Historical Writings* (Edinburgh, 1892, repr. 1979).

Roberts, Jane Annette, ed., *The Guthlac Poems of the Exeter Book* (Oxford, 1979).

Rodrigues, Louis J., ed. and trans, *Anglo-Saxon Verse Charms, Maxims, and Heroic Legends* (Pinner, Middlesex, 1993).

Rule of S. Benet: Latin and Anglo-Saxon Intelinear Version, Henri Logeman, ed., EETS Original Series, Vol. 90 (London, 1888).

Sacramentary of Ratoldus, Nicholas Orchard, ed., HBS, Vol. 116 (London, 2005).

Sæmundsson, M. V., ed., *Galdrar á Íslandi: Íslensk Galdrabók*, 2nd edn (Reykjavik, 1992).

Saxon Genesis: An Edition of the West Saxon Genesis B and the Old Saxon Vatican Genesis, Alger N. Doane, ed. (Madison, 1991).

Storms, Godfrid, ed. and trans, *Anglo-Saxon Magic* (The Hague, 1948).

Swanton, Michael, ed. and trans, *Anglo-Saxon Prose* (London, 1975).

Three Coronation Orders, John W. Legg, ed., HBS, Vol. 19 (London, 1900).

Toal, M. F., ed., *The Sunday Sermons of the Great Fathers*, 4 Vols. (San Francisco, 2000).

Two Anglo-Saxon Pontificals: (The Egbert and Sidney Sussex Pontificals), H. M. J. Banting, ed., HBS, Vol. 104 (London, 1989).

Vercelli Book, George Philip Krapp, ed., ASPR, Vol. 2 (London, 1932).

Vercelli Book: A Late Tenth-Century Manuscript Containing Prose and Verse, Vercelli Biblioteca Capitolare CXVII, Celia Sisam, ed., EEMF, Vol. 19 (Copenhagen, 1976).

Vercelli-Codex CXVII nebst Abdruck einiger altenglischer Homilien der Handschrift, Max Förster, ed. (Halle, 1913).

Vercelli-Homilien, Max Förster, ed. (Hamburg, 1964).

Vercelli Homilies and Related Texts, Donald G. Scragg, ed., EETS Original Series, Vol. 300 (Oxford, 1992).

Vitellius Psalter: Edited from British Museum MS Cotton Vitellius E. xviii, James L. Rosier, ed. (Ithaca, NY, 1962).

Wulfstan, *Wulfstan: Sammlung Englischer Denkmäler*, Arthur S. Napier, ed. (Berlin, 1883).

—— *The Homilies of Wulfstan*, Dorothy Bethurum, ed. (Oxford, 1971).

—— *Wulfstan's Canons of Edgar*, Roger Fowler, ed., EETS Original Series, Vol. 266 (London, 1972).

—— *Wulfstan's Canon Law Collection*, James E. Cross and Andrew Hamer, eds (Cambridge, 1999).

Secondary Sources

A Catalogue of the Harleian Manuscripts in the British Museum, 4 Vols. (London, 1808–12).

Alamichel, Marie-Françoise and Derek Brewer, eds, *The Middle Ages After the Middle Ages in the English Speaking World* (Cambridge, 1997).

Amies, Marion, "The "Journey Charm": A Lorica for Life's Journey', *Neophilologus*, 67 (1983), 448–62.

Amsler, Mark, *Etymology and Grammatical Discourse in Late Antiquity and the Early Middle Ages* (Amsterdam, 1989).

Anderson, G. K., *Literature of the Anglo-Saxons* (Princeton, 1949).

Århammar, Nils, ed., *Aspects of Language: Studies in Honour of Mario Alinei, Vol. 1: Geolinguistics* (Amsterdam, 1986).

Arnovick, Leslie K., *Written Reliquaries: The Resonance of Orality in Medieval English Texts* (Amsterdam, 2006).

Arthur, Ciaran, '*Ex Ecclesia*: Salvific Power beyond Sacred Space in Anglo-Saxon Charms', *Incantatio*, 3 (2013), 9–32.

—— 'Giving the Head's Up in Ælfric's *Passio Sancti Edmundi*: Postural Representations of the Old English Saint', *PQ*, 92 (2013), 315–34.

—— 'Ploughing through Cotton Caligula A. VII: Reading the Sacred Words of the *Heliand* and the *Æcerbot*', *RES*, 65 (2014), 1–17.

—— 'Three Marginal Notes in London, British Library, MS Cotton Caligula A. vii', *N&Q*, 62 (2015), 211–17.

—— 'The Gift of the Gab in Post-Conquest Canterbury: Mystical "Gibberish" in London, British Library, MS Cotton Caligula A. xv', *JEGP*, forthcoming.

Baker, Peter S., 'Byrhtferth's *Enchiridion* and the Computus in Oxford, St John's College 17', *ASE*, 10 (1981), 123–42.

Banham, Debby, 'The Staff of Life: Cross and Blessings in Anglo-Saxon Cereal Production', in *Cross and Cruciform in the Anglo-Saxon World: Studies to Honor the Memory of Timothy Reuter*, Sarah Larratt Keefer, Karen Louise Jolly, and Catherine E. Karkov, eds (Morgantown, 2010), pp. 279–318.

Banks, R. A., 'The Uses of Liturgy in the Magic, Medicine, and Poetry of the Anglo-Saxons', in *The Timeless and the Temporal: Writings in Honour of John Chalker by Friends and Colleagues*, Elizabeth Maslen, ed. (Exeter, 1993), pp. 19–40.

Barkley, Heather, 'Liturgical Influences on the Anglo-Saxon Charms against Cattle Theft', *N&Q*, 44 (1997), 450–2.

Barrow, Julia, 'The Chronology of the Benedictine "Reform"', in *Edgar, King of the English 959–975: New Interpretations*, Donald G. Scragg, ed. (Woodbridge, 2008), pp. 211–23.

—— *The Clergy in the Medieval World: Secular Clerics, Their Families and Careers in North-Western Europe, c. 800-c. 1200* (Cambridge, 2015).

Baycroft, Timothy and David Hopkin, eds, *Folklore and Nationalism in the Long Nineteenth Century* (Leiden, 2012).

Bedingfield, M. Bradford, *The Dramatic Liturgy of Anglo-Saxon England* (Woodbridge, 2002).

Berschin, Walter, 'Elements in Medieval Latin Manuscripts', in *Sacred Nectar of the Greeks: the Study of Greek in the West in the Early Middle Ages*, M. W. Herren, ed. (London, 1988), pp. 85–104.

Biggam, C. P., ed., *From Earth to Art: The Many Aspects of the Plant World in Anglo-Saxon England* (Amsterdam, 2003).

Billett, Jesse D., *The Divine Office in Anglo-Saxon England, 597 – c. 1000*, HBS Subsidia Series, Vol. 7 (Woodbridge, 2014).

Birkett, Tom, 'Runes and *Revelatio*: Cynewulf's Signatures Reconsidered', *RES*, 65 (2014), 771–89.

—— 'Unlocking Runes? Reading Anglo-Saxon Runic Abbreviations in Their Immediate Literary Context', *Futhark*, 5 (2015), 91–114.

—— *Reading the Runes in Old English and Old Norse Poetry* (Abingdon, 2017).

Bischoff, Bernhard, *Mittelalterliche Studien, Ausgewählte Aufsätze zur Schriftkunde und Literaturgeschichte*, 3 Vols. (Stuttgart, 1966–81).

Bischoff, Bernhard and Michael Lapidge, *Biblical Commentaries from the Canterbury School of Theodore and Hadrian* (Cambridge, 1994).

Bitterli, Dieter, *Say what I Am Called: The Old English Riddles of the Exeter Book and the Anglo-Latin Riddle Tradition* (Toronto, 2009).

Blair, Peter Hunter, *The World of Bede* (Cambridge, 1970).

Blair, John, *The Church in Anglo-Saxon Society* (Oxford, 2005).

Blake, N. F., 'The Scribe of the Exeter Book', *Neophilologus*, 46 (1962), 316–19.

Blom, Alderik, '*Linguae Sacrae* in Ancient and Medieval Sources: An Anthropological Approach to Ritual Language', in *Multilingualism in the Graeco-Roman Worlds*, Alex Mullen and Patrick James, eds (Cambridge, 2012), pp. 124–40.

Bonser, Wilfrid, 'The Seven Sleepers of Ephesus in Anglo-Saxon and Later Recipes', *Folklore*, 56 (1945), 254–6.

—— 'Anglo-Saxon Laws Relating to Theft', *Folklore*, 57 (1946), 7–11.

—— *The Medical Background of Anglo-Saxon England: A Study in History, Psychology, and Folklore* (London, 1963).

Borsje, Jacqueline, 'A Spell Called *Éle*', in *Ulidia 3: Proceedings of the Third International Conference on the Ulster Cycle of Tales*, Gregory Toner and Séamus MacMathúna, eds (Berlin, 2013), pp. 193–212.

Boryslawski, Rafal, 'The Elements of Anglo-Saxon Wisdom Poetry in the *Exeter Book* Riddles', *Studia Anglica Posnaniensia*, 38 (2002), 35–47.

Bosworth, Joseph, *A Compendious Anglo-Saxon and English Dictionary* (London, 1848).

Bozóky, Edina, 'Medieval Narrative Charms', in *The Power of Words*, James A. Kapalo, Eva Pocs, and William F. Ryan, eds (Budapest, 2013), pp. 101–16.

Braekman, Willy L., 'Notes on Old English Charms', *Neophilologus*, 64 (1980), 461–9.

—— 'Notes on Old English Charms II', *Neophilologus*, 67 (1983), 605–10.

Bragg, Lois, 'Runes and Readers: In and Around "The Husband's Message"', *Studia Neophilologica*, 71 (1999), 34–50.

Bredehoft, Thomas A., 'The Boundaries Between Verse and Prose in Old English Literature', in *Old English Literature in its Manuscript Context*, Joyce Tally Lionarons, ed. (Morgantown, 2004), pp. 139–72.

—— 'Filling the Margins of CCCC 41: Textual Space and a Developing Archive', *RES*, 57 (2006), 721–32.

Bremmer, Rolf, 'Mercury-Hermes and Woden-Odin as Inventors of Alphabets: A Neglected Parallel', in *Old English Runes and their Continental Background*, Alfred Bammesberger, ed. (Heidelberg, 1991), pp. 409–19.

—— 'Continental Germanic Influences', in *A Companion to Anglo-Saxon Literature*, Phillip Pulsiano and Elaine Treharne, eds (Oxford, 2001), pp. 375–87.

—— 'The Anglo-Saxon Continental Mission and the Transfer of Encyclopaedic Knowledge', in *The Foundations of Learning: The Transfer of Encyclopaedic Knowledge in the Early Middle Ages*, Rolf H. Bremmer Jr and Kees Dekker, eds (Leuven, 2007), pp. 19–50.

—— 'Old English "Cross" Words', in *Cross and Cruciform in the Anglo-Saxon World: Studies to Honor the Memory of Timothy Reuter*, Sarah Larratt Keefer, Karen Louise Jolly, and Catherine E. Karkov, eds (Morgantown, 2010), pp. 204–32.

Brennessel, Barbara, M. Drout and R. Gravel, 'A Reassessment of the Efficacy of Anglo-Saxon Medicine', *ASE*, 34 (2005), 183–95.

Brooks, Nicholas, 'The Career of St Dunstan', in *St Dunstan: His Life, Times and Cult*, Nigel Ramsay, Margaret Sparks, and Tim Tatton-Brown, eds (Woodbridge, 1992), pp. 1–24.

Brooks, Nicholas and Catherine Cubitt, eds, *St Oswald of Worcester: Life and Influence* (London, 1996).

Brown, George Hardin, 'Solving the "Solve" Riddle in B. L. MS Harley 585', *Viator*, 18 (1987), 45–51.

Brown, Michelle P., *The Book of Cerne: Prayer, Patronage, and Power in Ninth-Century England* (London, 1996).

—— 'Female Book Ownership and Production in Anglo-Saxon England: The Evidence of the Ninth-Century Prayerbooks', in *Lexis and Texts in Early English: Studies Presented to Jane Roberts*, C. J. Kay and L. M. Sylvester, eds (Amsterdam, 2001), pp. 45–63.

—— *Manuscripts from the Anglo-Saxon Age* (London, 2007).

Budny, Mildred, *Insular, Anglo-Saxon, and Early Anglo-Norman Manuscript Art at Corpus Christi College, Cambridge: An Illustrated Catalogue*, 2 Vols. (Kalamazoo, MI, 1997).

Butler, Robert M., 'Glastonbury and the Early History of the Exeter Book', in *Old English Literature in its Manuscript Context*, Joyce Tally Lionarons, ed. (Morgantown, 2004), pp. 173–215.

Caie, Graham, 'Codicological Clues: Reading Old English Christian Poetry in its Manuscript Context', in *The Christian Tradition in Anglo-Saxon England: Approaches to Current Scholarship and Teaching*, Paul Cavill, ed. (Cambridge, 2004), pp. 3–14.

Cain, Andrew, *The Letters of Jerome: Asceticism, Biblical Exegesis, and the Construction of Christian Authority in Late Antiquity* (Oxford, 2009).

Cain, Christopher M., 'Sacred Words, Anglo-Saxon Piety, and the Origins of the *Epistola Salvatoris* in London, British Library, Royal 2.A.xx', *JEGP*, 108 (2009), 168–89.

Calder, Daniel G., 'Theme and Strategy in *Guthlac B*', *Papers on Language and Literature*, 8 (1972), 227–42.

Cameron, Malcolm L., 'Bald's *Leechbook*: Its Sources and their Use in its Compilation', *ASE*, 12 (1983), 153–82.

—— 'Anglo-Saxon Medicine and Magic', *ASE*, 17 (1988), 191–215.

—— 'Bald's *Leechbook* and Cultural Interactions in Anglo-Saxon England', *ASE*, 19 (1990), 5–12.

—— *Anglo-Saxon Medicine* (Cambridge, 1993).

Carley, James P., *The Libraries of King Henry VIII* (London, 2000).

Cassiday, Augustine, 'St Aldhelm's Bees (*De Uirginitate Prosa*, cc. iv-vi): Some Observations on a Literary Tradition', *ASE*, 33 (2004), 1–22.

Cavell, Megan, 'Powerful Patens in the Anglo-Saxon Medical Tradition and Exeter Book *Riddle 48*', *Neophilologus*, 101 (2017), 129–38.

Cavill, Paul, *Anglo-Saxon Christianity* (London, 1999).

Chaney, William, 'Paganism to Christianity in Anglo-Saxon England', *Harvard Theological Review*, 53 (1960), 197–217.

Chardonnens, Lázló Sándor, 'An Arithmetical Crux in the Woden Passage in the Old English *Nine Herbs Charm*', *Neophilologus*, 93 (2009), 691–702.

Chave-Mahir, Florence, *L'exorcisme des possédés dans l'Église d'Occident (Xe-XIVe siècle)* (Turnhout, 2011).

Chickering, Howell, 'The Literary Magic of *Wið Færstice*', *Viator*, 2 (1972), 83–104.

Christie, Edward, 'The Image of the Letter: From the Anglo-Saxons to the Electronic Beowulf', *Culture, Theory and Critique*, 44 (2003), 129–50.

—— 'By Means of a Secret Alphabet: Dangerous Letters and the Semantics of *Gebregdstafas* (*Solomon and Saturn I*, Line 2b)', *Modern Philology*, 109 (2011), 145–70.

Clark-Hall, John R., *A Concise Anglo-Saxon Dictionary*, 2nd rev edn (New York, 1916).

Clarke, Catherine A. M., *Writing Power in Anglo-Saxon England: Texts, Hierarchies, Economies* (Cambridge, 2012).

Clements, Jill Hamilton, 'Reading, Writing and Resurrection: Cynewulf's Runes as a Figure of the Body', *ASE*, 43 (2014), 133–54.

Clemoes, Peter, *Interactions of Thought and Language in Old English Poetry* (Cambridge, 1995).

Conner, P. W., *Anglo-Saxon Exeter: A Tenth-Century Cultural History* (Woodbridge, 1993).

Contreni, John J., 'The Biblical Glosses of Haimo of Auxerre and John Scottus Eriugena', *Speculum*, 51 (1976), 411–34.

Cooper, Tracey-Anne, 'The Homilies of a Pragmatic Archbishop's Handbook in Context: Cotton Tiberius A. iii', *Anglo-Norman Studies*, 28 (2006), 47–65.

—— *Monk-Bishops and the English Benedictine Reform Movement: Reading London, BL, Cotton Tiberius A. iii in Its Manuscript Context* (Turnhout, 2015).

Copeland, Rita, *Rhetoric, Hermeneutics, and Translation in the Middle Ages: Academic Traditions and Vernacular Texts* (Cambridge, 1991).

Crawford, Jane, 'Evidences for Witchcraft in Anglo-Saxon England', *Medium Ævum*, 32 (1963), 99–116.

Cronyn, J. M. and C. V. Horie, 'The Anglo-Saxon Coffin: Further Investigations', in *St Cuthbert, his Cult and his Community to A.D.*

1200, Gerald Bonner, David W. Rollason, and Clare Stancliffe, eds (Woodbridge, 1995), pp. 247–56.

Cubitt, Catherine, 'The Tenth-Century Benedictine Reform in England', *Early Medieval Europe*, 6 (1997), 77–94.

—— 'Sites and Sanctity: Revisiting the Cult of Murdered and Martyred Anglo-Saxon Royal Saints', *Early Medieval Europe*, 9 (2000), 53–83.

—— 'Ælfric's Lay Patrons', in *A Companion to Ælfric*, Hugh Magennis and Mary Swann, eds (Leiden, 2009), pp. 165–92.

Dachowski, Elizabeth, *First Among Abbots: The Career of Abbo of Fleury* (Washington, 2008).

Davidson, H. R. Ellis, *Gods and Myths of Northern Europe* (Harmondsworth, 1964).

Deegan, Marilyn and Donald G. Scragg, eds, *Medicine in Early Medieval England: Four Papers* (Manchester, 1989).

Dekker, Kees, 'Pentecost and Linguistic Self-Consciousness in Anglo-Saxon England: Bede and Ælfric', *JEGP*, 104 (2005), 345–72.

Dendle, Peter, 'The Demonological Landscape of the *Solomon and Saturn* Cycle', *ES*, 80 (1999), 281–92.

Derolez, René, 'Ogam, "Egyptian", "African" and "Gothic" Alphabets: some Remarks in Connection with Codex Bernensis 207', *Scriptorium* 5.1 (1951), 3–19.

—— *Runica Manuscripta: The English Tradition* (Brugge, 1954).

Discenza, Nicole Guenther, 'Writing the Mother Tongue in the Shadow of Babel', in *Conceptualizing Multilingualism in Medieval England, c. 800 – c. 1250*, Elizabeth M. Tyler, ed. (Turnhout, 2011), pp. 33–55.

Doane, Alger N., *Anglo-Saxon Manuscripts in Microfiche Facsimile, Vol. 1: Books of Prayers and Healing* (Binghamton, 1994).

—— *Anglo-Saxon Manuscripts in Microfiche Facsimile, Vol. 15: Grammars / Handlist of Manuscripts*, A. N. Doane and M. T. Hussey, eds (Tempe, AZ, 2007).

Duckert, Audrey, 'Erce and other Possibly Keltic Elements in the Old English Charm for Unfruitful Land', *Names*, 20 (1972), 83–90.

Duclow, Donald F., 'Divine Nothingness and Self-Creation in John Scotus Eriugena', *Journal of Religion*, 57 (1977), 109–23.

Dumitrescu, Irina A., 'Bede's Liberation Philology: Releasing the English Tongue', *PMLA*, 128 (2013), 40–56.

Dumville, David D., 'The Anglian Collection of Royal Genealogies and Regnal Lists', *ASE*, 5 (1976), 23–50.

—— *Liturgy and the Ecclesiastical History of Late Anglo-Saxon England: Four Studies* (Woodbridge, 1992).

—— *English Caroline Script and Monastic History: Studies in Benedictinism, A.D. 950–1030* (Cambridge, 1993).

—— 'English Square Miniscule Script: The Mid-Century Phases', *ASE*, 23 (1994), 133–64.

Edlich-Muth, Miriam, 'Prosopopoeia: Sharpening the Anglo-Saxon Toolkit', *ES*, 95 (2014), 95–108.

Elsheikha, Hany and Jon S. Patterson, *Vetinary Parasitology* (Boca Raton, FL, 2013).

Estes, Heide, 'Colonization and Conversion in Cynewulf's *Elene*', in *Conversion and Colonization in Anglo-Saxon England*, Catherine E. Karkov and Nicholas Howe, eds (Tempe, AZ, 2006), pp. 133–51.

Fell, Christine, 'Runes and Semantics', in *Old English Runes and their Continental Background*, Alfred Bammesberger, ed. (Heidelberg, 1991), pp. 195–229.

Fife, Austin E., 'Christian Swarm Charms from the Ninth to the Nineteenth Centuries', *Journal of American Folklore*, 77 (1964), 154–9.

Fisher, Rebecca M. C., 'Writing Charms: The Transmission and Performance of Charms in Anglo-Saxon England', Unpublished Doctoral Thesis (University of Sheffield, England, 2011).

—— 'The Anglo-Saxon Charms: Texts in Context', *Approaching Methodologies*, 4 (2012), 108–26.

—— 'Genre, Prayers, and the Anglo-Saxon Charms', in *Genre – Text – Interpretation: Multidisciplinary Perspectives on Folklore and Beyond*, Frog and Kaarina Koski, eds (Helsinki, 2013), pp. 1–25.

Fleming, Damian, '*Hebraeam scire linguam*: Bede's Rhetoric of the Hebrew Truth', in *Imagining the Jew: Jewishness in Anglo-Saxon Literature and Culture*, Samantha Zacher, ed. (Toronto, 2016), pp. 63–78.

—— 'Hebrew Words and English Identity in Educational Texts of Ælfric and Byrhtferth', in *Latinity and Identity in Anglo-Saxon England*, Rebecca Stephenson and Emily Thornbury, eds (Toronto, 2016), pp. 138–57.

Foot, Sarah, *Veiled Women I: The Disappearance of Nuns from Anglo-Saxon England* (Aldershot, 2000).

Forbes, Helen Foxhall, *Heaven and Earth in Anglo-Saxon England: Theology and Society in An Age of Faith* (Farnham, 2013).

Förster, Max, 'Ein altenglisches Prosa-Rätsel', *Archiv für das Studium der neueren Sprachen und Literaturen*, 115 (1905), 392–3.

Fowler, Roger, 'A Late Old English Handbook for the Use of a Confessor', *Anglia*, 83 (1965), 1–34.

Frantzen, Allen J., 'The Tradition of Penitentials in Anglo-Saxon England', *ASE*, 11 (1982), 23–56.

Frantzen, Allen J. and John D. Niles, eds, *Anglo-Saxonism and the Construction of Social Identity* (Gainesville, 1997).

Frazer, James G., *The Golden Bough: A Study in Magic and Religion*, abridged edn (London, 1974).

Fulk, R. D. and Christopher M. Cain, eds, *A History of Old English Literature*, 2nd edn (Malden, Mass., 2005).

Fuller, Susan, 'Pagan Charms in Tenth-Century Saxony? The Function of the Merseburg Charms', *Monatschefte*, 72 (1980), 162–70.

Gameson, Richard, 'The Origin of the Exeter Book of Old English Poetry', *ASE*, 25 (1996), 135–85.

—— *The Scribe Speaks? Colophons in Early English Manuscripts* (Cambridge, 2001).

Garner, Lori-Ann, 'Anglo-Saxon Charms in Performance', *Oral Tradition*, 19 (2004), 20–42.

Garner, Lori Ann and Kayla M. Miller, ' " A Swarm in July": Beekeeping Perspectives on the Old English *Wið Ymbe* Charm', *Oral Tradition*, 26 (2011), 355–76.

Garnet, George, 'The Third Recension of the English Coronation *ordo*: The Manuscripts', *Haskins Society Journal*, 11 (1998), 43–72.

Gatch, Milton McC., 'The Office in Late Anglo-Saxon Monasticism', in *Learning and Literature in Anglo-Saxon England*, Michael Lapidge and Helmut Gneuss, eds (Cambridge, 1985), pp. 341–62.

Gay, David E., 'Anglo-Saxon Metrical Charm 3 Against a Dwarf: A Charm against Witch-Riding?', *Folklore*, 99 (1988), 174–7.

Gittos, Helen, 'Is there any Evidence for the Liturgy of Parish Churches in Late Anglo-Saxon England? The Red Book of Darley and the Status of Old English', in *Pastoral Care in Late Anglo-Saxon England*, Francesca Tinti, ed., Anglo-Saxon Studies, Vol. 6 (Woodbridge, 2005), pp. 63–82.

—— *Liturgy, Architecture, and Sacred Places in Anglo-Saxon England* (Oxford, 2013).

—— 'Sources for the Liturgy of Canterbury Cathedral in the Central Middle Ages', *The British Archaeological Association Conference Transactions*, 35 (2013), 41–58.

—— 'The Audience for Old English Texts: Ælfric, Rhetoric and "the Edification of the Simple" ', *ASE*, 43 (2014), 231–66.

—— 'Researching the History of Rites', in *Understanding Medieval Liturgy: Essays in Interpretation*, Helen Gittos and Sarah Hamilton, eds (Farnham, 2015), pp. 13–37.

Glosecki, Stephen, *Shamanism and Old English Poetry* (New York, 1989).

Gneuss, Helmut, 'The Origin of Standard Old English and Æthelwold's School at Winchester', *ASE*, 1 (1972), 63–83.

—— 'Anglo-Saxon Libraries from the Conversion to the Benedictine Reform', *Settimane di studio del Centro italiano di studi sull' alto medioevo*, 32 (1984), 643–88.

—— 'The Study of Language in Anglo-Saxon England', *Bulletin of the John Rylands Library*, 72 (1990), 3–32.

—— 'Origin and Provenance of Anglo-Saxon Manuscripts: The Case of Cotton Tiberius A III', in *Of the Making of Books: Medieval Manuscripts, their Scribes and Readers; Essays Presented to M. B. Parkes*, P. R. Robinson and Rivkah Zim, eds (Aldershot, 1997), pp. 13–49.

—— *Handlist of Anglo-Saxon Manuscripts: A List of Manuscripts and Manuscript Fragments Written or Owned in England up to 1100* (Tempe, AZ, 2001).

Gneuss, Helmut and Michael Lapidge, *Anglo-Saxon Manuscripts: A Bibliographical Handlist of Manuscripts and Manuscript Fragments Written or Owned in England up to 1100* (Toronto, 2014).

Godden, Malcolm, 'Ælfric's Changing Vocabulary', *ES*, 61 (1980), 206–23.

—— 'Prologues and Epilogues in the Old English *Pastoral Care*, and their Carolingian Models', *JEGP*, 110 (2011), 441–73.

Gordon, E. V., ed., *An Introduction to Old Norse*, 2nd rev edn (Oxford, 1957).

Graham, Timothy, 'Glosses and Notes in Anglo-Saxon Manuscripts', in *Working with Anglo-Saxon Manuscripts*, Gale R. Owen-Crocker, ed. (Exeter, 2009), pp. 159–204.

Grendon, Felix, 'Samuel Butler's God', *North American Review*, 208 (1918), 227–86.

—— 'Socialism in Thought and Action by Harry W. Laidler', *Political Science Quarterly*, 35 (1920), 484–6.

Gretsch, Mechthild, *The Intellectual Foundations of the English Benedictine Reform* (Cambridge, 1999).

—— 'The Roman Psalter, its Old English Glosses and the English Benedictine Reform', in *The Liturgy of the Late Anglo-Saxon Church*, M. Bradford Bedingfield and Helen Gittos, eds, HBS Subsidia Series, Vol. 5 (London, 2005), pp. 13–28.

—— 'Ælfric, Language, and Winchester', in *A Companion to Ælfric*, Hugh Magennis and Mary Swann, eds (Leiden, 2009), pp. 35–66.

Grübl, Doris, *Studien zu den angelsachsischen Elegien* (Marburg, 1948).

Gwara, Scott, 'Three Acrostic Poems by Abbo of Fleury', *Journal of Medieval Latin*, 2 (1992), 203–35.

—— 'Further Old English Scratched Glosses and Merographs from Corpus Christi College, Cambridge MS 326 (Aldhelm's *Prosa De Virginitate*)', *ES*, 3 (1997), 201–36.

Hall, Alaric, 'Calling the Shots: The Old English Remedy Gif Hors Ofscoten Sie and Anglo-Saxon "Elf-Shot"', *Neuphilologische Mitteilungen*, 106 (2005), 195–209.

—— 'Constructing Anglo-Saxon Sanctity: Tradition, Innovation and Saint Guthlac', in *Images of Sanctity: Essays in Honour of Gary Dickson*, Debra Higgs Strickland, ed. (Leiden, 2007), pp. 207–35.

—— *Elves in Anglo-Saxon England: Matters of Belief, Health, Gender and Identity* (Woodbridge, 2007).

—— 'Glosses, Gaps and Gender: The Rise of Female Elves in Anglo-Saxon Culture', in *Change in Meaning and the Meaning of Change: Studies in Semantics and Grammar from Old to Present-Day English*, Matti Rissanen, ed. (Helsinki, 2007), pp. 139–70.

Hall, J. R., 'Anglo-Saxon Studies in the Nineteenth Century: England, Denmark, America', in *A Companion to Anglo-Saxon Literature*, Phillip Pulsiano and Elaine Treharne, eds (Oxford, 2001), pp. 434–54.

Hall, Thomas N., 'Ælfric as Pedagogue', in *A Companion to Ælfric*, Hugh Magennis and Mary Swann, eds (Leiden, 2009), pp. 193–216.

Hamilton, Sarah, 'Remedies for "Great Transgressions": Penance and Excommunication in Late Anglo-Saxon England', in *Pastoral Care in Late Anglo-Saxon England*, Francesca Tinti, ed. (Woodbridge, 2005), pp. 83–105.

Hart, Cyril, 'The Ramsey *Computus*', *EHR*, 85 (1970), 29–44.

—— 'Byrhtferth and his Manual', *Medium Ævum*, 41 (1972), 95–109.

—— 'The Foundation of Ramsey Abbey', *Revue Bénédictine*, 104 (1994), 295–327.

Hassig, Debra, *Medieval Bestiaries: Text, Image, Ideology* (Cambridge, 1995).

Hebing, Rosanne, 'The Textual Tradition of Heavenly Letter Charms in Anglo-Saxon Manuscripts', in *Secular Learning in Anglo-Saxon England: Exploring the Vernacular*, Lázló Sándor Chardonnens and Bryan Carella, eds (Amsterdam, 2012), pp. 203–22.

Henel, Heinrich, 'Notes on Byrhtferth's *Manual*', *JEGP*, 41 (1942), 427–43.

—— 'Byrhtferth's *Preface*: The Epilogue of his Manual?', *Speculum*, 18 (1943), 288–302.

Hermann, John, 'The Pater Noster Battle Sequence in *Solomon and Saturn* and the *Psychomachia* of Prudentius', *Neuphilologische Mitteilungen*, 77 (1976), 206–10.

Heyworth, Melanie, 'The "Late Old English Handbook for the Use of a Confessor": Authorship and Connections', *N&Q*, 54 (2007), 218–22.

Hill, Joyce, 'The Exeter Book and Lambeth Palace Library MS 149: A Reconsideration', *ANQ*, 24 (1986), 112–16.

—— 'The Exeter Book and Lambeth Palace Library MS 149: The Monasterium of Sancta Maria', *ANQ*, 1 (1988), 4–9.

—— 'The Benedictine Reform and Beyond', in *A Companion to Anglo-Saxon Literature*, Phillip Pulsiano and Elaine Treharne, eds (Oxford, 2001), pp. 151–69.

—— 'Rending the Garment and Reading by the Rood: *Regularis concordia* Rituals for Men and Women', in *The Liturgy of the Late Anglo-Saxon Church*, M. Bradford Bedingfield and Helen Gittos, eds, HBS Subsidia Series, Vol. 5 (Woodbridge, 2005), pp. 53–64.

—— 'Ælfric: His Life and Works', in *A Companion to Ælfric*, Hugh Magennis and Mary Swann, eds (Leiden, 2009), pp. 109–37.

Hill, Thomas D., 'An Irish-Latin Analogue for the Blessing of the Sods in the Old English *Æer-bot* Charm', *N&Q*, 213 (1968), 362–3.

—— 'The *Æcerbot* Charm and its Christian User', *ASE*, 6 (1977), 213–21.

—— 'The Theme of the Cosmological Cross in Two Old English Cattle Theft Charms', *N&Q*, 25 (1978), 488–90.

—— 'Invocation of the Trinity and the Tradition of the Lorica in Old English Poetry', *Speculum*, 56 (1981), 259–67.

—— 'The Devil's Forms and the Pater Noster's Powers: The Prose Solomon and Saturn *Pater Noster* Dialogue', *SP*, 85 (1988), 164–76.

—— 'The Rod of Protection and the Witches' Ride: Christian and Germanic Syncretism in Two Old English Metrical Charms', *JEGP*, 111 (2012), 145–68.

Hines, John, 'The Dwarf Is Dead', *British Archaeology*, 157 (2017), 52–7.

Hofman, Petra, 'Infernal Imagery in Anglo-Saxon Charters', Unpublished Doctoral Thesis (University of St Andrews, Scotland, 2008).

Hofsetter, W., 'Winchester and the Standardization of Old English Vocabulary', *ASE*, 17 (1988), 139–61.

Hohler, Christopher, 'Some Service-Books of the Later Saxon Church', in *Tenth-Century Studies: Essays in Commemoration of the Millenium of the Council of Winchester and 'Regularis Concordia'*, David Parsons, ed. (London, 1975), pp. 60–83.

—— 'Review of Raymond J. S. Grant, ed., *Cambridge, Corpus Christi College MS 41: the Loricas and the Missal* (Amsterdam: Rodopi, 1979)', *Medium Aevum*, 49 (1980), 275–8.

Hollis, Stephanie, 'Old English "Cattle-Theft Charms": Manuscript Contexts and Social Uses', *Anglia*, 115 (1997), 139–64.

—— 'Scientific and Medical Writings', in *A Companion to Anglo-Saxon Literature*, Phillip Pulsiano and Elaine Treharne, eds (Oxford, 2001), pp. 188–208.

Holsinger, Bruce, 'The Parable of Cædmon's *Hymn*: Liturgical Invention and Literary Tradition', *JEGP*, 106 (2007), 149–75.

Holthausen, Ferdinand, 'Eine ae Interlinearversion des athanasischen Glaubensbekenntnisse', *Englische Studien*, 75 (1942–43), 6–8.

Horne, Thomas Hartwell, *A Catalogue of the Library of the College of St. Margaret and St. Bernard, Commonly Called Queen's College in the University of Cambridge*, 2 Vols. (London, 1827).

Howlett, David, *Sealed from Within: Self-Authenticating Insular Charters* (Dublin, 1999).

Hunt, Tony, *Popular Medicine in Thirteenth-Century England* (Cambridge, 1990).

Hutcheson, B. R., '*Wið Dweorh*: An Anglo-Saxon Remedy for Fever in its Cultural and Manuscript Setting', in *Secular Learning in Anglo-Saxon England: Exploring the Vernacular*, Lázló Sándor Chardonnens and Bryan Carella, eds (Amsterdam, 2012), pp. 175–202.

Hussey, Matthew T., 'Dunstan, Æthelwold, and Isidorean Exegesis in Old English Glosses: Oxford, Bodleian Library Bodley 319', *RES*, 60 (2009), 681–704.

James, M. R., *A Descriptive Catalogue of the Western Manuscripts in the Library of Queen's College, Cambridge* (Cambridge, 1905).

—— *A Descriptive Catalogue of the Manuscripts in the Library of Gonville and Caius College*, 2 Vols. (Cambridge, 1908).

Johnson, Richard F., 'Archangel in the Margins: St. Michael in the Homilies of Cambridge, Corpus Christi College 41', *Traditio*, 53 (1998), 63–91.

Jolly, Karen, 'Anglo Saxon Charms in the Context of a Christian Worldview', *Journal of Medieval History*, 11 (1985), 279–93.

—— 'Magic, Miracle, and Popular Practice in the Early Medieval West: Anglo-Saxon England', in *Religion, Science, and Magic: In Concert and Conflict*, Jacob Neuser and Ernest S. Frerichs, eds (Oxford, 1989), pp. 166–84.

—— 'Father God and Mother Earth: Nature Mysticism in the Anglo-Saxon World', in *The Medieval World of Nature: A Book of Essays*, Joyce E. Salisbury, ed. (New York, 1993), pp. 221–52.

—— *Popular Religion in Late Saxon England: Elf Charms in Context* (Chapel Hill, 1996).

—— 'Prayers from the Field: Practical Protection and Demonic Defence in Anglo-Saxon England', *Traditio*, 61 (2006), 95–147.

—— 'Tapping the Power of the Cross: Who and for Whom?", in *The Place of the Cross in Anglo-Saxon England*, Catherine E. Karkov, Sarah Larratt Keefer, and Karen Louise Jolly, eds (Woodbridge, 2006), pp. 58–79.

—— 'On the Margins of Orthodoxy: Devotional Formulas and Protective Prayers in Cambridge, Corpus Christi College MS 41', in *Signs on the Edge: Space, Text and Margin in Medieval Manuscripts*, Sarah L. Keefer and Rolf Bremmer, eds (Paris, 2007), pp. 135–83.

Jones, Charles W., 'A Legend of St. Pachomius', *Speculum*, 18 (1943), 198–210.

Jones, Christopher A., 'The Book of the Liturgy in Anglo-Saxon England', *Speculum*, 73 (1998), 659–702.

—— 'The Chrism Mass in Later Anglo-Saxon England', in *The Liturgy of the Late Anglo-Saxon Church*, M. Bradford Bedingfield and Helen Gittos, eds, HBS Subsidia Series, Vol. 5 (Woodbridge, 2005), pp. 105–42.

—— 'Ælfric and the Limits of "Benedictine Reform"', in *A Companion to Ælfric*, Hugh Magennis and Mary Swann, eds (Leiden, 2009), pp. 67–108.

Jones, Claire, '"Efficacy Phrases" in Medieval English Medical Manuscripts', *Neophilologische Mitteilungen*, 99 (1998), 199–210.

Jungmann, Joseph A., *The Mass of the Roman Rite: Its Origins and Development*, Francis A. Brunner, trans, 2 Vols. (New York, 1951).

Karkov, Catherine E., 'Abbot Ælfwine and the Sign of the Cross', in *Cross and Cruciform in the Anglo-Saxon World: Studies to Honor the Memory of Timothy Reuter*, Sarah Larratt Keefer, Karen Louise Jolly, and Catherine E. Karkov, eds (Morgantown, 2010), pp. 103–32.

Keefer, Sarah Larratt, 'Margin as Archive: The Liturgical Marginalia of a Manuscript of the Old English Bede', *Traditio*, 51 (1996), 147–77.

Keeler, Richard F. and Anthony T. Tu, eds, *Plant and Fungal Toxins: Handbook of Natural Toxins*, Vol. 1 (New York, 1983).

Ker, Neil R., 'Two Notes on MS Ashmole 328 (*Byrhtferth's Manual*)', *Medium Ævum*, 4 (1935), 16–19.

—— *Catalogue of Manuscripts Containing Anglo-Saxon* (Oxford, 1957).

Keynes, Simon, *Anglo-Saxon Manuscripts in Trinity College*, OEN Subsidia Series, Vol. 18 (Binghamton, 1992).

—— 'Edgar, rex admirabilis', in *Edgar, King of the English 959–975: New Interpretations*, Donald G. Scragg, ed. (Woodbridge, 2008), pp. 3–59.

Kiff-Hooper, J. A., 'Classbooks or Works of Art? Some Observations on the Tenth-Century Manuscripts of Aldhelm's *De Laude Virginitatis*', in *Church and Chronicle in the Middle Ages: Essays Presented to John Taylor*, Ian Wood and G. A. Laud, eds (London, 1991), pp. 15–26.

Kitzinger, Ernst, 'The Coffin-Reliquary', in *The Relics of St. Cuthbert*, C. F. Battiscombe, ed. (Oxford, 1956), pp. 202–307.

Knowles, David, *The Monastic Order in England: A History of its Development from the Times of St Dunstan to the Fourth Lateran Council 940–1216*, 2nd edn (Cambridge, 1963).

Knowles, David, C. N. L. Brooke, and Vera C. M. London, *The Heads of Religious Houses England and Wales I: 940–1216*, 2nd edn (Cambridge, 2004).

Kuhn, Sherman M., 'Review of Herbert Dean Meritt, ed., *Old English Glosses: A Collection* (Oxford: OUP, 1945)', *JEGP*, 45 (1946), 344–6.

Lapidge, Michael, 'The Hermeneutic Style in Tenth-Century Anglo-Latin Literature', *ASE*, 4 (1975), 67–111.

—— 'Dunstan and Hrabanus Maurus: zur Hs. Bodleian Auctarium F.4.32', *Anglia*, 96 (1978), 136–48.

—— 'Aldhelm's Latin Poetry and Old English Verse', *Comparative Literature*, 31 (1979), 209–31.

—— 'Æthelwold As Scholar and Teacher', in *Bishop Æthelwold: His Career and Influence*, Barbara Yorke, ed. (Woodbridge, 1988), pp. 89–117.

—— *Anglo-Latin Literature 900–1066* (London, 1993).

—— *The Anglo-Saxon Library* (Oxford, 2005).

Law, Vivien, *Wisdom, Authority and Grammar in the Seventh Century: Decoding Virgilius Maro Grammaticus* (Cambridge,1995).

—— *Grammar and Grammarians in the Early Middle Ages* (London, 1997).

Lawson, M. K., 'Archbishop Wulfstan and the Homiletic Element in the Laws of Æthelred II and Cnut', *EHR*, 107 (1992), 565–86.

Lees, Clare A. and Gillian R. Overing, 'Women and the Origins of English Literature', in *The History of British Women's Writing, 700–1500*, Liz Herbert McAvoy and Diane Watt, eds (New York, 2012), pp. 31–40.

Lehmann, R. P. M., 'The Old English Riming Poem: Interpretation, Text, and Translation', *JEGP*, 64 (1970), 437–49.

Lenker, Ursula, 'The Monasteries of the Benedictine Reform and the "Winchester School": Model Cases of Social Networks in Anglo-Saxon England', *European Journal of English Studies*, 4 (2000), 225–38.

—— 'Signifying Christ in Anglo-Saxon England: Old English Terms for the Sign of the Cross', in *Cross and Cruciform in the Anglo-Saxon World: Studies to Honor the Memory of Timothy Reuter*, Sarah Larratt Keefer, Karen Louise Jolly, and Catherine E. Karkov, eds (Morgantown, 2010), pp. 233–75.

Leventhal, Robert, 'The Emergence of Philological Discourse in the German States 1770–1810', *Isis*, 77 (1986), 243–60.

Levison, Wilhelm, *England and the Continent in the Eighth Century: The Ford Lectures* (Oxford, 1943).

Lindquist, Ivar, *Galdrar: De gamla germanska trollsångernas stil undersökt I samband med en svensk runinskrift från folkvandringstiden* (Göteborg, 1923).

Lionarons, Joyce Tally, *The Homiletic Writings of Archbishop Wulfstan* (Woodbridge, 2010).

Little, Lester K., *Benedictine Maledictions: Liturgical Cursing in Romanesque France* (Ithaca, 1993).

Liuzza, Roy M., 'The Sphere of Life and Death: Time, Medicine, and the Visual Imagination', in *Latin Learning and English Lore: Studies in Anglo-Saxon Literature for Michael Lapidge*, Katherine O'Brien O'Keeffe and Andy Orchard, eds (Toronto, 2005), pp. 28–52.

—— 'Prayers and/or Charms Addressed to the Cross', in *Cross and Culture in Anglo-Saxon England: Studies in Honor of George Hardin Brown*, Karen Jolly, Catherine E. Karkov, and Sarah Larratt Keefer, eds (Morgantown, 2008), pp. 276–320.

Longland, Sabrina, 'Pilate Answered: What I have Written I Have Written', *The Metropolitan Museum of Art Bulletin*, 26 (1968), 410–29.

López, Francisco José Álvarez, 'Monastic Learning in Twelfth-Century England: Marginalia, Provenance and Use in London, British Library, Cotton MS. Faustina A. X, Part B', *Electronic British Library Journal* (2012), no. 11, 1–8.

Loud, Graham A. and Martial Staub, eds, *The Making of Medieval History* (York, 2017).

Lucas, Peter J. and Jonathan Wilcox, *Anglo-Saxon Manuscripts in Microfiche Facsimile, Vol. 16: Manuscripts Relating to Dunstan, Ælfric, and Wulfstan; the 'Eadwine Psalter' Group*, A. N. Doane, ed. (Tempe, AZ, 2008).

Mackie, W. S., 'The Old English "Rhymed Poem"', *JEGP*, 21 (1922), 507–19.

MacLeod, Mindy and Bernard Mees, *Runic Amulets and Magic Objects* (Woodbridge, 2006).

Malone, Kemp, 'The Old English Period (to 1100)', in *A Literary History of England*, A. C. Baugh, ed., 2nd edn (London, 1967), pp. 1–106.

Marsden, Richard, 'Ælfric as Translator: The Old English Prose *Genesis*', *Anglia*, 109 (1991), 319–58.

McBrine, Patrick, 'The Journey Motif in the Poems of the Vercelli Book', in *New Readings in the Vercelli Book*, Samantha Zacher and Andy Orchard, eds (Toronto, 2009), pp. 298–317.

McGowan, Joseph, 'Four Unedited Prayers in London, Cotton Tiberius A. iii', *Medieval Studies*, 56 (1994), 189–216.

Meaney, Audrey L., 'Woden in England: A Reconsideration of the Evidence', *Folklore*, 77 (1966), 105–15.

—— 'Variant Versions of Old English Medical Remedies and the Compilation of *Bald's Leechbook*', *ASE*, 13 (1984), 235–68.

—— 'Ælfric's Use of his Sources in his Homily on Auguries', *ES*, 66 (1985), 477–95.

—— 'Women, Witchcraft, and Magic in Anglo-Saxon England', in *Superstition and Popular Medicine in Anglo-Saxon England*, Donald G. Scragg, ed. (Manchester, 1989), pp. 9–40.

—— 'The Anglo-Saxon View of the Causes of Illness', in *Health, Disease and Healing in Medieval Culture*, Sheila Campbell, Bert Hall, and David Klausner, eds (London, 1992), pp. 12–33.

—— '"And we forbeodað eornostlice ælcne hæðenscipe": Wulfstan and Late Anglo-Saxon and Norse "Heathenism"', in *Wulfstan, Archbishop of York: The Proceedings of the Second Alcuin Conference*, Matthew Townend, ed. (Turnhout, 2004), pp. 461–500.

Merrills, A. H., *History and Geography in Late Antiquity* (Cambridge, 2005).

Molyneaux, George, 'The *Old English Bede*: English Ideology or Christian Instruction?', *EHR*, 124 (2009), 1289–323.

Moran, Pádraic, 'Hebrew in Early Irish Glossaries', *Cambrian Medieval Celtic Studies*, 60 (2010), 1–21.

—— 'A Living Speech? The Pronunciation of Greek in Early Medieval Ireland', *Ériu*, 61 (2011), 29–57.

Morrish, Jennifer, 'Dated and Datable Manuscripts Copied in England During the Ninth Century: A Preliminary List' *Mediaeval Studies*, 50 (1988), 512–38.

Mostert, Marco, *The Political Theology of Abbo of Fleury: A Study of the Ideas about Society and Law of the Tenth-Century Monastic Reform Movement* (Hilversum, 1987).

—— 'Relations between Fleury and England', in *England and the Continent in the Tenth Century: Studies in Honour of Wilhelm Levison (1876–1947)*, David Rollason, Conrad Leyser, and Hannah Williams, eds (Turnhout, 2010), pp. 185–208.

Murphy, Patrick J., *Unriddling the Exeter Book Riddles* (Pennsylvania, 2011).

Murphy, G. Ronald, 'The Old Saxon *Heliand*', in *Perspectives on the Old Saxon Heliand: Introductory and Critical Essays, with an Edition* of the Leipzig Fragment, V. A. Pakis, ed. (Morgantown, 2010), pp. 34–62.

Nelson, Marie, 'The Paradox of Silent Speech in the Exeter Book Riddles', *Neophilologus*, 62 (1978), 609–15.

—— 'An Old English Charm against Nightmare', *Germanic Notes*, 13 (1982), 17–18.

—— '"Wordsige and Worcsige": Speech Acts in Three Old English Charms', *Language and Style*, 17 (1984), 57–66.

—— 'A Woman's Charm', *Studia Neophilologica*, 57 (1985), 3–8.

—— 'King Solomon's Magic: The Power of a Written Text', *Oral Tradition*, 5 (1990), 20–36.

Nelson, Janet, *Politics and Ritual in Early Medieval Europe* (London, 1989).

Niles, John D., 'The Æcerbot Ritual in Context', in *Old English Literature in Context*, John D. Niles, ed. (Cambridge, 1980), pp. 44–56.

—— *Old English Enigmatic Poems and the Play of the Texts* (Turnhout, 2006).

Nokes, Robert Scott, 'The Several Compilers of *Bald's Leechbook*', *ASE*, 33 (2004), 51–76.

North, Richard, *Heathen Gods in Old English Literature* (Cambridge, 1997).

Oakley, Thomas Pollock, *English Penitential Discipline and Anglo-Saxon Law in their Joint Influence* (Clark, NJ, 2003).

O'Brien, Bruce R., *Reversing Babel: Translation among the English during an Age of Conquests, c. 800 to c. 1200* (Newark, DE, 2011).

O'Brien O'Keeffe, Katherine, *Visible Song: Transitional Literacy in Old English Verse* (Cambridge, 1990).

Ó Carragáin, Éamonn, 'Rome, Ruthwell, Vercelli: "The Dream of the Rood" and the Italian Connection', in *Vercelli tra Oriente ed Occidente tra Tarda Antichità e Medioevo*, Vittora D. Corazza, ed. (Alessandria, 1999), pp. 59–99.

Ó Cróinín, Dáibhí, *Early Irish History and Chronology* (Dublin, 2003).

Ohrt, Ferdinand, *'Herba, Gratia Plena': Die Legenden der älteren Segensprüche über den gottlichen Ursprung der Heil- und Zauberkräuter* (Helsinki, 1929).

—— 'Om Galdersange', *Danske Studier*, 23 (1923), 186–89.

—— 'Om Merseburgformlerne som Galder', *Danske Studier*, 35 (1938), 125–37.

Okasha, Elizabeth, 'Old English hring in Riddles 48 and 59', *Medium Ævum*, 62 (1993), 61–9.

O'Leary, Aideen M., 'Apostolic *Passiones* in Early Anglo-Saxon England', in *Apocryphal Texts and Traditions in Anglo-Saxon England*, Kathryn Powell and Donald G. Scragg, eds (Cambridge, 2003), pp. 103–20.

Olsan, Lea, 'Latin Charms of Medieval England: Verbal Healing in a Christian Oral Tradition', *Oral Tradition*, 7 (1992), 116–42.

—— 'The Inscriptions of Charms in Anglo-Saxon Manuscripts', *Oral Tradition*, 14 (1999), 401–19.

—— 'Charms and Prayers in Medieval Medical Theory and Practice', *Social History of Medicine*, 16 (2003), 343–66.

—— 'Charms in Medieval Memory', in *Charms and Charming in Europe*, Jonathan Roper, ed. (Basingstoke, 2004), pp. 59–88.

—— 'The Marginality of Charms in Medieval England', in *The Power of Words: Studies on Charms and Charming in Europe*, James Kapaló, Éva Pócs, and William Ryan, eds (Budapest, 2013), pp. 135–64.

Orchard, Andy, *The Poetic Art of Aldhelm* (Cambridge, 1994).

—— 'Old Sources, New Resources: Finding the Right Formula for Boniface', *ASE*, 30 (2001), 15–38.

—— 'The Word Made Flesh: Christianity and Oral Culture in Anglo-Saxon Verse', *Oral Tradition*, 24 (2009), 293–318.

Orel, Vladimir, *A Handbook of Germanic Etymology* (Leiden, 2003).

O'Sullivan, Sinead, *Early Medieval Glosses on Prudentius' Psychomachia: The Weitz Tradition* (Leiden, 2004).

—— 'The Sacred and the Obscure: Greek and the Carolingian Reception of Martianus Capella', *Journal of Medieval Latin*, 22 (2012), 67–94.

Page, R. I., 'Roman and Runic on St Cuthbert's Coffin', in *St Cuthbert, his Cult and his Community to A.D. 1200*, Gerald Bonner, David W. Rollason, and Clare Stancliffe, eds (Woodbridge, 1995), 257–65.

—— *An Introduction to English Runes*, 2nd edn (Woodbridge, 1999).

Page, Sophie, *Astrology in Medieval Manuscripts* (Toronto, 2002).

Paxton, Frederick S., 'Anointing the Sick and the Dying in Christian Antiquity and the Early Medieval West', in *Health, Disease and Healing in Medieval Culture*, Sheila Campbell, Bert Hall, and David Klausner, eds (London, 1992), pp. 93–102.

Paz, James, 'Magic that Works: Performing *Scientia* in the Old English Metrical Charms and Poetic Dialogues of *Solomon and Saturn*', *Journal of Medieval and Early Modern Studies*, 45 (2015), 219–43.

Pearman, Tory Vandeventer, *Women and Disability in Medieval Literature* (New York, 2010).

Peck, Jeffrey M., '"In the Beginning Was the Word": Germany and the Origins of German Studies', in *Medievalism and the Modernist Temper*, R. Howard Bloch and Stephen G. Nichols, eds (Baltimore, 1996), pp. 127–47.

Pelteret, David A. E., 'A Cross and an Acrostic: Boniface's Prefatory Poem to his *Ars grammatica*', in *Cross and Cruciform in the Anglo-Saxon World: Studies to Honor the Memory of Timothy Reuter*, Sarah Larratt Keefer, Karen Louise Jolly, and Catherine E. Karkov, eds (Morgantown, 2010), pp. 53–102.

Pfaff, Richard W., *The Liturgy in Medieval England: A History* (Cambridge, 2009).

Pinto, L. B., 'Medical Science and Superstition: A Report on A Unique Medical Scroll of the Eleventh-Twelfth Century', *Manuscripta*, 17 (1973), 12–21.

Porter, David W., 'Isidore's *Etymologiae* at the School of Canterbury', *ASE*, 43 (2014), 7–44.

Prescott, Andrew, 'The Text of the Benedictional of St Æthelwold', in *Bishop Æthelwold: His Career and Influence*, Barbara Yorke, ed. (Woodbridge, 1988), pp. 119–47.

Priebsch, R., *The Heliand Manuscript: Cotton Caligula A VII in the British Museum* (Oxford, 1925).

Pulsiano, Phillip, 'British Library, Cotton Tiberius A. iii, fol. 59rv: An Unrecorded Charm in the Form of an Address to the Cross', *ANQ*, 4 (1991), 3–5.

—— *Anglo-Saxon Manuscripts in Microfiche Facsimile, Vol. 2: Psalters I*, A. N. Doane, ed. (Binghamton, 1994).

—— 'Abbot Ælfwine and the Date of the Vitellius Psalter', *ANQ*, 11 (1998), 3–12.

—— 'The Prefatory Matter of London, British Library, Cotton Vitellius E. xviii', in *Anglo-Saxon Manuscripts and their Heritage*, Phillip Pulsiano and Elaine M. Treharne, eds (Aldershot, 1998), pp. 85–116.

—— *Anglo-Saxon Manuscripts in Microfiche Facsimile, Vol. 4: Glossed Texts, Aldhelmiana, Psalms* (Binghamton, 1996).

Raaijmakers, Janneke, *The Making of the Monastic Community at Fulda, c. 744 – c. 900* (Cambridge, 2012).

Ramey, Peter, 'Writing Speaks: Oral Poetics and Writing Technology in the Exeter Book Riddles', *PQ*, 92 (2013), 335–56.

Rauer, Christine, 'Usage of the *Old English Martyrology*', in *The Foundations of Learning: The Transfer of Encyclopaedic Knowledge in the Early Middle Ages*, Rolf H. Bremmer Jr and Kees Dekker, eds (Leuven, 2007), pp. 125–46.

Raw, Barbara, *Trinity and Incarnation in Anglo-Saxon Art and Thought* (Cambridge, 2006).

Ray, Roger, 'Bede's *Vera Lex Historiae*', *Speculum*, 55 (1980), 1–21.

Regan, Catharine A., 'Patristic Psychology in the Old English "Vainglory"', *Traditio*, 26 (1970), 324–35.

Robinson, W. C., *Introduction to Our Early English Literature* (London, 1885).

Rohde, Eleanour Sinclair, *The Old English Herbals* (London, 1922).

Roper, Jonathan, 'Towards a Poetics, Rhetorics, and Proxemics of Verbal Charms', *Folklore*, 24 (2003), 7–49.

—— 'Typologising English Charms', in *Charms and Charming in Europe*, Jonathan Roper, ed. (Basingstoke, 2004), pp. 128–44.

Rose, Els, *Ritual Memory: The Apocryphal Acts and Liturgical Commemoration in the Early Medieval West (c. 500–1215)* (Leiden, 2009).

Rosenberg, Bruce A., 'The Meaning of Æcerbot', *Journal of American Folklore*, 79 (1966), 428–36.

Rowley, Sharon M., 'Nostalgia and the Rhetoric of Lack: The Missing Exemplar of Corpus Christi College, Cambridge, Manuscript 41', in *Old English Literature in its Manuscript Context*, Joyce Tally Lionarons, ed. (Morgantown, 2004), pp. 11–35.

—— *The Old English Version of Bede's Historia Ecclesiastica* (Cambridge, 2011).

Rubin, Stanley, *Medieval English Medicine* (New York, 1974).

Rupp, Katrin, 'The Anxiety of Writing: A Reading of the Old English *Journey Charm*', *Oral Tradition*, 23 (2008), 255–66.

Rust, Martha Dana, 'The Art of Beekeeping Meets the Arts of Grammar: A Gloss of "Columcille's Circle"', *PQ*, 78 (1999), 359–87.

Ryan, J. S., 'Othin in England: Evidence from the Poetry for a Cult of Woden in Anglo-Saxon England', *Folklore*, 73–4 (1962–3), 460–80.

Schipper, William, 'Hrabanus Maurus in Anglo-Saxon England: *In honorem sanctae crucis*', in *Early Medieval Studies in Memory of Patrick Wormald*, Stephen D. Baxter, Catherine Karkov, Janet L. Nelson, and David Pelteret, eds (Farnham, 2009), pp. 283–300.

Schramm, Percy E., *A History of the English Coronation* (Oxford, 1937).

Scragg, Donald G., 'The Compilation of the Vercelli Book', *ASE*, 2 (1973), 189–207.

—— *Superstition and Popular Medicine in Anglo-Saxon England* (Manchester, 1989).

—— 'Manuscript Sources of Old English Prose', in *Working with Anglo-Saxon Manuscripts*, Gale R. Owen-Crocker, ed. (Exeter, 2009), pp. 61–87.

—— 'Studies in the Language of Copyists of the Vercelli Homilies', in *New Readings in the Vercelli Book*, Samantha Zacher and Andy Orchard, eds (Toronto, 2009), pp. 41–61.

—— *A Conspectus of Scribal Hands Writing English, 960–1100* (Cambridge, 2012).

Shippey, Tom A., *Old English Verse* (London, 1972).

Sims-Williams, Patrick, *Religion and Literature in Western England 600–800* (Cambridge, 1990).

Singer, Charles, 'A Review of the Medical Literature of the Dark Ages, With a New Text of About 1110', *Proceedings of the Royal Society of Medicine*, 10 (1917), 107–60.

—— 'Early English Magic and Medicine', *Proceedings of the British Academy*, 9 (1919), 341–74.

Sisam, Kenneth, 'Anglo-Saxon Royal Genealogies', *Proceedings of the British Academy*, 39 (1953), 287–348.

—— *Studies in the History of Old English Literature* (Oxford, 1953).

Stanley, Eric G., *Imagining the Anglo-Saxon Past: The Search for Anglo-Saxon Paganism and Anglo-Saxon Trial by Jury* (Cambridge, 1975).

—— 'On the Laws of King Alfred: The End of the Preface and the Beginning of the Laws', in *Alfred the Wise*, Jane Roberts, Janet L. Nelson, and Malcolm Godden, eds (Cambridge, 1997), pp. 211–21.

Stanton, Robert, *The Culture of Translation in Anglo-Saxon England* (Cambridge, 2002).

—— 'Linguistic Fragmentation and Redemption before King Alfred', *The Yearbook of English Studies*, 36 (2006), 12–26.

Stephenson, Rebecca, 'Scapegoating the Secular Clergy: The Hermeneutic Style as a Form of Monastic Self-Definition', *ASE*, 38 (2009), 101–35.

—— *The Politics of Language: Byrhtferth, Ælfric, and the Multilingual Identity of the Benedictine Reform* (Toronto, 2015).

Storms, Godfrid, 'How Did the *Dene* and the *Geatas* Get Into *Beowulf*?', *ES*, 80 (1999), 46–9.

Strasser, Gerhard F., 'Ninth-Century Figural Poetry and Medieval Easter Tables – Possible Inspirations for the Square Tables of Trithemius and Vigenère?', *Cryptologia*, 34 (2009), 22–6.

Stroud, Daphne, 'The Provenance of the Salisbury Psalter', *The Library*, 6 (1979), 225–35.

Stuart, Heather, '"Ic me on þisse gyrde beluce": The Structure and Meaning of the Old English "Journey Charm"', *Medium Ævum*, 50 (1981), 259–73.

Swan, Mary, 'Identity and Ideology in Ælfric's Prefaces', in *A Companion to Ælfric*, Hugh Magennis and Mary Swann, eds (Leiden, 2009), pp. 247–70.

Tanke, John, 'Beowulf, Gold-Luck, and God's Will', *SP*, 99 (2002), 356–79.

Tatton-Brown, Tim, 'The City and Diocese of Canterbury in St Dunstan's Time', in *St Dunstan: His Life, Times and Cult*, Nigel Ramsay, Margaret Sparks, and Tim Tatton-Brown, eds (Woodbridge, 1992), pp. 75–88.

Taylor, Paul Beekman, 'Some Vestiges of Ritual Charms in *Beowulf*', *Journal of Popular Culture*, 1 (1967), 276–85.

Teeuwen, Mariken, 'Carolingian Scholarship on Classical Authors: Practices of Reading and Writing', in *Manuscripts of the Latin Classics 800–1200*, Erik Kwakkel, ed. (Leiden, 2015), pp. 23–52.

Thacker, Alan, 'Cults At Canterbury: Relics and Reform under Dunstan and His Successors', in *St Dunstan: His Life, Times and Cult*, Nigel Ramsay, Margaret Sparks, and Tim Tatton-Brown, eds (Woodbridge, 1992), pp. 221–46.

The Shaw Review, 8 (1965), 110.

Thompson, Victoria, *Dying and Death in Later Anglo-Saxon England* (Woodbridge, 2004).

Thomson, R. B., 'Two Astronomical Tractates of Abbo of Fleury', in *The Light of Nature: Essays in the History and Philosophy of Science Presented to A. C. Crombie*, J. D. North and J. J. Roche, eds (Dordrecht, 1985), pp. 113–33.

—— 'Further Astronomical Material of Abbo of Fleury', *Mediaeval Studies*, 20 (1988), 671–3.

Tolhurst, J. B. L., 'An Examination of Two Anglo-Saxon Manuscripts of the Winchester School: The Missal of Robert of Jumièges, and the Benedictional of Aethelwold', *Archaeologia*, 83 (1933), 27–44.

Tornaghi, Paola, 'Anglo-Saxon Charms and the Language of Magic', *Aevum*, 84 (2010), 439–64.

Townend, Matthew, 'Contextualizing the *Knútsdrapur*: Skaldic Praise-Poetry at the Court of Cnut', *ASE*, 30 (2001), 145–79.

—— 'Cnut's Poets: An Old Norse Literary Community in Eleventh-Century England', in *Conceptualizing Multilingualism in Medieval England, c. 800 - c. 1250*, Elizabeth M. Tyler, ed. (Turnhout, 2011), pp. 197–215.

Treharne, Elaine M., 'The Dates and Origins of Three Twelfth-Century Old English Manuscripts', in *Anglo-Saxon Manuscripts and their Heritage*, Phillip Pulsiano and Elaine M. Treharne, eds (Aldershot, 1998), pp. 227–53.

—— 'Producing A Library in Late Anglo-Saxon England: Exeter 1050–1072', *RES*, 54 (2003), 155–72.

—— 'Bishops and their Texts in the Later Eleventh Century: Worcester and Exeter', in *Essays in Manuscript Geography: Vernacular Manuscripts of the English West Midlands from the Conquest to the Sixteenth Century*, Wendy Scase, ed. (Turnhout, 2007), pp. 13–28.

—— 'Form and Function of the Exeter Book' in *Text, Image, Interpretation: Studies in Anglo-Saxon Literature and Its Insular Context in Honour of Éamonn Ó Carragáin*, Alastair J. Minnis and Jane A. Roberts, eds (Turnhout, 2007), pp. 253–66.

—— 'Manuscript Sources of Old English Poetry', in *Working with Anglo-Saxon Manuscripts*, Gale R. Owen-Crocker, ed. (Exeter, 2009), pp. 88–111.

—— 'The Bishops' Book: Leofric's Homiliary and Eleventh-Century Exeter', in *Early Medieval Studies in Memory of Patrick Wormald*, Stephen Baxter, Catherine E. Karkov, Janet L. Nelson, and David Pelteret, eds (Farnham, 2009), pp. 521–37.

—— *Living Through Conquest: The Politics of Early English, 1020–1220* (Oxford, 2012).

Treharne, Elaine M., Orietta Da Rold, and Mary Swan, eds, *Producing and Using English Manuscripts in the Post-Conquest Period* (Turnhout, 2013).

Tupper, Frederick, *The Riddles of the Exeter Book* (Boston, 1910).

Turville-Petre, Edward O. G., *Myth and Religion of the North* (London, 1964).

Vanderputten, Stephen, 'Debating Reform in Tenth- and Early Eleventh-Century Female Monasticism', *Zeitschrift für Kirchengeschichte*, 125 (2014), 289–306.

Vaughan-Sterling, Judith A., 'The Anglo-Saxon Metrical Charms: Poetry as Ritual', *JEGP*, 82 (1983), 186–200.

Vleeskruyer, Rudolf, *The Life of St Chad: An Old English Homily* (Amsterdam, 1953).

Voigts, Linda, 'Anglo-Saxon Plant Remedies and the Anglo Saxons', *Isis*, 70 (1979), 250–69.

—— 'The Latin Verse and Middle English Prose Texts on the Sphere of Life and Death in Harley 3719', *The Chaucer Review*, 21 (1986), 291–305.

Voth, Christine, 'An Analysis of the Tenth-Century Anglo-Saxon Manuscript London, British Library, Royal 12. D. xvii', Unpublished Doctoral Thesis (Cambridge University, England, 2014).

Watkins, Calvert, *How to Kill a Dragon: Aspects of Indo-European Poetics* (Oxford, 1995).

Watkins, Carl S., *History and the Supernatural in Medieval England* (Cambridge, 2007).

Webster, Leslie, 'The Iconographic Programme of the Franks Casket', in *Northumbria's Golden Age*, Jane Hawkes and Susan Mills, eds (Stroud, 1999), pp. 227–46.

—— 'Visual Literacy in a Protoliterate Age', in *Literacy in Medieval and Early Modern Scandinavian Culture*, P. Hermann, ed. (Odense, 2005), pp. 21–46.

—— 'Encrypted Visions: Style and Sense in the Anglo-Saxon Minor Arts AD 400–900', in *Anglo-Saxon Styles*, Catherine E. Karkov and George Hardin Brown, eds (Albany, NY, 2012), pp. 11–30.

Wentersdorf, Karl P., 'The Old English "Rhyming Poem": A Ruler's Lament', *SP*, 82 (1985), 265–94.

Weston, L. M. C., 'The Language of Magic in Two Old English Metrical Charms', *Neuphilologische Mitteilungen*, 86 (1985), 176–86.

—— 'Women's Medicine, Women's Magic: The Old English Metrical Childbirth Charms', *Modern Philology*, 92 (1995), 279–93.

Whitelock, Dorothy, 'Wulfstan and the So-Called Laws of Edward and Guthrum', *EHR*, 56 (1941), 1–21.

—— 'Wulfstan and the Laws of Cnut', *EHR*, 63 (1948), 433–52.

Wieland, Gernot R., 'The Glossed Manuscript: Classbook or Library Book?', *ASE*, 14 (1985), 153–73.

—— 'A Survey of Latin Manuscripts', in *Working with Anglo-Saxon Manuscripts*, Gale R. Owen-Crocker, ed. (Exeter, 2009), pp. 113–58.

Wilcox, Jonathan, 'Ælfric in Dorset and the Landscape of Pastoral Care', in *Pastoral Care in Late Anglo-Saxon England*, Francesca Tinti, ed. (Woodbridge, 2005), pp. 52–62.

—— *Anglo-Saxon Manuscripts in Microfiche Facsimile, Vol. 17: Homilies by Ælfric and other Homilies*, A. N. Doane and M. T. Hussey, eds (Tempe, AZ, 2008).

Wildhagen, Karl, *Das Kalendarium der Handschrift Vitellius E XVIII (Brit. Mus.): Ein Beitrag zur Chronologie und Hagiologie Altenglands* (Halle, 1921).

Willetts, P. J. 'A Reconstructed Astronomical Manuscript from Christ Church Library Canterbury', *The British Museum Quarterly*, 30 (1965), 22–30.

Williamson, Craig, *The Old English Riddles of the Exeter Book* (Chapel Hill, 1977).

Willis, Geoffrey G., *Further Essays in Early Roman Liturgy* (London, 1968).

Wormald, Patrick, 'Æthelwold and his Continental Counterparts: Contact, Comparison, Contrast', in *Bishop Æthelwold: His Career and Influence*, Barbara Yorke, ed. (Woodbridge, 1988), pp. 13–42.

Wright, Charles D., *The Irish Tradition in Old English Literature* (Cambridge, 1993).

—— 'Vercelli Homilies XI-XIII and the Anglo-Saxon Benedictine Reform: Tailored Sources and Implied Audiences', in *Preacher, Sermon, and Audience in the Middle Ages*, Carolyn Meussig, ed. (Leiden, 2002), pp. 203–27.

Yorke, Barbara, 'Æthelwold and the Politics of the Tenth Century', in *Bishop Æthelwold: His Career and Influence*, Barbara Yorke, ed. (Woodbridge, 1988), pp. 65–88.

Zacher, Samantha, *Preaching the Converted: The Style and Rhetoric of the Vercelli Book Homilies* (Toronto, 2009).

Zacher, Samantha and Andy Orchard, 'Introduction', in *New Readings in the Vercelli Book*, Samantha Zacher and Andy Orchard, eds (Toronto, 2009), pp. 3–11.

Ziolkowski, Jan M., 'Theories of Obscurity in the Latin Middle Ages', *Mediaevalia*, 19 (1996), 101–70.

Zironi, Alessandro, 'Marginal Alphabets in the Carolingian Age: Philological and Codicological Considerations', in *Rethinking and Recontextualizing Glosses: New Perspectives in the Study of Late Anglo-Saxon Glossography*, Patrizia Lendinara, Loredana Lazzari, and Claudia Di Sciacca, eds (Turnhout, 2011), pp. 353–71.

Zoëga, Geir T., *A Concise Dictionary of Old Icelandic* (Oxford, 1910).

Websites

Dictionary of Old English Corpus (Toronto, 2009):
<http://0-tapor.library.utoronto.ca/doecorpus/> accessed 26 September 2017.

Köbler, Gerhard, *Neuenglisch-althochdeutsches Wörterbuch* (2006):
<http://www.koeblergerhard.de/germanistischewoerterbuecher/alt hochdeutscheswoerterbuch/neuenglisch-ahd.pdf> accessed 26 September 2017.

The Production and Use of English Manuscripts 1060 to 1220 (published online 2010–13):
<http://www.le.ac.uk/english/em1060to1220> accessed 26 September 2017.

Vercelli Book Digitale:
<http://vbd.humnet.unipi.it/?p=2047> accessed 26 September 2017.

Wallis, Faith, *The Calendar and the Cloister: Oxford, St John's College, MS 17* (Montreal, 2007):
<http://digital.library.mcgill.ca/ms-17> accessed 26 September 2017.

General Index

Index of Manuscripts

ANGLO-SAXON STUDIES